BISHOPS AND THE POLITICS OF PATRONAGE IN MEROVINGIAN GAUL

BISHOPS AND THE POLITICS OF PATRONAGE IN MEROVINGIAN GAUL

GREGORY I. HALFOND

CORNELL UNIVERSITY PRESS
Ithaca and London

Copyright © 2019 by Cornell University

All rights reserved. Except for brief quotations in a review, this book, or parts thereof, must not be reproduced in any form without permission in writing from the publisher. For information, address Cornell University Press, Sage House, 512 East State Street, Ithaca, New York 14850. Visit our website at cornellpress.cornell.edu.

First published 2019 by Cornell University Press

Library of Congress Cataloging-in-Publication Data

Names: Halfond, Gregory I., author.
Title: Bishops and the politics of patronage in Merovingian Gaul / Gregory I. Halfond.
Description: Ithaca [New York] : Cornell University Press, 2019. | Includes bibliographical references and index.
Identifiers: LCCN 2018053416 (print) | LCCN 2018055361 (ebook) | ISBN 9781501739323 (pdf) | ISBN 9781501739354 (epub/mobi) | ISBN 9781501739316 | ISBN 9781501739316 (cloth ; alk. paper)
Subjects: LCSH: Bishops—Gaul—Temporal power. | Bishops—Political Activity—Gaul. | Church and state—Gaul. | Merovingians. | Episcopacy—History. | France—Politics and government—To 987. | France—Church history—To 987.
Classification: LCC BX1905 (ebook) | LCC BX1905 .H35 2019 (print) | DDC 274.4/02—dc23
LC record available at https://lccn.loc.gov/2018053416

Contents

Acknowledgments vii
Abbreviations ix
Map x

	Introduction	1
1.	Episcopal Service to the Court	28
2.	Royal Patronage and Its Benefits	63
3.	Unity in Disunity: The Limits of Corporate Solidarity	95
4.	Disunity in Unity: Territorial Integration and Its Effects	120
	Conclusion	160

Bibliography 169
Index 197

Acknowledgments

This book never would have seen the light of day without the help and support of numerous individuals. At Cornell University Press, I would like to thank Bethany Wasik, Karen Hwa, and especially Mahinder Kingra, who shepherded this project from its beginnings through publication, providing both encouragement and invaluable advice for improving the final product. Kate Gibson and the staff of Westchester Publishing Services meticulously proofread the manuscript, saving me from many an error. Bernard S. Bachrach, Yaniv Fox, and Jamie Kreiner all read and commented on earlier drafts of the manuscript, and I am deeply indebted to them, as well as to the two anonymous readers for Cornell University Press, for their expert advice, criticism, and suggestions. At Framingham State University I would like to thank my colleague Dave Merwin for generously providing the map, as well as the staff at the Whittemore Library, especially Danielle Lamontagne and Kieran Shakeshaft, for helping me to secure the many resources that I required to complete this book. Finally, I would like to thank my family: Jay and Gayle Halfond, Rebecca Lahue, Jeanne Halfond, and especially Larissa, Benjamin, and Milo Halfond, to whom this book is lovingly dedicated.

Abbreviations

AASS	Acta sanctorum, ed. Jean Bolland et al. (Brussels and Antwerp, 1643–1940)
AASS OSB	Acta sanctorum ordinis sancti Benedicti, ed. Luc d'Achery and Jean Mabillon (Paris, 1668–1701)
CCSL	Corpus Christianorum: Series Latina (Turnhout, Belgium, 1953–)
ChLa	Chartae Latinae Antiquiores. Facsimile Edition of the Latin Charters Prior to the Ninth Century, ed. Albert Bruckner, Robert Marichal, et al. (Olten/Lausanne/Dietikon-Zürich, 1954–98)
MGH	Monumenta Germaniae Historica
AA	Auctores antiquissimi (Berlin, 1877–1919)
LL nat. Germ.	Leges nationum Germanicarum (Hanover, Germany, 1892–1969)
SRG	Scriptores rerum Germanicarum (Hanover, Germany, 1871–2007)
SRM	Scriptores rerum Merovingicarum (Hanover, Germany, 1885–1951)
SS	Scriptores (Folio) (Hanover, Germany, 1826–2009)
PL	Patrologia Latina, Patrologiae cursus completus, series latina, ed. J.-P. Migne (Paris, 1844–64)
SC	Sources Chrétiennes (Paris, 1942–)

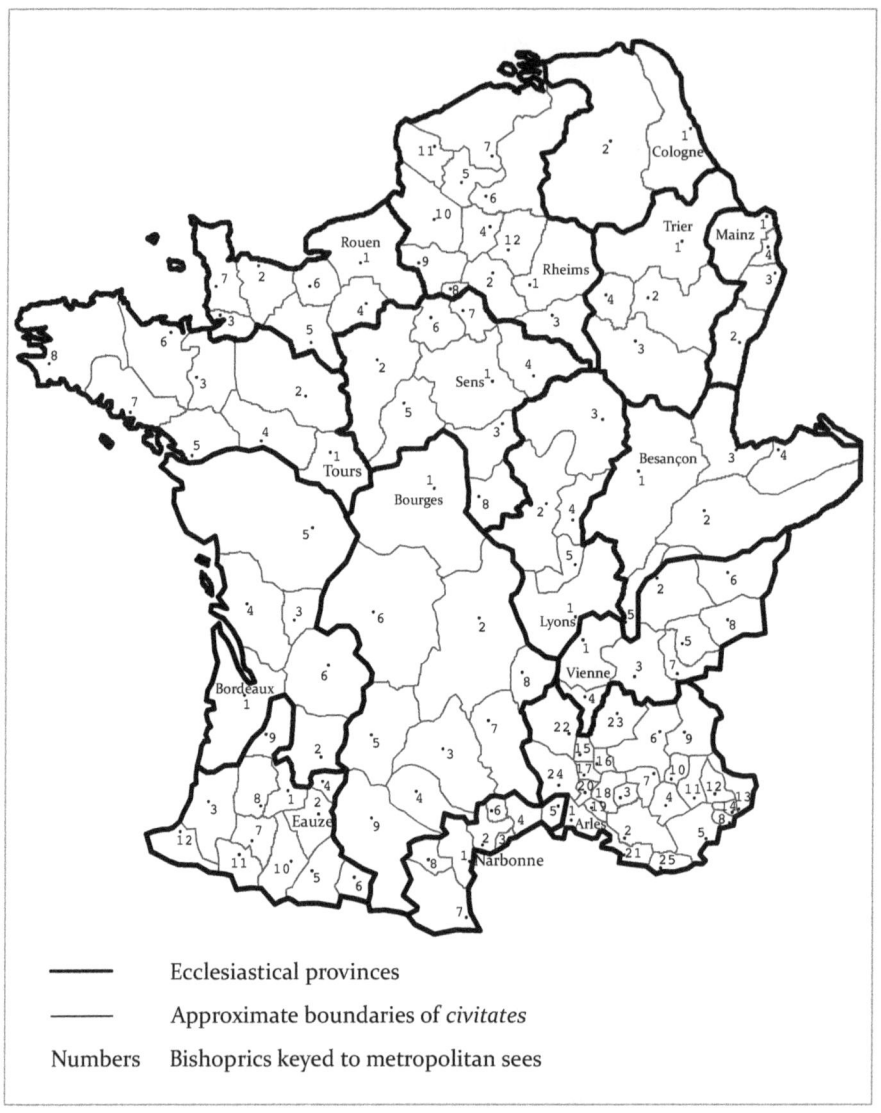

This map draws on, among other sources, earlier maps by Edward James, *The Origins of France: From Clovis to the Capetians, 500–1000* (New York: St. Martin's, 1982), xiii–xvii, xix–xx; Gregory Halfond, *The Archaeology of Frankish Church Councils, AD 511–768* (Leiden: Brill, 2010), 265–66; and, most recently, Alexander C. Murray, ed., *A Companion to Gregory of Tours* (Leiden: Brill, 2015), 584–91.

1. **Lyons (Lugdunensis Prima)**
2. Autun
3. Langres
4. Chalon-sur-Sâone
5. Mâcon

1. **Rouen (Lugdunensis Secunda)**
2. Bayeux
3. Avranches
4. Evreux
5. Sées
6. Lisieux
7. Coutances

1. **Tours (Lugdunensis Tertia)**
2. Le Mans
3. Rennes
4. Angers
5. Nantes
6. Corseul/Alet
7. Vannes
8. Osismes/Carhaix

1. **Sens (Lugdunensis Senonia)**
2. Chartres
3. Auxerre
4. Troyes
5. Orléans
6. Paris
7. Meaux
8. Nevers

1. **Bourges (Aquitanica Prima)**
2. Clermont-Ferrand
3. Rodez
4. Albi
5. Cahors
6. Limoges
7. Javols/Mende
8. Velay
9. Toulouse

1. **Bordeaux (Aquitanica Secunda)**
2. Agen
3. Angoulême
4. Saintes
5. Poitiers
6. Périgueux

1. **Eauze (Novempopulana)**
2. Auch
3. Dax
4. Lectoure
5. Saint-Bertrand-de-Comminges
6. Couserans (Saint-Liziers)
7. Lescar (Béarn)
8. Aire-sur-Adour
9. Bazas
10. Tarbes
11. Oloron
12. Bayonne

1. **Trier (Belgica Prima)**
2. Metz
3. Toul
4. Verdun

1. **Rheims (Belgica Secunda)**
2. Soissons
3. Châlons-en-Champagne
4. Vermand/Noyon
5. Arras
6. Cambrai
7. Tournai
8. Senlis
9. Beauvais
10. Amiens
11. Thérouanne
12. Laon

1. **Mainz (Germania Prima)**
2. Strasbourg
3. Speyer
4. Worms

1. **Cologne (Germania Secunda)**
2. Tongres/Maastricht/Liège

1. **Besançon (Maxima Sequanorum)**
2. Avenches/Lausanne
3. Basel
4. Windisch/Constance
5. Belley

1. **Vienne (Viennensis)**
2. Geneva
3. Grenoble
4. Valence
5. Tarentaise
6. Martigny (Valais)/Sion
7. Saint-Jean-de-Maurienne
8. Aosta

1. **Narbonne (Narbonensis Prima)**
2. Béziers
3. Agde
4. Maguelonne
5. Nîmes
6. Lodève
7. Elne
8. Carcassonne

1. **Arles (Narbonensis Secunda)**
2. Aix-en-Provence
3. Apt
4. Riez
5. Fréjus
6. Gap
7. Sisteron
8. Antibes
9. Embrun
10. Digne
11. Senez
12. Glandève
13. Cimiez/Nice
14. Vence
15. Saint-Paul-Trois-Châteaux
16. Vaison
17. Orange
18. Carpentras
19. Cavaillon
20. Avignon
21. Marseilles
22. Alba/Viviers
23. Die
24. Uzès
25. Toulon

BISHOPS AND THE POLITICS OF PATRONAGE IN MEROVINGIAN GAUL

Introduction

A Burgundian Prelude

In preparation for a major ecclesiastical council scheduled to assemble in September 517 in the parish of Epaone, the provincial metropolitan of Vienne, Alcimus Ecdicius Avitus (ca. 494–518), worked in collaboration with his colleague, the metropolitan of Lyons, to secure the attendance of the bishops of the Burgundian regnum. In a surviving epistle whose original recipient is uncertain, Avitus frankly acknowledged the burden of conciliar attendance. Not only were there the predictable hardships associated with travel, the council's dates of assembly—September 6 through September 15—coincided with the autumn harvest, thereby distracting attendees from the supervision of agricultural labor on those personal and diocesan lands under their management.[1] Avitus went so far as to acknowledge that the onus of conciliar attendance might be considerable enough to persuade some bishops to concoct excuses to avoid having to make the journey to Epaone. Nevertheless, he maintained, the very real responsibilities of episcopal officeholders in their respective dioceses ought not to distract them from the obligations of *caritas*. As Avitus

---

1. Danuta Shanzer and Ian Wood, trans., *Avitus of Vienne: Letters and Selected Prose* (Liverpool: Liverpool University Press, 2002), 309n7, question Avitus's claim that Epaone (Albon) was centrally located within the Burgundian regnum, although they acknowledge that the parish was accessible by river.

concluded, "The immensity of fraternal love and pastoral care only can be demonstrated through great labor."[2]

In this epistle, composed near the end of his life, Avitus acknowledged both the burdens and joys of serving in episcopal office. While bishops had to balance their local and collective responsibilities, they also could enjoy, when gathered together as a group, comradery and conversation with other men of similar rank, knowledge, and experience.[3] While individual bishops did not necessarily live up to all of the expectations associated with their office, as Avitus himself recognized all too well, collectively they shared a common bond grounded in both shared responsibilities and a membership in an exclusive fraternal *ordo episcoporum*. Such membership did not necessitate an abandonment of individual identity or agency but rather afforded bishops an opportunity to define common goals and to communicate policy through a collective voice that transcended diocesan borders.

This collective voice, particularly as articulated in council, could provide an effective medium for negotiating with the royal court. But what of those occasions when the court was unreceptive to episcopal pleading? While it is uncertain whether the decision to convoke a council in 517 originated with the Burgundian monarchy,[4] any goodwill engendered by the convocation gave way promptly to a sudden and rapid deterioration of relations between the episcopate and King Sigismund (516–23) over charges of incest laid against the royal treasurer Stephanus.[5] Shortly after Avitus's death, his former colleague Viventiolus of Lyons convoked another council at Lyons (518/23), at which

---

2. Avitus of Vienne, *Opera*, ed. Rudolf Peiper, MGH AA 6.2 (Berlin: Weidmann, 1883), no. 90 (98): "Ceterum dilectionis fraternae ac pastoralis diligentiae magnitudo nisi laboris magnitudine non probatur." See also *Concilia Galliae: A.511–A.695*, ed. Charles de Clercq, CCSL 148A (Turnhout, Belgium: Brepols, 1963), 22–23. See Shanzer and Wood, *Avitus of Vienne*, 308–10, for a translation of, and a commentary on, this epistle. Unless stated otherwise, all references to Merovingian-era conciliar *acta* are to de Clercq's edition, while references to the acts of earlier Gallic councils are to the edition of Charles Munier, ed., *Concilia Galliae: A.314–A.506*, CCSL 148 (Turnhout, Belgium: Brepols, 1963).

3. As suggested by Avitus's instructions for sending clerical delegates to the council. Avitus of Vienne, *Opera*, no. 90 (98): "Et tales dignetur eligere, quos episcoporum concilio non minus scientia quam reverentia iure faciat interesse; cum quibus delectet summos pontifices conferre sermonem; quos ad definitiones pro episcopo suo continendas subscribendasque cum fuerit sollertia eligi, sit auctoritas legi."

4. Shanzer and Wood, *Avitus of Vienne*, 23, suggest that Sigismund may have convoked the council in conjunction with his promulgation of the *Liber Constitutionum*. A second convocation letter sent out by Avitus's colleague, the metropolitan Viventiolus of Lyons (*Concilia Galliae: A.511–A.695*, 23–24), explains that laymen were to be invited to the Council of Epaone so that they in turn might inform the *populus* of bishops' decisions. It is possible that this information was filtered through the royal court.

5. Council of Epaone (517), c. 30. While the specific case of Stephanus was discussed in a conciliar context before the Council of Lyons (518/23), it is unknown whether it was at Epaone or another meeting.

he and his episcopal colleagues agreed to what has been described as a "unanimous vote of no confidence" against the king and threatened to cloister themselves within monasteries until Sigismund relented.[6] This was a remarkable display of group solidarity in the face of what must have been immense royal pressure. That said, only eleven bishops subscribed to the acts of the Council of Lyons, compared to the more than twice as many—twenty-four in all, not including an additional clerical delegate—who had been present at Epaone.[7] So it is quite possible that not all Gallo-Burgundian bishops were equally enthusiastic about directly challenging the monarchy. But any tensions between the episcopate and the monarchy—or, for that matter, within the Burgundian episcopate—soon were rendered moot by increasing Frankish military pressure on the kingdom, which in short order would erase the political border between the two Gallic regna, a border that largely had obstructed collaboration between the bishops living on the two sides of the secular divide.

With the annexation by the Franks of the kingdom of Burgundy in 534, the bishops of the defunct regnum were integrated into the Frankish episcopacy and within four years were attending councils along with bishops from throughout Merovingian Gaul.[8] Along with their Provençal colleagues, who similarly were absorbed into a Frankish ecclesiastical federation three years later, the Burgundian prelates now joined a much wider community of bishops, with whom they were expected to share that same fraternal bond about which Avitus had written back in 517. Several episcopal sees from the former Burgundian regnum were represented at the Council of Orléans (538), at which efforts were made to ease the integration.[9] *Regulae* published originally at Epaone

---

6. Council of Lyons (518/23), c. 1 (and c. 4[6]). On these events, see Paul Mikat, *Die Inzestgesetzgebung der merowingisch-fränkischen Konzilien (511–626/27)* (Paderborn, Germany: Ferdinand Schöningh, 1994), 106–15; Ian Wood, "Incest, Law and the Bible in Sixth-Century Gaul," *Early Medieval Europe* 7, no. 3 (1998): 291–303, at 299–301 (quote on 301); Karl Ubl, *Inzestverbot und Gesetzgebung: Die Konstruktion eines Verbrechens (300–1100)* (Berlin: Walter de Gruyter, 2008), 118–37; and Angela Kinney, "An Appeal against Editorial Condemnation: A Reevaluation of the *Vita Apollinaris Valentinensis*," in *Edition und Erforschung lateinischer patristischer Texte*, ed. Victoria Zimmerl-Panagl, Lukas J. Dorfbauer, and Clemens Weidmann (Berlin: De Gruyter, 2014), 157–77, at 162–67. As the terms *concilium* and *synodus* are both used in Gallic sources to indicate episcopal gatherings, I use their English equivalents interchangeably unless otherwise indicated. On conciliar terminology, see Adolf Lumpe, "Zur Geschichte der Wörter *Concilium* und *Synodus* in der antiken christlichen Latinität," *Annuarium Historiae Conciliorum* 2, no. 1 (1970): 1–21.

7. Only nine subscriptions, however, follow the more conciliatory addendum to the *acta*. Council of Lyons (518/22), *subscriptiones*: "Domni quoque gloriosissimi regis sententia secuti id temperamenti praestitemus, ut Stephano praedicto vel Palladiae usque ad orationem plebis, quae post evangelia legitur, orandi in locis sanctis spatium praestarimus." We can but speculate as to whether this signifies a further breakdown in episcopal consensus. See, e.g., Ubl, *Inzestverbot und Gesetzgebung*, 134.

8. For the possibility that Iulianus of Vienne attended the Council of Orléans (533), see chapter 4.

9. In the case of the Provençal bishops, it appears that some effort was made to ease integration by addressing issues known to be of concern to the southerners, despite their collective absence from

(517) were adopted as precedent by the attendees at Orléans.[10] Additionally, the first among the metropolitans to attach their names to the conciliar *acta* were Bishops Lupus of Lyons and Pantagatus of Vienne, indicating that they assumed positions of leadership at the council commensurate with their metropolitan status and seniority. Although the council's acts do not explicitly acknowledge the monarchy's (likely) convocation, both metropolitans dated their subscriptions to Childebert I's twenty-sixth regnal year, a small but significant gesture of recognition of Burgundy's recently transformed political status.[11]

While individual Burgundian bishops would display regionalist sentiments at various times in the future, there is no reason to think that at the moment of unification the Burgundian episcopate en masse resisted integration into the *regnum Francorum*, as integration augured easier, and more regular, interprovincial collaboration between members of the same order.[12] The Frankish monarchy, for its part, actively encouraged the assimilation and cooperation of the ecclesiastical, as well as secular, elites of Burgundy.[13] The Merovingians, for neither the first nor the last time, effectively promoted episcopal unity within their borders. In so doing, however, they exposed a fundamental paradox: the episcopal *ordo*, which theoretically transcended political borders and obligations, never functioned in isolation from temporal conditions. This was a consequence not only of the imposition of regnal borders on a universal order but also of the Frankish monarchy's acknowledgment that bishops possessed an *auctoritas* not dependent solely on royal delegation. It was this distinct authority that made bishops ostensible partners of the monarchy in the promotion of public order. But if the functioning of the episcopal *ordo* was necessarily circumscribed by temporal conditions, precisely what effects did the participation of Gallo-Frankish bishops in supraregional politics have on the corporate integrity of their order?[14]

In considering this question—one that surprisingly has received little sustained scholarly attention—it is unnecessary, even unwise, to presume an

---

the council. See William Klingshirn, *Caesarius of Arles: The Making of a Christian Community in Late Antique Gaul* (Cambridge: Cambridge University Press, 1994), 258–59.

10. Odette Pontal, *Histoire des conciles mérovingiens* (Paris: Éditions du Cerf, 1989), 110.

11. Orléans (538), *subscriptiones*.

12. On the question of Burgundian regionalism, see Yaniv Fox, "Image of Kings Past: The Gibichung Legacy in Post-conquest Burgundy," *Francia* 42 (2015): 1–25.

13. On Childebert I's efforts to align himself with local Burgundian elites by, among other means, episcopal appointments, see Yaniv Fox, "New *Honores* for a Region Transformed: The Patriciate in Post-Roman Gaul," *Revue belge de Philologie et d'Histoire* 93 (2015): 249–86, at 256–57.

14. I use the descriptor *Gallo-Frankish* here and elsewhere not as indicator of ethnicity but rather to identify the geographical and political context in which these prelates operated.

inherently oppositional relationship between bishops and the monarchy.[15] Contemporary canonical and royal legislation alike presuppose collaboration, and periodic conflicts and tensions between individual prelates and monarchs did not alter this sociopolitical ideal. Conversely, it is crucial not to conflate public engagement with secularization, a phenomenon not infrequently associated with the Gallic episcopate of the Merovingian era. Prayer and pastoral care, no less so than court attendance, were meant to benefit the wider lay community and its rulers. Some bishops, of course, could be men of wealth, whose political activities reflected the values of the aristocratic milieu in which they were raised. However, these values did not define the episcopal office; in fact, there is good reason to think that the opposite was the case.[16] Modern scholarship has been too quick to generalize about the episcopal *ordo* from the ambitions of those exceptional bishops who waded so confidently into the affairs of the court. It is true that some bishops spent considerable time at, or in communication with, royal courts, enjoying the benefits of *Königsnähe* (proximity to the king); for other prelates this contact was more irregular, and for others still, possibly nonexistent.[17]

Consequently, any consideration of the aforementioned question must necessarily consider those other bishops—that is, those whose public activities did not include sharing food, conversation, and counsel with the king at the royal villa. These prelates were no less immune to the stresses shouldered by all bishops within the *regnum Francorum*, whose office demanded the harmonization of sometimes-oppositional personal aspirations, corporate responsibilities, and the solicitations and demands of the royal court. While there was ostensible group consensus regarding some general principles on the proper balance of a bishop's responsibilities, ultimately the burden fell to individuals to achieve this balance in the course of their daily routines and lives. And, as we shall see, these personal choices could and did trigger reverberations—

---

15. Conversely, the ideological basis for episcopal participation in secular politics, as well as its various displays, has been the subject of extensive scholarly attention (see chapter 1). An important exception to the foregoing observation is Paul Fouracre, "Why Were So Many Bishops Killed in Merovingian Francia?," in *Bischofsmord im Mittelalter*, ed. Natalie Fryde and Dirk Reitz (Göttingen, Germany: Vandenhoeck and Ruprecht, 2003), 13–35, which explores the dangers inherent in factional politics. I have taken inspiration from Fouracre's approach and conclusions, which are informed by, but do not necessarily assume the orthodoxy of, earlier scholarship on the political activities of the Gallo-Frankish episcopate. He singles out in particular German-language scholarship on *Bischofsherrschaft* and its assumptions about the growing secularization of Frankish bishops in the seventh and eighth centuries.

16. Jamie Kreiner, *The Social Life of Hagiography in the Merovingian Kingdom* (Cambridge: Cambridge University Press, 2014), 140–88.

17. Chris Wickham, *Framing the Early Middle Ages* (Oxford: Oxford University Press, 2005), 200, suggests that aristocratic identity in Merovingian Gaul owed more to "title and *Königsnähe* . . . than simple de facto control over a county."

sometimes barely discernable, occasionally cataclysmic—through the ties that bound a bishop to his fraternal brethren.

Episcopal Diversity in Merovingian Gaul: Individuality and Corporatism

The avoidance of generalization about bishops is necessary not only in regard to the specific question of their political engagement. By one reasonable estimate between two thousand and three thousand men held episcopal office in Merovingian Gaul.[18] The most common quality shared among these numerous individuals from the perspective of modern scholars is their anonymity or near anonymity. Put simply, most Gallo-Frankish bishops did not achieve a reputation, for better or for worse, that survived much beyond their lifetimes. The *subscriptiones* appended to conciliar *acta*, as well as episcopal lists compiled in subsequent centuries, preserve the names of additional prelates unnamed in contemporary or near-contemporary historical or hagiographical sources. So too do surviving funerary epitaphs, which also can provide some biographical details.[19] But the fact remains that we know very little about the majority of episcopal officeholders in Merovingian Gaul: among the 50 percent or fewer bishops of this period identifiable by name, only a small handful apparently merited significant literary commemoration.

So, even if we leave aside such immeasurable qualities as piety, personality, and contemporary and posthumous influence, generalizing about even the comparatively tangible socioeconomic and familial backgrounds of Gallo-Frankish bishops necessitates caution.[20] It has been customary among modern scholars to identify this community as inherently aristocratic. This generalization, to a considerable extent, has been confirmed by prosopographical analyses, and there is no reason to doubt that access to episcopal office could be eased by a candidate's local prominence and his relationships with

---

18. Dietrich Claude, "Die Bestellung der Bischöfe im merowingischen Reich," *Zeitschrift der Savigny-Stiftung für Rechtsgeschichte Kanonistische Abteilung* 49 (1963): 1–75, at 4, citing Louis Duchesne, *Fastes épiscopaux de l'ancienne Gaule* (Paris: Albert Fontemoing, 1907–15), who identifies by name approximately one thousand bishops for this same period.

19. On the epitaphs, see Martin Heinzelmann, *Bischofsherrschaft in Gallien* (Munich: Artemis Verlag, 1976).

20. Henry G. J. Beck, *The Pastoral Care of Souls in South-East France during the Sixth Century* (Rome: Apud Aedes Universitatis Gregorianae, 1950), 36, observes that a lack of biographical information about individual bishops prohibits a "true and accurate moral cross-section of sixth-century prelates."

regional and national potentates.²¹ Members of prominent local families and former courtiers alike demonstrably found their way into the episcopate in significant numbers: among the roughly forty Gallic inscriptions dating between AD 450 and 600 that reference individual bishops, we find over a third of all prelates claiming such honorifics and status indicators as *nobilis*, *illustris*, and *clarissimus*.²² In their education, cultural interests, and even perhaps personal ambitions, these prelates may not have differed too greatly from their lay relations.²³ But beyond affirming the likely prevalence of socioeconomic elites among the Gallo-Frankish bishops, it is difficult to quantify or qualify the backgrounds of the majority of these men with any greater precision. As the researches of Steffen Patzold have demonstrated, the commonly perceived correlation between senatorial status and episcopal office relies as much on extrapolation from demonstrable cases as it does on broad prosopographical analysis.²⁴

---

21. See, e.g., Heinzelmann, *Bischofsherrschaft in Gallien*; Martin Heinzelmann, "Prosopographie et recherche de continuité historique: L'exemple des V–VII siècles," *Mélanges de l'École française de Rome: Moyen Age, Temps Modernes* 100, no. 1 (1988): 227–39, at 233–34; and Martin Heinzelmann, "L'aristocratie et les évêchés entre Loire et Rhin jusqu'à la fin du VII siècle," in *La christianisation des pays entre Loire et Rhin (IV–VII siècle)*, ed. Pierre Riché (Paris: Éditions du Cerf, 1993), 75–90. See also Ian Wood, "The Ecclesiastical Politics of Merovingian Clermont," in *Ideal and Reality in Frankish and Anglo-Saxon Society: Studies Presented to J. M. Wallace-Hadrill*, ed. Patrick Wormald, Donald Bullough, and Roger Collins (Oxford: Blackwell, 1983), 34–57, at 37–40; Raymond Van Dam, *Leadership and Community in Late Antique Gaul* (Berkeley: University of California Press, 1985), 133–34, 203–12, 228–29; Reinhold Kaiser, "Les évêques et leurs pouvoirs," in *La Neustrie: Les pays au nord de la Loire de Dagobert à Charles le Chauve (VIIe–IXe siècles)*, ed. Patrick Périn and Laure-Charlotte Feffer (Rouen, France: Musées et monuments départementaux de Seine-Maritime, 1985), 99–101; and Ralph Mathisen, *Roman Aristocrats in Barbarian Gaul* (Austin: University of Texas Press, 1993), 89–104. But on the more humble origins of the lower clergy, see Jens-Uwe Krause, "Überlegungen zur Sozialgeschichte des Klerus im 5/6 Jh. n. Chr.," in *Die Stadt in der Spätantike—Niedergang oder Wandel?*, ed. Jens-Uwe Krause and Christian Witschel (Stuttgart, Germany: Franz Steiner Verlag, 2006), 413–39.

22. Mark A. Handley, *Death, Society and Culture: Inscriptions and Epitaphs in Gaul and Spain, AD 300–750* (Oxford: British Archaeological Reports, 2003), 54. While the total number of comparable inscriptions dating to AD 600–750 is considerably less, the portion of bishops claiming status indicators remains at roughly a third (Handley, 55).

23. Ian Wood, "Administration, Law, and Culture in Merovingian Gaul," in *The Uses of Literacy in Early Medieval Europe*, ed. Rosamond McKitterick (Cambridge: Cambridge University Press, 1990), 63–81, at 76–78. On the community of courtiers (which included several future bishops) that coalesced in the courts of Chlothar II and Dagobert I, see also Yitzhak Hen, *Roman Barbarians: The Royal Court and Culture in the Early Medieval West* (New York: Palgrave, 2007), 94–123; Barbara Rosenwein, *Emotional Communities in the Early Middle Ages* (Ithaca, NY: Cornell University Press, 2006), 130–62; and Sebastian Scholz, *Die Merowinger* (Stuttgart, Germany: Kholhammer Verlag, 2015), 23–29.

24. Steffen Patzold, "Zur Sozialstruktur des Episkopats und zur Ausbildung bischöflicher Herrschaft in Gallien zwischen Spätantike und Frühmittelalter," in *Völker, Reiche und Namen im frühen Mittelalter*, ed. Mathias Becher and Stefanie Dick (Munich: Wilhelm Fink, 2010), 121–140; Steffen Patzold, "Bischöfe, soziale Herkunft und die Organisation lokaler Herrschaft um 500," in *Chlodwigs Welt: Organisation von Herrschaft um 500*, ed. Mischa Meier and Steffen Patzold (Stuttgart, Germany: Steiner, 2014), 523–43; Steffen Patzold, "Die Bischöfe im Gallien der Transformationszeit: Eine sozial homogene

Additionally, there is no reason to assume that those socioeconomic elites who took episcopal office were themselves a homogenous group. As Yaniv Fox has observed in his study of elite support for Columbanian monasticism, "There was a social hierarchy and differentiations of status even within the group broadly labeled 'aristocratic.' The chaotic nature of social interaction means that finding a precise definition of class whose criteria apply to all of its members is virtually impossible."[25] Thus, some bishops were scions of families of supraregional influence and wealth, while others were the members of families of more localized and modest influence. Some owed their offices to their own local status or familial claims to specific sees, others to royal intervention, regardless of their attachment or lack thereof to their designated *civitas*. Citing Patzold's work, Peter Brown has argued convincingly that diversity, ultimately, was a defining characteristic of the Gallo-Roman episcopate, and he consequently has rejected the generalization of the latter as an institution ripe for conquest and domination by a tenacious, grasping senatorial aristocracy intent on maintaining its civic influence in the post-Roman era by alternate means.[26]

While in the following pages every effort will be made to avoid broad generalizations about the Gallo-Frankish bishops as a community of distinct individual personalities, this study does assume the existence of an episcopal corporate body with a superseding identity and voice, which intentionally distinguished members from both laypersons and lower clerics.[27] A consequence

---

Gruppe von Amtsträgern?," in *Antike im Mittelalter: Fortleben, Nachwirken, Wahrnehmung*, ed. Sebastian Brather, Hans Ulrich Nuber, Heiko Steuer, and Thomas Zotz (Ostfildern, Germany: Thorbecke, 2014), 179–93; Steffen Patzold and Conrad Walter, "Der Episkopat im Frankenreich der Merowingerzeit: Eine sich durch Verwandtschaft reproduzierende Elite?," in *Verwandtschaft, Name und soziale Ordnung (300–1000)*, ed. Steffen Patzold and Karl Ubl (Berlin: De Gruyter, 2014), 109–39. Patzold and Walter's study has been critiqued by Hans Hummer, *Visions of Kinship in Medieval Europe* (Oxford: Oxford University Press, 2018), 152–53, for maintaining "an implicit biological standard" for kinship. Hummer, in turn, suggests that "the fate of Gregory [of Tours]' carnal family, as well as those of Sidonius, Ruricius, and Avitus, was inseparable from the episcopal 'families' to which they and theirs were bound." Gregory specifically "defined his kinship as an episcopal network" (Hummer, 139–77; quote on 177).

25. Yaniv Fox, *Power and Religion in Merovingian Gaul* (Cambridge: Cambridge University Press, 2014), 51. See also Peter Brown, *Through the Eye of a Needle: Wealth, the Fall of Rome, and the Making of Christianity in the West, 350–550 A.D.* (Princeton, NJ: Princeton University Press, 2012), 421–23.

26. Peter Brown, "The Study of Elites in Late Antiquity," *Arethusa* 33, no. 3 (2000): 321–46, at 335–38; Brown, *Through the Eye*, 494, 506; Peter Brown, *The Ransom of the Soul: Afterlife and Wealth in Early Western Christianity* (Cambridge, MA: Harvard University Press, 2015), 169–70.

27. In practice, efforts by Gallic ecclesiastics to define and enforce distinctions between themselves and the laity were complicated by the existence of populations such as ascetics, *conversi*, and ecclesiastical dependents, which transcended normative categories; see Lisa Kaaren Bailey, *The Religious Worlds of the Laity in Late Antique Gaul* (London: Bloomsbury, 2016), 21–51, who suggests greater overlap between the lower clerical orders and the laity than between the latter and the ecclesiastical leadership.

of the gradual emergence of monarchical episcopacy in the early church, the notion of episcopal corporatism developed concurrently with the governing organ of the ecclesiastical council.[28] In third-century North Africa, Bishop Cyprian of Carthage (d. 258) convoked a series of early councils whose protocol derived ultimately from that of the Roman Senate (although it has been suggested plausibly that Cyprian had more local sources of inspiration, such as municipal councils).[29] Cyprian's promotion of conciliar governance was predicated on his belief that "the episcopate is one, each part of which is held by an individual for the whole."[30] In his letters, he referred frequently to the episcopal collective as a *collegium*, a flexible term applied in late antiquity to various forms of organized groups of individuals.[31] While Merovingian-era Gallic writers, for the most part, did not adopt Cyprian's precise phraseology to describe episcopal officeholders collectively—preferring instead *ordo*, which likewise implied a shared corporate identity—the organization in Gaul of councils, beginning in the fourth century, as a governing institution for regulating ecclesiastical policy at the provincial and interprovincial levels echoed concurrent trends elsewhere in the wider Mediterranean world in the conceptualization and exercise of episcopal power.[32]

---

28. On episcopal authority in the early church, see Stuart George Hall, "Institutions in the Pre-Constantinian *ecclēsia*," in *The Cambridge History of Christianity*, vol. 1, *Origins to Constantine*, ed. Margaret M. Mitchell and Frances M. Young (Cambridge: Cambridge University Press, 2006), 413–33, at 416–21. On conciliar theory, see Hermann Josef Sieben, *Die Konzilsidee in der Alten Kirche* (Paderborn, Germany: Ferdinand Schöningh, 1979), 515–16, who identifies "horizontal consensus"—i.e., consensus not simply among conciliar participants but also among the churches (*consensio universitatis*)—as one of the fundamental components of conciliar authority in late antiquity.

29. Cf. Pierre Batiffol, "Le règlement des premiers conciles africains et le règlement du sénat romain," *Bulletin d'ancienne littérature et d'archéologie chrétiennes* 3 (1913): 3–19; and Philip R. Amidon, "The Procedure of St. Cyprian's Synods," *Vigiliae Christianae* 37 (1983): 328–39.

30. Cyprian of Carthage, *De catholicae ecclesiae unitate*, ed. Maurice Bévenot, CCSL 3 (Turnhout, Belgium: Brepols, 1972), chap. 5: "Episcopatus unus est cuius a singulis in solidum pars tenetur." On Cyprian's collegial ideal, see François Decret, *Early Christianity in North Africa*, trans. Edward L. Smither (Eugene, OR: Cascade Books, 2009), 76; and Allen Brent, *Cyprian and Roman Carthage* (Cambridge: Cambridge University Press, 2010), 328.

31. See, e.g., Cyprian of Carthage, *Sancti Cypriani episcopi epistularium*, 3 vols., ed. G. F. Diercks, CCSL 3B-D (Turnhout, Belgium: Brepols, 1994–99), eps. 55.1, 7–8; 21, 24, 30; 59.5, 10; 68.3–4. On *collegia*, see Lellia Cracco Ruggini, "Guilds," in *Late Antiquity: A Guide to the Postclassical World*, ed. Glen Warren Bowersock, Peter Brown, and Oleg Grabar (Cambridge, MA: Belknap Press of Harvard University Press, 1999), 479–81.

32. For uses of *ordo*, see, e.g., Gregory of Tours, *Decem libri historiarum*, ed. Bruno Krusch and Wilhelm Levison, MGH SRM 1.1 (Hanover, Germany: Hahn, 1951), 10.19; Gregory of Tours, *Liber in gloria martyrum*, ed. Bruno Krusch, MGH SRM 1.2 (Hanover, Germany: Hahn, 1885 [reprint 1969]), chap. 55; Gregory of Tours, *Liber in gloria confessorum*, ed. Bruno Krusch, MGH SRM 1.2 (Hanover, Germany: Hahn, 1885 [reprint 1969]), chap. 75; Venantius Fortunatus, *Carmina*, ed. Friedrich Leo, MGH AA 4.1 (Berlin: Weidmann, 1881), 3.5, 4.8, 9.1; *Passio Desiderii episcopi Viennensis*, ed. Bruno Krusch, MGH SRM 3 (Hanover, Germany: Hahn, 1896), chap. 7; *Vita Balthildis*, ed. Bruno Krusch, MGH SRM 2 (Hanover, Germany: Hahn, 1888), chap. 6; Council of Marseilles (533), *acta*; Council of

The Gallo-Frankish bishops were conscious of their affiliation with an exclusive order, the rights and responsibilities of which were consistently being defined and redefined, particularly within a conciliar context, and expressed through liturgy, dress, physical space (e.g., the cathedra and *domus episcopi*), preaching, and a self-styled "special relationship" with the saints.[33] In so doing, they refined and intensified contemporaneous efforts to "other" the clergy promoted by both clerics themselves and their lay congregants.[34] Upon their ordination, the Gallo-Frankish bishops consciously assumed the persona of *patres sanctissimi*, inheriting and continuing a tradition of ecclesiastical governance with origins among the apostles of Christ.[35] They constituted "a brotherhood of apostolic successors" who shared a common authority grounded in their individual reception of the pneuma (the spirit from God), their perceptible ascetic and righteous presentation and actions, and their public

---

Tours (567), *epistula ad plebem*; and Council of Chalon-sur-Saône (647/53), c. 20. See also the contemporary Visigothic Sisebut, *Vita vel passio Desiderii episcopi Viennensis*, ed. Bruno Krusch, MGH SRM 3 (Hanover, Germany: Hahn, 1896), chap. 10. On the corporate implications of *ordo*, see Michael Kulikowski, "Ordo," in *Late Ancient Knowing: Explorations in Intellectual History*, ed. Catherine M. Chin and Moulie Vidas (Oakland: University of California Press, 2015), 175–96, at 178–79. On efforts in the late antique Latin West to define the rank and qualities of the individual ecclesiastical orders, see Roger E. Reynolds, *The Ordinals of Christ from Their Origins to the Twelfth Century* (Berlin: Walter de Gruyter, 1978), 28–35. One text falsely credited to Saint Jerome, *De septem ordinibus ecclesiae*, ed. Athanasius Walter Kalff (PhD diss., University of Würzburg, 1935), may have been written in early fifth-century southern Gaul, but seventh-century Iberia also is a possibility; see Reynolds, *Ordinals of Christ*, 31–32. This text and the Gallic *Statuta ecclesiae antiqua* (ca. 476/85), credited to Gennadius of Marseilles, were sources for Isidore of Seville's subsequent, and more prominent, *De ecclesiasticis officiis*, ed. Christopher M. Lawson, CCSL 113 (Turnhout, Belgium: Brepols, 1989). On the *Statuta ecclesiae antiqua*, see *Les Statuta ecclesiae antiqua: Édition, études critiques*, ed. Charles Munier (Paris: Presses Universitaires de France, 1960), 209–36; and Lotte Kéry, ed., *Canonical Collections of the Early Middle Ages (ca. 400–1140)* (Washington, DC: Catholic University of America Press, 1999), 7. On its treatment of the clerical hierarchy, see also Alexandre Faivre, *Naissance d'une hiérarchie: Les premières étapes du cursus clérical* (Paris: Éditions Beauchesne, 1977), 181–98.

33. Michael E. Moore, *A Sacred Kingdom: Bishops and the Rise of Frankish Kingship, 300–850* (Washington, DC: Catholic University of America Press, 2011), 1–202; Kirsten DeVries, "The Episcopate as *Ethnos*: Strategies of Distinction and Episcopal Identity in Merovingian Gaul," in *Emotions, Communities, and Difference in Medieval Europe: Essays in Honor of Barbara H. Rosenwein*, ed. Maureen C. Miller and Edward Wheatley (Abingdon, England: Routledge, 2017), 143–59 (quote on 150). On liturgy, see Bernard Jussen, "Liturgie und Legitimation: Wie die Gallo-Romanen das Römische Reich beendeten," in *Institutionen und Ereignis: Über historische Praktiken und Vorstellungen gesellschaftlichen Ordnens*, ed. Reinhard Blänkner and Bernhard Jussen (Göttingen, Germany: Vandenhoeck and Ruprecht, 1998), 75–136. An English translation of the latter has been published as Bernard Jussen, "Liturgy and Legitimation, or How the Gallo-Romans Ended the Roman Empire," in *Ordering Medieval Society: Perspectives on Intellectual and Practical Modes of Shaping Social Relations*, ed. Bernard Jussen, trans. Pamela Selwyn (Philadelphia: University of Pennsylvania Press, 2001), 147–99. Yitzhak Hen, *The Royal Patronage of Liturgy in Frankish Gaul to the Death of Charles the Bald (877)* (Woodbridge, England: Boydell and Brewer, 2001), 28, 33, observes that individual bishops had considerable flexibility in determining liturgical celebrations, readings, and prayers.

34. Brown, *Through the Eye*, 517–22.

35. Moore, *Sacred Kingdom*, 162–63.

actions taken on behalf of others: what Claudia Rapp has labeled spiritual, ascetic, and pragmatic authority.[36] These qualities, of course, were not necessarily visible in equal measures among episcopal officeholders, nor were they necessarily equally valued as fixed standards across time and space. Steffen Diefenbach has suggested, for instance, that in sixth-century Gaul it was *sanctitas*—corporate, as opposed to personal—that increasingly became the defining virtue of the Gallic episcopate, whereas previously the juxtaposition of a (negated) high social status and *humilitas* had justified the authority of individual prelates. This increased emphasis on a communion between living bishops and their saintly predecessors effectively was a form of collective "self-sanctification."[37] In brief, an ordained bishop's personal authority was grounded in his membership within a sacred order and that order's ability to act in concert. Although he might bring to his office personal wealth and status, his spiritual authority was understood to be delegated directly by God.

While the episcopal *ordo*, conceptually, was supraregional, in administrative practice it fragmented among the "micro-Christendoms" of the early medieval Mediterranean, whose contours were defined at least in part by political geography.[38] The sometimes-uneasy balance of universal and regional expressions of corporate identity is particularly perceptible in the context of ecclesiastical legislating. Membership in a common order empowered bishops to contribute to an evolving tradition of canon law, with a faith that their consensus with each other and with ecclesiastical tradition ensured the orthodoxy of their pronouncements.[39] Nevertheless, the great majority of episcopal

---

36. J. M. Wallace-Hadrill, *The Frankish Church* (Oxford: Clarendon, 1983), 94; Julia Barrow, "The Bishop in the Latin West 600–1100," in *Celibate and Childless Men in Power: Ruling Eunuchs and Bishops in the Pre-modern World*, ed. Almut Höfert, Matthew M. Mesley, and Serena Tolino (London: Routledge, 2018), 43–64, at 44; Claudia Rapp, *Holy Bishops in Late Antiquity: The Nature of Christian Leadership in an Age of Transition* (Berkeley: University of California Press, 2005), 16–18. On bishops as apostolic successors, see also Isidore of Seville, *De ecclesiasticis officiis* 2.5–7.

37. Steffen Diefenbach, "'Bischofsherrschaft': Zur Transformation der politischen Kultur im spätantiken und frühmittelalterlichen Gallien," in *Gallien in Spätantike und Frühmittelalter: Kulturgeschichte einer Region*, ed. Steffen Diefenbach and Gernot M. Müller (Berlin: De Gruyter, 2013), 91–149.

38. For this terminology, see Peter Brown, *The Rise of Western Christendom: Triumph and Diversity, A.D. 200–1000*, rev. ed. (Oxford: Wiley, 2013), 13–17.

39. Sieben, *Die Konzilsidee in der Alten Kirche*, 25–380. The literature on consensus as an episcopal (and, by extension, conciliar) value is vast, but see in particular Jürgen Hannig, *Consensus Fidelium* (Stuttgart, Germany: Anton Hiersemann, 1982), esp. 64–79; Rachel L. Stocking, *Bishops, Councils, and Consensus in the Visigothic Kingdom, 589–633* (Ann Arbor: University of Michigan Press, 2000); Gregory Halfond, *The Archaeology of Frankish Church Councils, AD 511–768* (Leiden: Brill, 2010), 8–9, 87–89, 153–56; Steffen Patzold, "'Konsens' und 'consensus' im Merowingerreich," in *Recht und Konsens im frühen Mittelalter*, ed. Verena Epp and Christoph H. F. Meyer (Ostfildern, Germany: Jan Thornbecke Verlag, 2017), 265–97, at 285–89; and Stefan Esders, "Zwischen Historie und Rechtshistorie: Der *consensus iuris* im frühen Mittelalter," in Epp and Meyer, *Recht und Konsens im frühen Mittelalter*, 427–74, at 447–55.

councils that produced canonical *regulae* in these centuries purposefully addressed local conditions and concerns, seeking not ecumenical application but rather the enforcement of (ostensibly) universal standards locally.[40] While participating bishops assembled with personal, even conflicting, expectations and priorities, their published *acta* communicated their decisions in a single voice, articulating common rules for the governance of those dioceses located within the region or regions represented at the council. The relevance of these rules for unrepresented regions—including other, possibly distant, micro-Christendoms—was determined not so much by the authors of the *acta* as by the recipients, who were best situated to determine applicability to local concerns and conditions.[41]

In Merovingian Gaul specifically, episcopal councils functioned as representative organs of an administrative structure that remained notably stable over the course of the period, despite some variation in the total number of recognized and occupied episcopal sees, which, at any given time, numbered over one hundred.[42] In much of Gaul, this ecclesiastical apparatus closely followed the model of secular provincial organization laid out in the *Notitia Galliarum*, a list originally composed on the orders of the imperial usurper, Magnus Maximus (AD 383–88).[43] Evidence for the continued relevance, if not rigidity, of the Gallic church's provincial system can be found not only in its utilization for conciliar convocation and quite possibly protocol, episcopal ordination procedures, and intraecclesiastical justice. At the same time, individual metro-

---

40. Helmut Reimitz, *History, Frankish Identity and the Framing of Western Ethnicity, 550–850* (Cambridge: Cambridge University Press, 2015), 123, observes that the *acta* of the Council of Orléans (511), as preserved in Cologne, Erzbischöfliche Diözesan- und Dombibliothek cod. 212, conclude with the statement, "Expliciunt canones francisci."

41. Halfond, *Archaeology*, 174–79.

42. On the approximate number of episcopal sees in Merovingian Gaul, see Claude, "Die Bestellung der Bischöfe im merowingischen Reich," 4. Ian Wood, *The Transformation of the Roman West* (Leeds: Arc Humanities Press, 2018), 58, estimates as many as 130 dioceses, although it is not clear if this tally includes sees in Visigothic Narbonensis Prima. For a litany of vacated, merged, and newly founded dioceses between the fifth and seventh centuries, see Florian Mazel, *L'évêque et le territoire: L'invention médiévale de l'espace (Ve–XIIIe siècle)* (Paris: Éditions du Seuil, 2016), 35–36. In regard to individual sees, Mazel suggests that these were defined not by firm territorial borders but rather by those institutions and persons over whom an individual bishop exercised his authority at any given moment. On northern Gaul specifically, see also Margarete Weidemann, "Die kirchliche Organisation der Provinzen Belgica und Germania vom 4. bis zum 7. Jahrhundert," in *Willibrord, zijn wereld en zijn werk*, ed. Petronella Bange and Anton Gerard Weiler (Nijmegen, Netherlands: Centrum voor Middeleeuwse Studies, 1990), 285–316.

43. As shown by Alexander C. Murray, ed., *A Companion to Gregory of Tours* (Leiden: Brill, 2015), 584–91, through a comparison of the *Notitia* and a list of Merovingian-era dioceses, the most significant discrepancies between the two can be found in Southeast Gaul. On the *Notitia*, see Jill Harries, "Church and State in the *Notitia Galliarum*," *Journal of Roman Studies* 68 (1978): 26–43. In addition, there are cases—most notably those of Amandus and Boniface—of bishops appointed (initially) without assigned sees.

politans sometimes struggled to assert their authority over suffragan bishops and sees, and the imposition of royal borders that quite often traversed ecclesiastical boundaries further compromised metropolitan claims of jurisdiction. Chapter 3 will examine in greater detail the conflicts that could arise out of efforts by provincial metropolitans to assert their jurisdictional prerogatives. But the fact remains that the basic administrative structure of the Gallic church survived, albeit with modifications, into the Carolingian era. In both a practical and a symbolic sense, it united the Gallic bishops in a common spiritual and organizational hierarchy that embodied within the borders of the *regnum Francorum* the values and prerogatives of a universal order.[44] In this sense at least, it seems appropriate to refer collectively to the administrative structure governed by the episcopal *ordo* as a "Gallo-Frankish church."

As this Gallo-Frankish church was structured as a federation of dioceses, individual bishops could enjoy considerable autonomy as well as responsibilities within their dioceses, even under the theoretical oversight of a watchful metropolitan.[45] From the perspective of their parishioners, they embodied not merely ecclesiastical *auctoritas* but also, more broadly, a governing authority—albeit typically not the sole governing authority—within the *civitas*.[46] Through diverse acts of *caritas* and *intercessio*, they functioned as patrons of their respective communities.[47] But with such power came responsibility. While some prelates assumed office following lengthy careers in public or clerical service, their new office required commitments of time and energy no less demanding or taxing than their previous responsibilities. These prescribed duties, no less than titles or vestments, served to define the common identity of the episcopate. While the pastoral duties of bishops theoretically were paramount, their prescribed administrative duties very easily could come to dominate their busy schedules. Certainly, if contemporary canons are any indication, episcopal conciliar attendees recognized their supervision of clerical and lay dependents and the management of ecclesiastical property as particularly significant concerns requiring regular review and discussion. Both duties also could necessitate contact with local or court officials if disputes over jurisdiction or property ownership arose. The Gallo-Frankish episcopate

---

44. Halfond, *Archaeology*, 66–69, 200–8. For earlier views, see, e.g., Emile Lesne, *La hiérarchie épiscopale: Provinces, métropolitains, primats en Gaule et Germanie* (Lille, France: Facultes Catholiques, 1905); Pontal, *Histoire des conciles mérovingiens*, 255–57.
45. On the Gallic church as a federation, see Jean Gaudemet, *Les sources du droit de l'Eglise en Occident* (Paris: Éditions du Cerf/Editions du CNRS, 1985), 110.
46. Edward James, *The Origins of France: From Clovis to the Capetians, 500–1000* (New York: St. Martin's, 1982), 49.
47. Jill Harries, *Sidonius Apollinaris and the Fall of Rome* (Oxford: Clarendon, 1994), 207–18; Klingshirn, *Caesarius of Arles*, 235–36.

implicitly followed the rule set down at the Council of Chalcedon (451), which held that such contact was appropriate when it was in the interest of the church or its dependents.[48] But while such duties might raise a bishop's social profile, they also contributed to the heavy burden of the office. There is likely more than a little truth to the observation that "the ordinary prelate of this period . . . was more conscious of the obligations of his office than of its grandeur."[49]

So, if the episcopal office was so great a burden, why did so many individuals seek—even compete for—the chance to occupy it? For some, of course, it was not necessarily a choice. While the reluctant bishop is something of a literary topos of the period, there is no question that some individuals recognized the office as a distraction from other personal priorities, regardless of whether they were ascetic or secular in nature.[50] Conversely, among those bishops who began their careers as secular officeholders, and who owed their appointment to the monarchy, some may have viewed their ecclesiastical appointment as merely the next stage of a *cursus honorum*. For others, who may have devoted the bulk of their adult lives to the religious life, an episcopal see represented not simply a "promotion" and a personal honor but also an opportunity to craft and implement a spiritual and administrative agenda for both a local community and a broader ecclesiastical confederation. Of course, those who long had served their local communities in more humble roles may have viewed the episcopate as an earned position. Gregory of Tours included in his *Historiae* several infamous examples of clerics denied episcopal offices to which they felt entitled, and warned of the destabilizing effects such discontents could have on a diocese.[51]

---

48. Council of Chalcedon (451), c. 3: "Decrevit itaque sanctum hoc magnumque concilium, nullum deinceps, non episcopum non clericum vel monachum, aut possessiones conducere aut negotiis saecularibus sese miscere, praeter pupillorum, si forte curam inexcusabilem leges inponant, aut civitatis episcopus ecclesiasticarum rerum sollicitudinem habere praecipiat, aut orphanorum et viduarum earumque, quae sine ulla provisione sunt, personarum, quae maxime ecclesiastico indigent adiutorio, propter timorem Domini causa deposcat. Si quis autem transgredi de cetero statuta temptaverit, huiusmodi ecclesiasticis increpationibus subiacebit." For the text, see *Decrees of the Ecumenical Councils*, ed. Norman P. Tanner (London: Sheed and Ward; Washington, DC: Georgetown University Press, 1990), 88.

49. Beck, *Pastoral Care of Souls*, 4. See also Jamie Kreiner, "About the Bishop: The Episcopal Entourage and the Economy of Government in Post-Roman Gaul," *Speculum* 86, no. 2 (2011): 321–60, at 337–38.

50. Peter Norton, *Episcopal Elections 250–600: Hierarchy and Popular Will in Late Antiquity* (Oxford: Oxford University Press, 2007), 71–78, 191–202, provides examples.

51. Most infamously Cato, priest of Clermont, and Riculf, priest of Tours: Gregory of Tours, *Decem libri historiarum* 4.5–7, 5.49. On conflicts between bishops and their clergy, see also Brown, *Through the Eye*, 490–92. On the clerical *cursus* in theory and practice, see Robert Godding, *Prêtres en Gaule mérovingienne* (Brussels: Société des Bollandistes, 2001), 32–49.

Along with the honor of the office itself, bishops managed sometimes considerable staff and financial resources, and the perceived power and wealth associated with the office may well have added to its appeal, and not necessarily only to the more unscrupulous of episcopal candidates. In a study of the Merovingian-era episcopate, Jamie Kreiner has explored the symbolic significance of the episcopal entourage, which could include a variety of clerics, servants, and relations. This potentially "ostentatious sight," in Kreiner's words, acted as "a kind of gauge for [a bishop's] influence: the people whose loyalty he moved represented an extension of him, his capabilities, and his resources."[52] But while on the one hand an expression of personal pride, the entourage also was a visual demonstration of the capabilities and dignity of the office itself.

Building projects too served as a physical manifestation of the power of the episcopal office, as well as the worthiness of its occupants. Venantius Fortunatus commemorated in verse the completion of a number of such projects, rarely failing to make an explicit connection between the erected edifice and its financier. For instance, in his commemoration of the dedication of the new cathedral at Nantes circa 556/73, the poet dutifully assigned all honor and applause to Bishop Felix.[53] Although Felix's metropolitan, Eufronius of Tours, was in attendance as well, as were the majority of the latter's suffragans, the glory of the moment belonged to Felix himself, with all other pontifices and *ministri* surrounding him ("circumdant") in support and solidarity.[54] Even if we discount the various accusations subsequently leveled against Felix by Eufronius's successor, Gregory, it still is very easy to imagine the bishop of Nantes's personal pride in seeing his work celebrated and commemorated.[55]

The poet too recognized the obvious significance of building projects for the public and the posthumous reputations of the episcopal dedicatees of his poems.[56] But expressions of power like elaborate processions and monumental architecture did not necessarily negate an understanding on the part of episcopal officeholders that this power theoretically was grounded in the office itself. Where pride in office ended and personal pride began rarely is clearly identifiable from our sources. We need not deny the ostensible piety of many Gallo-Frankish bishops while acknowledging that these same individuals may

---

52. Kreiner, "About the Bishop," 343–44. More broadly, Wood, *Transformation of the Roman West*, 66, estimates that individual Gallic bishops supervised on average upwards of one hundred clerics.

53. Fortunatus, *Carmina* 3.6.46.

54. Fortunatus 3.6.45. On the attendees, see Gregory Halfond, "Charibert I and the Episcopal Leadership of the Kingdom of Paris (561–567)," *Viator* 43, no. 2 (2012): 1–28, at 14–17.

55. For a reevaluation of the relationship between Felix and Gregory, see William McDermott, "Felix of Nantes: A Merovingian Bishop," *Traditio* 31 (1975): 1–24.

56. Judith George, *Venantius Fortunatus: A Latin Poet in Merovingian Gaul* (Oxford: Clarendon, 1992), 108–23.

have been drawn to their offices by a range of personal and circumstantial factors. Former lay officials, for example, could embrace the dignity of episcopal office, while career clerics could abuse the unique power with which they had been entrusted.

Once in office, however, regardless of piety or aptitude, an individual prelate was incorporated into a larger *ordo*, whose collective personality and voice superseded his own when his and his colleagues acted in concert.[57] And while the burdens of office were indeed very real, the assumption of a corporate identity not only endowed members with a status that, in theory, superseded noble birth, wealth, and social prominence, it also incorporated members into an exclusive "community of shared obligation," whose members struggled collectively to achieve solidarity.[58] It was this community whose obligations, virtues, and communal spirit Avitus of Vienne had extolled in his convocation epistle of 517.

The Merovingian kings and queens, as I have suggested, similarly recognized, and even embraced, the existence of a superseding episcopal corporate order.[59] In identifying episcopal collaborators, the Merovingians naturally prioritized individuals from whom they could expect cooperation or who represented a diocese in which the monarchy maintained a strategic interest. Nevertheless, the services performed by these bishops on behalf of the royal court were predicated on their membership within a common order with recognized moral and administrative *auctoritas*. Despite this acknowledgment of corporate exceptionalism, the monarchy's necessarily unequal treatment of individual representatives of the Gallo-Frankish episcopal *ordo* proved ultimately to be a destabilizing influence on corporate solidarity.

Arguments and Methods

The following chapters explore the challenge for individual prelates to balance their personal and corporate responsibilities and priorities. While prior stud-

---

57. DeVries, "Episcopate as *Ethnos*," 153–54, rightly identifies the authority inherent in the episcopal voice, as utilized for preaching, prayer, and song, but does not distinguish between individual and corporate voices.

58. I borrow this conceptualization of community from Gervase Rosser, *The Art of Solidarity in the Middle Ages: Guilds in England, 1250–1555* (Oxford: Oxford University Press, 2015), 192.

59. As observed by Bruno Dumézil, "Incarnating Authority, Exercising Authority: The Figure of the King in the Merovingian Era," in *Absentee Authority across Medieval Europe*, ed. Frédérique Lachaud and Michael Penman (Woodbridge, England: Boydell, 2017), 21–36, Merovingian political culture similarly permitted a distinction between the reigning monarch and the responsibility for the care of the realm (regnum) that he exercised but did not solely possess.

ies of Gallo-Frankish bishops largely have singled out for emphasis one or the other of these overlapping identities, thereby implicitly endorsing an unnecessarily bifurcated perspective of the episcopate, for the reasons just outlined, an approach that embraces both individuality and corporatism can more precisely and comprehensively assess the experiences of these bishops. While Merovingian Francia is the geographical focus of this book, the perspective adopted here by no means is assumed to be exclusive to a single micro-Christendom. As the episcopal *ordo* was conceptually universal, regional variations on corporate identity united local networks of individual bishops throughout the former Roman West. Whenever possible, this study distinguishes those sources that preserve the corporate voice of the episcopate, particularly conciliar *acta*, charters, and multiauthored epistles. Certainly, such documents were not necessarily written by committee, and they may purposefully conceal any disagreement that may have preceded their publication. However, the subscriptions appended to conciliar acts, charters, and epistles do indicate the ostensible consensus of all of the signatories, whose individual contributions effectively are limited to their membership within a larger order. It was, in no small way, this corporatization of individual personalities that gave such documents their authority.

Chapter 1 surveys those services to the court most closely and habitually associated with the Gallo-Frankish episcopal *ordo* of the Merovingian era: counseling rulers; securing *pax* and administrative order through mediation, legislation, and judicial action; and normalizing political partitions provoked by war, treaty, or royal succession. While individual bishops might, of course, perform a variety of additional services for the royal regime—or none at all, for that matter—as an order the episcopate assented to the monarchy's expectation of collaboration and recognized this service as indicative of both personal and corporate status. As this expectation was grounded first and foremost in the spiritual *auctoritas* of the collective, other relevant factors such as individual social status or prior service to the court—which so often are the primary focus of modern efforts to define *Bischofsherrschaft* (literally, episcopal rule or lordship)—can be understand as being of secondary importance. Bishops certainly were not the only individuals capable of transcending the distance between the *civitas* and the court; they were unique, however, in their collective membership in an administrative structure ostensibly independent from—but collaborative with—royal administration.

Chapter 2 surveys the means by which the royal court solicited support and service from bishops. These forms of solicitation were expectedly diverse and included the nomination of individual candidates for episcopal election, displays of mercy or largesse either unsolicited or in response to petitions, and, perhaps most significantly, the formal recognition of the episcopate's corporate authority by, among other means, an embrace of conciliarism.⁶⁰ The Merovingians themselves, despite the occasional (and infamous) outburst about bishops who enjoyed all too much wealth and power, clearly recognized the advantages of a strong episcopate and did not attempt in any systematic way to redefine individual prelates as mere royal agents apart from their shared corporate identity.⁶¹ The monarchy furthermore relied on venerable traditions of patronage in defining their relationships both with individual bishops and with the corporate order. While, not surprisingly, the strategic allocation of this patronage could be perceived by individual bishops as inconsistent or unjust, the episcopate was just as committed as the monarchy to patronage as a social and economic instrument. Although this commitment most frequently has been identified in modern scholarship in relation to episcopal management of cults of sanctity, bishops in fact utilized patronage in maintaining personal relationships with a variety of persons both within and beyond their dioceses. Additionally, as individuals and as an *ordo*, they embraced the tangible benefits of royal beneficence, financial or otherwise. This receptivity, while in no way evidence for sycophancy, nevertheless placed recipients in dependent relationships with the monarchy, relationships that in some cases necessarily took precedence over corporate loyalties.

In an effort to contextualize more precisely the threat posed by royal patronage for episcopal corporate integrity, chapter 3 explores the causes of internal divisions that could form within the Gallo-Frankish episcopate, including both interpersonal disputes between prelates and the involvement of bishops in regnal or factional politics. While some interpersonal conflicts could be narrow, even petty, political differences easily could exacerbate tensions between prelates. It is well known that involvement in secular politics proved deadly for some unfortunate prelates. But its effects on the corporate integrity of the episcopate could be equally decisive. While there is no evidence to suggest either the formation of political blocs constituted primarily or entirely by bishops in Merovingian Gaul or the longevity of the majority of identifiable political factions that included episcopal partisans, a significant number of bishops

---

60. I employ the term *conciliarism* here and elsewhere following the definition of Paul Valliere, *Conciliarism: A History of Decision-Making in the Church* (Cambridge: Cambridge University Press, 2012), 7: "decision-making by means of . . . formally constituted, trans-local leadership assemblies called together to resolve issues affecting the life and ministry of the church."

61. The best-known example of such an outburst is that of Chilperic I: Gregory of Tours, *Decem libri historiarum* 6.46: "Ecce pauper remansit fiscus noster, ecce divitiae nostrae ad eclesias sunt translatae; nulli penitus nisi soli episcopi regnant." On this claim, cf. the responses of Wallace-Hadrill, *Frankish Church*, 124; and Jean Durliat, *Les finances publiques de Dioclétien aux Carolingiens (284–889)* (Sigmaringen, Germany: Jan Thorbecke Verlag, 1990), 138.

did affiliate with various political coalitions, and in some cases their relationships with their episcopal brethren consequently were damaged. Aside from the short-term injuries to corporate solidarity caused by political partisanship, it is not evident that long-term consequences included the often-assumed secularization of the episcopate. Instead, the long-standing expectation that bishops would contribute to royal efforts to promote public peace and order continually found new institutional and ideological expressions between the sixth and eighth centuries.

Periods of hostility between rival Frankish regna or between aristocratic factions most obviously provoked bishops to declare or act on political allegiances. However, as examined in chapter 4, moments of political unification could prompt similar responses. This phenomenon is explored through three case studies: the royal regimes of Clovis I (ca. 481/82–511) and Chlothar II (584–629) and the mayoral career of Pippin II (d. 714) before and after the Battle of Tertry (687). While all three leaders famously triumphed over their political opponents in military confrontations, they also were masters of diplomacy, skillfully and strategically directing their patronage toward individuals and institutions whose loyalty and support they pursued. However, in their efforts to encourage unified political support, Clovis, Chlothar, and Pippin unintentionally applied stress to the corporate integrity of the episcopate by requesting the allegiance of bishops, some of whom were unwilling or unable to grant it. More generally, as new regimes and borders were defined and redefined, affected bishops—regardless of personal political loyalties—often had no choice but to reorient themselves in relation to these structural changes that impacted the administration and integrity of the Gallo-Frankish church.[62] But rather than simply embrace secularism in response to political pressures and solicitations, Gallic bishops continued to endorse their long-standing ideal of corporate unity, even in moments of dramatic political change or transformation.

A Note on Sources

In an effort to distinguish, and indeed honor, the diversity of episcopal voices and perspectives from Merovingian Gaul, the sometimes-deafening voices of the major historical and hagiographical narrative sources for the period—in particular Gregory of Tours, the seventh-century Fredegar chronicler, and the

---

62. Louis Duchesne, *L'eglise au VI siècle* (Paris: Fontemoing, E. de Boccard, Successeur, 1925), 529–30; James, *Origins of France*, 197.

anonymous author of the *Liber historiae Francorum*—will not be permitted to drown out all others. This is not to say that these sources will be purposefully neglected, but rather that they will be treated as texts that co-opt rather than preserve individual episcopal identities and voices in service of their authors' narrative goals.

Gregory's authorial program has been discussed, debated, and dissected at length by modern scholars, who—despite their various interpretive differences—largely agree on the quality of the bishop's long-underappreciated skills as a narrative architect; the impact of his theological, political, and ideological perspectives on his historical writings; and the centrality of bishops to his worldview and literary corpus.[63] A diverse cast of prelates populates Gregory's writings, some holy, some mediocre, some utterly venal, and it simply is not possible to pursue any remotely comprehensive study of the Gallic episcopate during the entirety of the Merovingian era and ignore the biographical information provided by Gregory. At the same time, however, if we have no choice but to approach these individuals through the filter of the bishop of Tours, then it is necessary to identify more precisely the significance of this filter.

Even a cursory reading of the *Historiae* reveals that Gregory did not naively believe that only holy men were drawn to episcopal office, or that the office itself somehow purified the souls of its occupants. But, conversely, the bishop of Tours was no mere cynic who viewed contemporary ecclesiastical institutions as hopelessly corrupt. As perhaps the most forceful and articulate proponent of *Bischofsherrschaft* in sixth-century Gaul, Gregory—in Martin Heinzelmann's words—favored a "clericalization of society," in which bishops assumed a public role alongside the monarchy to ensure that "the values of the eternal *ecclesia Dei* were to be applied to the social values of Merovingian society."[64] Gregory acknowledged the obvious disconnect between his ideal and the contemporary reality, and Heinzelmann has suggested that the social message encoded in the *Historiae* was aimed first and foremost at the Merovingians themselves, lest they neglect to their detriment the counsel and coop-

---

63. See, for example, Giselle de Nie, *Views from a Many-Windowed Tower: Studies of Imagination in the Works of Gregory of Tours* (Amsterdam: Rodopi, 1987); Ian Wood, "The Secret Histories of Gregory of Tours," *Revue belge de philologie et d'histoire* 71 (1993): 253–70; Adriaan Breukelaar, *Historiography and Episcopal Authority in Sixth-Century Gaul* (Göttingen, Germany: Vandenhoeck and Ruprecht, 1994); Walter Goffart, *The Narrators of Barbarian History*, paperback ed. (Notre Dame, IN: University of Notre Dame Press, 2005), 112–234; Martin Heinzelmann, *Gregory of Tours: History and Society in the Sixth Century*, trans. Christopher Carroll (Cambridge: Cambridge University Press, 2001); Kathleen Mitchell and Ian Wood, eds., *The World of Gregory of Tours* (Leiden: Brill, 2002); and Murray, *Companion to Gregory of Tours*.

64. Heinzelmann, *Gregory of Tours*, 181–91 (quotes on 189, 191).

eration of bishops. Gregory furthermore distinguished between the episcopal office and its occasionally unworthy occupants. His *Historiae* offers several examples of the episcopal ideal, including, it has been observed, the bishop of Tours himself. As Kathleen Mitchell recognizes in her influential study of sanctity in the *Historiae*, "The bishop Gregory, in fact, served the historian Gregory as one of his best interpreters of the essential relationship between Christian belief and public action. He was one of his own best saints."[65] Those bishops who compared unfavorably to Gregory's model were not indicative of a dysfunctional episcopate, but rather their flaws put into relief the ideal promoted—and ostensibly embodied—by the bishop of Tours himself.

Gregory's construction of an episcopal ideal based on himself, sanctified exemplars like Martin of Tours, and even some contemporaries and near contemporaries raises the question of whether a reader can even trust the veracity of the characterizations of the individual prelates who populate the *Historiae*. Or, to put it another way, does Gregory's work necessarily reduce real persons to literary exempla? Such questions reflect broader epistemological concerns about the use of Gregory's historical writings as reliable sources while recognizing that they were part of the same socio-theological project that also produced the (less credible to many modern readers) *Miracula*.[66] Recognizing the deep significance of Gregory's complex worldview for his historical writings does not, of course, reduce them to "mere" literary artifacts. As Alexander C. Murray has cautioned, "Recognizing Gregory's point of view obviously requires more on our part than a reliance on old clichés about his naiveté and superstition. But, on the other hand, we should not jump to the conclusion that Gregory was the Loki of 6th-century history."[67]

I therefore follow Murray—and others—in assuming that Gregory did not unashamedly invent those events and persons about which he wrote, while still recognizing the bishop's narrative as a filter that complicates, and even at times distorts, our perceptions of his times. As I have suggested, since Gregory's writings are the sole source of biographical information on literally dozens of the bishops mentioned in the following pages, to simply ignore his work on the grounds that his personal values and experiences influenced his narrative would be both excessive and counterproductive. Instead, I have approached

---

65. Kathleen Mitchell, "Saints and Public Christianity in the *Historiae* of Gregory of Tours," in *Religion and Society in the Early Middle Ages: Studies in Honor of Richard E. Sullivan*, ed. T. F. X. Noble and John Contreni (Kalamazoo, MI: Medieval Institute Publications, 1987), 77–94, at 82.
66. Allen E. Jones, *Social Mobility in Late Antique Gaul* (Cambridge: Cambridge University Press, 2009), 68–69.
67. Alexander C. Murray, "The Composition of the *Histories* of Gregory of Tours and Its Bearing on the Political Narrative," in Murray, *Companion to Gregory of Tours*, 63–101, at 101.

Gregory's episcopal portraits not as objective representations but rather as subjective re-creations of individual personalities, some known personally to the historian, the others known only through the writings or memories of others. So, for example, Gregory writes disapprovingly in his *Historiae* of the arrogance of Bishop Leontius II of Bordeaux, who, it appears, promoted his own diocese as an "apostolic see."[68] While Gregory and Leontius were contemporaries, there is no reason to think that they ever enjoyed significant personal contact, let alone an intimate relationship.[69] Conversely, Leontius was very well known to Gregory's kinsman and predecessor as bishop of Tours, Eufronius, who likely was the source of Gregory's rather unflattering portrait. In the case of Leontius, we are fortunate to have sources other than Gregory alone for his life and career, including several poems by Venantius Fortunatus in which Leontius was the dedicatee; in many other cases, we are not so lucky.[70] In such instances, without compelling evidence to the contrary, I have not assumed that Gregory's information is necessarily factually suspect, particularly when the prelate in question was known personally to the bishop of Tours. Conversely, I also have assumed that Gregory chose selectively, and accentuated accordingly, that personal information deemed relevant to his narrative program, and that his episcopal portraits are fundamentally reflective of the historian's perception of his subjects.

While not as frequently praised for their literary skills as Gregory, the Fredegar chronicler, the unknown author of the *Liber historiae Francorum*, and the anonymous and identifiable hagiographers of Merovingian Francia, like the bishop of Tours, need to be approached not as naïve chroniclers but rather as deliberative narrative architects. As both the Fredegar *Chronica* and the *Liber historiae Francorum*—particularly the former, which names more than two dozen prelates in the interpolated passages of books 1–3 and in book 4—have much to say about the Gallo-Frankish church and its bishops, it is essential to approach this information with the same caution and attention to authorial agenda as with Gregory's more expansive and elaborate work. In the case of

---

68. Gregory of Tours, *Decem libri historiarum* 4.26: "Igitur postquam presbiter Parisiacae urbis portas ingressus regis praesentiam adiit, haec affatus est: 'Salvae, rex gloriosae. Sedis enim apostolica eminentiae tuae salutem mittit uberrimam.'"

69. On Leontius and his family, see Elie Griffe, "Un évêque de Bordeaux au VIe siècle: Léonce le Jeune," *Bulletin de littérature ecclésiastique* 64 (1963): 63–71; Karl Friedrich Stroheker, *Der senatorische Adel im spatantiken Gallien* (Tübingen, Germany: Alma Mater Verlag, 1948), 188; Heinzelmann, *Bischofsherrschaft in Gallien*, 217–20; J. R. Martindale, ed., *The Prosopography of the Later Roman Empire* (Cambridge: Cambridge University Press, 1992), 3:774; and Luce Pietri and Marc Heijmans, eds., *Prosopographie de la Gaule chrétienne (314–614)*, Prosopographie chrétienne du Bas-Empire 4 (Paris: Association des amis du Centre d'histoire et civilisation de Byzance, 2013), 1145–49.

70. I.e., Fortunatus, *Carmina* 1.6, 1.8–20, 4.10.

the seventh-century version of the Fredegar chronicle, I have followed the current scholarly consensus that a single "author" working around AD 660 was responsible for the compilation of the chronicle.[71] Even though the Fredegar chronicler drew his material from a variety of sources, his selection and extensive editing and elaboration of source texts reflect an authorial program not limited solely to his continuation of Gregory's *Historiae*. Not only were the chronicler's interpolations of new material into existing texts sometimes quite extensive, they also provide additional information—of varying credibility—that fundamentally alters the source texts. To cite just one particularly infamous example, the chronicler inserts into his epitome of Gregory's account of the Gundovald conspiracy the names of supposed episcopal conspirators, Flavius of Chalon and Syagrius of Autun, of whose complicity Gregory does not so much as hint. There is simply no way to verify (or for that matter disprove) the chronicler's accusations, although circumstantial evidence at least suggests that they ought to be treated skeptically.[72] But while it is not possible to determine the veracity or source of these unsubstantiated charges, their inclusion ultimately tells us less about the Gundovald conspiracy, for which Gregory remains our best—if a problematic—source, and more about the Fredegar chronicler's complex, but generally tolerant, view of episcopal participation in secular politics.[73]

The Neustrian *Liber historiae Francorum* (ca. 727), while shorter than both Gregory's *Historiae* and the Fredegar chronicle, and generally less obviously concerned with the affairs of bishops, is no less carefully composed, and it is a crucial source for the political history of the later Merovingian era.[74] While the chronicler offers few substantial episcopal portraits, he or she shares the Fredegar chronicle's preference for terse and subtle editorializing regarding their actions. Despite the author's less obvious interest in ecclesiastical or

---

71. For the case for single authorship, see Walter Goffart, "The Fredegar Problem Reconsidered," *Speculum* 18 (1963): 206–41; and Alvar Erikson, "The Problem of Authorship in the Chronicle of Fredegar," *Eranos* 63 (1965): 47–76. See also Roger Collins, *Fredegar*, Authors of the Middle Ages 13 (Aldershot, England: Ashgate, 1996), 11–16. For the dating, see Collins, *Fredegar*, 82–3; and Roger Collins, *Die Fredegar-Chroniken* (Hanover, Germany: Hahn, 2007), 25–26.

72. Gregory Halfond, "All the King's Men: Episcopal Political Loyalties in the Merovingian Kingdoms," *Medieval Prosopography* 27 (2012): 76–96, at 88–89.

73. Fredegar, *Chronica*, ed. Bruno Krusch, MGH SRM 2 (Hanover, Germany: Hahn, 1888), 3.89.

74. Richard Gerberding, *The Rise of the Carolingians and the Liber Historiae Francorum* (Oxford: Oxford University Press, 1987); Philipp Dörler, "The *Liber Historiae Francorum*—a Model for a New Frankish Self-Confidence," *Network and Neighbours* 1 (2013): 23–43; Richard Broome, "Approaches to the Frankish Community in the *Chronicle of Fredegar* and *Liber Historiae Francorum*," in *The Long Seventh Century: Continuity and Discontinuity in an Age of Transition*, ed. Alessandro Gnasso, Emanuele E. Intagliata, and Thomas J. MacMaster (Oxford: Peter Lang, 2015), 61–86.

religious matters, there is no reason to assume his or her secular status.[75] The even more terse sixth-century *Chronica* of Bishop Marius of Avenches, for example, despite its author's known attachment to the episcopal *ordo*, on its surface suggests little interest in the church and its bishops, with references to only three named Gallic prelates, none of which offers a particularly flattering representation of the Gallo-Frankish episcopate.[76] While the sort of biographical details available for Gregory of Tours conceivably could shed additional light on the narrative programs of these chronicles, without such information it is all the more necessary not simply to contextualize those spare references to individual bishops within the narrative programs that can be inferred from the texts themselves but also to consider why certain prelates were singled out for special attention.

So, for example, leaving aside for now the well-known admiration of the anonymous author of the *Liber historiae Francorum* for Bishop Audoin of Rouen, the same chronicler conversely was disdainful of the participation of Bishop Dido of Poitiers in the Grimoald coup d'état. Dido, the uncle of Leudegar of Autun, of whom the chronicler writes approvingly, is not explicitly criticized for luring the royal heir Dagobert II (676–79) to Ireland in 656, but Grimoald's own treachery in the same chapter is condemned in the harshest terms. Dido is guilty not simply by association but for committing the same act of disloyalty for which Grimoald was convicted.[77] While the chronicler admired the Pippinids of the late seventh and early eighth centuries, he or she had no patience for those *nobiles* who undermined the integrity of the court and monarchy; his or her ideal was cooperation between the monarchy and nobility, with the latter providing that counsel necessary for the proper governance of the realm.[78] Dido is not unique among the named bishops in the *Liber historiae Francorum* for his political involvement, but unlike, for instance, Audoin and Leudegar of Autun, his actions did not align with those of the

---

75. Gerberding, *Rise of the Carolingians*, 169, suggests that it is a "reasonable assumption" that the chronicler lived in a monastery. For the possibility that the chronicler was a nun of the convent of Notre Dame in Soissons, see Janet Nelson, "Gender and Genre in Women Historians of the Early Middle Ages," in *The Frankish World, 750–900* (London: Hambledon, 1996), 183–97, at 194–95.

76. Marius of Avenches, *Chronica*, ed. and trans. Justin Favrod (Lausanne: Université de Lausanne, 1993), an. 565, 579.

77. *Liber historiae Francorum*, ed. Bruno Krusch, MGH SRM 2 (Hanover, Germany: Hahn, 1888), chap. 43. Cf. *Visio Baronti monachi Longoretensis*, ed. Wilhelm Levison, MGH SRM 5 (Hanover, Germany: Hahn, 1910), chap. 17, on which see Yitzhak Hen, "The Structure and Aims of the *Visio Baronti*," *Journal of Theological Studies* 47, no. 2 (1996): 477–97. On Dido, see also Gerberding, *Rise of the Carolingians*, 48–49, 60–61, 66; Paul Fouracre and Richard Gerberding, eds., *Late Merovingian France* (Manchester: Manchester University Press, 1996), 101, 103, 196, 317; and Fox, *Power and Religion*, 177, 191, 267.

78. Gerberding, *Rise of the Carolingians*, 166–72; Fouracre and Gerberding, *Late Merovingian France*, 80–81.

Franci and the realm, as understood by the chronicler. Dido, in other words, seems to have been singled out not as an exemplar of a secularized episcopate but rather as an unfortunate reminder of the damage caused by those who seek to overturn the existing political order.

A similar attention to authorial intent is required with hagiographical and epigraphic sources for individual episcopal lives. *Vitae*, of course, also contain their own unique array of interpretive challenges, and I have taken inspiration here in particular from Jamie Kreiner's study of Merovingian-era lives, which explores how hagiographers employed sophisticated narrative strategies to encourage readers to locate in the lives of individual holy men and women lessons on governance, justice, and social welfare.[79] Kreiner observes in several of the *vitae*, for instance, an association between the performance of episcopal duties and the rule of the regnum, with "the integrity of the kingdom . . . becoming the ultimate measure of bishops' pastoral efficacy."[80] Similar to episcopal epitaphs, hagiographies are essentially commemorative in nature, with the authors of the texts seeking conformity between biographical "reality" and socioreligious ideals. In Fortunatus's epitaphs for bishops, for example, there is a "typical sequence" of episcopal merits that includes, among others, "family and secular office holding, secular and religious . . . personal qualities of character[,] . . . charitable and pastoral works[,] . . . and building activities."[81] Despite the regularity of these virtues across his poetic corpus, Fortunatus did not simply invent the personal details that served as "proof" for these virtues; but these details nevertheless were selectively chosen and do not provide a complete, and even necessarily accurate, portrait of the dedicatee.

So, as with contemporary historical writings, we cannot simply strip away an ideological veneer of commemorative sources to get to the truth buried beneath, as this "factual" material is very much part of the programmatic effort to idealize an individual. As Mark Handley observes in his wide-ranging study of late antique Gallic and Iberian epigraphy, "We should place no more trust in an episcopal epitaph that says a bishop acted as a judge and as a 'father of the poor,' than we would were the source hagiographical. Of course these

---

79. Kreiner, *Social Life of Hagiography*.
80. Kreiner, 182.
81. Michael Roberts, *The Humblest Sparrow: The Poetry of Venantius Fortunatus* (Ann Arbor: University of Michigan Press, 2009), 17. Heinzelmann, *Bischofsherrschaft in Gallien*, 239–42, in his broader survey of episcopal epitaphs, stresses the primacy of paternal *pietas*, as well as *iustitia, integritas, moderatio*, and *eloquentia*. Rosenwein, *Emotional Communities*, 123, notes Fortunatus's own emphasis on episcopal paternalism. On Fortunatus's depiction of bishops, see also Brian Brennan, "The Image of the Merovingian Bishop in the Poetry of Venantius Fortunatus," *Journal of Medieval History* 18, no. 2 (1992): 115–39.

texts exaggerate the role of the bishop—this was their function."[82] Episcopal *vitae*, in turn, arguably tell us more about the social construction of the "saintly bishop" than about the bishops themselves. In this sense they provide alternative, but no less valid, perspectives on the episcopal office to those found in contemporary historical writings.[83] If, as Kreiner suggests, these lives both reflected and helped to define aristocratic values in the *regnum Francorum*, their importance for the construction of the episcopal corporate public image must not be underestimated.

While historical and hagiographical texts in particular, despite their interpretive challenges, are fundamental for this study, epistolary sources are just as important for their ostensible preservation of unique episcopal voices and their sometimes-contrasting perspectives on the duties, responsibilities, and self-image of the corporate episcopate. The conscious selection and editing of surviving letters for inclusion in early medieval epistolary collections means that we cannot read them as the pure, "unfiltered" products of their original authors, who themselves did not necessarily choose to reveal the entirety of their thoughts and personality in their correspondence. Individual letters, as well as the collections that compiled them, thus must be treated as consciously constructed artifacts, rather than as unfiltered and transparent transcriptions of personal communications.[84] Nevertheless, compared to the episcopal personalities whose presence in historical and hagiographical sources is dictated largely by their contribution to an authorial agenda of which they had no knowledge or possibly even agreement, the episcopal voices preserved through epistles are likely to retain at least a comparatively more potent individuality.[85]

---

82. Handley, *Death, Society and Culture*, 3.

83. As, for instance, Georg Scheibelreiter, *Der Bischof in merowingischer Zeit* (Vienna: Bohlau, 1983), 240, observes regarding the literary construction of an episcopal death: "The bishop to whom a biography is dedicated, or who is reckoned to be among the leading figures of his time, dies according to his 'ordo.'" See also Georg Scheibelreiter, "The Death of the Bishop in the Early Middle Ages," in *The End of Strife*, ed. David Loades (Edinburgh: T. and T. Clark, 1984), 32–43, at 33.

84. Christiana Sogno, Bradley K. Storin, and Edward J. Watts, "Introduction: Greek and Latin Epistolography and Epistolary Collections in Late Antiquity," in *Late Antique Letter Collections: A Critical Introduction and Reference Guide*, ed. Christiana Sogno, Bradley K. Storin, and Edward J. Watts (Oakland: University of California Press, 2017), 1–10, at 1.

85. The same might be said of episcopal testaments—i.e., Remigius, *Testamentum*, ed. Bruno Krusch, MGH SRM 3 (Hanover, Germany: Hahn, 1896), 336–47; Caesarius of Arles, *Sancti Caesarii episcopi Arelatensis Opera omnia*, ed. Germain Morin (Brugge, Belgium: Maretioli, 1937–42), 2:281–89; Bertram of Le Mans, *Das Testament des Bischofs Berthramn von Le Mans*, ed. Margarete Weidemann (Mainz, Germany: Verlag des Römisch-Germanischen Zentralmuseums, 1986); and Margarete Weidemann, ed., *Geschichte des Bistums Le Mans von der Spätantike bis zur Karolingerzeit* (Mainz, Germany: Verlag des Römisch-Germanischen Zentralmuseums in Kommission bei Habelt, 2002), 2:202–6 (Hadoindus of Le Mans). Besides the expected information on familial relations, landholdings, and affiliations with religious institutions, Bonnie Effros, *Caring for Body and Soul: Burial and the Afterlife in the*

This attention to both the diversity and accessibility of individual episcopal voices ultimately is what permits a contextualization of episcopal corporatism, the construction and integrity of which were both contingent on the divergent experiences and perspectives of the episcopal officeholders of Merovingian Gaul. Corporate solidarity was a goal, not a perpetual state of affairs, and any number of factors, personal and well as political, could shatter episcopal consensus. Nevertheless, between the sixth and mid-eighth centuries, the most predictably disruptive force remained the political activities of bishops. Bishops were not pseudo royal officials, although their performance of public service—locally, at court, or both—informed and complicated episcopal corporate identity. Even the most mundane and limited service could divide a bishop's attention and loyalty from his corporate obligations. The cumulative effect was not, however, gradually expanding, irreparable fissures but rather a stubborn determination not to allow the inevitable conflicts to permanently rend the fraternal bond shared between the apostolic successors of Merovingian Gaul.

Merovingian World (Philadelphia: University of Pennsylvania Press, 2002), 195–96, also observes in the charitable donations and emancipations prescribed in these wills a personal desire by the testators for personal salvation and a forgiveness of sin. On the wills, see also Josef Semmler, "Zum Testament des gallofränkischen Bischofs," in *Herrscher- und Fürstentestamente im westeuropäischen Mittelalter*, ed. Brigitte Kasten (Cologne, Germany: Böhlau Verlag, 2008), 573–97.

Chapter 1

Episcopal Service to the Court

In his recounting of Chlothar II's triumph over his dynastic rivals, the Fredegar chronicler, normally sympathetic to Chlothar, relates approvingly how the *beatissimus* bishop Austrenus of Orléans in 604 provided shelter to the Burgundian mayor Bertoald. Bertoald had been in flight from Chlothar's forces, after having been sent purposely into harm's way by Theuderic II (596–613), Brunhild (d. 613), and his political nemesis, the *patricius* Protadius.[1] It is unknown whether Austrenus, the brother of Bishop Aunacharius of Auxerre, ever was disciplined for his interference in the interregnal warfare that culminated in Chlothar's domination of the entirety of the *regnum Francorum*. Fredegar's account certainly does not suggest that Austrenus was motivated by crass partisanship in offering shelter to the mayor. Rather, the chronicler implies that it was the bishop's mercy that inspired his courageous actions. Nevertheless, Fredegar does not indicate that Bertoald claimed right of asylum within a specific ecclesiastical institution. Instead, Austrenus closed the gates of Burgundian Orléans behind the mayor, knowing full well that Bertoald was being pursued by an invading Neustrian army. Nor did the bishop give up the fugitive to the enemy when the besiegers surrounded the city. So, even while the bishop's motives in protecting Bertoald may well have been pious, he staked both his own life and those of the residents of

---

1. Fredegar, *Chronica* 4.25. For Fredegar's opinion of Chlothar II, see *Chronica* 4.42.

Orléans on the principle that the *civitas* belonged to the Burgundian court, and that the Neustrians besieging its defenses had no claim either to it or to the mayor within its walls. While Bertoald certainly had his personal enemies in Burgundy, Theuderic almost certainly would have been relieved upon learning of Austrenus's actions.

Austrenus seems to have been relatively unique among Merovingian-era bishops for his audacious display of political loyalty. Most prelates simply were never in the position of needing to prove their allegiances at great personal risk to themselves. This is not to say that the fidelity of bishops was irrelevant to the Merovingian rulers whom they served, but rather that this fidelity rarely was tested in so dramatic a fashion. But while the political integrity of the Frankish realm did not rest solely on the shoulders of local bishops, the Merovingians not only solicited episcopal prayers for themselves and the realm, they acted on the assumption that the cooperation of bishops was a necessary component of effective royal governance.[2] Why the Frankish monarchy should consistently maintain this conviction over the entirety of the Merovingian period is the primary issue addressed in this chapter. Rather than comprehensively survey the myriad forms that episcopal service to the court could take during these centuries, the focus instead will be on those responsibilities that became ingrained into the administrative practices and political culture of the Merovingian realm. These included offering counsel to rulers, legislating in council for the purpose of securing administrative order and peace in the realm, and legitimizing territorial claims and partitions. In encouraging these services, the Merovingians sought to take full advantage of the administrative and spiritual *auctoritas* of the episcopate without purposefully compromising either by forcing bishops into the role of quasi-secular officials.

Counsel and Personal Communications

After King Chilperic I (561–84) departed from the audience hall (*secretarium*) of the Basilica of Saint Peter in Paris in 577, the assembled council of bishops

---

2. For the royal solicitation of episcopal prayers, see, e.g., *Marculfi formulae*, ed. Karl Zeumer, MGH Legum Sectio 5: Formulae (Hanover, Germany: Hahn, 1886), 1.6. Liturgical examples of prayers for kings include: *The Bobbio Missal: A Gallican Mass Book*, ed. E. A. Lowe, Henry Bradshaw Society Publications 58 (London: Harrison and Sons, 1920), 151–53; *Missale Francorum*, ed. Leo C. Mohlberg (Rome: Herder, 1957), 20–21; and *Liber sacramentorum Romanae ecclesiae ordinis anni circuli (Sacramentarium Gelasianum)*, ed. Leo C. Mohlberg, Leo Eizenhöfer, and Petrus Siffrin (Rome: Herder, 1960), 213–18. On these, see Hen, *Royal Patronage of Liturgy*, 39–41.

and clerics remained behind to discuss the testimony that they had just heard.³ Although the trial of Bishop Praetextatus of Rouen had only just begun, the disconcerting presence of Chilperic himself at the proceedings, along with the appearance of a threatening crowd of Franci assembled outside the church, ensured a tense atmosphere within. Then, in the middle of the discussion, a Parisian archdeacon named Aetius entered the hall and addressed the bishops. His words startled the assembled prelates. In a pseudoprophetic speech, Aetius warned his clerical superiors that if they allowed the unjust prosecution of Praetextatus to continue, they would effectively forfeit their claim to be bishops of God.⁴

Sitting among the bishops in the basilica listening to this speech was Bishop Gregory of Tours, who insisted decades later that among his colleagues he alone had the courage to echo the archdeacon's admonishment. The speech that Gregory later recalled delivering at the Council of Paris (577) assumed the same prophetic tone that Aetius had employed.⁵ Gregory liberally paraphrased to his colleagues from the Old Testament prophet Ezekiel, who had cautioned, "But if the watchman sees the sword coming and does not blow the trumpet, so that the people are not warned, and the sword comes, and takes any one of them; that man is taken away in his iniquity, but his blood I will require at the watchman's hand" (Ezek. 33:6). In his *Historiae*, Gregory claims that he addressed his words specifically to those among his colleagues friendly to Chilperic, warning them of their own obligation to advise the king justly lest they, like the watchman who did not warn of an impending blow, allow his soul to be damned through sin. Gregory, by his own admission, met the same stony silence that greeted Aetius's speech. Undaunted, he continued his sermonizing, providing historical examples in support of his counsel. Again, according to Gregory, no one among the assembled body responded. However, among the conciliar attendees were two sycophants (*adolatores*) of Chilperic, Bertram of Bordeaux and Ragnemodus of Paris, who afterward informed the king of Gregory's opposition to the prosecution of Praetextatus. From Gregory's perspective, Bertram and Ragnemodus were guilty not of perfidy per se but rather of providing poor counsel to a king desperately in need of pious admonitions of the sort Gregory himself was prepared to deliver. When

---

3. On the basilica, see Jean-Charles Picard et al., *Province ecclésiastique de Sens (Lugdunensis Senonia)*, Topographie chrétienne des cités de la Gaule 8 (Paris: De Boccard, 1992), 116–19.

4. Gregory of Tours, *Decem libri historiarum* 5.18: "Audite me, o sacerdotes Domini, qui in unum collecti estis; aut enim hoc tempore exaltabitis nomen vestrum et bonae famae gratia refulgebitis, aut certe nullus vos amodo pro Dei sacerdotibus est habiturus, si personas vestras sagaciter non eregitis aut fratrem perire permittetis."

5. Heinzelmann, *Gregory of Tours*, 141.

Chilperic subsequently accused Gregory of refusing him *iustitia*, the bishop replied that all he could offer the king was counsel; only God could judge him.[6]

Chilperic, of course, was not unique among Frankish monarchs in his unresponsiveness to direct criticism from his bishops. The Merovingians, while occasionally receptive to artfully formulated admonitions, rarely responded positively to threats of spiritual sanctions. One of Gregory's own spiritual heroes, Nicetius of Trier, had gracelessly crossed this line with Chilperic's father, Chlothar I.[7] Possibly having gotten accustomed to the willingness of his previous royal masters, Theuderic I (511–34) and Theudebert I (534–47), to tolerate his reproaches, Nicetius went too far when he excommunicated Chlothar I. The king, taking advantage of the considerable ill will harbored against the bishop by some of his own episcopal colleagues, arranged for the metropolitan prelate's exile. Nicetius's banishment lasted through the remainder of the unforgiving king's lifetime.[8]

It seems, however, that more Merovingian bishops prudently followed the example of Nicetius's colleagues than that of Nicetius himself, cooperating, if sometimes only begrudgingly, with the royal court rather than sanctimoniously challenging its authority. This is not to accuse these prelates of cowardice or sycophancy, as did Gregory of Tours of his episcopal colleagues in his account of the Council of Paris (577). While the episcopal office theoretically armed bishops with the *auctoritas* to proffer spiritual counsel, the maintenance of an effective personal relationship with the court required a delicate

---

6. Gregory of Tours, *Decem libri historiarum* 5.18: "Si quis de nobis, o rex, iustitiae tramitem transcendere voluerit, a te corrigi potest; si vero tu excesseris, quis te corripiet? Loquimur enim tibi; sed si volueris, audis; si autem nolueris, quis te condemnavit, nisi is qui se pronuntiavit esse iustitiam." On *iustitia*, and its place among the cardinal virtues, see Sibylle Mahl, *Quadriga virtutum, Die Kardinalugenden in der Geistesgeschichte der Karolingerzeit* (Cologne, Germany: Böhlau, 1969). On its implementation in Merovingian Gaul, see Olivier Guillot, "La justice dans le royaume Franc à l'époque merovingienne," in *La giustizia nell'alto medioevo, secoli V–VIII* (Spoleto, Italy: Centro Italiano di Studi sull'Alto Medioevo, 1995), 653–731. On Praetextatus's trial, see Stefan Esders, *Römische Rechtstradition und merowingisches Königtum* (Göttingen, Germany: Vandenhoeck and Ruprecht, 1997), 443–49; Nira Gradowicz-Pancer, "Femmes royales et violences anti-épiscopales l'époque a mérovingienne: Frédégonde et le meurtre de l'évêque Pretextat," in *Bischofsmord im Mittelalter*, ed. Natalie Fryde and Dirk Reitz (Göttingen, Germany: Vandenhoeck and Ruprecht, 2003), 37–50; and Helmut Reimitz, "After Rome, before Francia: Religion, Ethnicity, and Identity Politics in Gregory of Tours' *Ten Books of Histories*," in *Making Early Medieval Societies: Conflict and Belonging in the Latin West, 300–1200*, ed. Kate Cooper and Conrad Leyser (Cambridge: Cambridge University Press, 2016), 58–79, at 61–67.

7. On Nicetius of Trier, see Nancy Gauthier, *L'évangélisation des pays de la Moselle: La province romaine de Première Belgique entre Antiquité et Moyen-Âge (IIIe–VIIIe siècles)* (Paris: E. de Boccard, 1980), 172–89; and Kevin Uhalde, *Expectations of Justice in the Age of Augustine* (Philadelphia: University of Pennsylvania Press, 2007), 62–65.

8. Gregory of Tours, *Liber vitae patrum*, ed. Bruno Krusch, MGH SRM 1.2 (Hanover, Germany: Hahn, 1885 [reprint 1969]), 17.1–3.

approach from both sides. Of course, these were not relationships between equals. Moreover, spiritual and royal authority had distinct sources and expressions that were not always fully compatible. This disparity is apparent in the often-repeated contemporary formula *canones et leges*. Both conciliar canons and royal legislation had binding authority in Merovingian Gaul and were thought to be complementary but not identical.[9] When kings cited canonical *regulae* in their own edicts, it rarely was without revision; they preferred to craft their own legal statements, rather than simply repeating verbatim the decisions of their bishops.[10] In the same way, bishops were considered by kings to be valued partners in the promotion of domestic peace and administrative order (*pax et disciplina*), in part because they did bring to bear different talents and resources toward this shared goal, not least of which was their pastoral and spiritual authority, which intimated a special competency in the promotion of justice.[11]

However, as the examples of Nicetius and Praetextatus suggest, monarchs and bishops sometimes disagreed when it came to actually defining *iustitia* in specific cases, particularly when it was the monarch's own judgment or actions that were in question. Episcopal counsel could, in theory, provide necessary guidance, but only when it was accepted as constructive rather than insolent or ill conceived. This required bishops to be diplomatic in their communications with the court, and conversely for the Merovingians to be receptive to advice grounded in moral judgment while at the same time being wary of *consilium perfidum*. In both interpersonal dialogues between bishops and monarchs and those communications in which the Gallo-Frankish episcopate assumed a corporate voice, the medium, message, and sincerity of the counsel all were determining factors in the receptivity of monarchs to counsel.

Like Gregory of Tours, the seventh-century Fredegar chronicler too endorsed the basic principle of episcopal counsel, while still providing several examples of bishops proffering specious advice. So, whereas the chronicler attributed the (initially) successful reign of Dagobert I (623–39) to his counselors Arnulf of Metz and later Cunibert of Cologne, he also credited the victory of Dagobert's father, Chlothar II, over his political enemies in part to the

---

9. Halfond, *Archaeology*, 137–42.
10. Halfond, 142–46.
11. On peace and order, see Alexander C. Murray, "*Pax et Disciplina*: Roman Public Law and the Merovingian State," in *Proceedings of the Tenth International Congress of Medieval Canon Law*, ed. Kenneth Pennington, Stanley Chodorow, and Keith H. Kendall (Vatican City: Biblioteca Apostolica Vaticana, 2001), 269–85; Thomas Renna, "The Idea of Peace in the West," *Journal of Medieval History* 6 (1980): 143–67, at 148–50; and Paul Kershaw, *Peaceful Kings: Peace, Power and the Early Medieval Political Imagination* (Oxford: Oxford University Press, 2010), 119–31. On late antique expectations of episcopal justice, see Uhalde, *Expectations of Justice*.

latter's execution of Bishop Desiderius of Vienne on the *consilium* of Aridius of Lyons.[12] The chronicler implies in these and other cases that episcopal office alone did not guarantee constructive, or even reliable, counsel, and that the Merovingians, with whom all final decisions lay, had to evaluate carefully the sources and motivations of all advice offered to them by their counselors. The chronicler here implicitly followed his predecessor Gregory, who credited the deaths of several Merovingians to their failure to follow episcopal counsel, and admitted that not all bishops were to be trusted.[13]

Also significant for the reception of episcopal counsel were the personalities of the parties and the context of the discourse, as the case of Nicetius suggests. It is unknown whether Nicetius's time in exile mellowed the cantankerous prelate, but it is clear that his relationship with Chlothar's son, Sigibert I (561–75), was considerably more sociable than with the latter's father. There is reason to think, however, that Sigibert himself initially was hesitant about recalling from exile the bishop who had excommunicated his father. The eighth-century *Vita Goaris* suggests that Nicetius actually was Sigibert's second choice for the episcopal see, after the hermit Goar, who refused the position.[14] Although the *vita*'s account admittedly is of questionable veracity, Sigibert certainly was aware that Nicetius was, even in the best of times, a difficult man, some of whose own episcopal colleagues supported his deposition. But Nicetius's force of personality also could be an attractive feature in a bishop whose *civitas* was under military threat by the king's brother, Chilperic. Perhaps trusting in Nicetius's ostensible gratitude for his recall, Sigibert not only restored Nicetius but also invited him to provide counsel at court.[15]

---

12. Fredegar, *Chronica* 4.32, 4.58. See also Gregory Halfond, "The Endorsement of Royal-Episcopal Collaboration in the Fredegar *Chronica*," *Traditio* 70 (2015): 1–28, at 7–8.

13. Failures to heed episcopal counsel: Gregory of Tours, *Decem libri historiarum* 3.6, 4.26, 4.51. On Egidius of Rheims's poor counsel, see Gregory of Tours, *Decem libri historiarum* 7.33, 10.19. On Gregory's ideal of episcopal counsel, see Breukelaar, *Historiography*, 252–54. In contrast to Gregory's *Historiae* and the Fredegar Chronicle, the *Liber historiae Francorum* devotes little attention to episcopal counsel, although the counsel of the Franci is a major theme: Gerberding, *Rise of the Carolingians*, 75–76, 168.

14. *Vita Goaris confessoris Rhenani*, ed. Bruno Krusch, MGH SRM 4 (Hanover, Germany: Hahn, 1888), chaps. 7–11. The *vita* also reports that during Nicetius's absence, a certain Rusticus held the episcopal seat of Trier. On the veracity of the *vita*'s account, see Eugen Ewig, *Trier im Merowingerreich: Civitas, Stadt, Bistum* (Trier, Germany: Paulinus Verlag, 1954), 88–90. Cf. Franz Josef Heyen, "St. Goar im frühen und hohen Mittelalter," *Kurtrierisches Jahrbuch* 1 (1961): 87–106, at 92–93; and Ferdinand Pauly, *Die Stifte St. Severus in Boppard, St. Goar in St. Goar, Liebfrauen in Oberwesel, St. Martin in Oberwesel*, Erzbistum Trier 2 (Berlin: De Gruyter, 1980), 161–64. Cf. also the comments of Krusch in his edition of the *Vita Goaris*, 403–5; and Gauthier, *L'évangélisation*, 170–71.

15. Gregory of Tours, *Liber vitae patrum* 17.5: "Regressus autem a rege evectu navali, obdormivit." On the context for Nicetius's restoration, see Gregory Halfond, "Negotiating Episcopal Support in the Merovingian Kingdom of Rheims," *Early Medieval Europe* 22, no. 1 (2014): 1–25, at 10–12.

Sigibert similarly was cautious in accepting the counsel of Bishop Germanus of Paris, whom the king knew to be on friendly terms with his brother Chilperic.[16] Germanus in 573 also had played a leading role at the Burgundian-sponsored Council of Paris, which had requested that Sigibert support the deposition of Bishop Promotus of Châteaudun, whose appointment had been prompted by Sigibert's efforts to extend his authority over the *civitas* of Chartres.[17] Gregory of Tours, from the perspective of hindsight, credited Sigibert's death to his refusal to heed Germanus's admonition not to depose his brother Chilperic. Nevertheless, the bishop of Tours acknowledged that Sigibert permitted Germanus to advise him right up until his untimely death.[18]

While the narrative histories, hagiographies, and royal diplomas of the Merovingian era affirm the acceptability, frequency, and benefits of episcopal counsel, the strongest evidence for the rhetorical strategies adopted by episcopal counselors can be found in the relatively slim corpus of epistolary communications between members of the Gallo-Frankish episcopate and the Merovingians.[19] Although it is likely that counsel most often was delivered orally in the presence of the ruler, such *viva voce* exchanges survive only in the filtered accounts of narrative sources and thus are less likely to reflect accurately the form or even the content of the original conversations.

The earliest surviving epistolary exchanges between bishops and the Merovingians are five letters dating to the reign of Clovis I. Significantly, the first of these epistles, written by Remigius of Rheims most likely upon the occasion of Clovis's succession as king in Belgica Secunda (traditionally dated to ca. 481/82), provides a rationale for why the yet-to-be converted ruler should include Catholic bishops among his *consiliarii*.[20] Remigius suggests that an

---

16. Gregory Halfond, "Sis Quoque Catholicis Religionis Apex: The Ecclesiastical Patronage of Chilperic I and Fredegund," *Church History* 81 (2012): 48–76, at 73.

17. *Concilia Galliae: A.511–A.695*, 211–17; Gregory of Tours, *Decem libri historiarum* 4.47. On this council, see Charles de Clercq, *La législation religieuse franque de Clovis à Charlemagne (507–814)* (Leuven, Belgium: Bibliothèque de l'Université, 1936), 47–48; Pontal, *Histoire des conciles mérovingiens*, 169–70; and Halfond, "Negotiating Episcopal Support," 21.

18. Gregory of Tours, *Decem libri historiarum* 4.51.

19. *Epistolae Austrasicae*, ed. Wilhelm Gundlach, MGH Epistolae 3 (Berlin: Weidmann, 1892), nos. 1, 2, 8, 9, 10 (112–13, 119–26); *Epistolae aevi Merowingici collectae*, ed. Wilhelm Gundlach, MGH Epistolae 3 (Berlin: Weidmann, 1892), nos. 3, 15 (437–38, 457–60); Avitus of Vienne, *Opera*, ep. 46 (75–76); Desiderius of Cahors, *Epistulae S. Desiderii Cadurcensis*, ed. Dag Norberg (Uppsala, Sweden: Almquist and Wiksell, 1961), nos. 1.3, 1.4, 1.5, 2.9, 2.17 (15–20, 57–58, 69–71); *Concilia Galliae: A.511–A.695*, 4, 111–12, 215–17 (Council of Orléans [511], Epistle to Clovis I; Council of Clermont [535], Epistle to Theudebert I; Council of Paris [573], Epistle to Sigibert I); *Vita Desiderii Cadurcae urbis episcopi*, ed. Bruno Krusch, MGH SRM 4 (Hanover, Germany: Hahn, 1902), chap. 14 (572–73). On the reflection in royal diplomas of episcopal counsel and participation in court discussions, see Kreiner, *Social Life of Hagiography*, 165n87 (with references).

20. *Epistolae Austrasicae* no. 2 (113–14). The epistle also has been dated to the aftermath of the Syagrian campaign ca. 486; see, e.g., Matthias Becher, *Chlodwig I: Der Aufstieg der Merowinger und das*

effective (episcopal) counselor can bolster a ruler's reputation (*fama*), and that Belgica Secunda would profit from the harmony between the king and his bishops. In the same letter, Remigius encourages Clovis's adoption of policies reflective of the social values of the church, specifically charity and justice.[21] In his second surviving letter to Clovis, written on the occasion of the death of the king's sister Albofledis, Remigius repeats his earlier recommendation that Clovis would rule most effectively with *consilia erectiora*, presumably again with the Gallic bishops in mind. In addition, he urges the king to devote himself fully to the maintenance of public order as the head of his people ("Populorum caput estis et regimen sustinetis").[22]

The three principles of *caritas*, *iustitia*, and *disciplina publica* (with its corollary *pax*) would form the ideological basis for much subsequent episcopal counsel to the Merovingian dynasty, and they are reflected as early as Clovis's own letter to the bishops of Aquitaine (507/8), in which the king committed, in principle, to the protection of ecclesiastical property and dependents and the charitable redemption of captives taken during his campaign against the Visigoths.[23] Clovis's acceptance of the general principle of episcopal counsel

---

Ende der antiken Welt (Munich: C. H. Beck, 2011), 153–54. Nevertheless, the dating I suggest in the text remains the most widely accepted; see Reinhold Kaiser and Sebastian Scholz, *Quellen zur Geschichte der Franken und der Merowinger: Vom 3. Jahrhundert bis 751* (Stuttgart, Germany: Kohlhammer, 2012), 100. However, cf. Penny MacGeorge, *Late Roman Warlords* (Oxford: Oxford University Press, 2002), 125–30, who suggests that the letter was written following an indeterminate (but presumably brief) period of unrest during which Clovis faced competition for his father's legacy in the province. Guy Halsall, "Childeric's Grave, Clovis' Succession, and the Origins of the Merovingian Kingdom," in *Cemeteries and Societies in Merovingian Gaul: Selected Studies in History and Archaeology, 1992–2009* (Leiden: Brill, 2010), 169–87, at 172, as well as his appended "Commentary" (188–97, at 191–93), implies a date between 474 and 500 but ultimately concludes that the letter is "undatable." More recently, Graham Barrett and George Woudhuysen, "Remigius and the 'Important News' of Clovis Rewritten," *Antiquité Tardive* 24 (2016): 471–500, who provide a thorough historiographical overview (and new edition), have suggested a late date, ca. 500/511. Cf. however Pablo Poveda Arias, "Clovis and Remigius of Reims in the Making of the Merovingian Kingdoms," *European Review of History/Revue européenne d'histoire*, published online, November 23, 2017 (https://doi.org/10.1080/13507486.2017.1397108), 1–22, at 3, who observes that Barrett and Woudhuysen's preferred reading of *secundum bellice* over the *Secundum Belgice* of Gundlach's edition does not preclude the possibility that the letter refers to an earlier campaign. On the inclusion of Remigius's letters among the *Epistulae Austrasicae*, see Graham Barrett and George Woudhuysen, "Assembling the *Austrasian Letters* at Trier and Lorsch," *Early Medieval Europe* 24, no. 1 (2016): 3–57, at 34–36.

21. *Epistolae Austrasicae* no. 2 (113): "Et beneficium tuum castum et honestum esse debet, et sacerdotibus tuis debebis deferre et ad eorum consilia semper recurre; quodsi tibi bene cum illis convenerit, provincia tua melius potest constare. Civos tuos erige, adflictos releva, viduas fove, orfanos nutre, si potius est, quam erudies, et omnes te ament et timeant. Iustitia ex ore vestro procedat, nihil sit sperandum de pauperes vel peregrinis, ne magis dona aut aliquid accipere vellis; praetorium tuum omnibus pateatur, ut nullus exinde tristis abscedat."

22. *Epistolae Austrasicae* no. 1 (112–13).

23. Clovis, *Epistola ad episcopos*, in *Capitularia regum Francorum*, ed. Alfred Boretius, MGH Legum Sectio 2: Capitularia regum Francorum (Hanover, Germany: Hahn, 1883), 1–2. On the dating of this

similarly was reaffirmed in 511, when he convoked the Council of Orléans (511). In their epistolary preface to the conciliar *acta*, addressed to Clovis, the conciliar attendees describe their canons as recommendations in response to the topical agenda (*tituli*) proposed by the king, suggesting that they understood Clovis's conciliar convocation as a request for episcopal counsel on specific issues of mutual concern.[24]

In contrast to the shared ecclesio-political values enshrined in these four letters, Avitus of Vienne, in an epistle to Clovis assumed to have been written on the occasion of the Frankish king's baptism, emphasizes a different range of royal virtues—namely, *fides, humilitas* (before God and his bishops), *misericordia*, and, somewhat surprisingly for a recent convert, mission.[25] While subsequent epistolary exchanges between Merovingian kings and bishops would promote in particular the first three of these virtues, it is striking that there should be so little overlap between Avitus's counsel and that of Remigius.[26]

---

letter, see Ian Wood, *The Merovingian Kingdoms: 450–751* (London: Longman, 1994), 47; William M. Daly, "Clovis: How Barbarian, How Pagan?," *Speculum* 69, no. 3 (1994): 619–64, at 645n80; and Danuta R. Shanzer, "Dating the Baptism of Clovis: The Bishop of Vienne vs. the Bishop of Tours," *Early Medieval Europe* 7, no. 1 (1998): 29–57, at 47–50. On the redemption of captives as an expression of *caritas*, see William Klingshirn, "Charity and Power: Caesarius of Arles and the Ransoming of Captives in Sub-Roman Gaul," *Journal of Roman Studies* 75 (1985): 183–203.

24. Council of Orléans (511), Epistle to Clovis: "Quia tanta ad religionis catholicae cultum gloriosae fidei cura vos excitat, ut sacerdotalis mentis afteetum sacerdotes de rebus necessariis tractaturos in unum collegi iusseritis, secundum voluntates vestras consultationem et titulos, quos dedistis, ea quae nobis visum est definitione respondimus."

25. Avitus of Vienne, *Opera*, ep. 46 (75–76). Remigius, in his first letter to Clovis, does credit the king's humility (presumably before God) for his success. On proselytization, also see *Epistolae Austrasicae* no. 8 (119–22), which is Nicetius of Trier's effort to persuade Chlothar I's daughter, Chlodosind, to preach the Catholic faith to her Lombard husband.

26. On the establishment of those virtues identified by Remigius and Avitus as fundamental components of the early medieval ideology of kingship, see Eugen Ewig, "Zum christlichen Königsgedanken im Frühmittelalter," in *Spätantikes und fränkisches Gallien*, 3 vols., ed. Hartmut Atsma et al. (Munich: Artemis, 1976–2009), 1:3–71; J. M. Wallace-Hadrill, *Early Germanic Kingship in England and on the Continent* (Oxford: Clarendon, 1971), 48–53; Marc Reydellet, *La royauté dans la littérature latine de Sidoine Apollinaire à Isidore de Séville* (Rome: École Française de Rome, 1981); Brian Brennan, "The Image of the Frankish Kings in the Poetry of Venantius Fortunatus," *Journal of Medieval History* 10, no. 1 (1984): 1–11; and P. D. King, "The Barbarian Kingdoms," in *The Cambridge History of Medieval Political Thought, c. 350–c. 1450*, ed. J. H. Burns (Cambridge: Cambridge University Press, 1988), 123–53 (with special attention paid to the Visigothic kingdom). On Gregory of Tours specifically, see also J. M. Wallace-Hadrill, "Gregory of Tours and Bede: Their Views on the Personal Qualities of Kings," in *Early Medieval History* (New York: Harper and Row, 1976), 96–114; Breukelaar, *Historiography*, 230–45 (who emphasizes the relevance of many of these same virtues to bishops and to secular elites); and Martin Heinzelmann, "Gregor von Tours: Die ideologische Grundlegung fränkischer Königsherrschaft," in *Die Franken—Wegbereiter Europas*, ed. Alfried Wieczorek et al. (Mainz, Germany: Verlag Philipp von Zabern, 1996), 1:381–88. Note, however, the observation of Gerd Althoff, *Family, Friends, and Followers: Political and Social Bonds in Early Medieval Europe*, trans. Christopher Carroll (Cambridge: Cambridge University Press, 2004), 106, that there was no hierarchy of royal virtues in this period.

While the latter emphasized such virtues as receptivity to episcopal counsel, justice, and public order, which not only were germane to a head of state but were in their essence qualities of effective royal governance, Avitus's moral program, while certainly applicable to royalty—*misericordia*, for instance, was understood during late antiquity as a particularly elite virtue associated with *caritas*—nevertheless emphasized qualities comparatively less exclusive to public administration.[27] Possibly Avitus's residency in the Burgundian regnum influenced the content of his letter of congratulations to a "foreign" king: he neither personally knew nor served Clovis. His concern may have been less with the latter's internal administration of the *regnum Francorum* than with his assumption of Catholic rule and the moral expectations that it entailed.[28]

The relevance of the major themes of the episcopal counsel of the reign of Clovis to subsequent generations of Merovingian rulers is apparent in two later letters of counsel, both effectively prototypical "mirrors for princes."[29] The first of these is a epistle sent by a Provençal bishop named Aurelianus to Theudebert I sometime in the late 530s that promotes many of the same royal virtues previously identified by Remigius and Avitus, utilizing in several cases identical vocabulary, including *misericordia, iustitia,* and *humilitas*.[30] A similar, but even lengthier, mirror was written for Clovis II (634–57) by an anonymous bishop circa 645.[31] It has been observed of this epistle that while it demonstrates significant stylistic and substantive parallels with both Remigius's correspondence with Clovis and Aurelianus's letter to Theudebert, its reliance on Old Testament themes and models—in particular Kings David and Solomon—is far more pronounced, perhaps reflecting a deepening "Christianization" of Frankish kingship in the seventh century.[32] The anonymous

---

27. Deborah M. Deliyannis, *Ravenna in Late Antiquity* (Cambridge: Cambridge University Press, 2010), 330n165. On *misericordia*, see also Hélène Petre, *Caritas: Etude sur le vocabulaire latin de la charité chrétienne* (Leuven, Belgium: Spicilegium Sacrum Lovaniense, 1948), 229–39. Roger Collins, "Theodebert I, 'Rex Magnus Francorum,'" in Wormald, Bullough, and Collins, *Ideal and Reality*, 7–33, at 22–23, notes that *humilitas* rarely was applied to Roman emperors outside of the Ambrosian tradition.

28. This is not to say, of course, that Avitus did not recognize as well the broader diplomatic implications of the conversion. See Shanzer and Wood, *Avitus of Vienne*, 25–26, 362–69.

29. On this genre, see Hans Hubert Anton, *Fürstenspiegel des frühen und hohen Mittelalters* (Darmstadt, Germany: Wissenschaftliche Buchgesellschaft, 2006).

30. *Epistolae Austrasicae* no. 10 (124–26). In addition, *concordia* is somewhat analogous to Remigius's emphasis on social order and cohesion. On the identity of Aurelianus and the dating of the letter, see Collins, "Theodebert," 18–21, who rejects an association with the similarly named bishop of Arles, who had been appointed by Childebert I. On the latter Aurelianus, see Klingshirn, *Caesarius of Arles*, 262–64.

31. *Epistolae aevi Merowingici collectae* no. 15 (457–60). On the identity of the addressee, see Reimitz, *History, Frankish Identity*, 264–65.

32. Yitzhak Hen, "The Uses of the Bible and the Perception of Kingship in Merovingian Gaul," *Early Medieval Europe* 7, no. 3 (1998): 277–89, at 284–85; Yitzhak Hen, "The Christianisation of Kingship," in *Der Dynastiewechsel von 751: Vorgeschichte, Legitimationsstrategien und Erinnerung*, ed. Mathias

episcopal author impresses on Clovis that just as the Israelite kings embodied such values as humility and justice and listened to the counsel of the prophets, he too should heed the advice of his bishops and senior counselors.³³

While these two letters reflect a continuing emphasis on the importance of episcopal counsel, as well as those specific virtues by which the Gallo-Frankish episcopate had defined good kingship since the time of Clovis, the means by which these same virtues might be promoted in more concrete contexts are suggested by that royal-episcopal correspondence concerned with issues of contention between kings and bishops. In such instances, it was not uncommon for policy recommendations to be couched in moralizing advice akin to that found in the aforementioned epistolary mirrors for princes. For instance, in 575, Germanus of Paris employed biblical parallelism when he wrote to Queen Brunhild in the hopes that she would intercede with her husband, Sigibert, in the manner of Queen Esther, as Sigibert pursued war against his brother Chilperic. Additionally, Germanus warned the queen that should Sigibert attempt to kill his brother, he risked the same divine punishments that struck such biblical fratricides as Cain and Absalom.³⁴ While his use of biblical parallels allowed Germanus to avoid a more candid reproach in his promotion of peace, he also informed Brunhild that rumors—to which (he insisted) he gave no credence—were circulating that it was she who was encouraging her husband's belligerence.³⁵ Proving these rumors wrong not only would benefit the queen's personal reputation but, more importantly, would encourage *pax* within the *regnum Francorum*.

Germanus and his episcopal colleagues similarly had avoided frank condemnation when they wrote directly to Sigibert two years earlier, following the

---

Becher and Jörg Jarnut (Münster, Germany: Scriptorium, 2004), 163–78, at 169; Hans-Hubert Anton, "Königsvorstellungen bei Iren und Franken im Vergleich," in *Das frühmittelalterliche Königtum: Ideele und religiöse Grundlagen*, ed. Franz-Reiner Erkens (Berlin: De Gruyter, 2005), 270–330, at 320–24; Reimitz, *History, Frankish Identity*, 264–66.

33. *Epistolae aevi Merowingici collectae* no. 15 (458): "Isti reges supradicti semper, prophetae Domini quod eis denuntiaverunt, intento sensu audierunt. Quamobrem, gloriosissime domine, modo oportet te, ut et sacerdotes audias et consiliarios seniores diligas simulque et illum, qui post te palatium tuum regit, et ad eorum doctrinam, quam tibi indicant, vigilanter adtendas, quia vulgari sermone ita dicitur: 'Qui cum pluribus consiliatur, solus non peccat.'" Clovis's brother, Sigibert III (ca. 633–ca. 656), received a letter from Bishop Desiderius of Cahors (post-639) following the death of Dagobert I. Desiderius of Cahors, *Epistulae S. Desiderii Cadurcensis* no. 1.3 (15–16). Much shorter than the two prototype princely mirrors, this letter similarly echoes traditional episcopal virtue of royal *caritas* by stressing that the new king should devote himself to *bona opera*.

34. *Epistolae Austrasicae* no. 9 (122–24).

35. *Epistolae Austrasicae* no. 9 (123): "Vulgi verba iterantes, quae nos maxime terrent, vestrae pietati in notitiam deponimus, quae ita disseminat—eloquentium ora detrahuntur—, quasi vestro voto, consilio et instigatione domnus gloriosissimus Sigibertus rex tam arduae hanc vellit perdere regionem. Non propterea haec dicimus, quasi a nobis credatur; sed supplicamus, ut nulla occansio tribuatur dicendi, unde vobis tam maximum et periculosum generetis blasphemium."

conclusion of their deliberations at the Council of Paris (573). In their epistle, the bishops politely credited Sigibert with helping to organize the synod, which he almost certainly had not. They took a generally conciliatory tone with the king who had arranged for the aforementioned election of Promotus as bishop of Châteaudun, asking Sigibert for his cooperation in the enforcement of their decision to depose Promotus.[36] Yet beneath this veneer of pleasantries is a frank condemnation of Sigibert's actions, as well as a demand that he not intervene as the bishops of a rival regnum attempted to nullify his earlier decree. The utilization of their corporate voice no doubt emboldened the bishops at Paris, as did the protection owed to them by Sigibert's brother Guntram (561–92). However, at the same time, they likely understood that an appeal to Sigibert's sense of *iustitia* was more likely to succeed than harsh criticism of his role in the Promotus affair.

Similarly eager to avoid too provocative a condemnation of royal action was Bishop Desiderius of Cahors in a letter to Dagobert I seeking to appeal a judicial decision by the king (ca. 630/39) in opposition to the interests of the church of Cahors.[37] The closest Desiderius came to explicit censure of Dagobert's verdict was a quotation of James 2:13: "For judgment is without mercy to one who has shown no mercy; yet mercy triumphs over judgment." But Desiderius "knew his limits" and followed this biblical quotation with an apology for his counsel.[38]

Rather less judicious than either Desiderius or Germanus and his colleagues was Bishop Leo of Sens, whose letter to Childebert I of 540 notably lacks the tact one would typically expect from a bishop responding to a royal order.[39] Childebert previously had requested that Leo, as provincial metropolitan, preside at, or least give his consent to, the ordination of a bishop for the *castrum* of Melun, which lay between Paris and Leo's own *civitas*. Sens, at the time of the request, was under the jurisdiction of Theudebert I, while Childebert claimed the nearby Melun.[40] In response to Childebert's request, Leo feigned surprise that the king would pursue the ordination without the approval of Theudebert and threatened ecclesiastical sanctions against any of his colleagues who might choose to cooperate with the king in violation of the canons. While Leo stops just short of threatening Childebert himself, rather

---

36. Council of Paris (573), Epistle to Sigibert (149–50): "Nuper etenim non absque coniventia gloriae vestrae, sicut credimus, evocati Parisius venientes." See Karl Joseph von Hefele, *Histoire des conciles d'après les documents originaux*, ed. and trans. Henri Leclercq (Paris: Letouzey et Ané, 1907–52), 3.1:197.
37. *Epistolae Desiderii episcopi* no. 1.5 (18–20).
38. Kreiner, *Social Life of Hagiography*, 85.
39. *Epistolae aevi Merowingici collectae* no. 3 (437–38).
40. Duchesne, *Fastes épiscopaux de l'ancienne Gaule*, 2:394.

discourteously he closes his letter by repeating his warning that should an ordination occur without the prior consent of himself, the pope, or a council of bishops, then both the officiates and the ordained prelate will earn excommunication.[41] Like the bishops at Paris (573), Leo's residency in a rival kingdom no doubt emboldened him to communicate more freely with his royal correspondent, although his letter lacks the social niceties with which the conciliar attendees at Paris had shrouded their equally obstinate response to a royal action. It is perhaps not surprising then that Leo's letter is unique within the corpus of episcopal correspondence with the Merovingian monarchy for its obstinacy and bold criticism of royal action.[42] As a general rule, as we have seen, such exchanges were more commonly characterized by episcopal deference, if not docile subservience, to royal authority, as well as tactful style that obfuscated provocative criticism of royal policy in part through appeals to broad moral principles and biblical models. While it is not possible to gauge with any precision the frequency by which kings consulted with bishops in the *regnum Francorum*, it is clear that certain expectations and rhetorical strategies retained their relevance over the course of the Merovingian era.

Administrative and Legislative Service

As their receptivity to episcopal counsel suggests, the Merovingians valued the ability of bishops to transcend the divide between court and local administration. The civic authority enjoyed by bishops in their respective communities has been a topic of particular fascination for modern historians, who continue to debate vigorously the means by which this *auctoritas* first was assumed by the Gallic episcopate. Was it, as some have argued, formally delegated by late Roman imperial authorities, or rather simply seized by ambitious bishops during a time of political and social transformation in late antique Gaul?[43] Or, as

---

41. *Epistolae aevi Merowingici collectae* no. 3 (438): "Nam gloria vestra optime debit et credire et scire, quia, si contra statuta canonum quicumque episcoporum sine consinsum nostrum Mecledone episcopum voluerit ordenare, usque ad pape notitiam vel sinodale audientiam tam hi, qui ordenaverint, quam qui ordenatus fuerit, a nostra erunt communione disiuncti."

42. While the criticism of royal policy in the canons of the Council of Paris (556/73) is similarly forthright, as suggested later, it was not directed toward the recipient of the conciliar *acta*—i.e., Charibert I. Similarly, as I have argued elsewhere, the object of the bishops assembled at Tours in 567 was reconciliation with Charibert, not further antagonism: Halfond, "Charibert," 23–27; Gregory Halfond, "Contextualizing the Council of Tours (567)," in *Proceedings of the Fourteenth International Congress of Medieval Canon Law*, ed. Joseph Goering, Stephan Dusil, and Andreas Their, Monumenta Iuris Canonici, Series C: Subsidia 15 (Rome: Biblioteca Apostolica Vaticana, 2016), 289–301.

43. On the alternatives of usurpation and delegation, see, respectively, the fundamental studies of Friedrich Prinz and Martin Heinzelmann: Friedrich Prinz, "Die bischöfliche Stadtherrschaft im

still others have suggested, are the alternatives of delegation and usurpation themselves misleading, and should we understand transformations of episcopal authority not in juridical terms at all but rather as a shift in cultural semantics and the self-expression of elite Gallo-Romans?[44] Or, perhaps, all three of these explanations may be problematic because of their assumption that scions of the old Gallic senatorial aristocracy monopolized the Gallic episcopate into the Merovingian era.[45] Despite the controversial origins of *Bischofsherrschaft*—a conceptual model that occasionally risks anachronism through generalization—there is broad agreement that the assumption of some measure of civic authority by individual bishops positioned them to facilitate communications between the court and *civitates*, although they more often than not had to share this power with local *seniores* and *cives*.[46] What distinguished these bishops from local secular elites and royal officials like *comites*

Frankenreich vom 5. bis zum 7. Jahrhundert," *Historische Zeitschrift* 217 (1974): 1–35; Friedrich Prinz, "Die Bischöfliche Stadtherrschaft im Frankenreich vom 5. bis zum 7. Jahrhundert," in *Bischofs- und Kathedralstädte des Mittelalters und der frühen Neuzeit*, ed. Franz Petri (Cologne, Germany: Böhlau, 1976), 1–26 (revised version of *Historische Zeitschrift* essay); Friedrich Prinz, "Der fränkische Episkopat zwischen Merowinger- und Karolingerzeit," in *Nascita dell'Europa ed Europa carolingia* (Spoleto, Italy: Centro Italiano di Studi sull'Alto Medioevo, 1981), 101–33; Friedrich Prinz, "Herrschaftsformen der Kirche vom Ausgang der Spätantike bis zum Ende der Karolingerzeit: zur Einführung ins Thema," in *Herrschaft und Kirche*, ed. Friedrich Prinz (Stuttgart, Germany: Hiersemann, 1988), 1–21; and Martin Heinzelmann, "Bischof und Herrschaft vom spätantiken Gallien bis zu den karolingischen Hausmeiern: Die institutionellen Grundlagen," in Prinz, *Herrschaft und Kirche*, 23–82. Steffen Patzold, "L'épiscopat du haut Moyen Âge du point de vue de la médiévistique allemande," *Cahiers de Civilisation Médiévale* 48 (2005): 341–58, at 351n59, observes that Prinz's 1988 essay constitutes an attempt to reconcile the author's position with that of Heinzelmann.

44. Bernhard Jussen, "Über 'Bischofsherrschaften' und die Prozeduren politisch-sozialer Umordnung in Gallien zwischen 'Antike' und 'Mittelalter,'" *Historische Zeitschrift* 260 (1994): 673–718; Bernhard Jussen, "Zwischen Römischem Reich und Merowingern: Herrschaft legitimieren ohne Kaiser und König," in *Mittelalter und Moderne: Entdeckung und Rekonstruktion der mittelalterlichen Welt*, ed. Peter Segl (Sigmaringen, Germany: Thorbecke, 1997), 15–29; Jussen, "Liturgie und Legitimation," 75–136.

45. See the introduction.

46. On the term *Bischofsherrschaft*, its meanings, and its historiography, see Hans Hubert Anton, "'Bischofsherrschaften' und 'Bischofsstaaten' in Spätantike und Frühmittelalter: Reflexionen zu ihrer Genese, Struktur und Typologie," in *Liber amicorum necnon et amicarum für Alfred Heit*, ed. Friedhelm Burgard (Trier, Germany: Verlag Trierer Historische Forschungen, 1996), 461–73; Patzold, "L'épiscopat du haut Moyen Âge"; and Diefenbach, "Bischofsherrschaft," 93–101, 123–27. On the civic responsibilities of bishops, see Jean Durliat, "Les attributions civiles des évêques mérovingiens: L'exemple de Didier, évêque de Cahors (630–655)," *Annales du Midi* 91 (1979): 237–54; Jean Durliat, "Evêque et administration municipale au VIIe siècle," in *La fin de la cité antique et le début de la cité médiévale*, ed. Claude Lepelley (Bari, Italy: Edipuglia, 1996), 273–86; Brigitte Beaujard, "L'évêque dans la cité en Gaule aux Ve et VIe siècles," in Lepelley, *La fin de la cité antique*, 127–45; and Nancy Gauthier, "Le réseau de pouvoirs de l'évêque dans la Gaule du Haut Moyen-Age," in *Towns and Their Territories between Late Antiquity and the Early Middle Ages*, ed. Gian Pietro Broglio, Nancy Gauthier, and Neil Christie, Transformation of the Roman World 9 (Leiden: Brill, 2000), 173–207, at 188–95. On the last point, see Simon T. Loseby, "Decline and Change in the Cities of Late Antique Gaul," in Krause and Witschel, *Die Stadt in der Spätantike*, 67–104, at 91–92.

(who might well come from the same families) was a corporate identity that existed independently of royal power and that was grounded in an authority intrinsic to their office. Bishops wielded a unique "soft" pastoral power and were expected to direct this power, in conjunction with the ecclesiastical resources under their supervision, to the benefit of a broadly defined "poor."[47] The Merovingians themselves were very conscious of this distinction and, more often than not, sought to use it to their advantage.

This is particularly conspicuous in the case of ecclesiastical councils. While councils could assemble independently of royal authority, particularly in the case of provincial and diocesan gatherings, rulers recognized the myriad advantages of actively encouraging, through royal convocation, the legislative and judicial business of the episcopate. It was common, for instance, for councils to be convoked at the conclusion of military campaigns for the purpose of reinforcing peace and administrative order.[48] As will be discussed in greater detail in chapter 4, this appears to have been Clovis's intent for the very first Frankish synod, the Council of Orléans (511), convoked by the king four years after his victory over the Visigothic king Alaric II (484–507). The council's attendance, almost certainly by design, reflected the recent absorption of numerous Gallic episcopal sees by the rapidly expanding Frankish regnum.[49] The location of the synod, similarly, was a deliberate choice: a northern Gallic city on the frontier of the defunct Visigothic kingdom was ideally positioned to integrate the diverse episcopal attendees into a single administrative order.[50] Finally, the legislative acts of the council, based in part on *tituli* supplied by Clovis, constituted a veritable "concordance" between the king and the politically unified episcopal sees of the realm, as they touched on issues of mutual concern with a notable effort at compromise between competing royal and episcopal priorities and legal expectations.[51] So, while Clovis's victory at

---

47. Brown, *Through the Eye of a Needle*, 496–509; Peter Brown, "From *Amator Patriae* to *Amator Pauperum* and Back Again: Social Imagination and Social Change in the West between Late Antiquity and the Early Middle Ages, ca. 300–600," in *Cultures in Motion*, ed. Daniel Rodgers, Bhavani Raman, and Helmut Reimitz (Princeton, NJ: Princeton University Press, 2014), 87–106, at 101–3.

48. E.g., the Councils of Paris (556/73), Tours (567), Mâcon (585), and Paris (614). See in general Gregory Halfond, "War and Peace in the *Acta* of the Merovingian Church Councils," in *The Medieval Way of War: Studies in Medieval Military History in Honor of Bernard S. Bachrach*, ed. Gregory Halfond (Farnham, England: Ashgate, 2015), 29–46, at 33–35.

49. Gregory Halfond, "Vouillé, Orléans (511), and the Origins of Frankish Conciliar Tradition," in *The Battle of Vouillé, 507 CE: Where France Began*, ed. Ralph Mathisen and Danuta Shanzer (Berlin: Walter de Gruyter, 2012), 151–65, at 154–58.

50. Halfond, 158–61, suggests Washington, DC, as a modern analogy.

51. Jean Heuclin, "Le Concile d'Orléans de 511, un premier concordat," in *Clovis: Histoire et mémoire*, ed. Michel Rouche (Paris: Presses de l'Université de Paris-Sorbonne, 1997), 1:435–50; Halfond, "Vouillé," 161–64; Becher, *Chlodwig I*, 245–46; Scholz, *Die Merowinger*, 61–68 (on the treatment of asylum law specifically), drawing from the observations of Stefan Esders, "Rechtsdenken und

Vouillé unified politically the majority of Gallic *civitates* under Frankish rule, the subsequent council extended this integration project to the affected episcopal dioceses.

Trusting in the capacity of councils to promote peace, the Merovingians convoked synods for that explicitly stated purpose, as well as for mediating between members of the royal family.[52] The success of mediation, however, depended as much on royal cooperation as on episcopal counsel, if not more. When in 573, for example, King Guntram convoked a synod in Paris to adjudicate a dispute between himself and Sigibert, neither brother, according to Gregory of Tours, was willing to listen to the advice of the bishops, blinded as they were by sin.[53] The bishops who attended a Lyonnais council in 581 at Guntram's request similarly failed to ease tensions between the king and his nephew Childebert II (575–96), although Gregory's account suggests that Guntram was less interested in the restoration of peace than in dealing with the implications of the broken treaty between Burgundy and Austrasia.[54] Certainly, peace did not immediately follow from the intervention of the episcopate.[55] Such failures to realize *pax* are less suggestive of a lack of royal receptivity to episcopal counsel than of the challenge of harmonizing royal and episcopal agendas.[56]

Royal agendas likewise could complicate the work of conciliar tribunals, as obviously was the case in Praetextatus of Rouen's trial. In some instances, of course, it was the monarchy that demanded the convocation of such tribunals in the first place, as these judicial forums allowed rulers to investigate and discipline bishops suspected of disloyalty to the regime, while ostensibly delegating judicial responsibilities to the episcopate. This is not to say that conciliar judicial hearings were ruses, kangaroo courts for prosecuting bishops who failed to toe the line. While royal involvement in these hearings certainly

---

Traditionsbewußtsein in der gallischen Kirche zwischen Spätantike und Frühmittelalter: Zur Anwendbarkeit soziologischer Rechtsbegriffe am Beispiel des kirchlichen Asylrechts im 6. Jahrhundert," *Francia* 20, no. 1 (1993): 97–125.

52. E.g., Councils of Tours (567), *praefatio*; Clichy (626/67), *praefatio*; and Bordeaux (662/67), *praefatio* (c. 4). See also Guy Halsall, *Warfare and Society in the Barbarian West, 450–900* (London: Routledge, 2003), 141; and Halfond, "War and Peace," 38–40.

53. Gregory of Tours, *Decem libri historiarum* 4.47: "Tamen per Andigavus regressus, ad eum rediit. Cum autem intentio inter Gunthchramnum et Sigyberthum regis verteretur, Gunthchramnus rex apud Parisius omnes episcopus regni sui congregat, ut inter utrusque quid veritas haberit edicerent. Sed ut bellum civili in maiore pernicitate cresceret, eos audire, peccatis facientibus, distulerunt."

54. Gregory of Tours, *Decem libri historiarum* 6.1: "Apud Lugdunum sinodus episcoporum coniungitur, diversarum causarum altercationis incidens neglegentioresque iudicio damnans. Sinodus ad regem revertitur, multa de fuga Mummoli ducis, nonnulla de discordiis tractans."

55. See, e.g., Gregory of Tours, *Decem libri historiarum* 6.3, 6.11, 6.31, 6.33.

56. Similarly, Fredegar, *Chronica* 4.53, credits Arnulf of Metz with helping to settle a dispute between Chlothar II and his son Dagobert in 625.

influenced deliberations and verdicts, it did not necessarily entirely negate the judicial independence of the participating bishops. Additionally, royal involvement in conciliar trials was not limited to "bad kings" like Chilperic, and guilty verdicts were not always foregone conclusions.

While Gregory of Tours was particularly and predictably scathing in his assessment of Chilperic's abuse of conciliar tribunals, it actually was Guntram of Burgundy among the sons of Chlothar I who seems to have taken the greatest advantage of this means of indirect episcopal discipline. The King of Burgundy convoked at least half a dozen synods for the purpose of judging prelates, most notably the Second Council of Mâcon (585), which dealt comprehensively with the involvement of bishops in the plot to secure a regnum for the royal pretender Gundovald.[57] Among the more than a dozen prelates implicated in the Gundovald affair by Gregory of Tours, only those either already dead or residing in a different regnum were absent from the council. Furthermore, Gregory's account is explicit that it was the king who determined which of the episcopal collaborators were to be publicly identified, penalized, or even exonerated by the council, although Guntram did choose to limit the scope of these prosecutions following a near-death experience.[58] However, for the most part, the guilty parties were not charged specifically with secular crimes (with the exception of Ursicinus of Cahors, who was found guilty of opening his *civitas* to Gundovald) and were subject to ecclesiastical justice rather than penalties imposed by the court. Those bishops, for example, who were implicated in the ordination of Faustianus of Dax were prosecuted, according to Gregory of Tours, for performing the ceremony on the orders of an illegitimate authority. The council determined that the bishops owed restitution to Faustianus himself, who had to give up his seat due to the irregularity of his ordination.[59] Thus, despite Guntram's undeniable influence over the proceedings, the conciliar attendees were able to stay mostly true to their

---

57. The Councils of Lyons (567/70), Paris (573), Chalon-sur-Saône (579), possibly Lyons (581), Troyes (585), Mâcon (585), and Unknown (588), on which see Halfond, *Archaeology*, 229–34. See Gregory Halfond, "Corporate Solidarity and Its Limits within the Gallo-Frankish Episcopate," in *The Oxford Handbook of the Merovingian World*, ed. Bonnie Effros and Isabel Moreira (Oxford: Oxford University Press, forthcoming), on the prosecution of episcopal collaborators in the Gundovald affair.

58. Gregory of Tours, *Decem libri historiarum* 8.20: "His etenim diebus Guntchramnus rex graviter aegrotavit, ita ut potaretur a quibusdam non posse prorsus evadere. Quod, credo, providentia Dei fecisset. Cogitabat enim multus episcoporum exsilio detrudere."

59. Gregory of Tours, *Decem libri historiarum* 8.20: "Faustianus autem, qui ex iusso Gundovaldi Aquinsi urbi episcopus ordinatus fuerat, ea condicione removitur, ut eum Bertchramnus Orestesque sive Palladius, qui eum benedixerant, vicibus pascerent centinusque ei aureus annis singulis ministrarent."

own stated principle that only prelates could adjudicate cases involving other ecclesiastics.[60]

Conversely, and ironically in light of Gregory's accusations against him, Chilperic seems to have been as willing as Guntram (if not more so) to show mercy and to permit conciliar attendees themselves to determine just verdicts. This was the case in Gregory's own conciliar trial at Berny in 580.[61] Chilperic also showed notable restraint in the case of Bishop Charterius of Périgueux, who had been accused of treason by one of Chilperic's *comites*. Gregory's own account of the investigation acknowledges the king's caution and prudence. Following the investigation, which uncovered a conspiracy against Charterius, Chilperic was "moved by mercy" to declare the bishop innocent of all charges.[62]

Despite Chilperic's perhaps exaggerated reputation for judicial meddling, the actions of his brothers and other members of the ruling dynasty suggest that such meddling was common, but that the Merovingians recognized the value of allowing the episcopate some measure of judicial autonomy. In most cases we simply cannot gauge the degree of royal pressure directed at conciliar tribunals, in part because these tribunals were usually populated by at least some prelates already predisposed toward the royal agenda. As we have seen, Nicetius of Trier's colleagues probably needed little royal encouragement to depose the cantankerous metropolitan. Similarly, according to Fredegar's account, Brunhild and Theuderic II had a willing collaborator in their prosecution of Bishop Desiderius of Vienne in the person of Aridius of Lyons.[63] Ebroin too, in his persecution of Leudegar of Autun, Chramlinus of Embrun, and other prelates, did not lack for episcopal allies.[64] Such cases serve as a reminder that the actions of conciliar tribunals were influenced by more than a single party's agenda. Bishops like Bertram of Bordeaux and Ragnemodus of Paris were not mere *adolatores*, despite what Gregory of Tours claimed. They made the conscious choice to abet Chilperic's persecution of Praetextatus, no doubt for a variety of personal, political, and perhaps even pious

---

60. Council of Mâcon (585), cc. 9–10.
61. Gregory of Tours, *Decem libri historiarum* 5.49.
62. Gregory of Tours, *Decem libri historiarum* 6.22: "Proclamante vero episcopo et dicente, quod saepius hic ingenia quaereret, qualiter eum ab episcopatu deiceret, rex misericordia motus, commendans Deo causam suam, cessit utrisque, deprecans clementer episcopum pro diacono, et supplicans, ut pro se sacerdos oraret. Et sic cum honore urbi remissus est."
63. Fredegar, *Chronica* 4.24. Yaniv Fox, "The Bishop and the Monk: Desiderius of Vienne and the Columbanian Movement," *Early Medieval Europe* 20, no. 2 (2012): 176–94, at 189–93, argues persuasively for the veracity of Fredegar's accusation against Aridius due to a rivalry between the latter and Desiderius.
64. Halfond, "Corporate Solidarity."

reasons. The majority of their colleagues present at the Basilica of Saint Peter in Paris, however, as even Gregory admits, did not play nearly so active a role in the deliberations. But even in their passivity they were making personal and conscious choices that influenced the direction of the proceedings.

If neither the legislative nor judicial actions of episcopal councils reveal them to be obsequious royal instruments, then we must consider the reasons why the Merovingians relied on them so heavily and consistently. Among the Merovingian kings it was, to the best of our knowledge, Guntram who took the greatest advantage of conciliarism in the governance of his regnum. Guntram sponsored the convocation of over a dozen councils during his reign, most of which assembled in close proximity to his residence at Chalon-sur-Saône, with the surrounding provinces of Lyons and Vienne the most heavily represented among the participating bishops.[65] Despite the large number of *civitates* under the king's rule, particularly following Chilperic's death in 584, fewer than a dozen bishops attended four or more councils convoked in Guntram's name. Not surprisingly these same bishops performed a variety of other services for the king, suggesting that they enjoyed a particularly intimate and collaborative relationship with Guntram.[66]

Thus, relying on the cooperation of these and other friendly prelates, Guntram encouraged the bishops of his kingdom to regularly assemble as a united body "pro causis publicis," with the confidence that conciliar agendas would reflect his own.[67] In his *edictum*, issued following the conclusion of the Second Council of Mâcon (585), the king went so far as to acknowledge that both regnal stability and the salvation of his subjects were dependent on the observance of both the *canones et leges*. Furthermore, he explicitly associated his own legislation with that defined by the council, whose participants, he insisted, possessed the *auctoritas* necessary for making law.[68] Yet, in his *edictum*, Guntram only cited a single canon composed by the conciliar attendees concerning the observance of the Sabbath.

---

65. Halfond, "All the King's Men," 81–84. Similarly, Guntram's brother Charibert primarily collaborated with bishops whose sees were located in the northern half of his regnum, particularly those in close proximity to his royal seat in Paris; see Halfond, "Charibert," 10–11.

66. Halfond, "All the King's Men," 84–95.

67. Council of Mâcon (581/83), *praefatio*.

68. Guntram, *Edictum*, in *Capitularia regum Francorum*, 10–12: "Dum pro regni ergo nostri stabilitate et salvatione regionis vel populi sollicitudine pervigili attentius pertractaremus, cognovimus infra regni nostri spatia universa scelera, quae canonibus et legibus pro divino timore puniri consuerunt, suadente adversio boni operis perpetrari, et ex hoc procul dubio consumi censentur aut gladio, dum divina iudicia non timentur; atque ita fit, ut admittendo illicita per ignorantiam multi depereant, et non solum praesentem vitam celerius cogantur amittere sed et inferni supplicia sustinere. . . . Cuncta ergo quae huius edicti tenore decrevimus, perpetualiter volumus custodiri, quia in sancta synodo Matisconensi haec omnia, sicut nostis, studuimus definire, quae praesenti auctoritate vulgamus."

This disconnect is telling. In general, the Merovingian kings were selective in those canons they adopted for their own legislation and did not hesitate to alter the basic substance of these precedents. The most well known example of this practice is the alteration and inclusion of several canons from the Council of Paris (614) in the subsequent *edictum* of Chlothar II, which nevertheless echoed Guntram's earlier legislation in its assertion that "canonical statutes must be observed in their entirety, and those that have been neglected for some time be observed from now on."[69] Like Guntram, Chlothar explicitly distinguished between royal and canon law, while still accepting the legislative authority of both. Conciliar *regulae* did not require his approval to be valid; nor did he consider it necessary to adopt in his own legislation the entirety of conciliar *acta* verbatim. Chlothar, like Guntram before him, treated canon law essentially as legislative precedent for his own lawmaking.[70] So, while it is an easy matter to identify the linguistic and substantive transformation of individual canonical rules into the chapters of royal edicts, the results must be read as original legal statements.[71]

The bishops who participated in councils convoked by Guntram shared his understanding of the distinction between royal and canon law. At the First Council of Mâcon (581/83) the bishops devised rules that assumed their own *auctoritas* to penalize laymen for transgressions against ecclesiastical statutes,[72] while several canons dealing with the Jews presupposed the intervention of secular authorities for the purpose of enforcement.[73] Canon 17, for instance, states that a Jewish slave owner who has converted his Christian slave should be "legali damnatione plectatur," presumably in reference to secular authorities.[74] The most explicit distinction made in the canonical acts between secular

---

69. Chlothar II, *Edictum*, in *Capitularia regum Francorum*, c. 1. On Chlothar's alterations to the acts of the council, see de Clercq, *La législation religieuse franque*, 58–61; Halfond, *Archaeology*, 143–44.

70. This is not the place to wade too deeply into the fraught question of the practical utility of written law in the *regnum Francorum*. Nevertheless, there seems to me considerable value in the suggestion of Alice Rio, *Legal Practice and the Written Word in the Early Middle Ages* (Cambridge: Cambridge University Press, 2009), 209–10, that "formulae and law do not represent two sides of a struggle between central power and local circumstances . . . but a dialogue between different negotiating positions." If royal legislation, as Rio argues, reflects to a certain extent a product of negotiation between the monarchy and aristocracy, and formulae a product of consensus seeking by the aristocracy locally, then conciliar *canones* might represent another voice in this broader conversation about the definition and application of normative legal standards. As officeholders whose influence and authority could transcend diocesan borders, bishops were positioned both to influence legal pronouncements originating in the court and to negotiate the application of (especially) ecclesiastical and religious *regulae*—themselves a product of negotiated consensus—within their respective *civitates*.

71. Halfond, *Archaeology*, 143–46.

72. Council of Mâcon (581/83), cc. 4, 7, 15, 18, 19, threaten excommunication against laymen, while c. 19 requires the performance of public penance.

73. Council of Mâcon (581/83), cc. 13, 14, 16, 17.

74. Council of Mâcon (581/83), c. 17.

and ecclesiastical authority can be found, however, in the strongly worded canon 7, which threatens secular *iudices* with excommunication should they attempt to prosecute a cleric without first consulting with the latter's bishop: "No cleric should suffer injury for any reason at the hands of a secular *iudex*, or be imprisoned without the agreement of his bishop. But if any *iudex* should by some chance dare to do this to someone's cleric lacking criminal grounds, that is, homicide, theft, or criminal mischief, let him be kept away from the threshold of the church for as long as the bishop of that place wishes."[75] It is important to note that the canon forbids not the prosecution of clerics by secular authorities but rather prosecution without episcopal approval. Furthermore, in its second half, the canon acknowledges that the prosecution of certain crimes is the prerogative of civil, rather than religious, authorities.

This pronouncement raises the essential question of where the jurisdictional divide between ecclesiastical and royal law was located in Merovingian Gaul. A broad survey of both royal and secular legislation suggests that this divide was moveable rather than stationary, and indeed shifted according to changing conditions, as well as the priorities and negotiated agendas of legislators. While both conciliar and royal legislation were scripted in accordance with legal precedent, there was no simple linear development of universally adopted rules, but only—at most—broadly defined principles. A basic example that illustrates this phenomenon is the elaboration of Chlothar I on previous conciliar legislation defining the church's right of asylum. Four Frankish synods confirmed this right in the first half of the sixth century: Orléans (511), canons 1–3; Orléans (538), canon 14; Orléans (541), canons 21 and 30; and Orléans (549), canon 22.[76] Chlothar, however, specifically had the first of these

---

75. Council of Mâcon (581/83), c. 7: "Ut nullus clericus de qualibet causa extra discussionem episcopi sui a seculare iudice iniuriam patiatur aut custodiae deputetur. Quod si quicumque iudex cuiuscumque clericum absque causa criminali, id est homicidio, furto, et maleficio, hoc facere fortasse praesumpserit, quamdiu episcopo loci ipsius visum fuerit, ab ecclesiae liminibus arceatur." Pontal, *Histoire des conciles mérovingiens*, 185, has written of this canon's innovative nature: "Pour la première fois un concile de la Gaule franque interdit expressément, sous peine de sanctions, aux clercs d'évoquer les litiges entre gens d'Église devant un juge civil."

76. In addition, see the Burgundian Council of Epaone (517), c. 39. On ecclesiastical asylum, see Edward James, "*Beati Pacifici*: Bishops and the Law in Sixth-Century Gaul," in *Disputes and Settlements: Law and Human Relations in the West*, ed. John Bossy (Cambridge: Cambridge University Press, 1983), 25–46, at 36–40; Esders, "Rechtsdenken und Traditionsbewußtsein"; Rob Meens, "The Sanctity of the Basilica of St Martin: Gregory of Tours and the Practice of Sanctuary in the Merovingian Period," in *Texts and Identities in the Early Middle Ages*, ed. Richard Corradini et al. (Vienna: Österreichischen Akademie der Wissenschaften, 2006), 277–87; Rob Meens, "Violence at the Altar: The Sacred Space around the Grave of St. Martin of Tours and the Practice of Sanctuary in the Early Middle Ages," in *Ritual and Space in the Middle Ages*, ed. Frances Andrews (Donington, England: Shaun Tyas, 2011), 71–89; and Karl Shoemaker, *Sanctuary and Crime in the Middle Ages, 400–1500* (New York: Fordham University Press, 2011).

councils in mind when he referred in his own legislation to the conciliar pronouncement that royal agents could not pursue fugitives into the atrium of a church. Unlike the attendees at Orléans, however, Chlothar made a distinction between churches with enclosed atria and those without, ordering that in the case of the latter the invisible atria should be defined as constituting that land within 120 feet of the church walls. While Chlothar's ruling did not necessarily undermine or weaken the conciliar definition of sacrosanct space, his own delineation of ecclesiastical space closed to royal agents was defined in terms quite different from those employed by the episcopal attendees of the four councils of Orléans, perhaps due to his wish to craft a clear normative rule of use to secular officials regardless of location.[77]

The fluctuation of this jurisdictional divide is similarly visible in the conciliar and royal legislation dealing explicitly with the judicial rights of *iudices* in relation to clerics. Sixth-century Gallic councils focused primarily on three related issues: private law suits involving clerics, the public prosecution of ecclesiastics on criminal charges, and the jurisdiction of secular judges in relation to free persons over whom the church claimed protection.[78] Regarding the first of these issues, the Council of Orléans (511) made an early allowance for suits to be brought against clerics, a sanction echoed several years later by the Burgundian Council of Epaone (517).[79] The Council of Orléans (541) similarly verified the admissibility of laymen bringing lawsuits against clerics, but attempted to limit the jurisdiction of such suits to episcopal courts unless both parties, as well as the head of the clerical litigant's church, agreed to bring the case before a *iudex publicus*.[80] The Council of Orléans (549), in turn, attempted to clarify the precise procedures by which lay and ecclesiastical disputants might settle their differences within the church's jurisdiction. The conciliar attendees insisted that disputants first attempt to settle their differences through informal means. Should that fail, the provincial metropolitan could then intervene. If the accused bishop or cleric involved in the dispute refused to accept the metropolitan's intervention, however, he would suffer excommunication. In turn, if the lay accuser's case was found to be frivolous,

---

77. Chlothar I, *Decretio*, in *Capitularia regum Francorum*, c. 14. Two generations later, Childebert II exempted abductors from the protection of ecclesiastical asylum: Childebert II, *Decretio*, in *Capitularia regum Francorum*, c. 4.

78. The issue of the legal treatment of unfree ecclesiastical dependents is purposely avoided here, as this generally was a matter of greater interest to secular legislators than to conciliar attendees—e.g., Childebert II, *Decretio*, in *Capitularia regum Francorum*, c. 13; *Lex Ribuaria*, ed. Franz Beyerle and Rudolf Buchner, MGH LL nat. Germ. 3.2 (Hanover, Germany: Hahn, 1954), 61.9, 61.20.

79. Councils of Orléans (511), c. 6; and Epaone (517), c. 24.

80. Council of Orléans (541), c. 20. C. 13 from the same council also forbid *iudices* from requiring *publicae actiones* of clerics; see also Clichy (626/67), c. 7.

then he too could be subject to excommunication. If the metropolitan himself failed to intervene, then a provincial synod would hear the dispute.[81]

While not concerned directly with formal suits, both the Council of Eauze (551) and the Council of Mâcon (581/83) addressed the related problem of intraecclesiastical disputes. The former forbade bishops and clerics in dispute from seeking the intervention of *laici* on pain of excommunication, citing for support canon 31 of the so-called Second Council of Arles (but mistakenly attributed to the Council of Orange).[82] The Council of Mâcon similarly mandated severe punishments (thirty-nine blows for junior clerics, thirty days' confinement for senior clerics) against ecclesiastics who sought the intervention of *iudices*.[83] The diocesan synod of Auxerre (561/605), convoked by Aunacharius of Auxerre, an attendee of the Council of Mâcon, distinguished between intraecclesiastical disputes and those between laymen and clerics. In the case of the former, the synod followed established conciliar principle in forbidding such cases to be brought before secular courts.[84] In the case of the latter, however, it permitted clerics to use lay proxies to argue their position in court.[85]

Regarding the secular prosecution of ecclesiastics on criminal charges, the Council of Epaone (517) directly influenced the pronouncement by the Frankish Council of Orléans (538) that clerics could, in fact, be brought *ad saecolare iudicium* with prior episcopal approval, a principle verified several years later by the Council of Orléans (541).[86] The Council of Mâcon (581/83), in contrast, emphasized more strongly than these earlier pronouncements the limits to secular jurisdiction, threatening excommunication against those secular judges who penalized clerics *absque causa criminale* and without episcopal approval.[87] The Council of Mâcon (585), in an unusually lengthy canon, sug-

---

81. Council of Orléans (549), c. 17.
82. Council of Eauze (551), c. 4. The same canon also forbids a cleric from seeking lay patronage in defiance of his bishop.
83. Council of Mâcon (581/83), c. 8.
84. Council of Auxerre (561/605), c. 35.
85. Council of Auxerre (561/605), c. 41.
86. Councils of Epaone (517), c. 11; Orléans (538), c. 35; and Orléans (541), c. 20. Epaone (517), c. 12, also allowed clerics guilty of a *crimen capitale* to be imprisoned within a monastery. As noted earlier, Orléans (541), c. 13, also attempted to forbid *iudices* from requiring *publicae actiones* of clerics.
87. Council of Mâcon (581/83), c. 7. Council of Mâcon (581/83), c. 13, following Clermont (535), c. 9, also weighed in on the question of who was eligible to hold public office—i.e., not Jews. C. 7 also parallels Auxerre (561/605), c. 43, authored by Aunacharius of Auxerre, an attendee of the Council of Mâcon. The date of the council is uncertain. The acts conclude with the statement: "Expliciunt sinodus Matascensis, qui factus est anno XXII regni domni nostri Gunthrammi regis, die kal. Novembris, indicione XV." Guntram's twenty-second regnal year corresponds to the year 583. The indiction date indicates the year 581. Friedrich Maassen, ed., *Concilia aevi Merovingici*, MGH Legum Sectio 3: Concilia, Tomus 1 (Hanover, Germany: Hahn, 1893), 155, prefers 583, as do Hefele and

gested that these earlier rules were not being enforced and that bishops themselves were being taken from their churches and imprisoned. The council responded by asserting the fundamental principle of a bishop's judgment by his colleagues.[88]

On the third issue, the Council of Tours (567) was the first Frankish council to intervene directly between secular *iudices* and those free persons under the protection of the church (in this case *pauperes*), and only the second to threaten disobedient *iudices* with ecclesiastical sanctions.[89] While the acts of Mâcon (585) permitted *iudices* to summon (*convenire*) widows and orphans in collaboration with a bishop or the latter's representative, the same council attempted to limit cases involving ecclesiastical freedmen to episcopal courts (while nevertheless allowing laymen to attend at episcopal discretion).[90] In a rather surprising expansion of episcopal jurisdiction, Childebert II in 596 identified bishops as the primary agents responsible for separating incestuous couples, supplementing their power of excommunication with the threat of property seizure.[91]

These conciliar precedents were reviewed, renewed, elaborated, and in some cases altered in the conciliar *acta* and royal *edicta* of the reign of Chlothar II and his seventh-century successors. On the issue of private law suits, Chlothar generally was content to allow—albeit selectively—conciliar precedent to stand. Both his *edictum* of 614 (implicitly) and the Council of Clichy of 626/27 (explicitly) followed the Council of Orléans (541) in allowing clerics to appear before secular courts with the permission of the bishop.[92] Chlothar did, however, encourage secular *iudices* to defend the property of churches and monasteries, and limited the jurisdictional rights of bishops in other *provinciae*, even those in which they possessed property.[93] The basic principle, however, would go unchanged during the remainder of the Merovingian period. The only subsequent council to address the issue of suits involving clerics, the Council of Saint-Jean-de-Losne (673/75), merely restated the Synod of Auxerre's

---

Leclercq, *Histoire des conciles*, 3.202. Duchesne, *Fastes épiscopaux de l'ancienne Gaule*, 1:371–72, prefers 581, as does Pontal, *Histoire des conciles mérovingiens*, 182.

88. Council of Mâcon (585), c. 9.

89. Council of Tours (567), c. 27. The same council (c. 16) also ordered *iudices*, on pain of excommunication, to assist in preventing monks from leaving their monasteries in order to wed. The first council to threaten excommunication against *iudices* was Orléans (538), c. 34. Cf. Eauze (541), c. 4, which does not explicitly specify *iudices*.

90. Council of Mâcon (585), cc. 7, 12. On c. 7, see Stefan Esders, *Die Formierung der Zensualität: Zur kirchlichen Transformation des spätrömischen Patronatswesens im früheren Mittelalter* (Ostfildern, Germany: Thorbecke, 2010), 47–48.

91. Childebert II, *Decretio*, in *Capitularia regum Francorum*, c. 2.

92. Chlothar II, *Edictum*, c. 4; Council of Clichy (626/27), c. 20.

93. Chlothar II, *Edictum*, cc. 14, 19. *Pauperes* in c. 14 most likely refers to monks.

allowance for lay representatives in secular courts (in this case in specific reference to cases involving bishops).[94]

The issue of private suits involving ecclesiastics also is addressed in Marculf's formulary in two related documents: the first a summons addressed to a bishop, requesting that either the prelate or his representative come to court to defend his claim to a disputed villa, and the second a communication in which the bishop is asked to intervene in a dispute between one of his dependents or ecclesiastical subordinates and a third party over a slave. If the dependent refused to give up the slave, the case would be transferred to the royal court. Procedurally, neither document conflicts with prior canonical or secular legal precedent, while nevertheless emphasizing the king as the final arbiter of *iustitia*, even in cases involving bishops.[95]

Regarding the second issue, the Council of Paris (614) followed sixth-century precedent in allowing criminal cases involving clerics to be tried in public courts with episcopal approval. Once again, excommunication was threatened against *iudices* who failed to seek prior approval.[96] Chlothar's edict confirmed this basic principle and added that those clerics convicted of capital crimes be tried *iuxta canones* with bishops present.[97] The Council of Clichy (626/27) similarly repeated the threat of excommunication against overzealous *iudices* without any significant elaboration.[98] In his *praeceptio*, however, Chlothar went further and extended to bishops (in the absence of the king) the right to "castigate" *iudices* for faulty judgments, effectively paving the way for a new trial.[99] This "veto" power thus confirmed bishops' long-standing claim of jurisdictional superiority over lay judges.[100] The later *Leges Alamannorum* would seem to confirm this principle, suggesting that the judicial summons of a

---

94. Council of Saint-Jean-de-Losne (673/75), c. 3.
95. *Marculfi formulae* 1.26–27. See Guillot, "La justice dans le royaume Franc," 686–89.
96. Council of Paris (614), c. 6.
97. Chlothar II, *Edictum*, c. 4. The eighth-century *Lex Baiwariorum*, ed. Ernst Maria Augustin Schwind, MGH LL nat. Germ. 5.2 (Hanover, Germany: Hahn, 1926), 1.10, does not mention the necessity of obtaining approval before summoning a prelate before a public court, but it does require that the latter be judged following the canons.
98. Council of Clichy (626/27), c. 7.
99. Chlothar II, *Praeceptio*, in *Capitularia regum Francorum*, c. 6. On the dating and authorship of the *Praeceptio*, see Esders, *Römische Rechtstradition*, 88–108. Cf. Ingrid Woll, *Untersuchungen zu Überlieferung und Eigenart der merowingischen Kapitularien* (Frankfurt: Peter Lang, 1995), 17–29, who identifies Chlothar I as the author. On the question of authorship, see, most recently, Marcelo Candido da Silva, "Le prince, la *lex* et la *iustitia*: Le Bréviaire d'Alaric et l'Édit attribué à Clotaire II," in *Le Bréviaire d'Alaric aux origines du code civil*, ed. Michel Rouche and Bruno Dumézil (Paris: Presses de l'Université de Sorbonne, 2008), 199–212.
100. Nevertheless, as Yaniv Fox, pers. comm., has suggested, in reality a bishop likely would have been sensitive to the status and influence of the individual *iudex* with whom he was interacting. Cf. Heinzelmann, "Bischof und Herrschaft," 63–68.

bishop had even greater weight than that of an *iudex* by threatening a greater fine against those who ignored directives enclosed with an episcopal *sigillum*.[101] The lone ecclesiastical council to weigh in on the issue of episcopal jurisdiction following Chlothar's death was Chalon-sur-Saône (647/53), which accused *iudices* of failing to seek the approval not only of bishops but also of archpriests and abbots, respectively, before intervening in parishes and monasteries.[102] Despite the canonical authors' protestations to the contrary, this canon went beyond the strictures of prior legislation, possibly in reflection of a seventh-century ruralization of the Gallo-Frankish church.

Finally, on the bishops' jurisdictional claims over protected groups, the Council of Paris (614) explicitly forbade the summoning of any and all freedmen before public courts on pain of excommunication (without any mention of the possibility of laymen attending the episcopal courts), while Chlothar's subsequent edict allowed freedmen to be summoned to secular courts if the bishop himself attended in the former's defense.[103] In addition, Chlothar in his edict permitted suits involving *homines ecclesiae* (presumably lay dependents) to be adjudicated by an *audientia publica* presided over by lay and ecclesiastical judges.[104] The king insisted, however, that should these *homines ecclesiae* be accused of criminal acts, then their cases must be heard before a public court.[105] Despite these limits on episcopal jurisdiction, the early seventh-century *Lex Ribuaria* asserted that freedpersons, as well as their children, were to remain under the patronage of the churches where they were manumitted.[106]

It is not surprising that we should fail to find seamless consistency, let alone uniformity, in two hundred years of conciliar and royal legislative activity. This

---

101. *Leges Alamannorum*, 2nd ed., ed. Karl Lehmann and Karl August Eckhardt, MGH LL nat. Germ. 5.1 (Hanover, Germany: Hahn, 1966), 22.2 (twelve vs. six *solidi*).

102. Council of Chalon (647/53), c. 11.

103. Council of Paris (614), c. 7; Chlothar II, *Edictum*, c. 7. See also Esders, *Die Formierung der Zensualität*, 48–50.

104. Chlothar II, *Edictum*, c. 5.

105. Chlothar II, *Edictum*, c. 15. While not explicitly addressing the issue of jurisdiction, a canon (c. 14) issued by an episcopal council sometime after 614—sometimes associated with Chlothar's assembly at Bonueuil in 616—also addresses the rights of freedmen. On this council, see Pontal, *Histoire des conciles mérovingiens*, 211–12.

106. *Lex Ribuaria* 61 (58). On the dating of the code, see Esders, *Die Formierung der Zensualität*, 50n148; Scholz, *Die Merowinger*, 214–16; Karl Ubl, *Sinnstiftungen eines Rechtsbuchs: Die Lex Salica im Frankenreich* (Ostfildern, Germany: Thorbecke, 2017), 106–7, 130–33. Esders, *Die Formierung der Zensualität*, 50–60, and "Early Medieval Use of Late Antique Legal Texts: The Case of the *Manumissio in Ecclesia*," in *Configuration du texte en histoire*, Proceedings of the Twelfth International Conference on Studies for the Integrated Text Science, ed. Osamu Kano (Nagoya: Nagoya University, 2012), 55–66, at 62–63, sees this chapter as signaling a break from Roman legal tradition. Cf. Alice Rio, *Slavery after Rome, 500–1100* (Oxford: Oxford University Press, 2017), 101–2, who expresses skepticism regarding Esder's argument that this policy effectively created a new "half-free" dependent class—i.e., *censuales*—in the East.

brief survey of a small body of canonical and capitulary decrees suggests merely that sixth- and seventh-century episcopal and royal legislators generally agreed on several broad principles: (1) it was permissible for laymen to bring private suits against ecclesiastics; (2) clerics could be tried in public courts with (at least) the prior approval of their bishop; and (3) bishops enjoyed a supervisory, if not necessarily absolute jurisdictional, power over dependent groups such as freedmen. However, the canons themselves suggest that in practice even these seemingly uncontroversial rules were negotiated, challenged, and in some instances simply ignored.

So, to return to the original question posed, of where the jurisdictional divide between the royal regime and the episcopate was located, the only possible answer is that this divide existed not as a stable boundary but rather as a frame of reference for negotiations between Gallo-Frankish bishops and the monarchy. Both agreed that the divide existed, and attempted to define and redefine it through legislation. Similarly, the explicitly recognized division between the *canones* and *leges* was not so clear-cut as even contemporaries suggested. *Canones* cited *leges*, *leges* cited *canones*, kings convoked councils and influenced their agendas, conciliar agendas could serve as the basis for royal edicts, and bishops did explicitly call on secular authorities to enforce their legislation.[107] But rhetorically and practically such distinctions mattered: they allowed bishops to claim independence from the royal court, while allowing the court to treat bishops as ostensibly independent partners in the promotion of peace and administrative order in the *civitates* of the regnum. The Merovingians never claimed the right to delegate authority to the episcopate, and there simply was no need to, as they recognized both formally and informally, time and again, the latter's separate and substantive spiritual, administrative, and legislative *auctoritas*. This apparent lack of dependence on delegated royal authority enhanced episcopal prestige, which, in turn, strengthened bishops' efficacy as royal confederates.

Bishops and Territorial Partitions

The Merovingians' reliance on episcopal cooperation was put to the test during the periodic territorial partitions and military conflicts that disrupted the *pax* of the Frankish kingdom. While royal control of an individual *civitas* certainly did not rest solely in the hands of the local bishop, the latter's support could prove important, particularly when public opinion within the *civitas* was

---

107. E.g., Clichy (626/27), c. 27.

divided. When, for instance, Caesarius of Arles was suspected of plotting to aid the Frankish armies besieging Arles in 508, it was considered a serious enough threat to warrant the bishop's confinement.[108] The Franks too quickly came to appreciate bishops' ability to sway public opinion and morale, muster troops in times of conflict, and coordinate and repair urban infrastructure.[109] Episcopal diplomatic skills also could prove vital in the defense of a *civitas*.[110] When Guntram launched a military expedition against the Bretons in 590, it was Bishop Regalis of Vannes who negotiated successfully on behalf of his *civitas* along with Duke Ebrachar to ensure that his fellow citizens were not blamed for their actions during the occupation.[111]

Especially in periods of territorial *divisio*, rival Merovingians scrambled to shore up episcopal support in vulnerable or strategically significant cities. This strategy was utilized, for example, by all of the sons of Chlothar I following the territorial partitions of 561 and 567.[112] In the partition of 561, for example, Sigibert, as king of Rheims, claimed two dozen cities across Northeast Gaul, Provence, and Aquitaine. Defending these dispersed territories proved difficult, as demonstrated by Chilperic's efforts to chip away at his brother's territories as early as 562, attacking Rheims and coming perilously close to Trier. It was within this context that Sigibert made the decision to recall Nicetius of Trier from exile, and later to appoint Nicetius's successor Magnericus, who would prove to be an Austrasian loyalist.[113]

Sigibert's brother Charibert I (561–67), in turn, responded ambitiously to the *divisio* of 561 with the convocation of an interprovincial council in Paris

---

108. *Vita Caesarii episcopi Arelatensis*, ed. Bruno Krusch, MGH SRM 3 (Hanover, Germany: Hahn, 1896), 1.29.

109. Friedrich Prinz, *Klerus und Krieg im früheren Mittelalter: Untersuchungen zur Rolle der Kirche beim Aufbau der Königsherrschaft* (Stuttgart, Germany: Hiersemann, 1971), 37–72; Leif Inge Ree Peterson, *Siege Warfare and Military Organization in the Successor States (400–800 A.D.)* (Leiden: Brill, 2013), 74, 223, 229–33, 322 (with the specific examples cited therein).

110. On the late antique hagiographical depiction of bishops as diplomats, see Andrew Gillett, *Envoys and Political Communication in the Late Antique West* (Cambridge: Cambridge University Press, 2003), 113–71, 233n46 (with specific references to episcopal envoys in primary sources), 267–72, who observes that "the encomiastic image of bishop as envoy . . . seems no longer to have attracted hagiographers by the late-sixth century" (269). Gillett notes, however, Gregory of Tours's (possibly exaggerated) attention to episcopal envoys in the *Historiae*.

111. Gregory of Tours, *Decem libri historiarum* 10.9. Fredegar, *Chronica* 2.53, similarly alludes to the diplomatic talents of the episcopate, interpolating into the chronicle of Hydatius an account of Bishop Anianus of Orléans's duplicitous (but ultimately effective) actions while serving as Aëtius's *legatio* to the Goths. The result was 350,000 dead barbarians and an unmolested Orléans.

112. On the partitions, see Eugen Ewig, "Die fränkischen Teilungen und Teilreiche (511–613)," in *Spätantikes und fränkisches Gallien*, 1:114–71, at 1:135–41.

113. Halfond, "Negotiating Episcopal Support," 9–12.

sometime between late 561 and early 564.[114] Several of this council's acts refer explicitly to the repercussions of the recent partition. The first canon, for instance, condemns those (presumably lay and ecclesiastical) elites who took advantage of shifting royal borders, declaring, "Nor may anyone seek to claim the property of God on account of the divisions between kingdoms, because the power of God encompasses under His special dominion the boundaries of all kingdoms."[115] It is telling that the canon does not reject completely the legality of the Merovingians' role in the alienation of ecclesiastical property specifically during the *divisio*, but merely requires that temporary grants of ecclesiastical land be made with episcopal approval and cooperation.[116] Another, more opaque, allusion to the *divisio* of 561 might be found in the sixth canon, which claimed that individuals had been wrongfully requesting from the Merovingians the property of others (*res alienas*).[117] In crafting this canon, the conciliar authors may well have been alluding to their own churches' lands, lost to new owners in other *regna*.[118] These canons and others reveal the Council of Paris's agenda to be less an attack on royal policy, as some have

---

114. Although this council is traditionally dated to 556/73, there are several good reasons to narrow this chronological range—i.e., the likelihood that the council's first canon was composed before the Council of Tours (567), c. 26, which replicates much of its text; the death of Paternus of Avranches in 564; the first canon's reference to a territorial division, which only would have made sense at a time when the Merovingian regnum was divided (i.e., between 556 and 558, or after 561); and the reflection of the political borders of the 560s in the conciliar subscriptions. See Halfond, "Charibert," 6–9. I nevertheless will retain the traditional dating in citing the council's canons due to its usage by modern editors of the Merovingian conciliar *acta*.

115. Council of Paris (556/73), c. 1: "Neque quisquam per interregna res Dei defensare nitatur, quia Dei potentia cunctorum regnorum terminos singulari dominatione concludit. Quod si presumserit, et ipsius offensam et praedictae damnationis periculum sustinebit." On the translation of *interregna* as "divisions between kingdoms," see Olivier Guillot, "'Assassins des pauvres': Une invective pour mieux culpabiliser les usurpateurs de biens d'église, aident à restituer l'activité conciliaire des Gaules entre 561 et 573," in *La culpabilité: Actes des XXèmes Journées d'histoire du droit*, ed. Jacqueline Hoareau-Dodinau and Pascal Texier (Limoges, France: Presses Universitaires de Limoges, 2001), 329–66, at 340n57. On the threat that *divisiones* could pose to property, see also the Council of Clermont (535), Epistle to Theudebert I. On this letter, see Elisabeth Magnou-Nortier, "A propos des rapports entre l'Eglise et l'Etat franc: La lettre synodale au roi Théodebert (535)," in *Societa, Istituzioni, Spiritualita: Studi in Onore di Cinzio Violante* (Spoleto, Italy: Centro italiano di studi sull'alto Medioevo, 1994), 1:519–34; Heike Grahn-Hoek, "Quia Dei potentia cunctorum regnorum terminos singulari dominatione concludit: Kirchlicher Einheitsgedanke und weltliche Grenzen im Spiegel der reichsfränkischen Konzilien des 6. Jahrhunderts," in *Religiöse Bewegungen im Mittelalter: Festschrift für Matthias Werner zum 65. Geburtstag*, ed. Enno Bünz, Stefan Tebruck, Helmut G. Walther, and Mathias Werner (Cologne, Germany: Böhlau, 2007), 3–54, at 11–16.

116. Halfond, "Charibert," 17–20.

117. Council of Paris (556/73), c. 6: "Et quia utilium rerum coepit causa tractare, hoc universitas praecaveri quoque debet, tam Sacerdotes quam principis omnesque populus, ut nullus res alienas conpetire a regis audeat potestate. Nullus viduam neque filiam alterius extra voluntatem parentum aut rapere praesumat aut regis beneficio estimet postulandam. Quod si fecerit, similiter ab ecclesiae communione remotus anathematis damnatione plectatur."

118. Halfond, "Charibert," 20–21.

argued, than an effort to harmonize episcopal and royal priorities in the reconstituted regnum of Paris. The *acta* implicitly position Charibert as the defender of ecclesiastical property and rights in opposition to his more covetous brothers.

While comparatively less is known about the ecclesiastical policies of Guntram and Chilperic in the years immediately following the death of Chlothar I, there is every reason to think that, like Sigibert and Charibert, they sought and leveraged the support of bishops in important *civitates*, as comparative evidence for the next major *divisio* (of 567) suggests. Following Charibert's death in that year, Chilperic began the process of strengthening his position in Paris, a *civitas* he had long coveted, by courting its bishop, Germanus. As suggested by the latter's interactions with the Austrasian branch of the royal dynasty detailed earlier, Chilperic seems to have succeeded in winning Germanus's approval.[119] Upon the bishop's death in 576, Chilperic likely played a role in the election of Germanus's former deacon, the aforementioned Ragnemodus, whose loyalty to the king led Gregory of Tours to dismiss him as an *adolator*.[120] Guntram too recognized the advantages of episcopal support in a contested *civitas*. In 568, amid the territorial restructuring following Charibert's death, Sigibert tried to seize Arles from his brother. At the time, Sigibert controlled a number of cities in Southeast Gaul, including several in relative proximity to the commercial route following the Rhône River, which linked Frankish Gaul to the Mediterranean.[121] Arles, however, along with a number of other nearby *civitates*, had been assigned to Guntram in the *divisio* of 561, thus preventing any one king from controlling completely the lower part of

---

119. On Chilperic's long-standing admiration for Germanus, see Halfond, "Sis Quoque Catholicis Religionis Apex," 72–73.

120. On Ragnemodus, see Halfond, 68.

121. For the characterization of Sigibert's territories as an "Austrasian corridor," see E.-H. Duprat, "Le couloir austrasien du VIe siècle," *Mémoires de l'Institut Historique de Provence* 20 (1943–44): 36–65; Rudolf Buchner, *Die Provence in Merowingischer Zeit* (Stuttgart, Germany: W. Kohlhammer, 1933), 10–11; and Ewig, "Die fränkischen Teilungen," 1:137. Simon T. Loseby, "Discussion," in *Franks and Alamanni*, ed. Ian Wood (Woodbridge, England: Boydell, 1998), 270–84, at 275, conversely suggests that Sigibert's Provençal inheritance (like other regnal partitions) was constituted on a framework "which [was] financial, not territorial." The aforementioned *civitates* included Marseille, on which see Simon T. Loseby, "Marseille: A Late Antique Success Story," *Journal of Roman Studies* 82 (1992): 165–85; and Simon T. Loseby, "Marseille and the Pirenne Thesis I," in *The Sixth Century: Production, Distribution, and Demand*, ed. Richard Hodges and William Bowden (Leiden: Brill, 1998), 203–29. Sigibert also ruled Avignon, whose toll station is alluded to in *Marculfi formulae*, supplementum no. 1. On tolls and toll stations in general, see Reinhold Kaiser, "Steuer und Zoll in der Merowingerzeit," *Francia* 7 (1979): 1–17. Sigibert also controlled Uzès and Viviers, which housed mints; see Loseby, "Marseille and the Pirenne Thesis I," 223. Sigibert's Provençal holdings were loosely connected to his territories in Aquitaine.

the Rhône.¹²² When Sigibert occupied Arles, it was thanks, in large part, to the efforts of Bishop Sapaudus that the operation proved unsuccessful, as the bishop was able to convince Sigibert's soldiers to abandon their position of safety behind the city walls to engage with Guntram's forces and then shut the gates behind them.¹²³

Like his brothers, Sigibert, who inherited roughly half a dozen *civitates* from Charibert in 567, quickly set about establishing relationships with their episcopal sees, generally with greater success than in Arles.¹²⁴ In Tours, Sigibert appealed to Bishop Eufronius by returning to him the contested villa of Nazelles, which Charibert pointedly had refused to do, and by promising not to levy any new taxes on the *populus* of Tours.¹²⁵ In patronizing Eufronius, Sigibert surely was aware that public sentiment among the leading *cives* of Tours was split, with a number of prominent individuals, in particular the *comes* Leudast, preferring Chilperic to his brother.¹²⁶ Despite Sigibert's deposition of the count shortly after taking control of the city, Chilperic's son Clovis briefly occupied Tours circa 569/70, until Sigibert's forces forced him to abandon the *civitas*.¹²⁷ Although Eufronius's actions during the occupation are undocumented, there is every reason to suppose that he maintained his loyalty to Sigibert, as he later helped to enact the king's agenda in the *civitas* of Poitiers, another *civitas* occupied by Chilperic with the aid of locals loyal to that king.¹²⁸

---

122. Halfond, "Negotiating Episcopal Support," 17–19. On Arles's political and economic significance, see Simon T. Loseby, "Arles in Late Antiquity: *Gallula Roma Arelas* and *Urbs Genesii*," in *Towns in Transition: Urban Evolution in Late Antiquity and the Early Middle Ages*, ed. Neil Christie and Simon T. Loseby (Aldershot, England: Ashgate, 1996), 45–70; and Wickham, *Framing the Early Middle Ages*, 665–67, the latter of whom identifies the *civitas* as a focal point for "city-based elite activity."

123. Gregory of Tours, *Decem libri historiarum* 4.30. It is likely that Sapaudus also was the manager of the papal estates in Provence, previously administered by his father, Placidus; see Gregory Halfond, "*Patrimoniolum Ecclesiae Nostrae*: The Papal Estates in Merovingian Provence," *Comitatus* 38 (2007): 1–18, at 10n49. The precise location of these estates, however, is unknown.

124. I.e., Tours, Avranches, Albi, Poitiers, Couserans, Aire, Bayonne, and part of the territory of Chartres.

125. Gregory of Tours, *Libri de virtutibus Sancti Martini episcopi*, ed. Bruno Krusch, MGH SRM 1.2 (Hanover, Germany: Hahn, 1885 [reprint 1969]), 1.29; Gregory of Tours, *Decem libri historiarum* 9.30.

126. Gregory of Tours, *Decem libri historiarum* 5.48. On the support for Chilperic among the *cives* of Tours, see Breukelaar, *Historiography*, 202–3; and Marc Widdowson, "Merovingian Partitions: A Genealogical Charter," *Early Medieval Europe* 17, no. 1 (2009): 1–22, at 12–15. On Gregory's usage of the word *civis*, see Jean Durliat, "*Episcopus, civis,* et *populus* dans les *Historiarum Libri* de Grégoire," in *Grégoire de Tours et l'espace gaulois*, ed. Nancy Gauthier and Henri Galinie (Tours: Revue archéologique du Centre de la France, 1997), 185–93; Simon T. Loseby, "Lost Cities: The End of the *Civitas*-System in Frankish Gaul," in Diefenbach and Müller, *Gallien in Spätantike und Frühmittelalter*, 223–52, at 232.

127. Gregory of Tours, *Decem libri historiarum* 4.45. See also Bernard Bachrach, *Merovingian Military Organization, 481–751* (Minneapolis: University of Minnesota Press, 1972), 38–39.

128. Halfond, "Negotiating Episcopal Support," 15. On the occupation of Poitiers, see Gregory of Tours, *Decem libri historiarum* 4.45. Cf. Michel Rouche, *L'Aquitaine, des Wisigoths aux Arabes, 418–781: Naissance d'une région* (Paris: Éditions Touzot, 1979), 68.

Sigibert's relationship with Poitiers's own bishop, Maroveus, however, likely was tenser. While it is possible that Sigibert instigated Maroveus's election circa 568, the king's patronage of Radegund's convent no doubt rankled the bishop, who bristled at the queen's influence in his diocese.[129] When Maroveus refused to participate in the installation of the relic of the True Cross in the convent, whose arrival in Gaul Sigibert helped to facilitate, it was Eufronius who stepped in to perform the ceremony.[130] Despite this, Maroveus, like Eufronius, seems to have remained faithful to Sigibert during Clovis's occupation. Sigibert certainly never attempted to discipline the bishop following his reclamation of the *civitas*, and in subsequent years, Maroveus proved himself to be an Austrasian loyalist.[131]

Along with Tours and Poitiers, Sigibert also claimed in 567 land in Chartres, which posed a different set of problems. The bulk of the *civitas*, including its urban core, was assigned to Guntram. Sigibert made no attempt to hide his desire to control the entirety of Chartres, which, if brought entirely under Austrasian control, could help to connect Sigibert's northeast territories to his Aquitanian holdings.[132] Rather than attempt to seize the *civitas* outright from Guntram, however, Sigibert created a new episcopal see in Châteaudun, as discussed earlier. The king ordered Bishop Egidius of Rheims to ordain Promotus, despite the fact that Egidius's metropolitan jurisdiction did not extend to Chartres. Guntram responded to Sigibert's provocation by convoking the

---

129. On Maroveus, see Margarete Weidemann, *Kulturgeschichte der Merowingerzeit nach den Werken Gregors von Tours* (Mainz, Germany: Verlag des Römisch-Germanischen Zentralmuseums, 1982), 1:180–82. On the likelihood that Maroveus was ordained in early 568, see Halfond, "Negotiating Episcopal Support," 16n81. On Sigibert's patronage of the Convent of the Holy Cross, see Gregory of Tours, *Decem libri historiarum* 9.40, 9.42; and Baudonivia, *Vita Radegundis Liber II*, ed. Bruno Krusch, MGH SRM 2 (Hanover, Germany: Hahn, 1888), c. 16. On the establishment of the Holy Cross, see Yvonne Labande-Mailfert, "Les debuts de Sainte-Croix," in *Histoire de l'Abbaye Sainte-Croix de Poitiers*, ed. Yvonne Labande-Mailfert et al. (Poitiers, France: Société des antiquaires de l'Ouest, 1986), 25–69.

130. On Radegund's request for the relic of the True Cross, see Averil Cameron, "The Early Religious Policies of Justin II," in *The Orthodox Churches and the West*, ed. Derek Baker, Studies in Church History 13 (Oxford: Blackwell, 1976), 51–67; George, *Venantius Fortunatus*, 62–67; and Isabel Moreira, "*Provisatrix Optima*: St. Radegund of Poitiers' Relic Petitions to the East," *Journal of Medieval History* 19 (1993): 285–305. On Maroveus's response, see Raymond Van Dam, *Saints and Their Miracles in Late Antique Gaul* (Princeton, NJ: Princeton University Press, 1993), 30–36; and Barbara Rosenwein, *Negotiating Space: Power, Restraint, and Privileges of Immunity in Early Medieval Europe* (Ithaca, NY: Cornell University Press, 1999), 52–58.

131. Gregory of Tours, *Decem libri historiarum* 7.24, 9.30 and 10.15. See also Halfond, "Negotiating Episcopal Support," 16–17. Maroveus had no reason to believe that shifting his allegiance to Chilperic would improve his uncomfortable position vis-à-vis Radegund, as Chilperic similarly patronized the Holy Cross; see Halfond, "Sis Quoque Catholicis Religionis Apex," 71. Nevertheless, Erin T. Dailey, *Queens, Consorts, Concubines: Gregory of Tours and the Women of the Merovingian Elite* (Leiden: Brill, 2015), 72, has hypothesized that Maroveus's name might indicate a relationship to the royal family, and to Chilperic specifically.

132. Ewig, "Die fränkischen Teilungen," 1:139.

aforementioned Council of Paris (573), whose admonitions Sigibert simply ignored, and Châteaudun remained an episcopal see for the remainder of Sigibert's reign.¹³³

Whereas Sigibert's ecclesiastical policies in Tours, Poitiers, and Chartres post-567 were motivated by a desire to cement or extend his royal influence in newly acquired *civitates*, the king of Rheims also sought episcopal support in pursuing his territorial ambitions in strategically significant *civitates* and regions not formally assigned to him in 561 or 567. Despite his failure in Arles, Sigibert sought to expand his influence over additional Provençal *civitates*. Before (or during) the campaign of 568, Sigibert seems to have made contact with Mundericus, an archpriest of Tonnerre and bishop-elect of Langres, which led to the latter's subsequent imprisonment by Chilperic on the grounds that the cleric was working against Guntram's interests by supplying Sigibert's forces in Arles. In return for his service and suffering, Sigibert named Mundericus bishop of the *vicus* of Alais within the *civitas* of Rodez.¹³⁴ The establishment of a brand-new episcopal see in Alais helped Sigibert to link his Provençal and Aquitanian territories.¹³⁵ Less certain is Sigibert's possible role in the near-contemporary election of Veranus of Cavaillon. The Carolingian-era *Vita Verani* fails to name the king responsible for the appointment, and those modern historians who accept the veracity of the account have not agreed on the identity of this otherwise anonymous Merovingian. Certainly, both Guntram and Sigibert would have recognized Cavaillon's strategic significance, as the *civitas* was positioned to connect Arles to the rest of Burgundian Provence or, alternatively, Austrasian Provence to Aquitaine.¹³⁶

While formal territorial partitions such as those of 561 and 567 encouraged rival Merovingians to cultivate episcopal allies, so too did military conflicts. During the campaign by the royal pretender Gundovald to establish a *regnum* in Frankish Gaul (ca. 582–85), the putative son of Chlothar I traded gifts for loyalty oaths (*sacramenta*) of the leading *cives* of occupied Aquitanian cities. The recipients of Gundovald's generosity included bishops, with no fewer than nine Aquitanian prelates identified by Gregory of Tours as collaborating

---

133. Council of Paris (573), *acta*; Gregory of Tours, *Decem libri historiarum* 7.17.
134. Gregory of Tours, *Decem libri historiarum* 5.5. Weidemann, *Kulturgeschichte*, 1.136, dates his appointment to ca. 570.
135. Halfond, "Negotiating Episcopal Support," 18.
136. *Vita Verani*, AASS Oct. vol. 8 (Paris: Palmé, 1870), 467–70, at 469. For the dating of the *vita*, see Robert Amiet, "Verano," in *Bibliotheca Sanctorum*, ed. Felippo Caraffa et al. (Rome: Citta Nuova Editrice for Istituto Giovanni XXIII della Pontificia Universita Lateranense, 1969), 12:1017–21. On the debate and the significance of the episode, see Halfond, "Negotiating Episcopal Support," 18n96.

with the pretender.[137] Similarly, the Fredegar chronicler implicates unnamed members of the Burgundian episcopate in the downfall of Brunhild and her family line, cooperating with the Burgundaefarones to further the cause of Chlothar II.[138] And when Ebroin broke out of Luxeuil in 675, following the assassination of Childeric II (662–75), he contacted his many allies, including several bishops, most notable Audoin of Rouen, who provided the resurgent mayor with practical military advice.[139] The Pippinids of the early eighth century similarly cultivated episcopal support in advancing their politico-military agenda. As he expanded his power into Neustria, Charles Martel sought to extend his control over significant episcopal sees while demonstrating a predictable intolerance for bishops who refused his overtures, as Rigobert of Rheims and others discovered to their dismay.[140]

This chapter began with the cautionary note that there was no uniform level of political engagement among the Gallo-Frankish episcopate of the Merovingian era. Many, if not most, bishops never were asked for their counsel, served as royal envoys, or directed cults of sanctity patronized by the royal dynasty. Nevertheless, the royal administration of the realm was predicated on the expectation of episcopal service. So, while few bishops ever had the opportunity to provide counsel to kings or queens, the Merovingians themselves consistently solicited episcopal guidance, even though they were not always prone to be receptive to what they heard. While a far greater percentage of bishops participated in conciliar activities, only occasionally, such as in the trial of Praetextatus of Rouen, did this participation constitute direct service to the royal court. Rather, the judicial and legislative business of ecclesiastical synods, particularly larger interprovincial gatherings, indirectly reinforced peace and administrative order in the realm, a goal of both the Merovingians and the episcopate. Equally implicit the majority of the time was the recognition that bishops provided for the territorial claims of their

---

137. I.e., Faustianus of Dax, Bertram of Bordeaux, Palladius of Saintes, Orestes of Bazas, Ursicinus of Cahors, Antidius of Agen, Ferreolus of Limoges, Nicasius of Angoulême, and Rufinus of Comminges. See Halfond, "Corporate Solidarity."

138. Fredegar, *Chronica* 4.41. In this context, I follow Alexander C. Murray, *Germanic Kinship Structure* (Toronto: Pontifical Institute of Mediaeval Studies, 1983), 93, in identifying the Burgundaefarones as "the Burgundian *leudes* of the Frankish king." See also Wolfgang Haubrichs, "'Leudes, fara, faramanni und farones': Zur Semantik der Bezeichnungen für einige am Konsenshandeln beteiligte Gruppen," in Epp and Meyer, *Recht und Konsens im frühen Mittelalter*, 235–63, at 259–63.

139. *Liber historiae Francorum*, 45.

140. Paul Fouracre, *The Age of Charles Martel* (Harlow, England: Pearson Education, 2000), 74, identifies "at least eight bishoprics which stretched from Rouen to Rennes" as falling under Charles's influence. On Rigobert, see *Vita Rigoberti episcopi Remensis*, ed. Wilhelm Levison, MGH SRM 7 (Hanover, Germany: Hahn, 1920), chaps. 9, 12.

royal masters. Typically, it was only in moments of major transformation, dispute, or crisis that bishops were called on to explicitly declare or demonstrate their own and their *civitas*'s political allegiance. While their actions, on their own, could be insufficient to achieve royal goals, the Merovingians consistently relied on the spiritual and temporal authority of bishops as indispensable contributors to effective royal governance. This recognition assumed—and by extension strengthened—the independent authority of the episcopate, as reflected in the oft-repeated (if not necessarily transparent) distinction between *canones* and *leges*. However, this recognition proved a double-edged sword, as the Merovingians quite understandably collaborated more often and closely with individual bishops than with the unified episcopate. This, in turn, had the unintended consequence of undermining that very corporate structure on which royal administration relied so heavily.

CHAPTER 2

Royal Patronage and Its Benefits

Patronage as a device for establishing and maintaining vertical relationships long predated the arrival of the Franks in Gaul. Patronage was ingrained in late Roman society and culture in part because of its transcendent properties: as Peter Brown has observed, patronage "derived [its] appeal from a proven ability to render malleable seemingly inexorable processes, and to bridge with the warm breath of personal acquaintance the great distances of the late-Roman social world."[1] While periodic political and military crises coincided with the breakdown of patronage networks and relationships, the social construct itself survived into and beyond the Merovingian era, and new affiliations repeatedly were established between a variety

---

1. Peter Brown, *The Cult of the Saints* (Chicago: University of Chicago Press, 1981), 65. On Roman ideology and institutions of patronage, see Richard P. Saller, *Personal Patronage under the Early Empire* (Cambridge: Cambridge University Press, 1982); Jens-Uwe Krause, *Spätantike Patronatsformen in Westen des Römischen Reiches* (Munich: C. H. Beck, 1987); Andrew Wallace-Hadrill, ed., *Patronage in Ancient Society* (London: Routledge, 1989); and Mathisen, *Roman Aristocrats in Barbarian Gaul*, 50–55. On the continued significance of patronage in the medieval era, see Marc Bloch, *Feudal Society*, trans. L. A. Manyon (Chicago: University of Chicago Press, 1961), 147. On cultural patronage specifically, see Rosamond McKitterick, "Royal Patronage of Culture in the Frankish Kingdoms under the Carolingians: Motives and Consequences," *Committenti e Produzione artistico-letteraria nell'alto medioevo occidentale* (Spoleto, Italy: Centro Italiano di Studi sull'Alto Medioevo, 1992), 93–129; Hen, *Royal Patronage of Liturgy*; Hen, *Roman Barbarians*.

of parties.² The Gallo-Frankish episcopate was well versed in the language and manners of patronage, assuming at various times the roles of both patrons and clients.³ The former role has received rather more attention, due to the focus of contemporary sources on the episcopal responsibility for the creation and care of cults of sanctity. Yet even in their devotion to the saints, bishops embodied the dual roles of client and patron.⁴ As Raymond Van Dam has observed of Bishop Gregory of Tours and his saintly patrons, "Both bishop and saints benefitted from this relationship."⁵ Additionally, bishops could assume the role of patron toward their diocesan congregants and dependents, providing not simply pastoral care but also charity for the vulnerable (e.g., widows and orphans), hospitality for travelers, justice, intercession with secular authorities, and financial support for civic construction projects.⁶ Such activities, particularly in their aggregate, could both exemplify and enhance an individual bishop's local authority and prestige.

Similarly, clientage offered bishops an established and respectable framework for interacting with royal authorities. So far as the evidence permits any generalizations, it is likely that most bishops in Merovingian Gaul did not challenge in any meaningful way their integral, but fundamentally subservient, position as a corporate body vis-à-vis the monarchy. Even Gregory of Tours, as forceful a contemporary proponent of *Bischofsherrschaft* as one could find, did not advocate for a Gallo-Frankish theocracy. His own ideal *regnum* assumed "a divine order for the king to govern and for the bishops to impose

---

2. John Drinkwater, "Patronage in Roman Gaul and the Problem of the Bagaudae," in Andrew Wallace-Hadrill, *Patronage in Ancient Society*, 189–203, at 200, observes that social disorder often was an effect, not a cause, of the breakdown of systems of patronage.

3. As seen, for example, in *Marculfi formulae* 2.42–43, sample letters intended to accompany and respond to gifts from one bishop to another. On these letters, see the commentary of Alice Rio, trans., *The Formularies of Angers and Marculf* (Liverpool: Liverpool University Press, 2008), 222–23.

4. See above all Brown, *Cult of the Saints*, on the relationship between the "invisible friends and protectors" and the "impresarios" who promoted their cults. See also John H. Corbett, "The Saint as Patron in the Work of Gregory of Tours," *Journal of Medieval History* 7 (1981): 1–13.

5. Raymond Van Dam, *Saints and Their Miracles in Late Antique Gaul* (Princeton, NJ: Princeton University Press, 1993), 6.

6. Heinzelmann, "Bischof und Herrschaft," 54–57. Along with the previously cited examples of Sidonius Apollinaris and Caesarius of Arles (introduction, n. 47), Gregory of Tours's assumption of the responsibilities of civic patronage long has been recognized; see, e.g., Heinzelmann, *Gregory of Tours*, 45. On the episcopal patronage of ecclesiastical dependents specifically, see Esders, *Die Formierung der Zensualität*, 37–73. On orphans and widows as exemplars of "respectable," but still vulnerable, congregants who demanded episcopal charity, see Peter Brown, *Poverty and Leadership in the Later Roman Empire* (Hanover, NH: University Press of New England, 2002), 58–59. On charitable institutions and practices, see also Thomas Sternberg, *Orientalium more secutus: Räume und Institutionen der Caritas des 5. bis 7. Jahrhunderts in Gallien* (Münster, Germany: Aschendorff, 1991); see 86–92 on hospitality specifically.

moral *'correctio.'*"⁷ As Gregory's own client, Venantius Fortunatus, suggested of Chilperic I in a panegyric delivered in 580, it was the king's duty not only to provide justice and security but also to assume his proper role as the "apex of the Catholic faith."⁸ The *Missa pro principe* inserted within the Bobbio Missal similarly beseeched God to assist the ruler toward *victoria* and *pax*, recognizing the king as a direct agent of God, as well as the figure ultimately responsible for ensuring (with God's help) those temporal conditions in which the *ecclesia* could thrive.⁹

Such statements reflected not simply a recognition of the legitimacy of royal power but also an optimism that the monarchy would use its power to the benefit of the body of all believers. The patronage of the Roman imperial government of the church offered a useful historical model for both kings and bishops, who generally agreed that the governance of the realm required strong, properly directed, royal rule, even if the latter sometimes preferred to think of secular largess as *oblationes* (offerings) or *munera* (gifts) rather than as *beneficia* (favors).¹⁰ Additionally, while the Gallo-Frankish bishops were

---

7. Heinzelmann, *Gregory of Tours*, 190, in reference to Guntram's *edictum*, over which Gregory (Heinzelmann argues) may have exercised an influence.

8. Fortunatus, *Carmina* 9.1.144: "Sis quoque catholicis religionis apex." On this panegyric, recited at Gregory's trial at Berny in 580, see Brian Brennan, "The Career of Venantius Fortunatus," *Traditio* 41 (1985): 49–78, at 74–75; Judith George, "Poet as Politician: Venantius Fortunatus' Panegyric to King Chilperic," *Journal of Medieval History* 15, no. 1 (1989): 5–18; and Simon Coates, "Venantius Fortunatus and the Image of Episcopal Authority in Late Antique and Early Merovingian Gaul," *English Historical Review* 115, no. 464 (2000), 1109–37, at 1135–36. George, "Poet as Politician," 12–13, reads lines 51–52 ("Noxia dum cuperent hostes tibi bella parare, pro te pugnavit fortis in arma fides") as a reference to Chilperic's reliance on the episcopate.

9. *Bobbio Missal: A Gallican Mass Book*, 151–53. On the *Missa* and its disputed origins, see Mary Garrison, "The *Missa pro principe* in the Bobbio Missal," in *The Bobbio Missal: Liturgy and Religious Culture in Merovingian Gaul*, ed. Yitzhak Hen and Rob Meens (Cambridge: Cambridge University Press, 2004), 187–205; Ian Wood, "Liturgy in the Rhone Valley and the Bobbio Missal," in Hen and Meens, *Bobbio Missal*, 206–18, at 212–14.

10. On the contemporary recognition of the compatibility of Christianity and monarchy, see Hen, "Christianisation of Kingship," 163–77. On the terminological preference, see Harries, *Sidonius Apollinaris*, 39–40. For the meaning(s) of *beneficium* in early medieval Francia, see Jan Frederik Niermeyer, *Mediae Latinitatis Lexicon Minus* (Leiden: Brill, 2002), 121–27; and Paul Fouracre, "The Use of the Term *Beneficium* in Frankish Sources: A Society Based on Favours?," in *The Language of Gift in the Early Middle Ages*, ed. Wendy Davies and Paul Fouracre (Cambridge: Cambridge University Press, 2010), 62–88. On gift giving as an unequal, as opposed to a (balanced) reciprocal, exchange in ecclesiastical discourse, see Florin Curta, "Merovingian and Carolingian Gift Giving," *Speculum* 81, no. 3 (2006): 671–99, at 678, following Bernhard Jussen, "Religious Discourses of the Gift in the Middle Ages, Semantic Evidences (Second to Twelfth Centuries)," in *Negotiating the Gift: Pre-modern Figurations of Exchange*, ed. Gadi Algazi, Valentin Groebner, and Bernhard Jussen (Göttingen, Germany: Vandenhoeck and Ruprecht, 2003), 173–92. Conversely, the Merovingian conciliar *acta* do not employ *gratia* in a purely secular context, although see Gregory of Tours, *Decem libri historiarum* 5.18 ("regis gratiam") in reference to Bishop Praetextatus of Rouen and Chilperic I. Additional examples not involving bishops include Gregory of Tours, *Decem libri historiarum* 6.35, 7.22, 8.27, 10.5. On *gratia* in an early medieval context, see Gerd Althoff, "(Royal) Favor: A Central Concept in Early Medieval

habitually and explicitly hostile toward lower clerics and monks relying on secular *patrocinium*, particularly in conflicts with their ecclesiastical superiors, the bishops' primary concern in such cases was asserting episcopal jurisdictional prerogatives, not forbidding secular patronage of the church or its leadership.[11] For example, bishops in attendance at the Council of Orléans (511) formally permitted lower clerics to accept Clovis's *beneficia*, but only with the approval of their bishops.[12] Similarly, in his flattering description of King Theudebert I, Gregory of Tours explicitly praises the king's generosity toward *ecclesiae* and *pauperes* and his bestowal of numerous *beneficia*.[13] Audoin of Rouen too, in his *Vita Eligii*, describes admiringly the *beneficia* that the future saint secured from Dagobert I for the Church of Saint Martin.[14] But even in those cases when bishops preferred to avoid the traditional terminology of patronage to describe royal support, they enthusiastically assumed the role of grateful recipients. The sometimes substantial personal wealth and status of individual bishops similarly was no obstacle to their assumption of a client role vis-à-vis the Merovingians. Royal patronage of the aristocracy was an integral component of Merovingian governance through at least the mid-seventh century, after which court patronage increasingly was disseminated by the mayors of the palace.[15]

The Gallo-Frankish episcopate anticipated, and indeed relied on royal largess, and on an individual, a diocesan, and a corporate basis. This chapter will examine all three of these forms of patronage. In discussing the royal patronage of individual prelates, however, it is necessary to emphasize that in practice the distinction between the person of the bishop and the amalgamation of

---

Hierarchical Relations," in Jussen, *Ordering Medieval Society*, 243–69. See also Oliver Nicholson, ed., *The Oxford Dictionary of Late Antiquity* (Oxford: Oxford University Press, 2018), s.v., "gratia."

11. E.g., the Councils of Arles (442/506), c. 31; Clermont (535), c. 2; Orléans (538), c. 12 (11); Orléans (541), c. 25; Eauze (551), c. 4; Mâcon (581/83), cc. 10, 20; Paris (614), c. 5 (cf. Chlothar II, *Edictum*, c. 3); and Chalon-sur-Saône (647/53), c. 15.

12. Council of Orléans (511), c. 7: "Abbatibus, presbyteris omnique clero vel in relegionis professione viventibus sine discussione vel commendatione episcoporum pro petendis beneficiis ad domnus venire non liceat." It is very possible that when Remigius of Rheims advised Clovis that his "beneficium . . . castum et honestum esse debet" in a sentence otherwise concerned with the king's relationship with his bishops, the bishop assumed that this patronage would be directed toward the church; *Epistolae Austrasicae* no. 2 (113).

13. Gregory of Tours, *Decem libri historiarum* 3.25. Cf. Gregory of Tours, *Libri de virtutibus Sancti Martini episcopi* 1.25.

14. *Vita Eligii episcopi Noviomagensis*, MGH SRM 4, ed. Bruno Krusch (Hanover, Germany: Hahn, 1902), chap. 1.32. On the authorship of the *vita*, see Clemons M. M. Bayer, "Vita Eligii," in *Reallexikon der germanischen Altertumskunde*, 2nd ed., ed. Heinrich Beck, Dieter Geuenich, and Heiko Steuer (Berlin: Walter de Gruyter, 2007), 35:461–524; Charles Mériaux, "Du nouveau sur la Vie de saint Éloi," *Mélanges de science religieuse* 67, no. 3 (2010): 71–85.

15. Guy Halsall, *Settlement and Social Organization: The Merovingian Region of Metz* (Cambridge: Cambridge University Press, 1995), 38, 49–50; Ian Wood, *Merovingian Kingdoms*, 79.

properties, staff, congregants, and cults under his supervision often was blurry. Consequently, when a monarch patronized a bishop, in many cases his munificence formally was directed toward a diocese, its institutions, or the cults of sanctity maintained therein, rather than to the bishop who supervised the wealth, property, and spiritual obligations of the local church.

Episcopal Elections

The major exception to this rule was the involvement of the Merovingians in episcopal elections. The regularity of royal involvement in the selection of bishops in Merovingian Gaul is well established.[16] Less transparent is the episcopal attitude toward this practice. Royal interference in the election process did not inevitably impede, for example, the selection of qualified clerical candidates, nor did it preclude the involvement of the clergy and *cives* of the *civitas* in submitting nominations.[17] Conciliar *acta* offer the best evidence for an episcopal corporate attitude toward what amounted to a standard royal practice. Leaving aside for now the demonstrable fact that some of the episcopal authors of these acts owed their offices to royal support, Frankish conciliar canons that address the issue of royal participation in episcopal elections do not necessarily articulate a consistent policy, despite strong continuities in legal thought.[18] It is true that they drew from a canonical tradition dating back to the early fourth century that acknowledged, on the one hand, the responsibility of bishops, in particular metropolitans, for the ordinations of their provincial colleagues but also, on the other hand, the role of the local lay and clerical population in the selection process.[19] However, the reality of not only regular lay

---

16. Claude, "Die Bestellung der Bischöfe"; Ian Wood, "Ecclesiastical Politics of Merovingian Clermont"; Scheibelreiter, *Der Bischof in merowingischer Zeit*, 149–56; Christoph Müller, "Kurialen und Bischof, Bürger und Gemeinde—Untersuchungen zur Kontinuität von Ämtern, Funktionen und Formen der 'Kommunikation' in der gallischen Stadt des 4.–6. Jahrhunderts" (PhD diss., Albert-Ludwigs-Universität Freiburg, 2003), 200–303; Norton, *Episcopal Elections 250–600*, 115–17.

17. Bruno Dumézil, "La royauté mérovingienne et les élections épiscopales au VIe siècle," in *Episcopal Elections in Late Antiquity*, ed. Johan Leemans et al. (Berlin: De Gruyter, 2011), 127–43, at 133–34. On qualifications for episcopal office, see Susan Loftus, "Suitable Men to Enter the Episcopate in Late Antique Gaul: Ideal and Reality," *Journal of the Australian Early Medieval Association* 10 (2014): 23–46.

18. Cf. Pontal, *Histoire des conciles mérovingiens*, 258–60, who reads the canons collectively as an (unsuccessful) effort to limit royal input and involvement in elections. Cf. also Brigitte Basdevant-Gaudemet, "Childebert et les évêques: Note sur une procédure de désignation épiscopale," *Revue historique de droit français et étranger* 74 (1996): 567–72, at 567–69, who assumes that a consistent rule (i.e., election by the people and clergy and consecration by the metropolitan accompanied by his comprovincials) underlay the canonical legislating of the period.

19. Norton, *Episcopal Elections 250–600*, 20–51.

involvement in the nomination and selection of bishops but also contested elections regularly conflicted with legal theory, and the conciliar legislation of the Merovingian period is, in part, a response to a lack of procedural consistency. So, in other words, we cannot read the canons as evidence for actual practices, but rather for their articulation of an episcopal response to these practices.

As early as the Council of Orléans (511), bishops conceded the right of the king to intervene in the ordination of laymen to the clergy by granting him (or his delegates) the right of approval through an *iussio*. Only those laymen with preexisting familial ties to the clerical *ordo* could be ordained solely through episcopal impetus.[20] The immediate relevance of this early canon on subsequent conciliar rules regarding episcopal elections, however, appears to have been negligible. Not only is the canon entirely concerned with lower clerics, its concession to the monarchy likely was motivated by very different concerns from those that compelled the Merovingians to intervene in episcopal elections. The Orléans canon elaborates on established Roman legal precedent, limiting the ordination of some lay persons, possibly so as to prevent a swelling of the ranks of the clergy at the expense of the free lay population from whom *milites* and other royal servants were drawn.[21] In other words, there is no reason to think that the canon reflects Clovis's wish to monopolize the clerical staffs of Gallic churches with his supporters, an impractical goal at best. Despite the canon's dissimilar motivations, it nevertheless does constitute the first episcopal concession to the Merovingians in matters of clerical staffing, a necessary precedent for future rulings expanding this right to include episcopal elections themselves.

The first Frankish episcopal synod to address directly the possibility of lay interference in episcopal elections was the Council of Clermont (535), attended by bishops from the regnum of Theudebert I. In their *acta*, the bishops limited participation in the election to local *clerici* and *cives*, "[cum] consensu etiam metropoletani eiusdem provinciae," while explicitly forbidding candidates from seeking the *patrocinium* of powerful lay patrons.[22] The Council of Orléans (538), attended by bishops from the regna of Childebert I and Theudebert I, identified the same parties as electors but made no reference to the interference of external lay parties.[23] In contrast, the Council of Orléans (549), convoked by Childebert alone, raised once again the possibility of

---

20. Council of Orléans (511), c. 4.
21. De Clercq, *La législation religieuse franque*, 9; Daly, "Clovis," 660. Another plausible concern, as suggested by Yaniv Fox, pers. comm., may have been tax exemptions.
22. Council of Clermont (535), c. 2.
23. Council of Orléans (538), c. 3.

interference by influential persons but took pains to emphasize that these individuals did not, in fact, include kings, whose *voluntas* (consent) confirmed the choice of the electors. The same council also prohibited these same "powerful persons" from forcing candidates on the *clerici* and *cives* and dictated the procedures by which a layman might be elected bishop with no mention of royal consent as a prerequisite.[24] These canons effectively constitute an effort to maintain "free" episcopal elections while legitimizing royal involvement (via consent) and the ordination of individuals who may never before have held clerical office, including, presumably, former royal officials.

The Council of Paris, convoked ca. 561/64 in the regnum of Childebert's nephew, Charibert, reiterated the previous synod's insistence that only the *populi* and *clerici*, with the consent of the metropolitan and his provincial suffragans (who were to perform the ordination), could elect a new bishop, as well as its assertion that an episcopal candidate should not be forced on a *civitas*. However, it adopted a slightly altered policy toward lay involvement. Instead of singling out anonymous potentates for criticism, as had the Council of Orléans (549), the synod insisted that new bishops should not be imposed on the diocese "either by royal authority or an agreement contrary to the will of the metropolitan and the comprovincial bishops."[25] Despite its strong language, the canon does not necessarily constitute a novel prohibition of royal involvement in episcopal elections: it does not forbid kings from nominating or confirming nominated candidates, so long as the *populi* and *clerici* elect the candidate canonically with the approval of the other bishops of the province.[26] The concern here seems to be more with proper procedure and metropolitan prerogative than with preventing royal participation altogether.

Of course, nominating monarchs were not always as concerned with procedural niceties and metropolitan prerogatives as their bishops. This became clear shortly after the Council of Paris concluded its business, when Leontius of Bordeaux, an attendee of the synod, attempted to enforce its rulings by convoking

---

24. Council of Orléans (549), cc. 9, 10, 11. On the meaning of *voluntas* in c. 10, see Adolf Berger *The Encyclopedic Dictionary of Roman Law* (Philadelphia: American Philosophical Society, 1953), s.v. "voluntas." The Council of Orléans (541), in contrast, did not address the issue of episcopal elections directly, but only the question of where the ordination should take place (c. 5). On possible readings of c. 10, see also Basdevant-Gaudemet, "Childebert."

25. Council of Paris (556/73), c. 8: "Nullus civibus invitis ordinetur episcopus, nisi quem populi et clericorum electio plenissima quesierit voluntate; non principes imperio neque per quamlibet conditionem contra metropolis voluntatem vel episcoporum comprovincialium ingeratur." On the dating of the council, see chapter 1, n. 114.

26. On the political context of this canon, see Halfond, "Charibert," 21–22. On its "revision" of the rule promulgated at Orléans (549), see Andreas Thier, *Hierarchie und Autonomie: Regelungstraditionen der Bischofsbestellung in der Geschichte des kirchlichen Wahlrechts bis 1140* (Frankfurt am Main: V. Klostermann, 2011), 215–17.

his own provincial meeting at Saintes to depose Bishop Emerius of Saintes, originally appointed to his seat by Chlothar I without metropolitan consent. The Council of Saintes then appointed—presumably without bothering to consult the *cives* and *clerici* of Saintes—Heraclius, a presbyter of Bordeaux. When Charibert learned of Leontius's actions, he simply voided the council's orders, exiled Heraclius, and fined Leontius.[27] While Leontius's efforts to assert metropolitan privilege were ham-fisted and politically naïve, there is no question that conciliar legislation including that of the Council of Paris left sizable procedural loopholes for the Merovingians to take advantage of in justifying their continued intervention in elections.

While it would be another fifty years before a Frankish council addressed through legislation the issue of lay involvement in episcopal elections, synods in the interim continued to wrestle with the repercussions of royal interference, most notably at the Council of Paris (573), where bishops from Guntram's kingdom attempted to eliminate the new episcopal see of Châteaudun.[28] The Council of Paris (614), while paying lip service to the participation of *cives* and local *clerici*, emphasized even more so than the Council of Paris (561/64) the role of the provincial metropolitan and his suffragans in the election. The former now was characterized unequivocally as an elector, as opposed to a mere consenting party.[29] While the canon also forbids simony, it does not identify a role for the monarchy in either the nomination or the election of episcopal candidates.[30] Chlothar rectified this lacuna a week later in his *edictum*, which included a new addendum to the canon: "If [the chosen individual] is worthy, he shall be ordained by the decree [*ordination*] of the king; certainly, if he is chosen from among the palace staff, he ought to be selected on account of his personal merit and learning."[31] Obviously, this policy exceeded any previous concessions made by the episcopate regarding royal participation in elections, which, for instance, made no explicit mention of the (perfectly normal) selection of former court officials to fill vacant sees. Furthermore, the role of the king now had been expanded beyond simply nomination or consent: it was solely his authority, communicated via an *ordinatio*, that initiated the ordination procedures, not the will of the electors.[32]

---

27. Gregory of Tours, *Decem libri historiarum* 4.26. On the dating of the Council of Saintes, see Halfond, "Charibert," 7–8.
28. Council of Paris (573), *acta*.
29. Thier, *Hierarchie und Autonomie*, 220–21, argues on semantic grounds against the view that the canon identifies metropolitans as the sole electors.
30. Council of Paris (614), c. 2.
31. Chlothar II, *Edictum*, in *Capitularia regum Francorum*, c. 1.
32. As Carlo Servatius, "'Per ordinationem principis ordinetur.' Zum Modus der Bischofsernennung im Edikt Chlothars II vom Jahre 614," *Zeitschrift für Kirchengeschichte* 84 (1973): 1–29, at 28, observes,

There was no immediate conciliar response to Chlothar's edict, so we have no way of knowing how his policies were received by the episcopal *ordo*. Of course, his legislation quite probably reflected the reality of royal involvement in episcopal elections, even more so than the legislation of the Council of Paris (614), which had ignored entirely the possibility of monarchical interference. So there is no reason necessarily to suppose widespread episcopal condemnation of his legislation. The Council of Clichy (626/27), which assembled over a decade after the publication of the edict, made no explicit references to royal involvement in elections, merely reiterating the expectation that the people and clergy of the city, along with the other bishops of the province, elect the new occupant of a vacant see. The attendees, however, did require the new occupant of an episcopal seat to be a native of the *civitas*, which theoretically reduced the number of potential candidates.[33] The canon certainly does not preclude royal involvement in the nomination process, but it can still be read as a concession to regional potentates attempting to monopolize local sees.

Such a concession, however, undoubtedly would have required royal approval. Chlothar convoked the Council of Clichy and was the recipient of its acts, whose servile tone toward the king has been noted by editors.[34] It seems unlikely that he would have approved of a canon that limited his previously asserted authority in the selection of new bishops. Certainly, there is no reason to assume that Chlothar made this concession from a position of weakness vis-à-vis the Frankish aristocracy. Rather, we might read this canon as a form of royal exemption, building on a legislative program begun by the king in 614. The Edict of Paris similarly had required *iudices* to be residents of their jurisdictional district of appointment, and Alexander C. Murray has observed that this concession "is as much a sign of the secondary importance of the office of count as it is of the influence of regional interests. In 614 Chlothar could afford to accommodate those who helped bring him to power by agreeing to draw his counts from the provinces in which they were to serve."[35] While the conciliar canon, in contrast, does not reflect the weakness of episcopal office—Murray notes in relation to chapter 12 of the *edictum* that bishops

---

Chlothar's edict had the effect of transforming the election proper into a mere nonbinding *petitio*. Additionally, in the same edict (c. 2), Chlothar banned the practice of bishops selecting their own successors, which similarly ensured the monarchy's role in the selection process. But cf. Thier, *Hierarchie und Autonomie*, 217–23, who argues for the edict's traditionalism.

33. Council of Clichy (626/27), c. 28.

34. Jean Gaudemet and Brigitte Basdevant-Gaudemet, eds., *Les canons des conciles mérovingiens (VIe–VIIe siècles)*, SC 354 (Paris: Cerf, 1989), 527.

35. Alexander C. Murray, "Immunity, Nobility, and the Edict of Paris," *Speculum* 69, no. 1 (1994): 18–39, at 30. For Murray's full discussion of chapter 12 of Chlothar's edict, see 27–30.

probably played some role in the selection of *comites*—it also does not suggest royal impotence.

The Council of Chalon-sur-Saône (647/53), unlike those synods held during the reign of Chlothar II, assembled when the Neustrian king, Clovis II, still was a minor.³⁶ Despite the conciliar acts crediting the council's convocation to Clovis, the initiative almost certainly came from Erchinoald, the mayor of the palace.³⁷ Unsurprisingly, the council's proscription regarding episcopal elections makes no mention of any royal role whatsoever. Instead, the canon merely reiterates the Council of Clichy's classification of the electors as comprising the *clerici*, *cives*, and *comprovinciales*.³⁸ The final Merovingian councils to deal with procedural issues surrounding episcopal elections were Saint-Jean-de-Losne (673/75) and Mâlay-le-Roi (677/79), which emphasized very different criteria for determining the legitimacy of episcopal elections. While the former insisted on the *consensus populi* for the legitimization of episcopal elections, the latter deposed Bishop Chramlinus of Embrun partly on the grounds that he had been appointed without the approval of Theuderic III (673, 675–90/91), ostensibly the convoking monarch.³⁹ While the councils' rulings were by no means mutually exclusive, the Mâlay-le-Roi meeting is unique among Merovingian-era synods for its deposition of a sitting bishop on the grounds of the absence of royal confirmation.

This brief survey of conciliar legislation, as suggested earlier, does not reveal a uniform policy (let alone practice) on episcopal elections in Merovingian Gaul, but only continuities in tradition and legal thought. The Gallo-Frankish councils never, for instance, abandoned their insistence that *clerici* and *cives* were qualified to serve as episcopal electors, although by the late seventh century the people sometimes were being characterized as consenters to ordinations rather than as electors proper. Conversely, the metropolitan and his suffragans only were explicitly identified as electors in the early seventh century. Furthermore, while no Merovingian councils ever attempted to ban outright royal involvement in episcopal elections, their precise role continued to be modified

---

36. On his year of birth (634), see Eugen Ewig, "Die Namengebung bei den ältesten Frankenkönigen und im merowingischen Königshaus," in *Spätantikes und fränkisches Gallien*, 3:163–211, at 3:208.
37. Pontal, *Histoire des conciles mérovingiens*, 217.
38. Council of Chalon-sur-Saône (647/53), c. 10.
39. Council of Saint-Jean-de-Losne (673/75), c. 5; *Die Urkunden der Merowinger*, ed. Carlrichard Brühl et al. (Hanover, Germany: Hahn, 2001), no. 122: "Dum et episcopos de regna nostra tam de Niuster et de Burgundia pro statu aeclesiae vel confirmacione pacis ad nostro palacio Maslaco villa iussemus advenire et aliqui ex ipsis, qui in infidilitate nostra fuerant inventi, per eorum cannonis fuirunt iudecati, inter quos adfuit Chramlinus, filius Miecio quondam, qui aepiscopatum Aebreduno civitate habuit, inventum est, quod sua praesumcione vel per falsa carta seu per revellacionis audacia, sed non per nostra ordenacione ipsum aepiscopatum reciperat, eciam nec sicut eorum cannonis contenent ad ipsum benedictum solemnetur episcopi non adfuirunt."

up through the reign of Chlothar II, when the *ordinatio* of the king became a mandated prerequisite for ordinations.

The mutability of conciliar rules regarding the royal role in episcopal elections further complicates any effort to compare legal theory with practical reality. The Merovingians did intervene in elections—this is not in dispute—and this involvement (as opposed to their support for particular candidates), as far as we know, rarely was questioned on principle. However, the actual frequency of royal intervention is difficult to gauge with accuracy, and we must be cautious not to overstate the regularity of these intrusions, particularly by any individual ruler. When a new king came to power, the episcopal sees of his regnum already were occupied by prelates chosen by different electors, and few, if any, Merovingians reigned long enough to oversee elections in every diocese of their kingdom. Additionally, the shifting of regnal borders brought sees whose occupants had been chosen by "foreign" electors under new regimes, complicating any royal efforts to pack local dioceses with hand-chosen partisans. Furthermore, contemporary accounts of elections reveal that royal involvement frequently was solicited by the electors themselves or by disputing candidates. In such cases, it simply is not possible to say whether royal interference would have occurred regardless of the *petitio*.[40]

Most significantly of all, our knowledge of the selection process for the vast majority of those several thousand bishops who held office between circa 500 and 750 is extremely sparse, particularly for the later seventh and early eighth centuries. Furthermore, in many cases, royal nomination only can be inferred rather than proved, such as when an elected prelate held secular office under the reigning monarch and pursued no clerical career in the interim. However, former courtiers probably only accounted for a minority of royal appointees to the episcopate, let alone of all ordained bishops. Bruno Dumézil has tallied that between 500 and 614 at least twenty-six former clerics were nominated by the royal court, compared to only eleven secular officeholders.[41] One could add to this latter tally at least three additional sixth-century secular officeholders

---

40. Susan Loftus, "Episcopal Elections in Gaul," in Leemans et al., *Episcopal Elections in Late Antiquity*, 423–36, at 434–36 (with specific examples cited therein).

41. Dumézil, "La royauté mérovingienne," 133–35. In the cases of three of the former secular officeholders, Albinus of Uzès, Flavius of Chalon, and Ursicinus of Cashors, royal nominations are inferred. Gregory of Tours relates, for instance, that Albinus was supported by the *patricius* Dynamius of Marseilles, and probably by extension Guntram of Burgundy, but against the wishes of Childebert II (Gregory of Tours, *Decem libri historiarum* 6.7). Dumézil observes that nine of the nominated clerics came from *civitates* different from the seas to which they were appointed, while several more were exiles or fugitives.

turned bishops.[42] Of these fourteen former courtiers, no fewer than five, more than one-third, were nominated by a single king: Guntram of Burgundy.[43] For the seventh century, we can identify roughly an equivalent number of appointments of former secular officials in which the court played a role.[44] The spotty statistical information available suggests that when the Merovingians were intervening in episcopal elections, much of the time they were supporting candidates qualified under canon law for the office. More importantly, this evidence cannot demonstrably prove that the majority, let alone the entirety, of bishops ordained in the Merovingian period were royal appointees, merely that court involvement in elections was not infrequent.

This observation is borne out by the formulary evidence. For its emphasis on procedure, Marculf's formulary is especially valuable. Four documents in the late seventh-century formulary (nos. 1.5–7 and *supplementum* no. 6) touch on election protocol.[45] Whereas numbers 1.5 and 1.6 and *supplementum* number 6 are models for royal letters or charters (no. 1.6 being a condensed version of no. 1.5), number 1.7 is intended to convey the *consensus civium* regarding nominations. Alice Rio has noted several reasons to be cautious about reading this latter document as evidence for the survival of "democratic" episcopal elections. First of all, it is not obvious from the document precisely who these *cives* were; there is no reason to think that they constituted a representative cross section of the *civitas*'s population. Additionally, Rio argues on the basis of the document's location in the formulary, following the two royal letters, that the *consensus civium* formula was intended to confirm the royal

---

42. Servatius, *"Per ordinationem,"* 16–17, who records thirty appointments of former secular officeholders for the entirety of the sixth and seventh centuries, includes several sixth-century individuals not named by Dumézil: Austrapius of Champtoceaux, Desiderius of Eauze (his secular office-holding status is uncertain), Gregory of Langres (a Burgundian, not Frankish, *civitas*, and probably elected canonically), Maracharius of Angoulême (his royal nomination cannot be confirmed), and Nicetius of Dax. Neither Dumézil nor Servatius includes Priscus of Lyons (see n. 64 of this chapter).

43. Gregory of Tours, *Decem libri historiarum* 5.45 (Flavius of Chalon), 8.22 (Gundegisel of Bordeaux), 8.39 (Licerius of Arles); Fredegar, *Chronica* 3.89 (Cariatto of Geneva); Edmond Le Blant, ed., *Inscriptions chrétiennes de la Gaule antérieures au VIIIe siècle* (Paris: L'Imprimerie Impériale, 1856–65), 1:60–61 (no. 26) (Priscus of Lyon).

44. Servatius, *"Per ordinationem,"* 18–19, identifies as certain appointments Arnulf of Metz, Audoin of Rouen, Desiderius of Cahors, Leudegar of Autun, and Nivardus of Rheims. He identifies an additional eight former officeholders who may have received some form of royal backing: Ansbert of Rouen (whose *vita* reports that he was elected canonically with a *petitio* sent to the king for confirmation), Bonitus of Clermont (on whom, see chapter 4), Burgundofaro of Meaux (on whose appointment, see Fox, *Power and Religion*, 66), Eligius of Noyon, Genesius of Lyons (on whom, see the discussion later in this chapter), Lantbert of Lyons (on whom, see the discussion later in this chapter), Reolus of Rheims, and Rusticius of Cahors.

45. On the dating of the formulary, I follow Rio, *Legal Practice*, 82–88.

choice.⁴⁶ Finally, as Rio has argued at length in her study of the Frankish formularies, these collections "are essentially descriptive material turned into normative form," with limited value as evidence for local conditions.⁴⁷ So, the *consensus civium* document included by Marculf should be read in a similar manner as the conciliar canons examined earlier: as an effort to standardize practice.

When read in this light, the document embodies several general principles regarding election protocol. While Rio's suggestion that this document in practice might have been utilized more as a "legal fiction" cannot be dismissed, the formula maintains that the nomination of a bishop begins within the diocese itself, with the choice justified by the consensus of the electors, while the king is responsible for ordering the installation of the new bishop, effectively confirming the selection of the electors.⁴⁸ It surely is not a coincidence that the formula recalls the procedures mandated by Chlothar's *edictum* of 614, although consensus documents already were being employed back in the sixth century. Gregory of Tours's uncle Gallus, for example, was ordained on the orders of King Theuderic, following his receipt of a *consensus civium* delivered by the *clerici* of Clermont.⁴⁹

The preceding two documents (nos. 1.5 and 1.6), both royal *praeceptiones* ordering the installation of a new bishop, flesh out the formulary's expectations regarding the royal role.⁵⁰ Both are addressed by a king to a (presumably) metropolitan bishop, requesting the performance of the ordination ceremony in collaboration with the latter's comprovincials. In both documents, the king intimates that the nominee was chosen by himself in consultation with his *pontifices et proceres*. No mention at all is made of the *consensus civium* as a prerequisite for the king's decision, which could support the view that the latter was more a formality, perhaps even one pursued after the election was a fait accompli.⁵¹ On the other hand, there is no reason to assume that the

---

46. Rio, *Formularies of Angers and Marculf*, 139. Cf. Claude, "Die Bestellung der Bischöfe," 22–26; and Alexander C. Murray, "The Merovingian State and Administration in the Times of Gregory of Tours," in Murray, *Companion to Gregory of Tours*, 191–231, at 225n98.

47. Rio, *Legal Practice*, 198.

48. *Marculfi formulae* 1.7: "Quoniam sanctae memoriae vir apostolicos ille, illius urbis episcopus, finem adpropinquantem, ab hac luce migravit, tempore naturae conplenti, ne distututae sint, quod absit, oves decidentae pastore, in loco eiusdem, suppliciter postolamus, ut instituere dignetis inlustrem virum illum, aut venerabilem illum, cathedrae illius successorem, in quo est praespicuetas sublimis, ingenuetas nationis, elegantia refulgens, diligentia castitatis, caritatis locuplex."

49. Gregory of Tours, *Liber vitae patrum* 6.3. For a similar communication of consensus involving one of Gregory's kinsmen, see Gregory of Tours, *Decem libri historiarum* 4.15.

50. Gregory of Tours, *Decem libri historiarum* 7.7, 7.31, refers to royal ordination orders as *praeceptiones*.

51. *Marculfi formulae*, 1.5–6. *Supplementum* no. 6, which likely was added to the collection shortly after its compilation, does allude to the *petitio* of the clergy and people for a specific candidate, a former

issuance of a *consensus civium* document precluded the need for a king to make the final determination on a suitable occupant for a vacant episcopal seat, as the case of Gallus of Clermont suggests.

Additionally, despite the absence of any direct reference to local elections in documents 1.5–6, the allusion to the king's collaboration with *pontifices et proceres* in his deliberating (*pertractantes*) over the naming of a new bishop might possibly be read as a reference to those local electors who made nominations to the court for the king's final approval. In other words, these deliberations may not have occurred at the court itself but rather through written communications. At the very least, the inclusion of document 1.7 in the formulary, regardless of its placement, would suggest that local elections still mattered in seventh-century Francia, even if these elections were based less on democratic voting than on occasionally contentious negotiations between the leading secular and ecclesiastical residents of a *civitas*.

In this context, a king or queen, despite his or her elevated power and status, was one more, albeit potentially crucial, voice in a wider negotiation that stretched from the *civitas* to the court. While Merovingian royal intervention could settle disputed elections, their choice certainly was governed by self-interest. Selecting a candidate to support might have implications for the court's relations with a range of local constituencies, secular and ecclesiastical. Ian Wood's classic case study of the episcopal elections of Clermont bears out this observation. As Wood observes at the outset of his examination, the circumstances surrounding individual elections rarely conformed to "ideal procedure," and "the canons were ignored if circumstances demanded; each episcopal election requires individual scrutiny."[52] In the case of Clermont, despite the politicking of local constituencies, the monarchy ultimately determined the outcome of every single election in the sixth century.[53]

One of the elections examined by Wood is that of Avitus in 571. Before the former archdeacon's ordination, he had been competing for office with another scion of a local aristocratic family, the presbyter Eufrasius, who had the support of the local *comes* Firminus.[54] Gregory of Tours, a possible relation of the winning party, claimed after the fact that Avitus had been elected canonically by the *clerici* and *populi*.[55] But despite his ostensibly canonical election, Avitus still found it necessary to travel to Metz in 571 to be ordained at Sigibert's

---

comes.

52. Ian Wood, "Ecclesiastical Politics of Merovingian Clermont," 42–43.
53. Wood, 46–47.
54. On Avitus, see Wood, 37–39; on Eufrasius and his ancestry, see Wood, 48.
55. On the uncertain relationship between Avitus and Gregory of Tours, see Heinzelmann, *Gregory of Tours*, 30n19.

court. Why the king should have supported Avitus over his own *comes* is unknown, although he must have trusted that the new bishop would represent his interests in a factionalized *civitas*.⁵⁶

As Wood's study demonstrates, at least through the late seventh century, local politics in Clermont could be both complex and contentious. Less than two decades before the election of 571, for example, Firminus had been deposed as count by Sigibert's brother Chramn, who in his place appointed Salustius, the son and grandson of previous counts and the brother of Eufrasius. Clearly, Firminus did not blame Eufrasius himself for his deposition, and it is unknown what personal or familial prejudices prompted him to take extraordinary measures to attempt to block Avitus's ordination. By the 570s, while Clermont was securely within Sigibert's control, the king of Rheims could not afford to take the chance that internal factionalism within a city on whose military resources he had come to rely might threaten his stake in Aquitaine, particularly as the city was located precariously on the border of Guntram's kingdom.⁵⁷ Chramn's revolt had shown clearly how local and royal politics could become inextricably entangled, exacerbating existing local tensions and fomenting new disputes. In Clermont itself, the *cives* became divided between supporters and opponents of the Merovingian prince.⁵⁸ This, of course, was the sort of situation that Sigibert hoped to avoid, ironically by intervening on behalf of one local faction against another.

While our knowledge of episcopal elections in Clermont is uniquely detailed, thanks in no small part to the historical diligence of one of that *civitas*'s former residents, Gregory of Tours, the electoral histories of other cities do demonstrate parallels. The metropolitan see of Lyons, to which Gregory similarly harbored personal ties, is a suggestive example. At the time the city was integrated into the Merovingian *regnum* (AD 534), the city's episcopal seat was probably occupied by Bishop Lupus, who was succeeded sometime in the late 530s or 540s by a certain Leontius (or Licontius), known only through the inclusion of his name in a ninth-century episcopal list.⁵⁹ The first Lyonnais bishop of the Merovingian period about whom we know more than a few scant details is Leontius's successor, Sacerdos, a patrician and relation of Gregory of

---

56. On the context of Avitus's election, see Ian Wood, "Ecclesiastical Politics of Merovingian Clermont," 44–45; Brian Brennan, "The Conversion of the Jews of Clermont in AD 576," *Journal of Theological Studies* 36 (1985): 321–37; and Halfond, "Negotiating Episcopal Support," 19.

57. Gregory of Tours, *Decem libri historiarum* 4.30.

58. Gregory Halfond, "Ecclesiastical Politics in the *Regnum Chramni*: Contextualizing Baudonivia's *Vita Radegundis* Ch. 15," *Journal of Ecclesiastical History* 68, no. 3 (2017): 474–92.

59. On Lupus and Leontius, see Alfred Coville, *Recherches sur l'histoire de Lyon* (Paris: Picard, 1928), 316–18; Duchesne, *Fastes épiscopaux de l'ancienne Gaule*, 2:157, 2:165–66; and Pietri and Heijmans, *Prosopographie de la Gaule chrétienne*, 1208–10 (Lupus).

CHAPTER 2

Tours who apparently enjoyed a close personal relationship with King Childebert I.[60] Whether this king played any role in Sacerdos's election is unknown. Sacerdos's claim to the episcopate of Lyons was strong in any case, as he was quite likely related to several prior occupants of the see, including possibly his immediate predecessor.[61] As he reached the end of his own days, Sacerdos apparently hoped to keep the episcopal see of Lyons within the family, as Gregory reports that his great-uncle, Bishop Nicetius, was elected circa 552 on Sacerdos's recommendation.[62] This recommendation was communicated personally by Sacerdos to Childebert. Thus, it was the king who most likely engineered the succession.[63]

Gregory provides no details, however, regarding the election of Nicetius's successor, Priscus.[64] At the time of his election in 573, Lyons was under the control of Guntram of Burgundy, whom Priscus previously had served as a *domesticus*.[65] While his epitaph describes him as being of noble birth, it is unknown whether his family had roots in Lyons itself, although it is conceivable, if by no means demonstrable, that Priscus was a member of the lineage descended from Priscus Valerianus, an early to mid-fifth-century *praefectus praetorio*, which had links to Lyons through Bishop Eucherius of Lyons (early to mid-fifth century).[66] Regardless of his ancestry, Priscus's earlier service to Guntram no doubt made him an attractive candidate for office, and it is reasonable to assume that the king had some say in his ordination. Raymond Van Dam has suggested that Gregory's hostility toward Priscus might have stemmed in part from the former's hope that he himself would be chosen to succeed Nicetius as the occupant of an episcopal seat that he may have viewed as

---

60. Gregory of Tours, *Liber vitae patrum* 8.3. Heinzelmann, *Gregory of Tours*, 22, suggests that the bishop was "perhaps the most dominant figure in Childebert's kingdom in the 540's." On Sacerdos, see Pietri and Heijmans, *Prosopographie de la Gaule chrétienne*, 1674–76. On his epitaph, see Heinzelmann, *Bischofsherrschaft in Gallien*, 130–37.

61. Christian Settipani, "Ruricius Ier évêque de Limoges et ses relations familiales," *Francia* 18, no. 1 (1991): 195–222, at 206–9, suggests kinship with Viventiolus, Rusticus, and Leontius. Sacerdos's son, Aurelianus, was bishop of Arles; see Le Blant, *Inscriptions chrétiennes de la Gaule*, 53–55 (no. 23); see also Heinzelmann, *Bischofsherrschaft in Gallien*, 146–52. His sister, Artemia, was the great-grandmother of Gregory of Tours.

62. On Nicetius, see Pietri and Heijmans, *Prosopographie de la Gaule chrétienne*, 1369–73; and Heinzelmann, *Bischofsherrschaft in Gallien*, 152–74.

63. Gregory of Tours, *Decem libri historiarum* 4.36; Gregory of Tours, *Liber vitae patrum* 8.3.

64. On Priscus, see Stroheker, *Der senatorische Adel*, 206; Martindale, *Prosopography of the Later Roman Empire*, 3:1052; Weidemann, *Kulturgeschichte*, 170; and Pietri and Heijmans, *Prosopographie de la Gaule chrétienne*, 1526–30.

65. Le Blant, *Inscriptions chrétiennes de la Gaule*, 1:60–61 (no. 26).

66. Le Blant, 1:60–61 (no. 26): "Progenie clarus." On this lineage, see Ralph Mathisen, *Ecclesiastical Factionalism and Religious Controversy in Fifth-Century Gaul* (Washington, DC: Catholic University of America Press, 1989), 79.

belonging to his family.⁶⁷ Priscus's efforts to prevent a cult of sanctity from developing around Nicetius no doubt also rankled Gregory.⁶⁸ Despite the hostility of Gregory—and possibly his extended family—to Priscus's election, the latter continued to serve Guntram without incident for many years.

Priscus himself was succeeded in the late 580s or early 590s by Aetherius, his old rival for the episcopal seat, a *pater patriae* who supposedly had enjoyed the favor of the citizens of the *civitas* before being passed over in favor of Priscus.⁶⁹ Aetherius enjoyed sociable relations with Guntram of Burgundy, but it is unknown whether the king formally confirmed the former's ordination after earlier rejecting his candidacy.⁷⁰ Fredegar records Aetherius's death in 602, and the subsequent ordination of Secundinus, but similarly provides no details on the circumstances surrounding the transfer of episcopal authority.⁷¹ Circumstantial evidence, however, can shed comparatively more light on the seating of Secundinus's own successor, Aridius, in 603.⁷² Aridius was very possibly not an ordained cleric at the time of his nomination to the episcopate, which may have received support from the royal court.⁷³ Despite this support, Yaniv Fox has hypothesized that Aridius's candidacy was opposed by his future archnemesis, Bishop Desiderius of Vienne. As Fox acknowledges, however, there were other factors that inflamed the tensions between the two bishops, so we cannot say with complete certainty that their rivalry stretched as far back as Aridius's ordination.⁷⁴

Unfortunately, Aridius is the last bishop of Lyons before Viventius, ordained in the mid-seventh century, about whose election we possess any evidence at all. The name of the early seventh-century bishop Treticus is suggestive of a possible relationship with Gregory of Tours, but this is no more than conjecture.⁷⁵ As for Viventius himself, according the ninth-century *vita* of the archdeacon Garmier (Baldomer), he was abbot of Saint-Just before his episcopal ordination, sometime after the assembly of the Council of Chalon-sur-Saône

---

67. Van Dam, *Saints and Their Miracles*, 61. Settipani, "Ruricius Ier," 206–9, suggests that Gregory's family's ties to the episcopal see of Lyons stretched back even further than Sacerdos.
68. Van Dam, *Saints and Their Miracles*, 61–62.
69. *Vita Nicetii episcopi Lugdunensis*, ed. Bruno Krusch, MGH SRM 3 (Hanover, Germany: Hahn, 1896), chap. 17 (524). On Aetherius, see Pietri and Heijmans, *Prosopographie de la Gaule chrétienne*, 61–65.
70. Gregory of Tours, *Decem libri historiarum* 10.28.
71. Fredegar, *Chronica* 4.22. On Secundinus, see Pietri and Heijmans, *Prosopographie de la Gaule chrétienne*, 1724.
72. On Aridius, see Pietri and Heijmans, *Prosopographie de la Gaule chrétienne*, 196–98.
73. Fox, "Bishop and the Monk," 189–90.
74. Fox, 190–91.
75. Tetricus of Langres was Gregory's great-uncle. A Bishop Tetricus also held the episcopal seat of Auxerre in the late seventh century. See Duchesne, *Fastes épiscopaux de l'ancienne Gaule*, 2:169, 2:186–87, 2:448.

(647/53).⁷⁶ Viventius is said to have chosen his own successor, Aunemund, who also had strong links to the courts of Dagobert I and then Clovis II, as well as a strong family presence in Lyons itself, where both his father and then his brother held the prefecture.⁷⁷ Presumably, all of these factors played a role in his selection as bishop. After Aunemund's downfall, most likely due to local factionalism, Queen Balthild herself seems to have engineered the ordination of his successor, the abbot and former loyal courtier of Clovis II, Genesius.⁷⁸ Genesius himself was succeeded by another abbot, Lantbert of Fontenelle, circa 678, who also enjoyed an impressive family pedigree, as well as connections to the Neustrian court. His election also supposedly took place in the presence of Theuderic III.⁷⁹

The final Merovingian-era Lyonnaise bishop about whose ordination we can hypothesize is Godinus. Ordained in the late 680s, he likely owed his office to the patronage of the Pippinids, who subsequently may have "promoted" him to the abbacy of Jumièges, although he may also have been the member of an aristocratic family of regional importance.⁸⁰ The subsequent episcopal history of the *civitas* is more difficult to unravel, as it was caught up in the political turmoil of the reign of Charles Martel. According to Ado of Vienne, Lyons was "devastated and laid to waste" by Charles's army in the 730s and went without a bishop for "several years."⁸¹ Charles may have been responsible for the selection of subsequently ordained Lyonnaise bishops, but details are entirely lacking.⁸²

---

76. *Vita Baldomeri*, AASS Feb. vol. 3 (Antwerp: J. Meursium, 1658), 683–84. Any relationship with Bishop Viventiolus of Lyons (on whom see Duchesne, *Fastes épiscopaux de l'ancienne Gaule*, 2:165) can be no more than conjectural. Bishop Candericus of Lyons subscribed to the acts of the Council of Chalon-sur-Saône (647/53).

77. On Aunemund and his *vita*, see the commentary of Fouracre and Gerberding, *Late Merovingian France*, 166–79.

78. *Vita Balthildis*, chap. 4. On Wilfrid's claim that Balthild was responsible for Aunemund's death, see Janet Nelson, "Queens as Jezebels: Brunhild and Balthild in Merovingian History," in *Politics and Ritual in Early Medieval Europe* (London: Hambledon, 1986), 1–48, at 34–38.

79. Ian Wood, "Saint-Wandrille and Its Hagiography," in *Church and Chronicle in the Middle Ages: Essays Presented to John Taylor*, ed. Ian Wood and G. A. Loud (London: Hambledon, 1991), 1–14, at 1–3; and John Howe, "The Hagiography of Saint-Wandrille (Fontenelle) (Province of Haute-Normandie)," in *L'hagiographie du haut moyen âge en Gaule du Nord*, ed. Martin Heinzelmann (Stuttgart, Germany: Jan Thorbecke, 2001), 127–92, at 153, date his *vita* to ca. 800. On the account of his election in the *Vita Ansberti*, see Coville, *Recherches sur l'histoire de Lyon*, 422 (who dates the election to 678/79).

80. Jean Laporte, "Les listes abbatiales de Jumieges," in *Jumieges. Congres scientifique du XIII centenaire, Rouen, 10–12 June 1954* (Rouen, France: Lecerf, 1955), 435–66, at 451; Gerberding, *Rise of the Carolingians*, 98; Rosenwein, *Negotiating Space*, 87–88. Yaniv Fox, pers. comm., suggests that he was a descendant of the mayor Warnachar, who had a son named Godinus.

81. Ado of Vienne, *Chronicon*, ed. J. P. Migne, PL 123 (Paris: Garnier Brothers, 1879), col. 122, on which see Fouracre, *Age of Charles Martel*, 92–93.

82. Foaldus and Madalbertus of Lyons may have held office during Charles's reign, but their tenures in office cannot be dated with any certainty: Duchesne, *Fastes épiscopaux de l'ancienne Gaule*, 2:171.

This brief tour through the episcopal history of Lyons in the Merovingian period suggests that royal patronage was a habitual, but not the sole, factor influencing the choice of new bishops. Local conditions, family connections, and prior office-holding experience (ecclesiastical or secular) mattered a great deal and informed royal decisions. While kings could impose former courtiers with few local connections upon a *civitas*, particularly in factionalized cities a consensus candidate, or at least a candidate able to muster significant local support, was a far better choice, for even a carefully vetted candidate could face significant local opposition. Most famously, Gregory of Tours, who was uncanonically ordained at Rheims on the order of Sigibert I, found that his claims of kinship with prior occupants of the see, as well as his personal devotion to Martin of Tours, in no way shielded him from attacks by those who considered him an interloper.[83]

Petitions and Royal Grants

When challenged locally, as was Gregory of Tours, support from the court could prove to be a decisive factor in propping up a compromised episcopate. Even in times when a bishop's personal authority was not being directly challenged, prelates regularly sought and received direct access to the monarchy, bringing with them petitions and requests for royal support.[84] Gregory of Tours records several such "episcopal embassies" with varying agendas, most taking the form of physical journeys to royal residences. Such embassies could require significant time and logistical commitment on the part of the prelate, who might have to be absent from his *civitas* for a significant period of time. In 588, for example, Gregory of Tours set out from his own *civitas* to Metz to meet with Childebert II (whether he was summoned or traveled on his own volition is not clear), only to be immediately redirected to Chalon-sur-Saône on an embassy to Guntram's court, a total journey of nearly 800 kilometers as the crow flies. His return journey (assuming that he traveled directly to Tours) would have required him to travel an additional 360 kilometers. Assuming that Gregory was able to travel between 30 and 40 kilometers per day, he would have spent a minimum of thirty-nine days in transit, not even counting the time he would have spent at his two destinations.[85] Journeys such as

---

83. Van Dam, *Saints and Their Miracles*, 63–66. On Gregory's claims of kinship with prior bishops of Tours, see Heinzelmann, *Gregory of Tours*, 12–18.
84. Scheibelreiter, *Der Bischof in merowingischer Zeit*, 177–80.
85. Gregory of Tours, *Decem libri historiarum* 9.20. On the logistics of food rations and animal transport, see Donald Engels, *Alexander the Great and the Logistics of the Macedonian Army* (Berkeley:

this would have been costly, due to the need to purchase provisions and lodging for both the traveler and any servants in the traveling party.[86] If formal lodging was not available, a bishop might have to set up camp under the stars. This was the experience of Malluf of Sens, who we are told spent three long nights in a tent (*tentorium*) waiting to meet with Chilperic I. Unfortunately for Malluf, the king's delay was due in part to his untimely assassination, and the bishop was forced to bury the king with whom he had planned to meet.[87]

Such sacrifices of time and expense nevertheless were justified when a petition was successful. Episcopal petitions could be of a personal nature, on behalf of a second party, or on behalf of a local community. In the case of the first two forms of petition, bishops regularly contacted the royal court to appeal prior judicial verdicts, including those made against themselves.[88] In such cases, it is clear that the Merovingians enjoyed the right to review prior verdicts, including those made by ecclesiastical courts. The perpetually troublesome brothers Bishops Sagittarius and Salonius, for example, appealed their deposition by a council of their episcopal peers directly to Guntram of Burgundy, who approved their *petitio* to travel to Rome to present their case before Pope John III.[89] Similarly successful was Praetextatus of Rouen, whose restoration after Chilperic's death was tenuous until formally approved by Guntram in 584. In Praetextatus's case, Guntram first considered leaving the matter to an episcopal synod but was convinced that such a formality was unnecessary.[90]

Of course, the Merovingians were selective in choosing which prior verdicts to overturn, and petitioners could not assume a favorable response. A bishop whose petition was received as ill-considered or even insulting might receive more than a mere polite refusal. One such unsuccessful petitioner was the deposed bishop Promotus of Châteaudun, who met with Guntram the same year as Praetextatus. Guntram had taken advantage of Sigibert's death

---

University of California Press, 1978), 123–30. On travel speeds in the early medieval period specifically, see Michael McCormick, *Origins of the European Economy* (Cambridge: Cambridge University Press, 2001), 476–81; and Rosamond McKitterick, *Charlemagne: The Formation of a European Identity* (Cambridge: Cambridge University Press, 2008), 182.

86. On provisions, see Lionel Casson, *Travel in the Ancient World* (Baltimore: Johns Hopkins University Press, 1994), 154–55, 176–78. On inns and lodgings, see Samuel Dill, *Roman Society in Gaul in the Merovingian Age* (London: Macmillan, 1926), 238–39.

87. Gregory of Tours, *Decem libri historiarum* 6.46.

88. The subject of Desiderius of Cahors's petition to the mayor Grimoald alluded to in *Epistulae S. Desiderii Cadurcensis* no. 1.6 (20–22) is unknown.

89. Gregory of Tours, *Decem libri historiarum* 5.20. Another case that reached the papacy was an appeal by Sapaudus of Arles to Pope Pelagius I (AD 557): *Epistolae Arelatenses genuinae*, ed. Wilhelm Gundlach, MGH Epistolae 3 (Berlin: Weidmann, 1892), no. 52 (75–76).

90. Gregory of Tours, *Decem libri historiarum* 7.16. For another example of a successful petition for royal mercy, see 9.13 (Egidius of Rheims).

to facilitate the removal of the bishop from his subdiocese within the territory of Chartres, whose bishop, Pappolus, urged the king to refuse Promotus's plea for reconsideration. According to Gregory of Tours, not only did the king refuse Promotus, he sent the bishop back home to live with his mother.[91] Similarly unsuccessful was a newly elected bishop of Saintes, Heraclius, whose claim that he had been appointed by the "apostolic" bishop of Bordeaux, Leontius, failed to impress King Charibert I, who was enraged that his father's choice for the episcopal see had been deposed without his knowledge by the Council of Saintes (561/67). Charibert not only refused the petition, he exiled Heraclius in a wagon (*plaustrum*) filled with thorns.[92] While Charibert's response may have been somewhat excessive, it is not altogether surprising that petitions concerned with legal controversies should occasionally elicit strong responses from the court, whose members—the monarchy especially—might have a personal stake in their outcomes.

This also was true with those private suits involving the personal or institutional property of a bishop, which were argued in royal courts. As with cases in which prelates defended themselves against charges of violating criminal or canon law, a successful outcome in civil actions could not be assumed. Beracharius of Le Mans, for instance, failed circa 660/73 to convince a royal *placitum* held under the auspices of Chlothar III (657–73) that he should be allowed to retain property donated by a certain Ermelenus to Saint Denis.[93] Leaving aside the merits of the bishop's case, his was one of several related property disputes in which Chlothar found in favor of the monastery, and the king's verdict had as much to do with protecting the interests of Saint Denis as it had with justice.[94]

In contrast to the experience of the bishop of Le Mans, in 657 Praejectus of Clermont won his property dispute with Hector the *patricius* of Marseilles in the king's court, only to be murdered upon returning to his city, quite possibly as revenge for Hector's own assassination, suggesting that as with episcopal elections, royal verdicts in civil cases required the consensus of affected parties to be implemented successfully.[95] Praejectus's case, while concerned

---

91. Gregory of Tours, *Decem libri historiarum* 7.17.
92. Gregory of Tours, *Decem libri historiarum* 4.26.
93. *Die Urkunden der Merowinger* no. 95 (243–46).
94. *Die Urkunden der Merowinger* nos. 93, 94, 95 (239–46).
95. *Passio Praeiecti episcopi et martyris Arverneni*, ed. Bruno Krusch, MGH SRM 5 (Hanover, Germany: Hahn, 1910), chaps. 23–30; *Passio Leudegarii episcopi et martyris Augustodunensis I*, ed. Bruno Krusch, MGH SRM 5 (Hanover, Germany: Hahn, 1910), chaps. 9–11. On the problem of consensus, see Paul Fouracre, "'Placita' and the Settlement of Disputes in Later Merovingian Francia," in *The Settlement of Disputes in Early Medieval Europe*, ed. Wendy Davies and Paul Fouracre (Cambridge: Cambridge University Press, 1986), 23–43, at 38.

with the property bequeathed the church by Hector's mother-in-law, Claudia, stirred up various factions associated with the two litigants. As Paul Fouracre and Richard Gerberding have noted in their commentary on Praejectus's *vita*, even the bishop's hagiographer recognized that Hector's assassination was not due directly to his suit against Praejectus, but rather to his unintentional cultivation of enemies within the court.[96]

In regard to the second form of *petitio*, Edward James has demonstrated how the late antique principle of episcopal *intercessio* not only retained its value in the Merovingian period but was particularly valued by those charged with political crimes.[97] Furthermore, as early as Clovis's epistle to the bishops of Aquitaine (ca. 507/8), the Merovingians recognized the episcopal responsibility to intercede on behalf of prisoners of war.[98] While a bishop's success in obtaining royal concessions might be due to any combination of rhetorical skill, personal relationships with the monarch (*Königsnähe*) and high court officials, and the legitimacy of the petitions themselves, there is no doubt that a prelate's ability to intercede successfully with the court on behalf of petitioners, criminal or otherwise, could bolster his personal reputation. It even might be interpreted posthumously as evidence of sanctity.

According to the *acta* of Aunemund of Lyons, for example, the bishop was so successful a petitioner that it was believed that "no one might acquire anything to their advantage unless he [Aunemund] obtained it from King Chlothar III by his own entreaty."[99] Ironically, according to Aunemund's hagiographer, it was the bishop's intimacy with the court that aroused great jealousy against him. Eligius of Noyon too, according to his biographer Bishop Audoin of Rouen, even before his episcopal ordination took advantage of his ability to successfully petition Dagobert I to beg for concessions for the poor, as well as land on which to found a monastery.[100] Audoin himself had similar

---

96. Fouracre and Gerberding, *Late Merovingian France*, 263–64.

97. James, "*Beati Pacifici*," 34–44. James recognizes ecclesiastical sanctuary as a manifestation of episcopal intervention on behalf of the accused. Fouracre, "'Placita,'" 32, reads c. 2 of the Council of Bordeaux (662/75) as evidence for widespread clerical involvement in "the legal affairs of lay persons." See also Bruno Dumézil, "La confiscation punitive en Gaule romano-barbare," in *Expropriations et confiscations dans les royaumes barbares: Une approche régionale*, ed. Pierfrancesco Porena and Yann Rivière (Rome: École Française de Rome, 2012), 51–68, at 65, who suggests limited success in episcopal petitions aimed at reversing royal property confiscations.

98. Clovis, *Epistola ad episcopos*, in *Capitularia regum Francorum*. See also Klingshirn, "Charity and Power."

99. *Acta Aunemundi alias Dalfini episcopi*, AASS Sept. vol. 7, chap. 2: "A regibus tamen et proceribus ita habebatur acceptus, ut, quicquid ab eis peteret, impetraret, nullusque de aliqua re ad suum profectum quidquam valebat impetrare, nisi sua suggestione Clotario tertio principi deportaret qui eius de lavacro sacro fontis filiolus fuerat."

100. *Vita Eligii episcopi Noviomagensis*, chaps. 1.14–15.

success in helping Filibert procure the land for the future monastery of Jumièges from Clovis II and Balthild.[101]

And it was not only male petitioners who took advantage of episcopal *intercessio*. In the *vitae* of female saints, it is a relatively common topos for the saint to seek the intercession of a bishop either to enter a cloister or to obtain a position of leadership within the convent. In his *vita* of Rusticula of Arles, probably composed not long after the saint's death circa 632, Florentius includes several interventions of this sort: first when the abbess Liliola of Arles asks Syagrius of Autun to assist her in convincing Guntram to help her to secure the release of Rusticula so that she might enter the convent, and later when Bishop Domnolus of Vienne intercedes on the saint's behalf with Chlothar II in order to convince the king that she is not his enemy.[102] Similarly, the hagiographers of Rusticula's older contemporary, Radegund, name several bishops who facilitated her transition from Chlothar I's side to the cloistered life, including Medard of Noyon, Pientius of Poitiers, and Germanus of Paris.[103] Whereas Radegund and Rusticula required episcopal assistance to enter their cloisters, several later *vitae* credit bishops with nominating sainted women to the office of abbess. The eighth-century life of Bertilla of Chelles suggests that she was made abbess on the orders of Queen Balthild, partly on the recommendation of Bishop Genesius of Lyon, who vouched for her character, while the Carolingian life of Anstrude of Laon credits an unnamed metropolitan bishop with recommending her as a replacement for Sadalberga.[104]

While episcopal petitions of a personal or intercessory nature could entail a range of royal concessions, petitions on behalf of a *civitas* or diocesan church or monastery typically involved financial concessions, sometimes of significant magnitude. When Clovis's troops plundered an unknown church and reportedly carried off an *urceus*, the bishop of the church—unconvincingly identified by the Fredegar chronicler as Remigius of Rheims—sent representatives to request its return. The object's considerable value, however, led infamously to a dispute between the king and one of his soldiers.[105] While no doubt the

---

101. *Vita Filiberti abbatis Gemeticensis et Heriensis*, ed. Wilhelm Levison, MGH SRM 5 (Hanover, Germany: Hahn, 1910), chap. 6; *Vita Balthildis*, chap. 8.

102. *Vita Rusticulae sive Marciae abbatissae Arelatensis*, ed. Bruno Krusch, MGH SRM 4 (Hanover, Germany: Hahn, 1902), chaps. 3, 9–12. On the *vita*, see Pierre Riché, "Note d'hagiographie mérovingienne: La *vita Rusticulae*," *Analecta Bollandiana* 72 (1954): 369–77.

103. Venantius Fortunatus and Baudonivia, *Vita Radegundis Libri II*, 1.12, 2.5, 2.7.

104. *Vita Bertilae abbatissae Calensis*, ed. Wilhelm Levison, MGH SRM 6 (Hanover, Germany: Hahn, 1913), chap. 4; *Vita Anstrudis abbatissae Laudunensis*, ed. Wilhelm Levison, MGH SRM 6 (Hanover, Germany: Hahn, 1913), chap. 4. Genesius also is credited in the *Vita Balthildis*, chap. 4, with soliciting financial support for the poor from Clovis II on Balthild's behalf.

105. Gregory of Tours, *Decem libri historiarum* 2.27; Fredegar, *Chronica*, 3.16.

urceus was a desirable prize, considerably more wealth was at stake when bishops negotiated with the court for famine or tax relief. Such petitions might be framed as requests in the interests of piety or charity. In his *Libri de virtutibus Sancti Martini episcopi*, Gregory contrasts the piety of Charibert and Sigibert by describing the latter's willingness to accede to a petition by Eufronius of Tours to return the villa of Nazelles to the Church of Saint Martin.[106] When *discriptores* came to Tours several decades later, after completing their work in Poitiers "at the invitation of Bishop Maroveus," Gregory himself appealed directly to Childebert II through *nuntii* to ask the king to preserve his *civitas'* tax exemption. Childebert agreed, according to Gregory, "pro reverentia sancti Martini."[107] In a similar expression of royal *caritas*, Theudebert I canceled the debt of no less than seven thousand gold pieces originally requested by the bishop of Verdun to relieve the destitution of the people.[108]

Seventh-century charters and formularies record a range of episcopal petitions, most significantly those requesting fiscal or juridical exemptions. Beginning with Burgundofaro's privilege for Rebais of 637, which probably coincided with a royal grant of immunity, episcopal exemptions excused monasteries from various forms of episcopal oversight, including a bishop's traditional authority over all ecclesiastical property within his diocese.[109] Although the impetus for the Rebais exemption came from a *petitio* by Audoin of Rouen (Rebais's founder), royal pressure certainly could prompt the issuance of episcopal privileges. This, in itself, was nothing new. The *acta* of the episcopal Council of Valence (583/85), which may have influenced the Rebais charter, while forbidding either kings or bishops from alienating donations to the Basilicas of Saint Marcel and Saint Symphorian, was confirmed by the subscriptions of seventeen bishops.[110] While it is thus tempting to read episcopal exemptions as evidence of episcopal acquiescence to royal power, it is worth recalling the observation of Barbara Rosenwein in regard to Landeric of Paris's

---

106. Gregory of Tours, *Libri de virtutibus Sancti Martini episcopi* 1.29.
107. Gregory of Tours, *Decem libri historiarum* 9.30.
108. Gregory of Tours, *Decem libri historiarum* 3.34.
109. On the typology of episcopal exemptions, see Eugen Ewig, "Beobachtungen zu den Klosterprivilegien des 7. und frühen 8. Jahrhunderts," in *Spätantikes und fränkisches Gallien*, 2:411–26, at 2:418. It is now generally accepted that the Rebais charter (despite interpolations) is generally authentic; on the scholarly debate, see Rosenwein, *Negotiating Space*, 67n29.
110. On the influence of the Council of Valence (583/85) on the contents of the charter, see Barbara Rosenwein, "One Site, Many Meanings: Saint-Maurice d'Agaune as a Place of Power in the Early Middle Ages," in *Topographies of Power in the Early Middle Ages*, ed. Mayke de Jong, Frans Theuws, and Carine Van Rhijn (Leiden: Brill, 2001), 271–90, at 281–82. On the Council of Valence (583/85), see de Clercq, *La législation religieuse franque*, 51; Pontal, *Histoire des conciles mérovingiens*, 172; and Halfond, *Archaeology*, 232. Similarly, Council of Orléans (549), c. 15, preserves against episcopal encroachment the integrity of the property belonging to the new *xenodochium* in Lyons founded by the royal family.

exemption for Saint Denis, whose issuance may very well have been encouraged by the monarchy: "The very act of issuing the exemption was recognition of his control over episcopal access.... The episcopal exemption willed (in neat reversal, like Burgundofaro's exemption) a blow to episcopal prestige that thereby rebounded to it."[111]

Bishops, in other words, might have been not only willing participants in the granting of monastic privileges but even the sole or collaborative instigators. It is not insignificant in this context that the earliest exemptions were granted by a small and intimate group of bishops.[112] Equally significant was the subscription of seventh-century lay and ecclesiastical parties alike to a Columbanian-derived ideology of monastic "sacred space."[113] But regardless of whether an individual exemption originated from a royal or episcopal impetus or, as often was the case, from a negotiated decision, the exemption customarily would be confirmed by the royal court, signifying the monarchy's support both for the legality of the grant and for the recipient institution. In some cases, a monarch might use the act of confirmation to expand the privileges denoted in the original charter, along with extending his or her own protection over the institution in question.[114] So, while recognizing the diversity of contexts and instigators that prompted the issuance of individual exemptions, as a body these privileges are the product of episcopal-monarchical collaboration and negotiation, with the *petitio* for confirmation signifying an episcopal recognition of the need for royal support to ensure the integrity and preservation of the grant.

As for the royal immunities sometimes paired with episcopal exemptions, these might be granted to episcopal churches, and not simply to cloisters. As with royal *Klosterpolitik*, a combination of pious and political intentions typically underlay the identification of recipients, and bishops could and did petition for immunities. Clovis III, for instance, granted immunity to the Church of Saint Mary in Maastricht circa 690/95, possibly as a countermeasure against

---

111. Rosenwein, *Negotiating Space*, 77.
112. As observed by Constance Bouchard, *Rewriting Saints and Ancestors: Memory and Forgetting in France, 500–1200* (Philadelphia: University of Pennsylvania Press, 2015), 209.
113. Rosenwein, *Negotiating Space*, 70–73. See also Albrecht Diem, "Monks, Kings, and the Transformation of Sanctity: Jonas of Bobbio and the End of the Holy Man," *Speculum* 82, no. 3 (2007): 521–59, at 534–38.
114. As suggested by *Marculfi formulae* 1.2. On the link between episcopal exemptions and royal immunities in the context of Balthild's *Klosterpolitik*, see Eugen Ewig, "'Das Privileg des Bischofs Berthefrid von Amiens für Corbie von 664 und die Klosterpolitik der Königin Balthild," *Spätantikes und fränkisches Gallien*, 2:538–83, at 2:576–83; Rosenwein, *Negotiating Space*, 78–81; and Nelson, "Queens as Jezebels," 38–43. See also the conclusion.

Pippinid encroachment to the benefit of Bishop Lambert.[115] Marculf's formulary contains a pair of model charters for such grants, which similarly suggest—disingenuously or not—that the charters were issued at the request of episcopal petitioners.[116] It has been suggested in regard to these model charters that such transactions "fulfilled the function of strengthening links of patronage and obligation between king and bishop," and similar transactions involving privileges would seem to confirm this observation.[117] Immunities, in general, were particularly generous forms of royal patronage. As Alexander C. Murray in particular has emphasized, "judicial" immunities, which exempt institutions from intrusion by royal agents, essentially were fiscal in intent as the costs related to justice and the courts.[118]

While *petitiones* were a means for bishops to coordinate local and court agendas, communications naturally traveled the opposite direction as well, with monarchs taking the initiative in offering goodwill gestures toward a particular episcopal see and its occupant.[119] This practice began as early as the reign of Clovis I, whose patronage of the see of Rheims significantly increased its property holdings.[120] This practice continued into the reigns of Clovis's sons and grandsons. Charibert, for instance, upon succeeding his father as royal master of Tours, followed Chlothar's example by promising to impose no new tax burdens on the *cives* of that city. When Eufronius of Tours appealed to the king that the *comes* Gaiso was seeking to reimpose taxes on the people and church of Tours in violation of this agreement, the king's response was to refuse any and all collected monies, allowing them instead to be transferred to Eufronius for use by the Church of Saint Martin.[121]

---

115. *Vita Landiberti episcopi Traeiectensis auctore Nicolao*, ed. Bruno Krusch, MGH SRM 6 (Hanover, Germany: Hahn, 1913), chap. 5. On the political context for the grant, as well as the reliability of the source, see Frans Theuws, "Maastricht as a Centre of Power in the Early Middle Ages," in de Jong, Theuws, and Van Rhijn, *Topographies of Power*, 155–216, at 183–84.

116. *Marculfi formulae* 1.3–4.

117. Rio, *Formularies of Angers and Marculf*, 136.

118. Alexander C. Murray, "Merovingian Immunity Revisited," *History Compass* 8 (2010): 913–28, at 915–16.

119. For examples of royal generosity in regard to episcopal property (personal or diocesan) or jurisdiction, see, e.g., *Die Urkunden der Merowinger* nos. 79, 107, 118, 152, 163, and dep. 38, 80, 85, 95–97, 101–3, 110–20, 153, 156, 160, 191–92, 202, 210, 212, 212a, 227, 244, 246, 270, 273, 278–79, 287, 293, 313, 327, 340, 346, 362, 374–75, 378, 381–82, 387–88, 394–95, 407, 412. Note: dep. 38, 101–3, and 111–20 all are directed toward Bertram of Le Mans.

120. For an accounting based on Remigius's testament, see Noel Delgado, "The *Grand Testamentum* of Remigius of Reims: Its Authenticity, Juridical *Acta* and Bequeathed Property" (PhD diss., University of Minnesota, 2008), 131, who estimates that Clovis's donations accounted for 22 percent of the property under Remigius's supervision at the time of the bishop's death. It should be noted that this estimate is derived from the *grand testamentum*, whose authenticity Delgado supports, but traditionally has been doubted (see his helpful historiographical discussion on 68–99).

121. Gregory of Tours, *Decem libri historiarum* 9.30.

Similarly, the decision by kings and queens to fund the construction of new religious buildings could constitute a form of patronage, as could the distribution of gifts to individual prelates. Even Gregory of Tours's infamous bête noire Chilperic, as well as the ruler's demonized queen Fredegund, engaged in generous patronage with the goal of establishing or strengthening relationships with individual prelates. The *Praeceptio Chlotharii* refers explicitly to those gifts and immunities granted by the author's father to ecclesiastical institutions and persons.[122] Gregory himself acknowledges Chilperic's generosity toward a wide array of holy places, including the Churches of Saint Denis and Saint Vincent in Paris, a *civitas* over which the king long sought to extend his authority and with whose bishops he was friendly.[123] And despite Chilperic's sometimes tense relationship with Gregory, and the latter's accusation that the king did not respect the property and sacrosanctity of the Church of Saint Martin, the king was quick to condemn thieves who stole from the basilica, only sparing their lives when the bishop interceded on their behalf.[124] While there is no reason to doubt the king's sincerity in his veneration of Saint Martin, the timing of the theft in 581, one year after Gregory's trial at Berny, may suggest that the king was hoping to repair relations with the episcopal see of Tours.

As for Fredegund, in his testament of 616 Bishop Bertram of Le Mans recalls his receipt of the villa of Bonnelles in Étampes as a gift from the widowed Fredegund and her son Chlothar II during the period of her regency, 596/97.[125] Chlothar and Fredegund's generosity toward Bertram can be explained at least in part by the latter's long-standing loyalty toward the Neustrian branch of the royal family. While it was Guntram of Burgundy who originally appointed Bertram, upon the latter's death in 592 the bishop shifted his allegiance to the young Chlothar.[126] This proved in the short term to be a poor decision, as Childebert II soon seized Le Mans and deposed Bertram.[127] When Fredegund's forces retook the *civitas* in 596 following Childebert's death, she made it a point to recall the long-suffering Bertram. Even after the queen's death, Chlothar continued to patronize generously the loyal bishop.[128]

---

122. Chlothar II, *Praeceptio*, in *Capitularia regum Francorum*, cc. 11–12. See chapter 1, n. 99, on the question of authorship.
123. Halfond, "Sis Quoque Catholicis Religionis Apex," 72–73.
124. Gregory of Tours, *Decem libri historiarum* 5.14, 6.10.
125. Bertram of Le Mans, *Das Testament*, 8–9 (no. 1). Fredegund and Chlothar conquered Étampes in 596 upon the death of Childebert II: Fredegar, *Chronica* 4.17. Fredegund died within a year of the victory.
126. Gregory of Tours, *Decem libri historiarum* 8.39, 9.18, 9.41.
127. Ian Wood, *Merovingian Kingdoms*, 207.
128. Bertram of Le Mans, *Das Testament*, 86–88.

Patronizing the Corporate Episcopate

As the next chapter will explore in greater detail, the Merovingians' patronage of individual prelates and episcopal sees could have the consequence of weakening the corporate spirit of the episcopal *ordo*. Conversely, the royal patronage of the Gallo-Frankish episcopate as a united body strengthened its corporate identity. We already have had occasion to note several of the forms that this patronage took: (1) a formal recognition of the Gallo-Frankish episcopate's independent authority; (2) the consequential recognition that this authority could be expressed through binding canonical legislation or (3) judicial verdicts within a negotiated jurisdictional space; (4) the royal convocation of ecclesiastical councils at which bishops assumed a corporate voice; and (5) the (selective) royal enforcement of *regulae* and verdicts pronounced at these councils.

The two primary venues in which the Merovingians could communicate and negotiate with the episcopate as a corporate body thus were councils and the court. Of course, not even the largest of conciliar gatherings included the entire assembled body of sitting bishops. Not one of the great sixth-century councils of Orléans, nor even the Council of Paris (614), convened while Chlothar II was sole reigning monarch, was attended by every bishop in the realm.[129] So, in all councils, the episcopal attendees constituted essentially a representative body, a role of which they were very conscious. While the *subscriptiones* of the participants were sufficient to prove the consensus underlying their *acta*, and by extension the orthodoxy and authority of those acts, in a few cases conciliar attendees sent copies of their decisions to bishops not in attendance, requesting that the latter subscribe as well.

The authors of the acts of the Council of Paris (561/64), for example, quoted the Roman legal principle of "that which affects all must have the consent of all" as an explanation for their relatively unusual request.[130] There is no reason to imagine, however, that in this instance episcopal attendees made copies of their acts to be sent to every one of their colleagues beyond the

---

129. See, for convenience, the maps of the councils' attendance in Pontal, *Histoire des conciles mérovingiens*.

130. Council of Paris (556/73), c. 9: ". . . Et quia huic definitioni cuncti fratrum interesse minime potuerunt, hoc etiam omnis congregatio sacerdotum Christo propitiante decrevit, ut constitutio praesens, quantis oblata fuerit, subscriptionibus eorum debeat roborare, quatenus in hoc, quod ab universis observandum est, universitas debeat consentire." On this canon, see the remarks of Gaudemet and Basdevant-Gaudemet, *Les canons des conciles mérovingiens*, 422n3. See also Gregory of Tours, *Decem libri historiarum* 5.49, on the Council of Berny.

borders of the *regnum Chariberthi*.¹³¹ While the authority of conciliar canons was not supposed to be limited by geographical or political space, their practical application often was. So, when conciliar attendees like those who attended the Council of Paris assumed their representative role, they were representing both the universal episcopate and the episcopal leadership of the realm. It was the latter function, naturally, that was of primary concern to royal convokers of ecclesiastical councils. The Merovingians, as we have seen, encouraged episcopal conciliarism with the expectation that canonical *regulae* would complement (or inform) royal *leges* in the promotion of public order.

In the context of the court, the Merovingians similarly surrounded themselves with a select group of bishops whose counsel was valued and loyalty secure. The monarchy's reliance on these episcopal courtiers easily can be seen in the latter's regular influence on, and subscription to, royal acts. Of the nearly eighty Merovingian royal diplomas with at least partial claim to authenticity, no fewer than nine were witnessed by, or the result of deliberations with, bishops.[132] These references to episcopal (and lay) counselors were clear evidence of the consensus underlying the acts. In turn, episcopal reputations could be enhanced by their service to the realm, as suggested by hagiographers' close attention to this phenomenon.[133]

However, in their own legislating and codification of law, the Merovingians more often addressed the episcopate as a corporate body (or as representatives thereof) than as unique individuals. Codified Frankish law generally addressed bishops in the contexts of justice and jurisdiction—for example, the value of their wergild and their jurisdictional authority. On the issue of wergilds, the Frankish law codes vary in their particulars but agree on the high social value of an episcopal life. Whereas the *Pactus legis Salicae* does not mention bishops at all, which would be expected if the code was compiled before Clovis's conversion,[134] the seventh-century *Lex Ribuaria* pays them greater attention, assigning their wergild at nine hundred solidi.[135] The *Lex Baiwariorum*, in contrast, describes a rather more elaborate compensation formula for the wergild. Depending on the wealth of the perpetrator, he would have to pay either gold equivalent in weight to a *tunica plumbea* or property of an equal

---

131. Halfond, "Charibert," 20. The sporadic inclusion of the canons in near-contemporary canonical collections may speak to their limited circulation.
132. *Die Urkunden der Merowinger* nos. 80, 81, 85, 94, 122, 131, 136, 141, 149.
133. Kreiner, *Social Life of Hagiography*, 156–88.
134. Karl Ubl, "L'origine contestée de la loi salique: Une mise au point," *Revue de l'Institut français d'histoire en Allemagne* 1 (2009): 208–34; Ubl, *Sinnstiftungen eines Rechtsbuchs*, 92–97, 108–12 (suggesting a composition date of ca. 475–486/87); Étienne Renard, "Le *Pactus legis Salicae*, règlement militaire romain ou code de lois compilé sous Clovis?," *Bibliothèque de l'École des chartes* 167 (2009): 321–52.
135. *Lex Ribuaria* 40.9.

value if he did not possess gold. If he did not possess enough moveable or immoveable property, his only alternative was to subject himself and his family to servile labor on behalf of the church.[136] In a similar confirmation of episcopal status as in its counterparts, the *Leges Alamannorum* suggest that injured or murdered bishops should be compensated in the same manner as *duces*.[137] Besides its attention to the bodies of bishops, this code also recognizes the inviolability of episcopal space, requiring those who trespass with arms into the *curtis* of an episcopal residence or into the *domus* proper to pay a fine (eighteen solidi for the former violation, and double that for the latter).[138]

On the issue of episcopal jurisdiction, royal capitularies have comparatively more to say than the codified laws, although the latter, as discussed in the preceding chapter, do address certain procedural details (such as in regard to judicial summons), as well as confirming episcopal oversight over dependent groups. The *Lex Baiwariorum*, for example, contains an unusual chapter tasking bishops (with royal or ducal consent) with tracking down and retrieving abducted nuns. Nevertheless, the punishment for unrepentant abductors—exile—presumably would be implemented by the secular authorities.[139] In contrast, Chlothar II's earlier *edictum* made no reference to any episcopal responsibility for retrieving abductees in its lengthy chapter on abduction.[140]

While the capitularies similarly recognize episcopal jurisdiction over both clerical and lay persons, and by extension the public authority and social prominence of those who held episcopal office, they also occasionally identify some limitations on episcopal power, particularly in cases in which it might challenge royal prerogatives and status. Chlothar II, for instance, mandated episcopal forgiveness of wayward clerics upon royal request, while also warning bishops (along with other *potentes*) not to seize the property of others.[141] Rather less certain an effort to limit episcopal power is the first chapter of the edict of Chlothar's father, Chilperic. Concerned with the proper procedures for the summoning of the accused to the *mallus*, the chapter states, "Those things which have been proclaimed in the churches shall be announced to those living where the court convenes."[142] This statement has been read as a

---

136. *Lex Baiwariorum* 1.10.
137. *Leges Alamannorum* 11.
138. *Leges Alamannorum* 9. The next chapter (10) applies the same principle (with differing compensation) to priests.
139. *Lex Baiwariorum* 1.11.
140. Chlothar II, *Edictum* c. 18.
141. Chlothar II, *Edictum* cc. 3, 20. In the same edict (c. 19), Chlothar also forbids bishops from exercising authority outside their territorial jurisdiction.
142. *Capitularia regum Francorum* 10 (c. 9): "Illas et marias qui nuntiabantur ecclesias nuntientur consistentes ubi admallat." Franz Beyerle, "Das legislative Werk Chilperichs I," *Zeitschrift der Savigny-*

manifestation of Chilperic's ostensible anticlericalism and his desire to "limit the social role of the churches."[143] However, the chapter does not explicitly prohibit the announcement of future court summons in churches; its intent seems to be to mandate the repetition of summons in the location of the *mallus* itself.[144] This reading would align the chapter more closely not only with those other chapters in the edict concerned with ensuring attendance at court following a summons but also with the *Pactus legis Salicae*, which similarly was attentive to this problem.[145]

While Chilperic may have had his doubts about the excesses of what modern historians have labeled *Bischofsherrschaft*, there is no evidence to suggest that either he or his descendants made it a legislative priority to strip away the civic prerogatives of bishops.[146] In this sense, Chilperic's edict is not so far removed from that of his brother Guntram as sometimes has been imagined. Guntram's edict, in fact, arguably was far more explicit in its recognition of the limits of episcopal power. As Martin Heinzelmann has argued, Guntram recognized in his edict the limitations faced by bishops in enforcing "moral *correctio*," and the need for secular assistance and royal oversight. Guntram, as Heinzelmann shows, was even confident enough in his responsibilities as a Christian king to correct the theology of the bishops who attended his council in Mâcon (585).[147]

While Guntram's edict arguably is the most explicit statement of Christian kingship as understood by the Merovingians, his recognition of bishops as unequal partners of the monarchy in the assurance of the realm's moral health was a shared value of his royal kin. While bishops were not royal agents simply by virtue of their office and ordination, there was without question an

---

Stiftung für Rechtsgeschichte, Germanische Abteilung 78 (1961): 1–38, at 10, 16–17, reads "marias" as "wargos" (outlaws). Cf. Maurizio Lupoi, *The Origins of the European Legal Order*, trans. Adrian Belton (Cambridge: Cambridge University Press, 2000), 372n40; and Michael Glatthar, "Der Edictus Chilperichs I. und die Reichsversammlung von Paris (577)," *Deutsches Archiv für Erforschung des Mittelalters* 73 (2017): 1–74, at 56–64 (suggesting alternatively *iniurias*). Glatthar (1–49) dates the *edictum* to summer 577.

143. Heinzelmann, *Gregory of Tours*, 185. Heinzelmann's argument (184–85) follows that of Beyerle, "Das legislative Werk Chilperichs I," 37.

144. Halfond, "Sis Quoque Catholicis Religionis Apex," 66–67.

145. E.g., *Pactus legis Salicae*, ed. Karl Eckhardt, MGH LL nat. Germ. 4.1 (Hanover, Germany: Hahn, 1962), chaps. 1, 47.2, 49, 50.4, 52.1, 56, 73, 102. On the relationship between the edict and the *Pactus*, see Ubl, *Sinnstiftungen eines Rechtsbuchs*, 122–24; and Glatthar, "Der Edictus Chilperichs I," 43. On summoning, see Ian Wood, "Jural Relations among the Franks and Alamanni," in *Franks and Alamanni in the Merovingian Period*, ed. Ian Wood (Rochester, NY: Boydell, 1998), 213–26, at 216–17.

146. Cf. Heinzelmann, *Gregory of Tours*, 185, who suggests that Chilperic's decree was "almost certainly accompanied by other comparable decrees [intended] to limit the social role of the churches."

147. Heinzelmann, 185–91.

expectation of reciprocity in return for generous patronage from the court. Bishops were expected to utilize royal sponsorship to effect moral correction, provide counsel, ensure peace and administrative stability, and enforce justice, but they also "repaid" their royal patrons through the performance of undeniably secular duties. But consciously reciprocal actions were not the only episcopal response to royal patronage. As the following chapters will explore, royal patronage, particularly of individual prelates, had the (usually unintended) consequence of threatening the corporate solidarity of the Gallo-Frankish episcopate.

Chapter 3

Unity in Disunity
The Limits of Corporate Solidarity

"You love a pretty girl from any land, not out of any generosity, not for the love of God. You will never be *righteous* as long as you hold to such a road. By your long 'tail'—Is it long enough or not?—by everything, order yourself to be castrated so that you not perish through such things, because God will judge fornicators."[1] So wrote Bishop Importunus of Paris to Bishop Frodebert of Tours (ca. 664/66) in the midst of one of the more colorful epistolary exchanges to have survived from seventh-century Francia. So colorful, in fact, that both the authenticity and the sincerity of the correspondence have been questioned.[2] Consisting of a total of five epistles appended to a collection of formulae (BN lat. 4627), the corpus employs rhyme, sarcasm, and creative personal and political insults in what has been described alternatively as a "Merovingian street fight" and "stylized ritual competitive

---

1. Importunus of Paris, Epistle 3 to Frodebert of Tours, trans. Danuta R. Shanzer, in Danuta R. Shanzer, "The Tale of Frodebert's Tail," in *Colloquial and Literary Latin*, ed. Eleanor Dickey and Anna Chahoud (Cambridge: Cambridge University Press, 2010), 376–405, at 401.

2. On the letters, their authorship, and their authenticity, see Gerard J. J. Walstra, ed., *Les cinq épîtres rimées dans l'appendice des formules de Sens* (Leiden: Brill, 1962); Shanzer, "Tale of Frodebert's Tail"; Yitzhak Hen, "Changing Places: Chrodobert, Boba, and the Wife of Grimoald," *Revue belge de philologie et d'histoire* 89, no. 2 (2012): 225–44; and Vida Alice Tyrrell, "Merovingian Letters and Letters Writers" (PhD diss., University of Toronto, 2012), 166–80.

abuse . . . a consensual co-performance."³ The correspondence, which commences with Frodebert's complaints regarding the quality of grain sent by the addressee to Tours, rapidly devolves into a volley of mutual abuse with no conclusive ending. The final word, such as it is, seemingly belongs to Importunus, who urges unnamed *domnae sanctae* of Tours to ignore his opponent's ostensible lies.⁴ It seems that not long after the apparent conclusion of their correspondence, Importunus died, and whether he ever reconciled with Frodebert is unknown.

While it is not demonstrable beyond all doubt that Frodebert and Importunus were the true authors of the epistles that bear their names, the correspondence nevertheless is indicative of very real epistolary exchanges between bishops in which conflicts alternately were exacerbated and resolved through the written word.⁵ Around 512, for example, Bishop Remigius of Rheims received a letter signed by the bishops of Paris, Sens, and Auxerre. Although this letter does not survive, Remigius's response does, and it paraphrases the former's contents. The exchange, it seems, was prompted by the actions of a presbyter named Claudius, originally ordained by Remigius at Clovis's request. Following his ordination, Claudius (by Remigius's own admission) committed a *sacrilegium* of some sort, for which Remigius ordered him to perform *paenitentia*. Remigius's episcopal colleagues were furious at what they viewed as too light a punishment, and they reprimanded the bishop of Rheims that he should never have ordained Claudius in the first place. This admonition alone was offensive to the senior prelate, but his episcopal colleagues were not content with a mere rebuke. They accused Remigius of performing an uncanonical ordination in return for a bribe (*praemium*). Confident in their own moral righteousness, the bishops concluded, "It would have been better if you [Remigius] had never been born." Remigius's response, while avoiding such unseemly ad hominem attacks, was furious. Citing his age and seniority (no fewer than fifty-three years in office), he declared that in all of his years of service to the church, he had never been addressed with such insolence, and

---

3. See, respectively, Hen, "Changing Places," 232; and Shanzer, "Tale of Frodebert's Tail," 393. On the manuscript and its contents, see Rio, *Legal Practice*, 51–54, 256–57, who suggests that the letters were included among the formulary documents as stylistic models, under the assumption that "insulting missives clearly had their place among the range of writings necessary for a bishop to conduct his affairs in Merovingian Francia" (52).

4. On the voice of ep. 5, see Shanzer, "Tale of Frodebert's Tail," 395–96.

5. See also, e.g., Ruricius of Limoges, *Fausti aliorumque epistulae ad Ruricium aliosque*, ed. Bruno Krusch, MGH AA 8 (Berlin: Weidmann, 1887), no. 2.33 (336); *Epistolae Austrasicae* nos. 3, 11 (113–14, 126–27); and Desiderius of Cahors, *Epistulae S. Desiderii Cadurcensis* nos. 1.16, 2.21 (39–41, 75–76).

proceeded to lecture his colleagues on the virtues of charity and mercy.[6] As we only have Remigius's side of the dispute, it is impossible to say whether his critics' charges had any legitimacy. Nevertheless, this exchange between four senior prelates, including two metropolitans, is a reminder that the sort of episcopal squabbling found in the correspondence between Importunus and Frodebert had a long history in Merovingian Gaul.

Interpersonal Conflicts between Bishops

That interpersonal conflicts between bishops could weaken episcopal consensus and corporate solidarity is not, in itself, surprising. At any given time, over one hundred men held episcopal office in the *regnum Francorum*; the notion that universal harmony should perpetually prevail among them probably would have struck even these bishops themselves as naïve. They recognized that consensus, even within the episcopate, was a goal not easily realized, and whose accomplishment was, in fact, a sign of intervention by the Holy Spirit.[7] Yet consensus remained an episcopal priority of paramount importance, despite the difficulty of its realization, as evidenced by the attention paid to the ideal by successive Gallic church councils. Four conciliar canons issued between 541 and 614 explicitly dictate procedures for intra-episcopal conflict resolution. There is no reason to assume, of course, that any one of these four canons was regularly or universally enforced; their value lies primarily in their recognition of the reality—and, indeed, probability—of conflicts, and in their articulation of basic principles for resolution. The earliest of these *canones*, issued by the Council of Orléans (541), identifies competing property claims as the basis for episcopal conflicts, as well as the necessity to resolve these disagreements quickly before they escalate. The canon also endorses the selection of external mediators, either fellow bishops or chosen arbiters (*electi iudices*), to help the parties reach a resolution.[8] The use of mediators subsequently would be endorsed by both the Council of Tours (567), a meeting of the prelates of the *regnum Chariberthi*, and the Council of Lyons (567/70), attended by bishops from the *regnum Gunthramni*. The former proposed that

---

6. *Epistolae Austrasicae* no. 3 (113–14). On the dating of the letter, see Michel Rouche, *Clovis* (Paris: Fayard, 1996), 456.
7. Lisa Kaaren Bailey, *Christianity's Quiet Success: The Eusebius Gallicanus Sermon Collection and the Power of the Church in Late Antique Gaul* (Notre Dame, IN: University of Notre Dame Press, 2010), 40–41.
8. Council of Orléans (541), c. 12. On the terminology utilized here, see Halfond, "Corporate Solidarity."

presbyteres fill this role, or else an episcopal council should the disputing parties be unable to reach an agreement. The latter recommended that provincial councils settle intraprovincial conflicts, while metropolitan bishops resolve differences between their respective suffragans.[9] The Council of Paris (614) adopted the Council of Lyons's preference for metropolitan arbiters while explicitly forbidding this role to be assumed by an *iudex publicus*.[10] In addition to their endorsement of mediation, these four canons collectively suggest a preference for internal adjudication, rather than in the context of a comital or royal *placitum*.[11] Or, to put it another way, they advocate resolution processes that, beyond the particulars of specific conflicts, reaffirm the integrity of the episcopal *ordo* through collegial mediation.

Excluding disputed episcopal elections (which, by definition, were not conflicts between ordained bishops) and formal conciliar trials, the several dozen interpersonal conflicts between Gallo-Frankish prelates recorded in contemporary sources mostly are over matters profane and not spiritual, let alone theological. A rare sixth-century exception, albeit from outside the Frankish realm, was a conflict between Bishops Cyprian of Toulon and Maximus of Geneva. Around 524/33, Cyprian was criticized by his episcopal colleague for referring to the incarnated God's suffering (*Deum hominem passum*).[12] In a lengthy epistolary response, Cyprian defended his orthodoxy by stringing together several pages' worth of biblical citations.[13] Additionally, he suggested somewhat patronizingly that his accuser reexamine the writings of Hilary of Poitiers and the *Libellus emendationis* of the Gallic monk Leporius and then promptly send his response to Cyprian or, if he wished, through the latter's metropolitan, Caesarius of Arles. This name-dropping almost certainly was a not-so-subtle reminder of Caesarius's recent diplomatic victory over the metropolitan see of Vienne.[14] It is unknown whether Maximus ever responded to Cyprian's epistle, and the bishop of Geneva died before his see and that of his correspondent were represented at the Council of Orléans (541), following the Frankish annexation of the Burgundian and Provençal *civitates*. Therefore, we can never know whether the two old nem-

---

9. Council of Tours (567), c. 2; Council of Lyons (567/70), c. 1.

10. Council of Paris (614), c. 13. On the influence of the Council of Lyons, see Halfond, "Corporate Solidarity."

11. The dearth of disputes between bishops in the corpus of Merovingian royal *placita* may be reflective of this preference. On the corpus, see Werner Bergmann, "Untersuchungen zu den Gerichtsurkunden der Merowingerzeit," *Archiv für diplomatik* 22 (1976): 1–186.

12. On the two bishops, and their identification as the correspondents in dispute, see Pietri and Heijmans, *Prosopographie de la Gaule chrétienne*, 537–41, 1305–7.

13. *Epistolae aevi Merowingici collectae* no. 1 (434–36).

14. Tyrrell, "Merovingian Letters and Letters Writers," 248–49.

eses would have been willing to put aside their differences to subscribe to the council's acts as collaborators in consensus.

While scriptural and patristic texts occasionally were quoted in other recorded interpersonal disputes between bishops, the absence of major doctrinal controversies within the Gallic church in the Merovingian period probably limited the number of cases akin to that of Cyprian and Maximus. This is not to say, of course, that Gallic bishops were completely detached from the Christological and Trinitarian discussions that so occupied their Mediterranean colleagues, but only that such debates did not lead to major schisms within the Gallo-Frankish church.[15]

Furthermore, agreement on the basic dictates of Christian orthodoxy did not in any way preclude disagreements regarding ecclesiastical policy, royal politics, or—as in the case of Importunus and Frodebert—commercial transactions. In fact, a substantial number of recorded interpersonal episcopal conflicts revolved around property or jurisdictional disputes. Typically, in these cases, disputed property was institutional, not personal. While the wealthier members of the episcopate occasionally found themselves in court over disputed property—Cautinus of Clermont, Gregory of Tours tells us, went systematically after all of those properties bordering his own, some of which very well may have belonged to fellow bishops—it is to be expected that conflicts between episcopal sees were less likely to be over personal possessions.[16] As a federation, the Gallic churches by the sixth century collectively had accumulated a substantial territorial patrimony.[17] And as individual episcopal sees through donations and bequests gradually acquired additional properties beyond the borders of their own *civitas*, and as the number of rural churches multiplied, conflicts predictably mounted.[18] In the early sixth century, for instance, Ruricius of Limoges and Cronopius of Périgueux both claimed Gemiliacum (Jumilhac-le-Grand), which was virtually equidistant from the two episcopal sees.[19] In such cases, it may not have been ill intent that motivated usurpation, but simply an uncertainty of jurisdiction.

---

15. Ian Wood, "The Franks and Papal Theology, 550–660," in *The Crisis of the Oikoumene*, ed. Celia Martin Chazelle and Catherine Cubitt (Turnhout, Belgium: Brepols, 2006), 223–41.

16. Gregory of Tours, *Decem libri historiarum* 4.12.

17. Emile Lesne, *Histoire de la propriété ecclésiastique en France* (Lille, France: Rene Giard, 1910–43), 1:153; A. H. M. Jones, "Church Finance in the Fifth and Sixth Centuries," *Journal of Theological Studies*, n.s., 11, no. 1 (1960): 84–94, at 84–85; Ian Wood, "Entrusting Western Europe to the Church, 400–750," *Transactions of the Royal Historical Society* 23 (2013): 37–73; Wood, *Transformation of the Roman West*, 96–102.

18. On the growing number of rural churches, see Edward James, *The Franks* (Oxford: Blackwell, 1988), 149–51. On the treatment of both urban and rural churches as properties, see Susan Wood, *The Proprietary Church in the Medieval West* (Oxford: Oxford University Press, 2006), 25–30.

19. Ruricius of Limoges, *Fausti aliorumque epistulae ad Ruricium aliosque* no. 2.6 (316).

It is true that Gregory of Tours suggested of the bishops of his own time that the acquisition of an episcopate could sometimes arouse *avaritia* in its occupant, as was the case with Cautinus. Gregory implies that base motives similarly compelled Innocentius of Rodez, immediately (*confestim*) upon his ordination, to claim parishes then under the supervision of his neighbor, Ursicinus of Cahors. While a conciliar tribunal sided with Ursicinus (Gregory seems to imply justly), Innocentius had been confident enough in his case to press it for several years.[20] Gregory himself was involved in at least one property dispute in the early 570s over a *villa ecclesiae* possessed by the diocese of Tours but coveted by his suffragan Bishop Felix of Nantes, with whom he enjoyed a sometimes contentious relationship. The villa itself seems to have been located outside Tours, perhaps even within the territory of Nantes itself.[21]

While Gregory may have seen ill will motivating Felix's claims, the latter probably viewed the matter rather differently. Similarly, it is unlikely that malicious intent motivated Leudegar of Autun to side with the *patricius* Hector of Marseilles against Praejectus of Clermont over property claimed both by Hector and by the diocese of Clermont.[22] Praejectus's own hagiographer, who has very little positive to say about Hector, implicates Leudegar in Hector's *scelus* without explicitly condemning him, while also admitting that Praejectus struggled to convince the court of his position.[23] Even Bishop Mummolus of Uzès, whom we are told resorted to attempted murder when Amandus sought to found a monastery at Nant with the support of Childeric II, may have been motivated less by *invidia* than by a belief that his jurisdictional rights were being threatened.[24] So, without denying that base motives ever played a role in fomenting disputes, in most recorded cases both sides were confident of their own diocese's legal right to disputed property.

---

20. Gregory of Tours, *Decem libri historiarum* 6.38 (*diocesis*). On the terminology of *parish* and *diocese*, as well as the absence of formalized parish divisions in the sixth century, see Georg Scheibelreiter, "Church Structure and Organisation," in *The New Cambridge Medieval History*, vol. 1, c. 500–c. 700, ed. Paul Fouracre (Cambridge: Cambridge University Press, 2005), 675–709, at 686. On parishes, see also Christine Delaplace, ed., *Aux origines de la paroisse rurale en Gaule méridionale, IVe–IXe siècles* (Paris: Editions Errance, 2005).

21. Gregory of Tours, *Decem libri historiarum* 5.5. On the villa, see McDermott, "Felix of Nantes," 11–12.

22. *Passio Praeiecti* chaps. 23, 25–27; *Passio Leudegarii I* chap. 9.

23. On the latter point, see Fouracre and Gerberding, *Late Merovingian France*, 263.

24. *Vita Amandi prima*, ed. Bruno Krusch, MGH SRM 5 (Hanover, Germany: Hahn, 1910), chap. 23. To cite an additional example from the early Pippinid era, the hostility of the bishops of Mainz and Rheims toward Boniface probably had less to do with their morals than with their efforts to preserve their own jurisdictional authority: see Boniface, *S. Bonifatii et Lulli epistolae*, ed. Ernst Dümmler, MGH Epistolae 3 (Berlin: Weidmann, 1892), nos. 24, 60, 87 (273–74, 323–24, 369–72). On these conflicts, see Fouracre, *Age of Charles Martel*, 133–34.

Additional factors could cause or aggravate property or jurisdictional disputes, such as shifting regnal borders. The long-standing jurisdictional dispute between the metropolitan sees of Arles and Vienne in southern Gaul, for example, which had been exacerbated by new regnal borders in the later fifth century, continued into the sixth century with neighboring *civitates* disputed and usurpations alleged.[25] Another, more egregious case involved parishes belonging to the episcopal see of Turin, which were seized (along with moveable goods) by the Franks and turned into a new episcopal see by Guntram of Burgundy, Saint-Jean-de-Maurienne. Pope Gregory the Great in 599 attempted to intervene on behalf of Bishop Ursicinus of Turin, first by asking Syagrius of Autun to use his influence with the Merovingians to intercede on Ursicinus's behalf. Not taking any chances, however, Gregory additionally sent separate letters directly to both Theuderic II and Theudebert II, but there is no reason to believe that his pleas were heard, as Maurienne remained an episcopal see.[26]

While property disputes might be provincial or interprovincial in nature, a strictly provincial form of jurisdictional conflict that afflicted the Gallo-Frankish episcopate concerned metropolitan prerogatives. As previously suggested, it is tempting both to over- or underestimate the structural integrity of the provincial administration of the Gallic church in the Merovingian era.[27] Conciliar evidence, for example, indicates that metropolitan power was consistently recognized and utilized for the convocation and operation of ecclesiastical councils, the administrative embodiment of the corporate church, and not merely those convoked within individual provinces.[28] That said, even in the age of Gregory of Tours, provincial metropolitans often struggled to assert their authority over their suffragans, as the frosty relationship between Gregory and Felix of Nantes suggests. The likelihood that Nicetius of Trier's own suffragans were relieved at his exile already has been noted, as has Leontius of Bordeaux's clumsy and politically naïve deposition of a suffragan whose election he had not approved. Even more challenging were cases in which metropolitan bishops—often frustratingly—attempted to assert their will over bishops not technically under their supervision.

---

25. *Epistolae Arelatenses genuinae* nos. 23–25, 47 (33–36, 69–70). On the background for this jurisdictional dispute, see Klingshirn, *Caesarius of Arles*, 65–71, 129–32.

26. On the lost parishes, see Gregory I, *Registrum epistularum*, ed. Dag Norberg, CCSL 140 (Turnhout, Belgium: Brepols, 1972), eps. 9.215, 9.227 (775–76, 801–2). For an additional example of shifting royal borders prompting a jurisdictional dispute, see the discussion of Châteaudun in chapter 1.

27. Compare Halfond, *Archaeology*, 200–208, to Pontal, *Histoire des conciles mérovingiens*, 255–57, both of whom utilize conciliar evidence in consideration of this question.

28. Halfond, *Archaeology*, 67–69.

Contained within the *Epistolae Austrasicae* is a letter from Remigius of Rheims to Falco of Maastricht in which the metropolitan accuses Falco of interfering in his province by performing ordinations in the Church of Mouzon circa 500/33. This was an indiscretion that Remigius did not take lightly, furiously writing, "If your holiness was unaware of the canons, it was imprudent for you to transgress before learning them."[29] While it is true that Mouzon was approximately 90 kilometers as the crow flies from Rheims, the tone of Remigius's letter strongly suggests the metropolitan's confidence that Mouzon was securely within his own jurisdiction. It is possible as well that Falco's audacity may have been prompted by a lack of episcopal supervision within his own province, as the metropolitan see of Cologne possibly was vacant at the time.[30] Remigius may have recognized in Falco a potential regional rival.

Remigius's contemporary, Caesarius of Arles, likely suspected similar motivations on behalf of the bishop of Aix.[31] In 514 Caesarius wrote to Pope Symmachus to complain that the bishop was purposely avoiding meetings convoked by Caesarius in his role as provincial metropolitan, such as episcopal ordinations and ecclesiastical synods.[32] One could hardly blame the reluctant bishop, whose *civitas* had long claimed a metropolitan status, which it fought a losing battle to maintain between the fifth and early sixth centuries.[33] But the showdown with Caesarius proved decisive, as Symmachus not only confirmed that the bishop of Arles's powers as metropolitan extended over Aix but officially named Caesarius papal *vicarius*.

Despite this victory, Caesarius's successors would find it progressively more challenging to assert their papal-granted authority in a new Frankish context. In 557, for example, Sapaudus of Arles had to appeal to the papacy when, against his protests, Childebert I disregarded canonical rules regarding the summoning of bishops to trial.[34] Such defensiveness on the part of Gallo-Frankish bishops from the perspective of hindsight is understandable, if not always defensible. While the provincial organization of the Gallic church was, in theory, orderly and stable, the reality often proved rather more complex. Regnal borders shifted, metropolitans struggled to assert or even to expand their authority within and beyond their own provinces, and the sometimes uncertain

---

29. *Epistolae Austrasicae* no. 4 (115–16).
30. Duchesne, *Fastes épiscopaux de l'ancienne Gaule*, 2:179.
31. The name of the reigning bishop is unknown. It is possible that Maximus of Aix, who was in office by 524, was the subject of Caesarius's ire. See Duchesne, 1:280.
32. *Epistolae Arelatenses genuinae* nos. 28–29 (40–42).
33. Mathisen, *Ecclesiastical Factionalism*, 22–24, 103, 118–19, 219–21; Klingshirn, *Caesarius of Arles*, 129–30, 137.
34. *Epistolae Arelatenses genuinae* no. 52 (75–76).

or shifting jurisdictional status of rural churches had the potential to foment disagreements. So, despite the broad structural integrity of the provincial system during the Merovingian period, particularly in local contexts metropolitan jurisdiction often was the subject of sometimes-contentious negotiation.

A third major source of conflict within the episcopal ranks is similarly suggestive of an ecclesiastical governance model that generally was stable in the aggregate but subject to dissent and dispute in specific situations: the participation of bishops in church councils. Gallic conciliar canons were unambiguous regarding the necessity and authority of these meetings. Provincial councils were supposed to be held either annually or biannually, and the canons forbade all excuses but illness for absenteeism.[35] We know from a variety of sources, however, that bishops did not always attend councils to which they were summoned. Ruricius of Limoges's absence from the Council of Agde (506) earned him a gentle rebuke from Caesarius of Arles, the council's president. Ruricius, who claimed the perfectly allowable excuse of ill health, nevertheless was annoyed enough by Caesarius's letter to post a defensive rejoinder in which he suggested that Caesarius owed his reputation to the status of his *civitas*, rather than to his toil on behalf of the church.[36] Similarly defensive to criticism of his conciliar absenteeism was Mappinus of Rheims, whose fellow metropolitan, Nicetius of Trier, had sent him a rebuke around 550. Mappinus, unlike Remigius, excused his absence from the Council of Toul on the more questionable grounds that he had not learned of its agenda in time.[37]

Furthermore, while conciliar acts of this period were composed so as to avoid any hint of a lack of consensus, there is no reason to think that conciliar participants approached every agenda item from the position of unanimity. Gregory of Tours's aforementioned account of Praetextatus's conciliar trial, for example, suggests a great deal of uncertainty and dissension among his episcopal judges.[38] And, in at least one case, despite the considerable efforts of a council president, true consensus never was achieved. In May 533, Caesarius of Arles gathered fourteen of his suffragans, along with one clerical

---

35. The following Gallic canons mandated annual attendance: Councils of Agde (506), c. 49; Orléans (533), c. 2; Orléans (538), c. 1; Orléans (541), c. 37; Orléans (549), c. 23; Chalon-sur-Saône (647/53), preface; Eauze (551), c. 7; Germania (742), c. 1; and Soissons (744), c. 2. The following canons concern biannual provincial councils: Councils of Riez (439), c. 7; Orange (441), c. 28; Tours (567), c. 1; and Ver (755), c. 4. See also Avitus of Vienne's convocation letter for the Council of Epaone (517): *Concilia Galliae: A.511–A.695*, 22–23. On the required attendance of bishops at councils, see also Councils of Epaone (517), c. 1; Orléans (533), c. 1; Orléans (538), c. 1; Orléans (549), c. 18; Eauze (551), c. 7; Tours (567), c. 1; Mâcon (585), c. 20; and Saint-Jean-de-Losne (673/75), c. 21.

36. Caesarius of Arles, *Sancti Caesarii episcopi Arelatensis Opera omnia* eps. 3–4 (2:5–8).

37. *Epistolae Austrasicae* no. 11 (126–27).

38. Gregory of Tours, *Decem libri historiarum* 5.18.

representative, in the city of Marseilles to consider the case against one of their colleagues, Contumeliosus of Riez, who had been accused of "multa turpia et inhonesta," including sexual indiscretions and alienating ecclesiastical property.[39] Following Contumeliosus's admission of guilt, the council ordered him to be confined in a monastery as penance. The acts' failure to indicate the permanency of this arrangement, as William Klingshirn has shown, reveals a significant rift between Caesarius and his suffragans, many of whom believed Caesarius's call for Contumeliosus's deposition was too harsh and joined the latter in rejecting "Caesarius' calls for radical changes in their pastoral practices and way of life, and continued to run their dioceses as they saw fit."[40]

Having failed to achieve consensus at Marseilles, Caesarius next solicited the support of Pope John II (533–35) to pressure his suffragans into supporting his own position.[41] But John's successor, Agapitus I (535–36), believing a false report that Caesarius had approved Contumeliosus's return from monastic seclusion to Riez, convoked a court of appeal in Rome to retry the accused prelate.[42] Whether this court of appeals ever assembled is unknown. But regardless of the ultimate outcome of the affair, in this case at least, the consensus among Caesarius's suffragans appears to have been stronger than that between the metropolitan and his comprovincials.

Another notable case of episcopal dissent regarding a conciliar verdict occurred several decades later, following the Council of Saintes (561/67), which deposed Bishop Emerius of Saintes. Upon the conclusion of the council's business, the newly appointed bishop Heraclius was sent to Paris with a copy of the conciliar *acta*. He stopped in Tours and while there requested of Bishop Eufronius that he too subscribe to the acts. Eufronius refused. Gregory of Tours believed that subsequent events ultimately proved his kinsman's wisdom, as both Heraclius and Leontius of Bordeaux, the convoker of the Council of Saintes, were duly punished by Charibert for their insolence.[43] Gregory does not explicitly say, however, whether Eufronius was motivated more by political acumen or by a sincere belief that Leontius had wrongly deposed Emerius despite his uncanonical consecration.[44] Leontius's failure to attend the Council of Tours (567), which almost certainly assembled after the

---

39. Council of Marseilles (533), *acta*. On this council's attendance and acts, see Pontal, *Histoire des conciles mérovingiens*, 84–86.
40. Klingshirn, *Caesarius of Arles*, 249–50 (whole discussion: 247–50).
41. *Concilia Galliae: A.511–A.695*, 86–96.
42. *Concilia Galliae: A.511–A.695*, 96–97.
43. Gregory of Tours, *Decem libri historiarum* 4.26.
44. On Gregory's account, see Luce Pietri, *La ville de Tours du IVe au VIe siècle: Naissance d'une cité chrétienne* (Rome: Ecole française de Rome, 1983), 240–42.

Council of Saintes, and over which Eufronius presided, suggests that relations between the two metropolitan bishops had yet to mend.[45] Leontius's absence, however, while significant due to his rank, reputation, and stature, was further evidence that he remained to some degree estranged from the small circle of bishops whose collaboration allowed them considerable influence in the ecclesiastical governance of the *regnum Chariberthi*.[46] In fact, his absence arguably confirmed the integrity (and insularity) of that group of prelates whose consensus and collaboration remained relatively stable during the seven years of Charibert's reign.

This survey of some of the major themes of interpersonal disputes between Gallo-Frankish prelates suggests several important points. The first is that these disputes, while often contentious, bitter, and sometimes unresolved, did not on their own permanently or irreparably undermine corporate integrity of the united Gallic episcopate, even within the borders of an individual sub-kingdom. By their nature, property issues usually were limited to a pair of competing sees, while jurisdictional disputes rarely extended beyond one or two provinces. While, in theory, conciliar disputes might include a broader range of bishops, most known examples are relatively small in scale and longevity.

A second observable feature is the regular reliance on arbiters—fellow bishops, the royal court, or even the pope—to settle disputes. This reliance on mediators reflects the spirit, if not always the letter, of contemporary conciliar legislation that defines procedures for dispute settlement. As the canons themselves offered a multiplicity of possible protocol, there is no reason to assume any greater uniformity in practice. That said, the canons offered useful guidance and in certain cases do appear to have been inspirational, such as the intervention by the provincial metropolitan of Bourges, and subsequently by a council, in the dispute between Innocentius of Rodez and Ursicinus of Cahors, thus mirroring the procedures defined by the Council of Lyons, which had assembled about fifteen years earlier.[47]

Finally, the secular focus of most of these interpersonal disputes already has been noted. While there were notable exceptions beyond the epistolary exchange between Cyprian and Maximus, such as Avitus of Vienne's annoyance with a Lyonnaise bishop who shared theological texts with the Arians,

---

45. That Leontius was still alive at the time of the Council of Tours is suggested by his correspondence with Fortunatus after ca. 568. See Brennan, "Career of Venantius Fortunatus," 63.

46. I.e., Eufronius of Tours, Praetextatus of Rouen, Germanus of Paris, Domitianus of Angers, Domnolus of Le Mans, Felix of Nantes, and Victorius of Rennes. See Halfond, "Charibert," 9–17.

47. Gregory of Tours, *Decem libri historiarum* 6.38. In general, however, Rio, *Legal Practice*, 202, is surely correct that "the manner in which parties [in dispute] wished to proceed in particular cases had at least as much influence in forging agreements as the formal procedures set down in written law."

the participation of bishops in the dispute fomented by the monk Agrestius over Columbanus's legacy in the 620s, and the dispute between Norbert of Clermont and Godinus of Lyons over the body of Saint Bonitus following the latter's death circa 706, at least among known conflicts these are the exceptions to the rule and, in the case of Agrestius, may have been prompted in part by factors and motivations not entirely spiritual in nature.[48] We cannot extrapolate from this, of course, that the Gallo-Frankish bishops were comparatively materialistic and unconcerned with spiritual matters. Besides their occasional conflicts, these same bishops also regularly collaborated with their colleagues in charitable pursuits, pastoral care, clerical ordinations, ecclesiastical legislating, and the dedication of new religious buildings. Such collaborative initiatives not only reflected episcopal corporatism at its best, they strengthened through their recurrence an ecclesiastical superstructure that transcended diocesan boundaries and—by extension—the authority of individual representatives of the order. Bishops, of course, were administrators as well as pastors, and it was in the former role apparently that they most often came into conflict with their colleagues.[49]

The Structural Integrity of Provincial Governance

With this last point in mind, we now must consider whether there existed any inherent structural conditions within the institutional Gallic church that encouraged breakdowns in consensus. Earlier, it was suggested that the provincial system on which the Gallic church's corporate organization was based was generally stable during the course of the Merovingian era, but with some important caveats. While the provinces and diocesan organization within these provinces remained relatively constant from the early sixth through the eighth century, created in this period were (sometimes short-lived) new sees, such as Alais, Châteaudun, and Saint-Jean-de-Maurienne. Additionally, as already has been noted, the authority of metropolitan bishops was far from uniform and had as much to do with the personality of individual prelates as the size, wealth, and status of their see. It could prove challenging, for instance, for younger metropolitans to exert their will on older, more experienced colleagues, who

---

48. Avitus of Vienne, *Opera* ep. 28 (58–59); Jonas of Bobbio, *Vitae Columbani abbatis discipulorumque eius libri duo auctore Iona*, ed. Bruno Krusch, MGH SRM 4 (Hanover, Germany: Hahn, 1902), 2.9–10; *Vita Boniti episcopi Arverni*, ed. Bruno Krusch, MGH SRM 6 (Hanover, Germany: Hahn, 1913), chap. 32.

49. This was the case in the Gallic church before the Merovingian era. See, for example, the discussion of the fifth-century Chelidonius affair by Mathisen, *Ecclesiastical Factionalism*, 147–66.

unsurprisingly did not enjoy being lectured to by men they considered to be their juniors.

An additional factor that impacted the structural integrity of the provincial system was the grafting of (shifting) regnal borders on the Gallic provinces. Did this development render increasingly irrelevant the provincial identities of individual sees? The subscriptions appended to conciliar acts suggest that provincial membership remained a basic criterion in determining the attendance of councils, except in cases in which provincial and royal borders came into conflict. In other words, neither royal nor provincial borders exclusively determined conciliar attendance in the Merovingian era.[50] One might examine, for example, the Council of Chalon-sur-Saône (647/53), which was one of the final Merovingian councils for which we possess a subscription list. The council was attended exclusively by bishops from the Neustro-Burgundian kingdom, then ruled by Clovis II. Six metropolitan bishops were in attendance, representing the provinces of Lyons, Vienne, Rouen, Sens, Bourges, and Besançon. Both Latinus of Tours and Theodorius of Arles's attendance also had been requested, but while the former sent a delegate, the latter simply refused to come when he learned that he was to be charged with official misconduct at the council.[51]

The six metropolitans were joined by thirty-three of their suffragans, as well as six clerical representatives, all of whom came from the aforementioned provinces, including Arles. In the acts, the metropolitans subscribed first, reflecting their senior status, followed by their suffragans, and finally by the clerical delegates. While most of the represented provinces were not represented by the entirety of their episcopal cohort, this was very much the norm for Gallic councils.[52] Thus, while the anachronistic, but regularly employed, terminology of *national council* is ostensibly applicable to Chalon-sur-Saône, this term obscures the fact that within the confines of the Neustro-Burgundian kingdom, provincial identities were still very much relevant for the administrative organization of the episcopate as late as the mid-seventh century.

In addition to the evidence provided by conciliar acts, there are additional reasons to think that the superimposing of Frankish regna on older ecclesiastical borders did impact the integrity of the provincial system without wholly undermining it. The establishment of the *regnum Francorum* in Gaul effectively had undermined the traditional Roman provinces' role in secular administration,

---

50. Halfond, *Archaeology*, 67–69.
51. Council of Chalon-sur-Saône (647/53), ep. to Theodorius (*Concilia Galliae: A.511–A.695*, 309–10).
52. J. Champagne and R. Szramkiewicz, "Recherches sur les conciles des temps mérovingiens," *Revue historique de droit français et étranger* 49 (1971): 5–49, at 19.

and provincial identity became primarily an ecclesiastical designation.[53] Furthermore, as Simon T. Loseby has suggested, it is possible that *civitates* themselves began to lose their administrative significance in the seventh century, to be replaced structurally and ideologically by a *tria regna* model characterized in part by a "ruralisation of royal and aristocratic power."[54] These same processes, Loseby argues, affected the bishops in their cities but did not necessarily lead to a dramatic "deterritorialisation" of episcopal governance.[55] Even back in the sixth century those cities identified as metropolitan sees often were not those of the greatest political or even spiritual importance in Merovingian Gaul. Royal seats (*sedes regiae*), for instance, usually could be found elsewhere, and the larger interprovincial councils often were located in relative proximity to these political capitals rather than to metropolitan sees.[56] Tours was relatively unique among sixth-century metropolitan *civitates* in being home to a cult of sanctity with a national following: the cults of Geneviève (Paris), Vincent (Paris), Denis (Paris), Medard (Soissons), and Marcellus (Chalon-sur-Saône) all were centralized in political, not ecclesiastical, capitals.[57]

And yet, even as late as the early eighth century, as Charles Martel consolidated his hold over the Frankish kingdom, the provincial system of ecclesiastical governance retained its basic form and significance, if not always in specific instances its integrity.[58] Several metropolitan sees, such as Lyons, Vienne, and Rheims, are reported to have suffered as a result of Charles's policies, and eighth-century lacunae in the episcopal *fastes* have also been read as evidence for the breakdown in ecclesiastical governance. But without discounting several real instances of administrative disarray, as well as the allowance for some individual prelates to administer multiple *civitates* or to combine secular and episcopal offices, it is unwise to extrapolate from a handful of cases that a

---

53. Loseby, "Lost Cities," 230–31.
54. Loseby, 223–52 (quote on 240).
55. Loseby, 241.
56. On the *sedes regiae*, see Eugen Ewig, "Résidence et capitale pendant le Haut Moyen Age," *Revue historique* 230 (1963): 47–70; and Alain Dierkens and Patrick Périn, "Les *sedes regiae* mérovingiennes entre Seine et Rhin," in *Sedes Regiae (ann. 400–800)*, ed. Gisela Ripoll and Josep M. Gurt (Barcelona: Reial Academia de Bones Lletres, 2000), 267–304. On the locations of councils, see Halfond, *Archaeology*, 65–66.
57. Van Dam, *Saints and Their Miracles*, 24–28.
58. Timothy Reuter, "Kirchenreform und Kirchenpolitik im Zeitalter Karl Martells: Begriffe und Wirklichkeit," in *Karl Martell in seiner Zeit*, ed. Jörg Jarnut, Ulrich Nonn, and Michael Richter (Sigmaringen, Germany: Jan Thorbecke Verlag, 1994), 35–59, at 46–47, observes that whatever the extent of Charles's secularization of ecclesiastical property, it did not erase any existing dioceses.

majority, or even a sizable percentage, of *civitates* experienced similar turmoil during Charles's career.[59]

Similarly, while contemporary and near-contemporary sources do attest to improperly ordained bishops (including the occupants of some metropolitan sees) holding office in the early eighth century—that is, the *vocati episcopi*— their administrative authority does not seem to have differed in any meaningful way from that of their properly ordained peers.[60] Finally, there is reason to think that regardless of institutional integrity, bishops still thought of their corporate identity in terms of the old provincial model. Eugen Ewig has observed, for example, that the order of subscriptions attached to seventh- and eighth-century episcopal privileges suggests that bishops still cared a great deal about their traditions of corporate order and hierarchy.[61] In short, without denying that the Gallo-Frankish episcopate experienced institutional pressures and even transformations over the course of the first half of the eighth century, these forces did not erase the institutional apparatus on which episcopal corporate identity was based.

Political Engagement and Its Consequences

But while the grafting of royal borders on the existing provincial divisions of Gaul did not fundamentally undermine the stability of episcopal governance, Merovingian rule did expose and exacerbate fundamental weaknesses in the corporate episcopate. Among the explicitly attested cases of interpersonal conflicts between bishops, at least five were in part a consequence of bishops aligning themselves with competing political blocs.[62] Even the colorful Importunus-Frodebert exchange had a political dimension, with the former accusing the latter of an improper relationship with the wife of Grimoald, the disgraced mayor of the palace, before shutting her away in a monastery.[63] While the veracity of this accusation is unverifiable, one study of the correspondence has hypothesized that Frodebert (or Chrodebert) previously had occupied the episcopate of Paris with Grimoald's patronage and only moved

---

59. Halfond, *Archaeology*, 200–204.
60. Halfond, 204–7.
61. Eugen Ewig, "Beobachtungen zu den Bischofslisten der merowingischen Konzilien und Bischofsprivilegien," in *Spätantikes und fränkisches Gallien*, 2:427–55, at 437–46.
62. I.e., the disputes involving Palladius of Saintes and Bertram of Bordeaux; Chrodobert of Tours and Importunus of Paris; Leudegar of Autun and Diddo of Chalon; Leudegar and Bobo of Valence; and Domnolus of Vienne and Maximus (see unknown).
63. Importunus of Paris, Epistle 3 to Frodebert of Tours, in Shanzer, "Tale of Frodebert's Tail," 400–401.

to Tours following the failure of his former patron's coup d'état.[64] Regardless of the truth of the accusation, by identifying his correspondent with Grimoald, Importunus was using Frodebert's specific political loyalties, and not simply his involvement in court politics, as ammunition in their escalating war of words.

The preceding chapters have identified a number of the major gravitational forces that attracted bishops to royal courts, first and foremost the allure of patronage, one of the fundamental social and institutional constructs undergirding the episcopate. While the Gallo-Frankish episcopate never fractured into semipermanent political factions as a result of these gravitational forces, there is no question that the ecclesiastical hierarchy at any given time contained partisans of competing royal or aristocratic parties. This political partisanship, in turn, threatened the corporate integrity of the episcopate far more seriously than those purely interpersonal conflicts discussed earlier. This is not to say, of course, that partisanship did not breed or exacerbate interpersonal conflicts within the episcopate; on the contrary, such conflicts could be among the most vicious. Rather, political partisanship, unlike interpersonal conflicts, affected a wider range of individuals, was more likely to lead to violence, and, perhaps most significantly, forced individual bishops to balance—or even to choose between—corporate and political loyalties.

While some of these "macro" effects will be examined in greater detail in the next chapter, first it is necessary to address three problems related to the phenomenon of episcopal involvement in court politics: (1) the implications of partisanship for interpersonal relationships between bishops; (2) the composition of political blocs or factions, and the membership of bishops therein; and (3) the stability and permanency of political divisions within the episcopate. Regarding the first of these problems, the Importunus-Frodebert correspondence is suggestive of both the weight that accusations of political heterodoxy could carry in interpersonal disputes and the hostility that competing political loyalties could engender. Politics caused or exacerbated often vicious conflicts between bishops due to the natural danger that accompanied partisan behavior. Political involvement could and did lead to the deaths of bishops.[65] The looming threat of retribution from the court or a rival aristocratic faction within the court thus raised the stakes considerably in interpersonal disputes.

---

64. Hen, "Changing Places."
65. Fouracre, "Why Were So Many Bishops?" Martyrdom, however, was available even to those bishops who died violently; see Scheibelreiter, "Death of the Bishop," 41–43.

An example can be found in the breakdown of relations between Bishop Palladius of Saintes and his metropolitan, Bertram of Bordeaux, in the aftermath of the failed effort by Gundovald to secure a regnum in Frankish Gaul circa 585. Gregory of Tours, who supplies the details of the dispute, did not think much of either disputant, particularly Bertram, who had participated in Chilperic's earlier efforts to prosecute Gregory. Gregory also recognized in both bishops a dangerous absence of fidelity toward their royal masters. In the case of Palladius, his *civitas* was possessed by Guntram between 567 and 576, during which time the bishop (according to Gregory) was duplicitous in his communications with the king.[66] It is possible that Palladius's loyalties already lay at this point with Chilperic, who captured Saintes in 576.[67] Palladius's metropolitan, despite his kinship with Guntram, as already noted, was a faithful ally of the king of Soissons.[68] Perhaps it is not surprising, then, that the fissure between the two bishops occurred following Chilperic's death and the arrival of Gundovald in Aquitaine. In the short period between the king's death and the pretender's arrival, Guntram had claimed his brother's Aquitanian possessions, and several bishops of former Neustrian-controlled *civitates* saw in Gundovald an opportunity to escape Burgundian rule. Bertram, Gregory later claimed, was particularly eager to support Gundovald's cause, welcoming him to Bordeaux with open arms.[69] Palladius too seems to have been a willing partisan of the pretender.[70]

Both bishops' loyalty was tested by Gundovald's order that Bertram ordain the presbyter Faustianus as bishop of Dax in 585. According to Gregory of Tours, Gundovald sought to nullify Chilperic's *decreta* in cities previously ruled by the latter, including a *decretum* naming the *comes* Nicetius successor to the episcopal see of Dax.[71] Bertram, however, may not have been Gundovald's first choice to perform the ordination. Canonical rules dictated that Laban of Eauze, the metropolitan bishop with jurisdiction over Dax, perform the ordination. As Eauze was within Gundovald's sphere of influence, Laban's absence is all the more suspect. While it has been hypothesized that Bertram's involvement was due to a provincial restructuring, which resulted in Eauze losing its metropolitan status, this seems an unlikely scenario, as the ordination of

---

66. Gregory of Tours, *Decem libri historiarum* 8.2: "Sed et Palladius episcopus ob hoc maxime regem incurrerat, quod ei saepius fallacias intulisset."
67. Gregory of Tours, *Decem libri historiarum* 5.13.
68. Halfond, "Sis Quoque Catholicis Religionis Apex," 61, 69.
69. Gregory of Tours, *Decem libri historiarum* 7.31: "Erat tunc temporis Gundovaldus in urbe Burdegalensi a Berthramno episcopo valde dilectus."
70. Bernard Bachrach, *Anatomy of a Little War: A Diplomatic and Military History of the Gundovald Affair (568–586)* (Boulder, CO: Westview, 1994), 232n49.
71. Gregory of Tours, *Decem libri historiarum* 7.31.

Faustianus is the only known occasion in which the bishop of Eauze failed to fulfill his obligations as provincial metropolitan.[72] It seems more likely that Laban either implicitly or explicitly expressed a disinterest in performing the ordination, requiring Gundovald to turn instead to a more willing metropolitan collaborator.[73] While Gregory of Tours does not delineate the full attendance of the council at which the ordination was performed, it appears that some, but not all, of Laban's provincial colleagues were in attendance.[74]

As Gregory does not suggest any reasons to doubt Bertram's own devotion toward Gundovald, the bishop of Bordeaux's claim that he could not perform Faustianus's ordination due to eye trouble should be understood as a judicious act of caution rather than an indicator of any wavering loyalty toward the pretender. Bertram proposed that Palladius attend the council in his stead, which raises the question of why this particular bishop was nominated. Considering the later disintegration of the relationship between the two bishops, it is tempting to think that the nomination simply was a ruse on Bertram's part to force his suffragan into a precarious situation while at the same time preserving his own safety. This explanation, however, is unconvincing for several reasons. First of all, Gregory of Tours is explicit that the fallout between the bishops was the result of the discovery of their participation in the Faustianus affair. Additionally, Gregory suggests that Guntram (apparently rightly) did not believe that Palladius was coerced into performing the ordination, while also implying that Palladius had welcomed Gundovald into his *civitas*.[75] There seems little reason to doubt Gregory on either of these two points. As already suggested, Palladius had little love for Guntram and, like other Aquitanian bishops, may have viewed Gundovald as an attractive alternative following Chilperic's death.

Guntram himself seems to have differentiated little between the actual roles played respectively by Bertram and Palladius in weighing their guilt. Palladius's initial decision to attempt to claim all responsibility for Faustianus's ordination may have been motivated in part by the fact that it was his fellow bishops, and not Guntram himself, who initially interrogated him at Orléans in July 585. Perhaps he hoped that loyalty toward a metropolitan bishop might be received more positively by this particular audience. But Palladius's full

---

72. Cf. Auguste Longnon, *Géographie de la Gaule au VIe siècle* (Paris: E. Martinet, 1878), 185–86, 589.
73. Halfond, "Corporate Solidarity."
74. Bachrach, *Anatomy of a Little War*, 99–100. For example, Orestes of Bazas was in attendance.
75. Gregory of Tours, *Decem libri historiarum* 8.2: "Discussi enim ante paululum fuerant a reliquis episcopis et optimatibus regis, cur Gundovaldum suscepissent, cur Faustianum Aquis episcopum ad praeceptionem eius levissimam ordinassent. . . . Cum haec rege nuntiata fuissent, valde commotus est, ita ut vix obtineri possit, ut eos ad convivium provocaret, quos antea non viderat."

explanation for his actions, as related by Gregory, was that following word of Bertram's illness, he (Palladius) was manhandled by the pretender's men and forced to perform the ordination against his will. In other words, it was not corporate loyalty that motivated his actions at all but rather brute force. Palladius's explanation also left open the question of whether Bertram would have performed the ceremony had his health permitted. It is no wonder, then, that this excuse convinced few and seems to have led directly to the breakdown in relations between Bertram and Palladius, which also occurred during the Orléans sojourn.[76]

Gregory, who was present at the event, specifically states that the argument began at a dinner hosted by Guntram following the king's public humiliation of Palladius during a Sunday mass. No doubt this embarrassment had exacerbated tensions all the more, and it is also possible that alcohol consumed at the meal may have been another contributing factor, as Gregory relates that the argument was received as hilarious by many of those in attendance, with the exception of those "qui alacriores erant scientiae."[77] In any case, what is not clear from Gregory's account is whether the accusations hurled across the table had anything whatsoever to do with the Faustianus affair or merely referred to various "adulteries and fornications." Perhaps, in spite of their fury, both bishops recognized the risk in bringing up the matter that so infuriated the king.

Regardless, relations between the two bishops continued to deteriorate as Guntram began actively to prosecute prelates who had collaborated with Gundovald. In the months before the Council of Mâcon, which assembled a mere three months after the Orléans sojourn, Bertram, probably uncertain of the precise penalties he would face at the council, spent the intervening time trying to solicit written collaboration of Palladius's guilt from the latter's own clergy. Bertram probably had very good reason to be concerned: while his eventual punishment would be relatively light—he and his collaborators would have to supply the deposed Faustianus with annual stipends of food and money—it seems rather likely, considering his prior activities, that he was among those bishops that Guntram originally had planned to exile following the council.[78] Gregory's account implies that Palladius had become aware of this conspiracy against him by the time the council assembled (it is possible that the evidence was formally presented at the meeting) but only was able

---

76. Gregory of Tours, *Decem libri historiarum* 8.7.
77. Gregory of Tours, *Decem libri historiarum* 8.7.
78. Gregory of Tours, *Decem libri historiarum* 8.20.

to act against his enemies within Saintes following Bertram's death shortly after the conclusion of the synod.[79]

Despite the raised tensions instigated by the looming threat of punishment, neither Bertram nor Palladius suffered much more than humiliation and moderate discomfort as a result of their dispute. The same could not be said, however, in the case of Bishop Leudegar of Autun's conflicts with bishops allied to his political nemesis Ebroin, in particular Desideratus (Diddo) of Chalon-sur-Saône and Bobo of Valence, who rallied to the mayor's side upon his escape from Luxeuil in 675. Bobo and Diddo may have had very good reasons (beyond their political loyalties and their purported desire for financial gain) to harbor such animosity toward Leudegar: both, it seems, had been exiled by King Childeric II, whose establishment in Neustria Leudegar had helped to engineer.[80] It was the deposed Diddo who led the siege of Lyons later that same year, allegedly refusing to depart without seizing his enemy on account of "the mad yearning of his fury."[81] After Leudegar's surrender, Diddo was among those who oversaw the blinding of the imprisoned bishop, and he also apparently arranged for his colleague, the deposed Bobo, to take over the see of Autun.[82] As Leudegar's fate suggests, the tensions inherent in court politics easily could exacerbate existing conflicts between members of rival factions, even members of the same corporate order.[83]

In Leudegar's case, it is possible, at least in part, to reconstruct the membership of the opposing court factions.[84] As a general rule, prosopography can provide significant context for the actions of individual players in communication or competition with other influential persons, and competing political blocs do appear throughout Merovingian history. Additionally, a mapping of episcopal communications with royal courts reveals the existence of informal networks that regularly advised and supported individual political leaders.[85] But while bishops might wade into the treacherous waters of court affairs, even rallying with their colleagues in support of (or in opposition to)

---

79. Gregory of Tours, *Decem libri historiarum* 8.22.
80. Fouracre and Gerberding, *Late Merovingian France*, 241n130.
81. *Passio Leudegarii I* chap. 23.
82. *Passio Leudegarii I* chaps. 24–25.
83. Paul Fouracre, "The Incidence of Rebellion in the Early Medieval West," in Cooper and Leyser, *Making Early Medieval Societies*, 104–24, at 112–13, cautions against equating factions with specific regions, as most political conflicts and their participants were linked to the royal court. Cf. Wickham, *Framing the Early Middle Ages*, 193, who associates seventh-century Neustrian factionalism (in part) with the concentration of aristocratic landowning around the Paris basin.
84. Fouracre and Gerberding, *Late Merovingian France*, 197–98.
85. On the sons of Chlothar I, see, e.g., Halfond, "All the King's Men" (which, admittedly, is inconsistent in its use of the term *faction*); Halfond, "Sis Quoque Catholicis Religionis Apex"; Halfond, "Negotiating Episcopal Support"; and Halfond, "Charibert."

a particular individual or faction, what we do not find in Merovingian Gaul are purely episcopal factions competing with other episcopal factions as distinct secularized political blocs. When individual bishops or groups of bishops confronted each other over affairs of state, it was as members of broader coalitions consisting of both ecclesiastics and laymen. So, while bishops could and did act as political partisans, their engagement with nonaffiliated colleagues almost always was dictated by those secular persons whose causes they championed, as was the case, for instance, in those many conciliar trials where loyalists of the royal or mayoral convener prosecuted members of their own order at the ruler's request.

As a result, fractures within the episcopate resulting from political disputes, while sometimes disruptive and even violent, generally lacked permanency. Typically, they dissipated along with the ruler or court faction around or against whom the individual bishops rallied. However, while the immediate effects of these fractures generally were constrained to a single generation, their cumulative effects were not necessarily inconsequential: the body of the corporate episcopate carried the scars of decades of internal disputes. Still, it does not necessarily follow that the Gallo-Frankish episcopate became progressively, and inevitably, politicized—let alone secularized—between the sixth and eighth centuries, as its members engaged actively with imperial and royal courts long before the Merovingians solidified their control of Gaul. Similarly, it is impossible to prove on the basis of our meager sources a gradual acceptance on the part of bishops and secular rulers alike that the political fidelities and obligations of prelates were, in all practical ways, as integral to their group identity as those corporate ties by which the Gallic episcopate had always defined itself. But with these important caveats, there are several reasons to think that a common devotion to public service—an attitude whose diverse permutations frequently are pooled under the common rubric of *Bischofsherrschaft*—articulated as early as the sixth century was manifested in new and meaningful ways in the seventh and eighth centuries.

But in looking for reflections of this ideology in institutional change, we need to proceed with caution. Ewig's suggestion that "episcopal republics" emerged in some seventh-century *civitates* has proved controversial in recent years, with its critics charging that its view of a secularized episcopacy is too beholden to the prejudiced views of Boniface, and furthermore that it assumes too wide a gap between the court and regional politics.[86] Even scholars willing to accept the model's relevance for the careers of particular bishops have

---

86. Eugen Ewig, "Milo et Eiusmodi Similes," in *Spätantikes und Fränkisches Gallien*, 2:189–219, at 2:207–19. For criticism of this model, see chapter 4.

noted that these so-called republics were limited in number, as well as longevity, which in turn implies that they perhaps were not reflective of a major or widespread transformation in ecclesiastical and civic governance.[87] We will discuss these "republics" further in the next chapter. Similarly, while the handful of references in eighth-century documents to the aforementioned *vocati episcopi* do sometimes refer to men who combined comital and episcopal office or who never were canonically ordained as bishops, the malleability of the terminology and its selective employment are not necessarily suggestive of a major structural change in the episcopate.[88]

In contrast to episcopal "republics" and the so-called *vocati episcopi*, more certain evidence for an institutionalization of the secular political responsibilities of the episcopate in the later Merovingian period can be found in the blending of traditionally distinct episcopal and royal institutions of council and assembly. While mixed councils, as they sometimes are called, are strongly associated with the Carolingians, they have their roots in Merovingian practice, dating back to the late sixth century. The Council of Mâcon (585) was scheduled in conjunction with a subsequent royal assembly, at which the previously published canons were endorsed and adjoined to a corresponding royal *edictum*.[89] Guntram's collaborative venture may have served as a model for Chlothar II, who appears to have made semiregular use of conjoined meetings of *episcopi* and *proceres*, recognizing that their assembly confirmed his jurisdictional power over matters both spiritual and profane.

Subsequent seventh-century diplomas similarly reveal a royal preference for legislating and adjudicating with mixed groups of bishops and lay officials, although it is not always obvious whether these two bodies met separately or together.[90] While this preference would be more formally institutionalized by the Carolingians, it does suggest an evolving conception of the episcopal responsibility for governance in the Merovingian era: while bishops remained a distinct *ordo* among the office-holding elite, with unique responsibilities and privileges, their performance of certain common services alongside lay courtiers more clearly and systematically defined an assumed collaboration between

---

87. On the lack of longevity among episcopal republics, see Wickham, *Framing the Early Middle Ages*, 257. Those veritable episcopal "empires," which consisted of multiple *civitates*, similarly seem to have been relatively short-lived exceptions to the rule. Along with the infamous example of Milo of Trier, Hugo of Rouen and Savaric of Auxerre likewise found their assigned diocesan borders to be constraining; see Ewig, "Milo et Eiusmodi Similes," 2:190–99, 202, 204–5.

88. Halfond, *Archaeology*, 206–7.

89. Heinzelmann, *Gregory of Tours*, 185, also identifies the Councils of Lyons (572/73 and 581) as proto *conciliae mixtae*, although this seems more likely in the case of the former meeting.

90. Halfond, *Archaeology*, 195–97. Wood, *Transformation of the Roman West*, 87, sees in the frequency of episcopal participation in seventh-century royal courts a "triumph of the episcopate."

these two groups within the context of the court. In contrast to the image of bishops as near-autonomous lords of diocesan republics, the participation of so many prelates in assembly politics through the eighth century (and beyond) is more suggestive of an ongoing sense of shared obligation with collegial and secular colleagues alike for the maintenance of peace and public order.

Turning from institutions to ideology, additional evidence for the continued, if not necessarily expanding, significance of political activity for Gallo-Frankish bishops can be found in the written histories and hagiographies of the seventh and eighth centuries. While the religious focus of the Fredegar *Chronica* has been found lacking in comparison with the original ten-book version of Gregory's *Historiae*—despite the fact that both authors share an eschatological frame of reference—the seventh-century chronicle does contain substantial discussion of the activities of bishops, particularly in the political sphere.[91] Collectively, these mostly brief allusions endorse collaboration between court and episcopate, and relatedly the belief that the spiritual and civic obligations of bishops are not mutually exclusive.[92] While the chronicler avoids lengthy editorializing, let alone sermonizing, he nevertheless regularly evaluates explicitly individuals or their actions, thus articulating a unique authorial perspective. Notably, the chronicler recognized the normality of episcopal involvement in court and factional politics but apparently was less concerned with the partisanship of bishops than with what persons or factions they aligned themselves. Thus, he praises both Austrenus of Orléans and Arnulf of Metz as *beatissimus* in describing the former's aforementioned sheltering of Bertoald and the latter's collaborative effort with the Pippinids to undermine the Agilolfing magnate Chrodoald.[93] He similarly expresses approval of Cunibert of Cologne's political alliance with Pippin I.[94] On the other hand, he is explicit in his criticism of Leudemund of Sion for opposing Neustrian rule in Burgundy and implicit in his description of Bishops Palladius and Sidoc of Eauze's exile for encouraging the Basques to revolt against Chlothar II.[95] These cases, and others, suggest that the chronicler was generally sympathetic

---

91. The chronicler, of course, utilized the six-book version of the *Decem Libri Historiarum*, on which see Reimitz, *History, Frankish Identity*, 133–59, who suggests that the elimination of chapters on ecclesiastical subjects does not necessarily constitute a "secularization" of the work.

92. See Halfond, "Endorsement of Royal-Episcopal Collaboration," which identifies twenty-one occasions on which the Fredegar chronicler refers explicitly to the active involvement of a bishop in the affairs of the court.

93. Fredegar, *Chronica* 4.25, 4.52. In 4.53, the chronicler similarly praises Arnulf's *sanctitas* in reference to the bishop's peacemaking efforts between Chlothar and Dagobert I.

94. Fredegar, *Chronica* 4.85.

95. Fredegar, *Chronica* 4.43, 4.54.

to political partisanship in support of Chlothar, and to a lesser extent his son Dagobert I, as well as the Pippinids. Additionally, as a general rule, the chronicler is sympathetic toward the Burgundaefarones, with whom, he claims, the bishops of Burgundy plotted the elimination of Brunhild's line.[96]

The comparatively limited references to prelates in the *Liber historiae Francorum* similarly are suggestive of the anonymous author's views on episcopal participation in court politics. The chronicler, for example, describes Leudegar of Autun as *beatus* and as a *sanctus episcopus* in the context of that bishop's expression of support for the appointment of Leudesius as the new Neustrian mayor following the murder of Childeric II.[97] In the same chapter, however, the chronicler describes Audoin of Rouen as *beatus* in reference to the latter's providing of counsel to Ebroin, who ordered Leudegar's martyrdom.[98] While seemingly contradictory positions considering the two bishops' differing factional loyalties, Richard Gerberding has noted both the chronicler's comparatively "neutral" treatment of Ebroin (particularly in comparison to his depiction in the *Passio Leudegarii*) and his selective interest in the political effects of episcopal holiness.[99] The chronicler recognized the two bishops not simply as holy men but also as the scions of important Neustrian families (i.e., the Franci) active in the governance of the regnum, who nevertheless engaged in the factional politics that consumed the court in these years. For the chronicler, and, indeed, for Audoin and Leudegar themselves, these were not mutually exclusive categories.

Turning from historiography to hagiography, Jamie Kreiner has shown that the later Merovingian *vitae* should be read as exemplary texts intended to articulate not simply spiritual principles but also social and political values. These values included, she argues, the responsibility of bishops for both modeling and counseling the Merovingians to embrace the promotion and defense of the public welfare. Kreiner suggests that by the late Merovingian era "the integrity of the kingdom was becoming the ultimate measure of bishops' pastoral efficacy."[100] Like the aforementioned mixed assemblies, this notion subsequently was taken up by the Carolingians, with whom it generally is more closely associated. While, as Kreiner acknowledges, there is no reason to think that all (or even most) bishops managed to embody the values articulated by hagiographers, it nevertheless is significant that the aristocratic audience for whom the hagiographies were composed shared an assumption of

---

96. Halfond, "Endorsement of Royal-Episcopal Collaboration," 10–12.
97. *Liber historiae Francorum* chap. 45.
98. *Liber historiae Francorum* chaps. 42, 45, 47.
99. Gerberding, *Rise of the Carolingians*, 73–74, 84.
100. Kreiner, *Social Life of Hagiography*, 182 (whole discussion: 156–88).

episcopal responsibility for the assurance of effective royal governance. Bishops shared a corporate responsibility to participate actively in the court; their attendance was not simply an unintentional consequence of the social prominence of individual members of the *ordo*.[101] This was, in many ways, an echo of Gregory of Tours's own deeply held belief in episcopal public service as a social and political virtue, but generalized for a wider aristocratic milieu.

In short, over the course of the seventh and eighth centuries, the political engagement of the Gallo-Frankish episcopate was consistently validated, if not expanded. Yet this engagement frequently came at the expense of the corporate integrity of the episcopal order, due to individual bishops offering service to myriad, and often competing, parties. And while episcopal participation in partisan politics rarely produced permanent fissures, its short-term effects in particular could be quite significant, even traumatic. The following chapter will explore this phenomenon through specific case studies of the partisan activities of individual bishops during decisive moments of political transformation.

---

101. Cf. Laury Sarti, *Perceiving War and the Military in Early Christian Gaul* (Leiden: Brill, 2013), 307–12, who prioritizes familial links between bishops and lay aristocrats as an explanation for the "apparent commonness" between the two groups in the sixth and seventh centuries.

CHAPTER 4

Disunity in Unity
Territorial Integration and Its Effects

The transitory nature of those fractures within the Gallo-Frankish episcopate triggered by interregnal conflicts or aristocratic factionalism necessitates examining specific moments when these ruptures in fraternal consensus emerged in order to gauge their severity and consequences. The three case studies examined in this chapter have been selected not simply because of the availability of prosopographical information on the participants but also because they occurred at crucial junctures in the history of the *regnum Francorum*: its expansion under Clovis I at the turn of the sixth century, its reunification under Chlothar II at the beginning of the seventh, and the transformative era of Pippin II, whose descendants would supplant the Merovingians they formerly had served. In other words, these are ostensible periods of political unification, when conflict and factionalism might be less expected than in eras of civil war, such as during the reigns of the sons of Chlothar I. But these political realignments, in their own way, could be nearly as disruptive as periods of declared *bellum civile*, and equally encouraging of aristocratic factionalizing. Due to their distinctiveness, they cannot be said to represent the "status quo" in the *regnum Francorum*; rather, they demonstrate the transformative and often divisive impact of political change on the episcopate.

The Age of Clovis I

The military campaigns of Clovis I resulted not simply in the incorporation of dozens of episcopal sees into his expansionary regnum but also in the effective foundation of a "Frankish" church in Gaul. This was a national church not necessarily in the traditional sense of a *Landeskirche* or *Reichskirche* but rather as a composite of institutions and officeholders that shared a common attachment to a royal regime, which in return offered patronage and protection.[1] While the Council of Orléans (511) in many ways marked the culmination of this achievement, Clovis's efforts to cultivate episcopal allies very likely stretched back to the earliest years of his reign, before his conversion to Catholic Christianity.

Contemporary sources, admittedly, are relatively silent regarding the episcopal response to Clovis's overtures, which ultimately had major implications for the administration of their churches. As William Daly emphasized in the mid-1990s, contemporary (or even near-contemporary) documentary evidence for the reign of Clovis I is extremely limited, comprising roughly a dozen epistles written to, by, or about the king, the *Vita Genovefae*, and the acts of the First Council of Orléans (511).[2] These sources may be supplemented with caution by noncontemporary historical and hagiographical narratives, as well as by material evidence, but collectively constitute the most important, if necessarily fragmentary, sources for Clovis's ecclesiastical policies.[3] Among these, the *Vita Genovefae* has relatively little to say of direct relevance to contemporary relations between the Frankish king and the episcopal *ordo*, so it is to the letters and the conciliar acts that we must necessarily turn for insight into the Gallic bishops' responses to Clovis's campaigns and ecclesiastical policy.[4]

---

1. Cf., for example, Edgar Loening, *Geschichte des deutschen Kirchenrechts* (Strasbourg: Verlag Karl J. Trübner, 1878), 2:130, who credits the Merovingians with "creating" a *Landeskirche*, whose unity conformed to, and indeed was predicated on, royal borders. The characterization of the Gallo-Frankish church I offer in the introduction, in contrast, suggests an identity informed both by royal borders and by a preexisting attachment to a universal *ecclesia*.

2. Daly, "Clovis: How Barbarian, How Pagan?," 625. Regarding the *Pactus legis Salicae*, one would do well to recall the warning of Murray, "Merovingian State," 196–97: "The code is early: the first decades of the 6th century for the earliest redaction is a harmless, unobjectionable conjecture. The common scholarly assumption that Clovis issued it is something else. . . . Clovis is a possible candidate as its author (or instigator) but that is hardly grounds for the firm attributions that appear over and over again in modern scholarship." See also chapter 2, n. 134 for additional references.

3. The most significant nonliterary source for Clovis's reign is, of course, the grave of his father, Childeric, on which see Halsall, "Childeric's Grave," who dates the burial to sometime between 474 and 500.

4. Nevertheless, if one follows Genovefa's hagiographer in recognizing her as "bishoplike," then her encounters with the Merovingian dynasty may at least offer parallels with the latter's relations

The earliest of the epistles, Remigius of Rheims's first letter to Clovis, likely was written at a time when the Merovingian regnum was restricted to Belgica Secunda and did not include even the entirety of the province.[5] Clovis's first major military campaign, for instance, was directed against Syagrius, the self-styled *rex* of Soissons (486), and Belgica also was home to Clovis's Frankish ally in the Syagrian campaign, Ragnachar of Cambrai, and probably to the Frankish *rex* Chararic as well.[6] As discussed in chapter 1, Remigius's congratulatory epistle encouraged the young king to include episcopal voices among those whose counsel he solicited. While not necessarily constituting an "ultimatum" to the king, Remigius's advice certainly was couched in the awareness that Clovis could benefit from the local assistance offered by himself and his episcopal colleagues.[7] But the full extent to which Clovis took this advice to heart during the first decade of his reign is nearly impossible to gauge beyond the maintenance of a relationship with Remigius, which likely included generous gifts of property in the province.[8]

A century later, Gregory of Tours would write of Clovis's troops pillaging the *ecclesiae* of Belgica Secunda following the successful war with Syagrius.[9] But Gregory's account consciously foreshadows the king's eventual conversion, with explicit emphasis placed both on Clovis's paganism and on his willingness to accede to an episcopal request for the return of the famous "vase of Soissons."[10] Such a literary construct unfortunately offers minimal insight into Clovis's actual relationships with the bishops of annexed cities in the

---

with ordained bishops. See Lisa Bitel, *Landscape with Two Saints* (Oxford: Oxford University Press, 2009), 51–71. See also n. 24 of this chapter for examples.

5. See chapter 1, n. 20, on the dating of the epistle.

6. On the Syagrian campaign, see Bachrach, *Merovingian Military Organization*, 3–5. On Clovis's subsequent conflicts with Chararic and Ragnachar, see Gregory of Tours, *Decem libri historiarum* 2.41–42.

7. Yitzhak Hen, "The Church in Sixth Century Gaul," in Murray, *Companion to Gregory of Tours*, 232–55, at 237.

8. See the litany of over a dozen properties compiled by Delgado, "The *Grand Testamentum* of Remigius of Reims," 131. But see also the cautionary note above (chapter 2, n. 120).

9. Gregory of Tours, *Decem libri historiarum* 2.27: "Eo tempore multae aeclesiae a Chlodovecho exercitu depraedatae sunt, quia erat ille adhuc fanaticis erroribus involutus." While Gregory's account seems to place these events within Soissons itself, Fredegar, *Chronica* 3.16, unconvincingly relocates the famous seizure of a vase to Rheims. Cf. Jane Woodruff, "The *Historia Epitomata* (Third Book) of the Chronicle of Fredegar: An Annotated Translation and Historical Analysis of Interpolated Material" (PhD diss., University of Nebraska, 1987), 122–23; and Gerald Schwedler, "'Lethe and 'Delete'—Discarding the Past in the Early Middle Ages: The Case of Fredegar," in *Collector's Knowledge: What Is Kept, What Is Discarded*, ed. Ania-Silvia Goeing, Anthony T. Grafton, and Paul Michel (Leiden: Brill, 2013), 71–96, at 88. On the size of Syagrius's regnum, see the cautionary remarks of James, *Franks*, 70–71.

10. Becher, *Chlodwig I*, 161. Cf. David Jäger, *Plündern in Gallien 451–592: Eine Studie zu der Relevanz einer Praktik für das Organisieren von Folgeleistungen* (Berlin: De Gruyter, 2017), 241–46, for an alternative reading suggesting an effort by Gregory to craft a narrative with contemporary resonance.

former Syagrian realm. But regardless of the dubiousness of this particular account, it is by no means inconceivable that Clovis allowed the pillaging of churches at the same time that he was making diplomatic gestures to local prelates.[11]

Much of the difficulty in reconstructing Clovis's relationships with the bishops of Belgica Secunda lies in the paucity of evidence for the state of the provincial church of the 480s. Remigius's letter implies a well-staffed provincial episcopacy, and noncontemporary hagiographical sources credit Remigius himself with ensuring the occupancies of suffragan sees.[12] It certainly would be unwise to assume that all those *civitates* unrepresented at the First Council of Orléans nearly thirty years later were unoccupied at the time Remigius composed his epistle, as the still-living Remigius himself was absent from the synod. In general, those bishops from Belgica Secunda who were in attendance at Orléans seem to have been more recent appointees.[13] Indisputably occupied circa 480 was the episcopal see of Soissons, held by Principius, called "meus frater" by Remigius in his testament and usually assumed—following Hincmar's *vita*—to be a blood relation of the bishop of Rheims.[14] The episcopal list of Châlons-sur-Marne similarly does not suggest any significant breaks in occupancy during this period, despite a lack of biographical information on the probable occupants.[15] For the bulk of *civitates*, however, there is no strong evidence to suggest either continuous occupancy or vacancy. Nevertheless, in light of Remigius's comments in his letter, the former possibility is probably to be preferred, if not necessarily for each and every see. In all likelihood, Clovis assumed royal power in an ecclesiastical province with a functioning metropolitan government.

The subsequent expansion of Clovis's regnum was rapid, but only rarely was he able to bring entire provinces under his control as the result of single decisive campaigns. So, while he dominated most of Belgica Secunda by the

---

11. On the plundering of churches, see Miriam Czock, "*Wo gesündigt wird, kann der Sieg nicht gewonnen werden*: Plünderung von Kirchen im Krieg in den Werken Gregors von Tours (538–594)," in *Blick auf das Mittelalter: Aspekte von Lebenswelt, Herrschaft, Religion und Rezeption*, ed. Bodo Gundelach and Ralf Molkenthin (Herne, Germany: Gabriele Schäfer Verlag, 2004), 13–23; Laury Sarti, "The Military, the Clergy, and Christian Faith in Sixth-Century Gaul," *Early Medieval Europe* 25, no. 2 (2017): 162–85, at 172–77; and Jäger, *Plündern in Gallien*.

12. *Vita Vedastis episcopi Atrebatensis*, ed. Bruno Krusch, MGH SRM 3 (Hanover, Germany: Hahn, 1896), chap. 5 (seventh century); Hincmar of Rheims, *Vita Remigii episcopi Remensis*, ed. Bruno Krusch, MGH SRM 3 (Hanover, Germany: Hahn, 1896), chap. 16 (ninth century).

13. Halfond, "Vouillé," 157.

14. Remigius, *Testamentum* 336–37; Hincmar of Rheims, *Vita Remigii* chap. 1; Martin Heinzelmann, "Gallische Prosopographie (260–527)," *Francia* 10 (1982): 531–718, at 673 (Principius 2).

15. Duchesne, *Fastes épiscopaux de l'ancienne Gaule*, 3:93–96. Five bishops are attested between 461 and 535.

early 490s, he only took Cambrai after his defeat of the Visigoths in 507.[16] It also is unclear when Clovis brought the entirety of Belgica Prima under his control, or what role a siege of Verdun (ca. 486/87?), reported by a ninth-century *vita*, played in this process.[17] Sixth-century sources are similarly elusive about the annexation of Armorica, although it appears that this, too, seemingly required multiple military and diplomatic initiatives.[18] Even Clovis's famous victory at Zülpich (496/97) over the Alamanni, with whom he fought a second war circa 505/6, did not result immediately in a complete annexation of Alamannia.[19] This gradualist approach necessitated on Clovis's part not only patience and discretion but also judicious overtures toward potential allies. Nevertheless, while efforts have been made to piece together a precise military chronology of Clovis's campaigns between the Syagrian War of 486 and the Battle of Vouillé of 507, such efforts have necessarily been tentative and patchwork.[20] Equally controversial is the precise date of Clovis's baptism, traditionally assigned to the year 496 but more recently argued to have occurred as late as circa 508/9, and possibly preceded by a brief spell in which Clovis was an Arian Christian.[21]

But whatever his precise denominational state, it is likely that Clovis continued to make gestures toward the bishops of occupied and conquered cities into the 490s as a part of his broader diplomatic efforts to secure local allies. Writing more than half a century after the events described, Nicetius of Trier claimed in an epistle to the Lombard queen Chlodoswintha that a still-unbaptized Clovis paid homage to Saint Martin at his tomb in Tours sometime before the Battle of Vouillé. While no doubt this gesture was welcomed by the guardians of Martin's tomb, it in no way ensured the king's ability to hold on to Tours, which returned shortly thereafter to Visigothic rule.[22]

---

16. Gregory of Tours, *Decem libri historiarum* 2.42.

17. See Gauthier, *L'évangélisation*, 149–51, on Bertholdus, *Vita Maximini abbatis Miciacensis*, ed. Luc d'Achéry and Jean Mabillon, AASS OSB 1 (Paris: Louis Billaine, 1668), chaps. 3–6, likely the earliest version of the life. On the hagiographical tradition of Micy, see also Thomas Head, *Hagiography and the Cult of Saints: The Diocese of Orléans, 800–1200* (Cambridge: Cambridge University Press, 1990).

18. Bernard S. Bachrach, "Procopius and the Chronology of Clovis's Reign," *Viator* 1 (1970): 21–31.

19. John F. Drinkwater, *The Alamanni and Rome, 313–496: Caracalla to Clovis* (Oxford: Oxford University Press, 2007), 335–46.

20. See, e.g., Bachrach, "Procopius"; Ralph Mathisen, "The First Franco-Visigothic War and the Prelude to the Battle of Vouillé," in Mathisen and Shanzer, *Battle of Vouillé*, 3–9.

21. Shanzer, "Dating the Baptism of Clovis"; Ian Wood, "Gregory of Tours and Clovis," *Revue belge de philologie et d'histoire* 63 (1985): 249–72; Shanzer and Wood, *Avitus of Vienne*, 362–69. For the historiography of the debate over dating, see also Mark Spencer, "Dating the Baptism of Clovis, 1886–1993," *Early Medieval Europe* 3, no. 2 (1994): 97–116.

22. *Epistolae Austrasicae* no. 8 (119–22). On this letter, see Mathisen, "First Franco-Visigothic War," 4–5.

Additionally, Avitus of Vienne's letter of congratulations to Clovis, written on the occasion of the latter's baptism, notes the presence of "numerous" bishops at the event and offers a strong hint that invitations had been sent to prelates beyond the borders of the Frankish regnum, including possibly to Avitus himself. The epistle thus suggests that Remigius was not the only prelate with whom Clovis maintained friendly relations in these years.[23] While it seems probable that some element of political strategizing underlay Clovis's identification of episcopal contacts, the aforementioned accounts do not permit a more precise dissection of his diplomatic overtures.[24]

It is only during the Visigothic campaign and its aftermath (507–11) that surer and more substantial evidence for Clovis's cultivation of episcopal partnerships can be found. It is to this period that Clovis's lone surviving epistle dates, as well as the acts of the Council of Orléans (511), which assembled at the king's request. The epistle is addressed generally to the bishops of the Visigothic regnum, usually assumed to be those residing in Aquitaine, where the fighting took place. It is not impossible, however, that Clovis originally addressed his letter to all of the bishops of the Visigothic kingdom, including those occupying Provençal sees, if the extent of the Frankish victory was not yet clear. Regardless, Clovis does not name any individual addressees and claims in the epistle merely to be repeating orders given to his army before the commencement of hostilities regarding the unjust seizure of ecclesiastical property and dependents. Clovis's delineation of the procedures by which prelates could request the return of lay and ecclesiastical captives is a reminder that even at this late date—either after or on the eve of the king's own baptism—Clovis assumed that his military campaigns would necessarily entail the pillaging of church property. This adds some useful perspective on the alleged actions of his soldiers in Belgica Secunda following the conclusion of the Syagrian campaign.

Although the First Council of Orléans assembled four years after the Battle of Vouillé, its convocation should be understood—as argued in chapter 1—as a response to Clovis's recent victory. The council's *acta*, in fact, provide the most substantial evidence for the king's ecclesiastical policies during that brief interim. First of all, they suggest that considerable advance planning preceded the meeting itself. The Council of Orléans assembled in July 511, a relatively unusual month for Gallic conciliar gatherings due to the heat of summer.[25]

---

23. Avitus of Vienne, *Opera* ep. 46. See also Shanzer and Wood, *Avitus of Vienne*, 366.
24. We might also consider in this context Clovis's positive response to the petitions of Genovefa of Paris: *Vita Genovefae virginis Parisiensis*, ed. Bruno Krusch, MGH SRM 3 (Hanover, Germany: Hahn, 1896), chap. 56. See also chap. 26 on Childeric's earlier receptivity to the saint's *petitiones*.
25. Halfond, *Archaeology*, 263–64.

Although the council's location seems to have been selected in part for its geographical centrality, several of the thirty-two episcopal attendees had considerable journeys to and from the council. Bishop Lupus of Soissons, for instance, had to travel 215 kilometers as the crow flies in each direction. Assuming that the bishop was able to cover approximately 30 kilometers per day, it would have taken between seven and eight days for him to reach Orléans from his home city.[26] Additionally, Clovis's convocation letter also would have required time—albeit of indeterminate duration—to make its way to Soissons, particularly if the messenger made multiple stops along the way.[27] Presumably Clovis also allowed Lupus some time following his receipt of an invitation to make his preparations, assemble an entourage, and settle affairs at home before setting out. So, while it is impossible to say precisely how much time elapsed between the king's posting of a convocation letter and the arrival of the bishop of Soissons at the council, it is quite conceivable that this was a period of at least several months.

This rough estimate does not even take into account any planning that may have preceded the formal convocation of the synod. This planning may have been complicated by ongoing hostilities with the Ostrogoths following Vouillé. Clovis's inability to annex the entirety of Aquitaine limited the participation of bishops from the region. Indeed, the extent of Frankish expansion to the south effectively determined which bishops from Aquitaine were able to attend the council. Thus, the majority of prelates from Novempopulana were absent, as was the entirety of the Septimanian episcopate, whose province remained under Visigothic rule. The only significant absences of Aquitanian bishops from the council that cannot obviously be explained by recent military activity, restrictive political borders, or vacant sees are those of Agen and Limoges.[28] In the case of the former, not only was this same see unrepresented at the early Council of Agde (506), no named bishops even can be identified securely for this period. Ruricius of Limoges, who also was absent from the Council of Agde, was alive in 511, but he may once again have cited poor health for his absenteeism.[29]

---

26. On travel time, see chapter 2, n. 85.

27. On the continued significance of the *cursus publicus* for travel in Merovingian Gaul, see Erik Holmberg, *Zur Geschichte des Cursus Publicus* (Uppsala, Sweden: A. B. Lundequistska Bokhandeln, 1933), 148; and Stéphane Lebecq, "Entre antique tardive et très Haut Moyen Age: Permanence et mutations des systèmes de communications dans la Gaule et ses marges," in *Morfologie sociali e culturali in Europa fra tarda Antichita e alto Medioevo* (Spoleto, Italy: Centro Italiano di Studi sull'Alto Medioevo, 1998), 461–502, at 472–73.

28. Halfond, "Vouillé," 155.

29. Ralph Mathisen, trans., *Ruricius of Limoges and Friends: A Collection of Letters from Visigothic Gaul* (Liverpool: Liverpool University Press, 1999), 44.

While comparatively more bishops—a total of sixteen—represented the Lyonnaise provinces (Secunda, Tertia, and Senonia) at the council, there still were absences both explicable (e.g., unoccupied sees or those within the border of another regnum) and inexplicable. The order of episcopal subscriptions in the acts strongly suggests that collectively these northern bishops assumed office more recently than their Aquitanian counterparts, but whether Clovis himself played a substantial role in filling these seats is impossible to say.[30] Remigius's response to the critics of his ordination of Claudius alludes to Clovis's sponsorship of their own episcopal candidacies. But whether Clovis played a role in some or all three elections is not clear from Remigius's epistle, so we should be cautious in extrapolating too much about Clovis's personal attention to the filling of vacant sees in the Lyonnaise provinces.[31]

But arguably as significant as any possible royal involvement in episcopal elections was the inclusion of a significant number of relatively "junior" bishops in the deliberations at Orléans, whose tenure closely coincided chronologically with Frankish dominance of northern Gaul. Unlike their more seasoned Aquitanian counterparts, these bishops had comparatively less experience governing their dioceses under any other political regime and thus may have found acculturation into a Frankish-dominated ecclesiastical organization an easier transition. This did not necessarily ensure their pliancy at Clovis's council or other occasions requiring them to respond to the royal agenda toward the church. They governed their sees, however, with the reasonable expectation that they would live out the entirety of their tenures under Frankish rule.

The most difficult to explain absences from the council are those of the Belgian bishops, most notably that of Remigius himself. As previously noted, the location of the names of prelates from Belgica Secunda among the episcopal subscriptions in the conciliar acts suggests that those in attendance did not rank high in seniority compared to their colleagues. It is possible that distance

---

30. That the bishops largely subscribed to the acts in rank order as determined by longevity in office (with the metropolitans subscribing first) can be seen through a comparison with those subscriptions appended to the acts of the Council of Agde (506). The six bishops who subscribed to both sets of acts signed their names in the same order, with only one exception: Nicetius of Auch signed his name before Cronopius of Périgueux at Agde, but after him at Orléans. While Cronopius also signed after Lupicinus of Angoulême at both Orléans 511 and 533, the subscriptions attached to the acts of the latter council do not follow a strict order of rank; on this, see Pontal, *Histoire des conciles mérovingiens*, 103. It also should be noted that an exception to the rank order preserved in Paris Lat. 12097 is the subscription of Eufrasius of Clermont (ordained ca. 490) immediately before that of Camillianus of Troyes (ordained ca. 479); see Pietri and Heijmans, *Prosopographie de la Gaule chrétienne*, 415 and 665–67.

31. *Epistolae Austrasicae* no. 3 (113–14): "Tanto in me prorupistis felle commoti, ut nec episcopatus vestri detuleritis auctori."

prevented some of the prelates from this province from attending, or perhaps ill health. Less likely, as already suggested, was widespread vacancy in episcopal sees. While vacancies seem to have been more common in contemporary Germania Prima and Secunda, these do not appear to have been as widespread a phenomenon in the Belgian provinces, despite the total absence of bishops from Belgica Prima from the council.[32]

A similarly unlikely explanation for the lack of episcopal representation from Belgica Prima specifically is a "boycott" by northern ascetics of Clovis's ecclesiastical policies, which they saw as threatening to the *pax ecclesiae*.[33] This latter hypothesis is based on sparse, and mostly noncontemporary, evidence from three cities: Trier, Toul, and Verdun. The refusal of the hermit Goar of the episcopal see of Trier is described in the eighth-century *Vita Goaris*, which dates the incident to the reign of Sigibert and thus offers little evidence for ascetic traditions fifty years earlier.[34] In the case of Toul, a hypothesized eremitic retreat by Bishop Aper (or Epvre) has been proposed to explain his epithet of "confessor" and the decision not to inter his body in an existing episcopal necropolis.[35] His tenure cannot be securely dated, however, to the reign of Clovis. Aper's predecessor, Ursus, purportedly held office at the time Clovis defeated the Alamanni in 496, while his successor, Alodius, attended the Council of Orléans (549).[36] In the case of Verdun, it has been suggested that, following the death of Bishop Firminus, there was a break in succession due to a refusal by the presbyter Euspicius to take the episcopal seat offered to him by Clovis. This story comes from Bertarius's tenth-century *Gesta episcoporum Virdunensium*, which states that upon Euspicius's refusal, the seat went to his *nepos* Vito.[37] However, *nepos* could mean either nephew or grandson, and the *Gesta*, which was drawing from a dubious historical tradition associated with the monastery of Micy, does not indicate a delay in ordination.[38] In short, there is no reason to think that the bishops of Belgica Prima collectively

---

32. Halfond, "Vouillé," 156n26; Weidemann, "Die kirchliche Organisation der Provinzen Belgica und Germania," 291, 312 (map). Weidemann also suggests comparatively more contemporary diocesan vacancies in Lugdunensis Secunda. On Belgica Prima, cf. Godefroid Kurth, *Clovis* (Paris: Retaux, 1901), 2:140–41. For the episcopal lists of Belgica Prima, see Duchesne, *Fastes Épiscopaux de l'ancienne Gaule*, 3:32–33, 37–38 (Trier); 3:46–47, 54–55 (Metz); 3:61–63 (Toul); 3:68–70 (Verdun).
33. Heuclin, "Le Concile d'Orléans de 511," 1:439.
34. *Vita Goaris confessoris Rhenani*, cc. 7–11.
35. Gauthier, *L'évangélisation*, 230–31.
36. Gauthier, 153, 230. On the hagiographical tradition surrounding Aper, see Monique Goullet, "Les saints du diocèse de Toul," in Heinzelmann, *L'hagiographie*, 11–89, at 27–42.
37. Bertarius, *Gesta episcoporum Virdunensium*, ed. D. G. Waitz, MGH SS 4 (Hanover, Germany: Hahn, 1841), chap. 4.
38. Gauthier, *L'évangélisation*, 150–51, 221–22.

boycotted the Council of Orléans due to either their ascetic inclinations or any misgivings about Clovis's ecclesiastical policies.

The simplest, if perhaps somewhat counterintuitive, explanation for the absence of so many Belgian prelates from Orléans is that they were not invited or strongly encouraged to attend in the first place. As we have seen, the attendance of the Council of Orléans essentially consisted of three major groups of bishops: (1) a small number (four) of relatively junior bishops from Belgica Secunda; (2) a larger number (sixteen) of mostly junior bishops from the Lyonnaise provinces; and (3) a significant number (twelve) of comparatively senior bishops from recently annexed *civitates* in Aquitaine. What all three groups shared, of course, was a lack of lengthy tenure under Frankish rule. This was partly a reflection of the relative immediacy of Clovis's conquests in Gaul, but the absence of Remigius and other northern bishops living under Frankish rule suggests a conscious intent underlying the council's attendance. If the council did embody a "concordance" between the Gallic church and the Merovingians, it was a concordance with limited and specific intent, at least on Clovis's part: to acculturate bishops unfamiliar with his rule into an expanded *regnum Francorum*.[39] Clovis's decision to assign the Council of Orléans's presidency to Cyprian of Bordeaux, with whom the king likely became acquainted no later than winter 507/8, was not necessarily a slight against Remigius of Rheims.[40] Rather, it was an implicit acknowledgment of both the more recent and substantive conciliar activity of the southern prelates (Cyprian himself had attended the Council of Agde several years earlier) and Cyprian's presumed willingness, as a bishop new to Frankish rule, to facilitate a synodal agenda on behalf of Clovis.[41]

Irrespective of the likelihood that those bishops in attendance at Orléans participated partly out of a sense of compulsory obligation to their monarch, their presence had advantages beyond an opportunity to articulate a collaborative legislative agenda with the king. For the majority of attendees, the council was likely their first significant opportunity to act in concert with nonprovincial colleagues. The *acta* of the Council of Orléans constitute the first articulation of the common corporate voice of the Gallic episcopal *ordo* within

---

39. Halfond, "Vouillé," 154–58. Becher, *Chlodwig I*, 249–50, proposes two additional—but ultimately not demonstrable—hypotheses in regard to the absence of some northern prelates: (1) the creation of a northern subregnum by Clovis for his son Theuderic; and (2) disorder caused by Clovis extending his authority over other Frankish peoples. Nathan J. Ristuccia, *Christianization and Commonwealth in Early Medieval Europe* (Oxford: Oxford University Press, 2018), 33, goes so far as to suggest a specifically royal interest in standardizing liturgical practice—i.e., Rogationtide—via conciliar legislation.

40. Kurth, *Clovis*, 2:136; Becher, *Chlodwig I*, 248–49.

41. Halfond, "Vouillé," 160.

an expanded Frankish kingdom. While the ecclesiastical administration supervised by this order did not at this time, of course, align perfectly with the *Notitia Galliarum*—not least of all because of the political borders that still divided the *regnum Francorum* from the rest of Gaul—its representative breadth in geographic terms extended significantly beyond that of the Council of Agde. The Council of Orléans offered a forum for the thirty-two bishops in attendance to assert not only a corporate identity but also the supervisory authority of their common order over an ecclesiastical federation stretching from Belgica to Novempopulana. The "Gallo-Frankish church," from the perspective of these prelates, may have constituted not so much an awkward realignment of ecclesiastical provinces within secular borders but rather a veritable revival of Gallic episcopal corporatism.

This spirit of solidarity, however, may well have proved challenging to maintain once the council concluded its business, partly in consequence of individual prelates needing to negotiate their own relationships with the royal regime. This is suggested by Remigius's subsequent quarrel with the bishops of Paris, Sens, and Auxerre. Both Heraclius of Paris and Theodosius of Auxerre had attended the Council of Orléans (Leo of Sens was absent), but otherwise their personal relations with Clovis are unknown. That Clovis chose Paris as his political capital following Vouillé alone is not strong evidence for an intimate relationship between Heraclius and the king. In Remigius's defensive response to his accuser's claims that he had been bribed to ordain the priest Claudius, he stated that he had performed the rite on Clovis's orders. Clovis also would seem to be the implicit subject of the quoted sentence from the accusers' original letter: "Canonicum non fuisse, quod iussit" (What he [Clovis] ordered was not canonical).⁴² In other words, Remigius's response seems to imply that the original accusation against him was that he took bribes from the king to ordain unqualified applicants as presbyters. In contrast, it seems unlikely that Remigius's accusers were upset by either Claudius's prior lay status or Clovis's sponsoring his clerical ordination, as both Heraclius and Theodosius, only a short time earlier, had consented to a canon promulgated at Orléans that stated, "No layman may assume clerical office without the permission of the king or without the consent of an *iudex*."⁴³

While Clovis's death explains the willingness of Remigius's accusers to criticize the former king's actions, more difficult to explain is their bile toward the bishop of Rheims. It is possible, of course, that it was merely the latter's

---

42. *Epistolae Austrasicae* no. 3 (113–14).
43. Council of Orléans (511), c. 4: "Ut nullus saecularium ad clericatus officium praesumatur nisi aut cum regis iussione aut cum iudicis voluntate." Cf. Rouche, *Clovis*, 458–59.

presumed corruptibility that was at issue, but why should the bishops of Lugdunensis Senonia be so incensed at the metropolitan of Belgica Secunda, with whom they had not even had occasion to collaborate in council? There are several possibilities suggested by the letter. One is that Claudius held clerical office in Lugdunensis Senonia. Remigius's assumption that his episcopal colleagues would determine Claudius's punishment might be cited in support of this possibility. Thus, following Claudius's apparent theft of property from the otherwise unknown Celsus, he (Claudius) fled to Remigius, who then sheltered him from the harsh sentences threatened by the Lyonnais prelates and advocated on his behalf ("Nam pro Claudio fudi simplicem precem, quem vos non presbyterum scribitis, ut in me indignationem vestri pectoris proderitis").

A second possibility is that Claudius held office in Remigius's own province of Belgica Secunda, but Celsus (and perhaps other "victims" of Claudius) resided in Lugdunensis Senonia. This might explain Remigius's apparent bewilderment that he should be expected to know Celsus's whereabouts or even whether he was still living, while also accounting for the role of Remigius in Claudius's ordination. Unfortunately, the lack of any additional information on the majority of major players in this incident prevents us from choosing confidently between these two possibilities, although I lean slightly toward the former.

But whatever the case may be, Remigius's accusers also may well have been resentful of the leeway granted to the metropolitan bishop of Rheims by Clovis. Their essential accusation, of course, was that Remigius allowed royal patronage—or, as they preferred, bribery—to improperly influence his decision to ordain a candidate for the priesthood. This special relationship between Clovis and Remigius might very well have irked the latter's episcopal contemporaries, particularly if it infringed on their own administrative jurisdiction, as may well have been the case in this particular instance. As Remigius's dispute with Falco of Maastricht suggests, the bishop of Rheims was not reticent about exerting his influence beyond his own province when he believed it justified. In the case of Claudius's ordination, the opportunity of Clovis's recent death allowed bishops angered by Remigius's perceived abuses to attack the latter with impunity, in the process reminding him that his seniority mattered far less outside Belgica Secunda.

The impact of Clovis on episcopal solidarity in the Gallic church was not limited to Remigius's relationships with his episcopal peers. Although Clovis brought greater political unity to Gaul than it had experienced in the decades before his assumption of royal power, at his death the region was still divided among the Franks, Visigoths, Ostrogoths, and Burgundians. Just as Clovis's council of 511 was attended solely by bishops of the *regnum Francorum*, the episcopal attendance of those Gallic councils held in the twenty-five years after his death similarly was restricted by regnal borders. For example, there was no overlap in attendance between the Council of Orléans (511) and the Burgundian Council of Epaone six years later, although it is possible that the presiding metropolitans extended invitations to bishops whose *civitates* bordered the Burgundian regnum.[44] But these borders not only were impediments to travel; more significantly, they influenced the ways in which the Gallic bishops thought of their own corporate identity. Caesarius of Arles, for instance, failed to join many of his provincial colleagues at the Council of Orléans (541), or even to send a representative, which William Klingshirn has credited to the elderly bishop's realization that his see's primacy would not be recognized in any meaningful way within the expanded Frankish church.[45] Possibly more amenable to this new ecclesiastical union was Iulianus of Vienne, a relative of his predecessor Avitus, whose attendance at the Frankish Council of Orléans (533) would have preceded by one year the formal annexation of Burgundy.[46] But as the *subscriptiones* do not name his see, it is conceivable that the Iulianus who signed the acts should be associated with the contemporary bishop of Bigorre of the same name.[47] Nevertheless, an identification with the bishop of Vienne is probably the more likely, as there is no evidence that Bigorre was part of the *regnum Francorum* before 541. If this was the case, Iulianus's attendance at Orléans can be understood as a goodwill gesture toward the victorious Franks, as well as a recognition that his province was destined for integration into a Frankish *ecclesia*.

So, while Clovis's reign is, for understandable reasons, associated with political and ecclesiastical unity in Gaul, neither process was rapidly achieved or seamless. The Council of Orléans (511), from the safe perspective of hindsight, may have signified an origin point of an active ecclesiastical network within expanded Frankish political borders, but it was preceded and followed by continually shifting political borders that complicated any notions of a pan-Gallic episcopal corporate identity for contemporaries. And as Remigius's epistle to the Lyonnaise bishops suggests, even shared political allegiances did not necessarily ensure a smooth integration of bishops into a Gallo-Frankish church. And, not for the last time in Frankish Gaul, political considerations impacted

---

44. Pontal, *Histoire des conciles mérovingiens*, 64, 390–91 (map). On the possibility that Avitus of Vienne invited Quintianus of Clermont to attend Epaone, see Shanzer and Wood, *Avitus of Vienne*, 308.
45. Klingshirn, *Caesarius of Arles*, 258–60.
46. Heinzelmann, *Bischofsherrschaft in Gallien*, 222.
47. Pietri and Heijmans, *Prosopographie de la Gaule chrétienne*, 1079–81 (Iulianus 9, 11).

the cohesion of the episcopate, requiring or encouraging prelates in affected *civitates* to reorient themselves in response to political and military events and policies in which they often had little direct involvement.

Chlothar II and the Reunification of the *Regnum Francorum*

The unification of the Merovingian regna by Chlothar II, roughly a century after Clovis's death, would have struck most politically astute Franks of the 580s and 590s as a distinctly unlikely possibility. Not only were the Merovingian regna ruled during these years by a multiplicity of kings and queens regent, Neustria, following the death of Chilperic in 584, had lost considerable territory to rival kingdoms. But thanks in no small part to his mother's talent for maintaining aristocratic support during her regency, strategic missteps by his Austrasian and Burgundian rivals, his own political savvy, and simple good fortune, Chlothar found himself in 613 in a position that no Frankish king had enjoyed since his namesake, Chlothar I. Nevertheless, this moment of triumph took nearly thirty years to realize and would not have been conceivable without the consistent support of secular and ecclesiastical elites who recognized in Chlothar a vehicle for the realization of their own personal or familial agendas. In order to appreciate the significance of episcopal support during crucial junctures in Chlothar's political career, it is helpful to divide his reign into three major periods: the regency and collaborative rule of his mother, Fredegund (584–97), the decade and a half of conflict with Brunhild and her grandsons (597–613), and the years of Neustrian domination of the *regnum Francorum* (613–29). In each of the phases of the king's lengthy reign, he employed patronage—although not always successfully—as an instrument for soliciting episcopal support. While he achieved his political goal of ridding himself of long-standing Austrasian and Burgundian rivals, the administrative unity that he brought to the Frankish church proved tenuous, and ultimately fleeting.

Back in the early 580s, not simply Chlothar's political position but also his very life were under real threat in the aftermath of his father's death. Following the assassination of Chilperic I in 584, it was not even immediately obvious that the legitimacy of his ostensible heir would be recognized by his uncle Guntram and cousin Childebert II. This uncertainty seems to have encouraged the second attempt by a group of Austrasian and Neustrian magnates—which included a number of bishops—to establish a *regnum Gundovaldi* in Gaul, and it was the recognition of Chlothar's status by Guntram and the Neustrian elite that ultimately undermined the pretender's efforts.⁴⁸ Although Chlothar's position (and that of his mother) temporarily was secured, the Neustrian *regnum* lost considerable territory, being reduced initially to the *civitates* of Boulogne, Therouanne, Tournai, Arras, Amiens, Vermand-Noyon, Rouen, Beauvais, Coutances, Bayeux, Lisieux, Evreux, Rennes, Le Mans, Angers, and possibly Avranches.⁴⁹ This shrunken Neustrian *regnum*, the borders of which continued to fluctuate into the 590s, was ruled by Chlothar in collaboration with his mother, Fredegund, until her death in 597.

During these years, Fredegund strategically cultivated links with regional prelates, no doubt with the hope that their loyalties to Chlothar would persist beyond her own lifetime. Three anonymous bishops, for example, had accompanied the three hundred Neustrian *optimates* who swore an oath to Guntram in 585 that Chlothar was Chilperic's legitimate heir.⁵⁰ While it is unclear whether Gregory of Tours, our source for this information, personally had knowledge of the identities of these anonymous bishops, it is reasonable to suppose that their sees were located among the aforementioned *civitates*.⁵¹ An identifiable supporter of Chlothar in these early years of his reign was Bishop Bertram of Le Mans, who took office circa 586, following service as archdeacon of Paris under another loyalist of Chilperic, Ragnemodus. As discussed in chapter 2, Bertram's support for Chilperic's line led directly to his exile when Le Mans fell into the hands of Childebert II and Brunhild.⁵² Bertram only was able to recover his office when Le Mans returned to Neustrian rule in 596, at which time he was compensated by Fredegund and Chlothar with the gift of the villa of Bonnelles in Étampes.⁵³ Bertram's brothers, Bishops Ermenulfus of Evreux and Haimoaldus of Rennes, may well have shared Bertram's political loyalties during these years, although it is not possible to determine with absolute certainty whether they both already held episcopal seats during Fredegund's regency.⁵⁴

---

48. Walter Goffart, "The Frankish Pretender Gundovald, 582–585: A Crisis of Merovingian Blood," *Francia* 39 (2012): 1–27.

49. Bertram of Le Mans, *Das Testament*, 149–51.

50. Gregory of Tours, *Decem libri historiarum* 8.9.

51. To be sure, Fredegund still enjoyed episcopal support beyond the contracted borders of the Neustrian regnum. In 585, she purportedly employed Bishop Amelius of Bigorra-Tarbes as an envoy to Leuvigild of Spain, while two years later Palladius of Saintes was accused of similar secretive diplomatic work (Gregory of Tours, *Decem libri historiarum* 8.28, 8.43). Gregory is explicit, however, that those three bishops who traveled to Guntram's court to attest Chlothar's parentage came from cities inside Neustria.

52. Halfond, "Sis Quoque Catholicis Religionis Apex," 70–71.

53. Bertram of Le Mans, *Das Testament*, 8–9 (no. 1). Chlothar, following Fredegund's death, made many additional gifts to Bertram (86–88).

54. Bertram of Le Mans, *Das Testament*, 125–27. Both men held episcopal office by no later than 614; see Pietri and Heijmans, *Prosopographie de la Gaule chrétienne*, 644, 695. Judging solely on the basis

The only bishop of a *civitas* inherited by Chlothar upon his father's death whose loyalties are at all suspect is Leudovald of Bayeux. While Chilperic had still lived, circa 581, Leudovald served as a royal envoy, but five years later he protested the murder of Bishop Praetextatus of Rouen by Fredegund's agents by shuttering the churches of Bayeux.[55] Gregory of Tours reports that Fredegund, believing that Leudovald had ascertained her complicity in the assassination, attempted unsuccessfully to have the bishop killed.[56] Regardless of the veracity of this report, there are several reasons to suppose that any hostility between the queen and bishop subsequently was resolved: only one year later, Leudovald resumed his role as a Neustrian *nuntius*, traveling to Guntram's court to plea successfully for the release of the *legatus* Baddo, who had been accused—Gregory implies justly—of plotting the king of Burgundy's death.[57] Still in office in 614, Leudovald attended the Council of Paris, convoked on Chlothar's orders.[58] So, without necessarily doubting the veracity of Gregory of Tours's report, by the late 580s any ill will between Fredegund and Leudovald seems to have dissipated, and there is no evidence of any lingering animosity between the latter and Chlothar.[59]

While admittedly the evidence is sparse, there is no reason to conclude that there was significant episcopal opposition within Neustria to Fredegund or Chlothar during the years of the former's regency. Certainly, the posthumous demonization of Fredegund by Gregory of Tours cannot obscure the fact that both she and her husband had little difficulty attracting aristocratic or episcopal support during their lifetimes.[60] The Gundovald affair had provided these elites with the ideal opportunity to displace the Neustrian line, an opportunity that they chose not to take. Subsequent incursions into the Neustrian heartland by rival Merovingians similarly offered local elites the opportunity to realign themselves with more promising royal patrons. Yet the territory controlled by Fredegund circa 584 remained the solid foundation of her son's *regnum*, even when he lost significant territory to his familial rivals following his mother's death.[61] This rather surprising degree of regnal integrity may suggest a regional aristocracy generally unified in its political loyalties.

---

of the location of their names among the subscriptions attached to the acts of Paris (614), which admittedly do not follow a strict rank order among the suffragan bishops, Haimoaldus was senior in rank to his brother.

55. Gregory of Tours, *Decem libri historiarum* 6.3.
56. Gregory of Tours, *Decem libri historiarum* 8.31.
57. Gregory of Tours, *Decem libri historiarum* 8.44, 9.13.
58. Council of Paris (614), *subscriptiones*.
59. Halfond, "Sis Quoque Catholicis Religionis Apex," 59.
60. Halfond, "Sis Quoque Catholicis Religionis Apex."
61. Bertram of Le Mans, *Das Testament*, 160–67 (with maps).

Compared to the years of Fredegund's regency, we have more knowledge of Chlothar's ecclesiastical initiatives for the years between 597 and 613, thanks in no small part to the information supplied by seventh-century hagiographical sources including Jonas of Bobbio's *Vita Columbani*, as well as the Fredegar *Chronica*, the latter of which provides the most sustained narrative of Chlothar's political career. Fredegar generally approved of those episcopal officeholders who expressed a personal loyalty toward the king or who performed service on his behalf. This is in line with the chronicler's overall approval of Chlothar himself. Unlike Chlothar's son Dagobert, whose sins were believed by the chronicler to outweigh his more positive attributes, Chlothar himself is criticized only for his excessive interest in hunting and his faith in the counsel of women.[62] Conversely, Chlothar is praised for his generosity toward the church and its governors ("ecclesiarum et sacerdotum magnus muneratur").[63] The Fredegar chronicler's admiration for Chlothar probably was inherited in part from the prejudices of his sources, most notably the *Vita Columbani* and the Visigothic king Sisebut's *Vita Desiderii*, both of which incriminate Chlothar's old rivals Brunhild and Theuderic II.[64] Nevertheless, his generally positive assessment of the king also seems to have been a more personal reaction to Chlothar's favoritism toward those aristocratic factions preferred by the chronicler, such as the Austrasian Pippinids. Thus, when the chronicler describes Chlothar's relations with individual prelates, his descriptions are colored by these factional preferences, which generally supersede the chronicler's admiration for the king himself.

For example, as noted earlier, the chronicler praises the actions of the *beatissimus* Austrenus of Orléans, who welcomed into his city the Burgundian mayor Bertoald, following the latter's flight in 604 from the forces of Chlothar's son, Merovech, and the Neustrian mayor Landeric.[65] As suggested by this episode, the chronicler, who admired both Bertoald and Austrenus, recognized a common cause between members of the Burgundian aristocracy and the bishops. Thus, when the Burgundaefarones turned against Brunhild

---

62. Fredegar, *Chronica* 4.42. See also J. M. Wallace-Hadrill, *The Long-Haired Kings* (London: Methuen, 1962), 90–94; and Halfond, "Endorsement of Royal-Episcopal Collaboration," 11–12.

63. Fredegar, *Chronica* 4.42.

64. On the political biases of Fredegar's sources, see Ian Wood, "The *Vita Columbani* and Merovingian Hagiography," *Peritia* 1 (1982): 63–80, at 70–71; Jacques Fontaine, "King Sisebut's *Vita Desiderii* and the Political Function of Visigothic Hagiography," in *Visigothic Spain: New Approaches*, ed. Edward James (Oxford: Clarendon, 1980), 93–129; and T. M. Charles-Edwards, *Early Christian Ireland* (Cambridge: Cambridge University Press, 2000), 351–63. On Fredegar's knowledge of Sisebut's *vita*, see Ian Wood, "Forgery in Merovingian Hagiography," in *Fälschungen im Mittelalter*, Monumenta Germaniae Historica: Schriften 33 (Hanover, Germany: Hahn, 1988), 5:369–84, at 375.

65. Fredegar, *Chronica* 4.25.

in 613, Fredegar claims that they were joined in their plot by unnamed bishops.[66] Conversely, the chronicler is critical of bishops who attempted to undermine the resulting Neustro-Burgundian alliance, most notably Leudemund of Sion, who is accused of participating in a successful plot to murder Chlothar's newly appointed *dux*, Erpo, circa 613. The plotters, who also included the *patricius* Aletheus and the *comes* Herpin, then audaciously attempted to encourage the defection of the Neustrian king's own wife, Bertrude, with the plan of establishing a new royal dynasty in Burgundy. Leudemund fled after the plot (expectedly) failed, but he somewhat surprisingly was reprieved by Chlothar at the request of Abbot Eustasius of Luxeuil.[67] While Leudemund and his coconspirators represented a lingering local opposition to Chlothar in the Jura specifically, and possibly in Burgundy more generally, their actions were in direct opposition to Warnachar's faction, which had allied itself with Neustria. Therefore, it is not surprising that the Fredegar chronicler expresses little sympathy for their cause.

Seventh-century hagiographies corroborate the Fredegar chronicler's implication that the events of 613 compelled a number of prelates to respond in various ways to the new political reality of a unified regnum. For some bishops, such as Gaugericus of Cambrai, regime change prompted a formal declaration of loyalty to the king. Gaugericus's seventh-century *vita* relates that circa 613, the saint made the journey to Chlothar's villa at Chelles near Paris to pay his respects to the new ruler of Austrasia. At their meeting, Chlothar requested that the latter travel on to Tours to personally distribute alms to the poor on his behalf, an obvious gesture of trust.[68] Other bishops were not so obsequious. While Leudemund's conspiracy seems to have been an exceptional occurrence, bishops of other annexed *civitates* were not necessarily pleased with the elimination of their previous royal patrons.

An anecdote from Florentius's seventh-century *Vita Rusticulae* is particularly revealing. According to Florentius, the abbess of Saint Jean in Arles had been accused before the king by the *patricius* Ricomer "cum multis episcopis"—including an otherwise-unidentified Bishop Maximus—of favoring local rule

---

66. Fredegar, *Chronica* 4.41.
67. Fredegar, *Chronica* 4.43–44. See also Fox, *Power and Religion*, 45–46.
68. *Vita Gaugerici episcopi Camaracensis*, ed. Bruno Krusch, MGH SRM 3 (Hanover, Germany: Hahn, 1896), chaps. 9–10. In dating this episode, I follow Bruno Krusch, "Das Leben des Bischofs Gaugerich von Cambrai," *Neues Archiv der Gesellschaft für ältere deutsche Geschichtskunde* 16 (1891): 227–34, at 231–32. But cf. Charles Mériaux, "Une Vita mérovingienne et ses lectures du IXe au XIe siècle: Le dossier de saint Géry de Cambrai," in *L'hagiographie mérovingienne à travers ses réécritures*, ed. Monique Goullet, Martin Heinzelmann, and Christiane Veyard-Cosme (Ostfildern, Germany: Jan Thorbecke Verlag, 2010), 161–91, at 163–64, who dates the encounter to the preceding decade on the assumption that the mayor Landeric, mentioned in the passage, was replaced in office ca. 613.

by Brunhild's descendants.⁶⁹ In response to these denunciations, Rusticula called on her own regional allies to attest to her innocence, including Bishop Domnolus of Vienne. Domnolus supposedly went so far as to prophesy the death of the king's children if he refused to cease his prosecution of Rusticula, a threat that caused Chlothar to abandon quickly his original plan.⁷⁰ What made Domnolus's allegedly audacious behavior so unexpected was his own known ties—and almost certainly known to Chlothar—to Brunhild and her progeny. Domnolus had first occupied the episcopal see of Vienne circa 603–7, during the exile of the previous occupant, Desiderius. Following the latter's assassination, Domnolus was restored to office, likely with royal backing from Brunhild and Theuderic II, and still was in office in 614 when he attended the Council of Paris.⁷¹

At first consideration, it seems strange that Chlothar, an early patron of the cult of Desiderius, would be so receptive to the threats of a prelate later characterized by Sisebut as a pseudo-bishop and "servant of the devil."⁷² One interpretation of this unpleasant encounter places the meeting between bishop and king at the Council of Paris itself and credits Domnolus with a foolhardy "willingness to compromise his standing with a new sovereign."⁷³ The identification of the council is feasible, if not demonstrable, and the attendance at the synod of other episcopal loyalists of the old regime, such as Aridius of Lyons, may very well have emboldened Domnolus. Alternatively, we might consider the possibility that Domnolus was more deferential to Chlothar than suggested by Rusticula's hagiographer. After Desiderius's death and his own reappointment, Domnolus apparently made no effort to erase the memory of his controversial predecessor. On the contrary, he seems to have taken on the responsibility of formally interring the saint's body in a basilica known to Florentius as the *basilica sancti Desiderii*.⁷⁴ Domnolus's actions may have been prompted by a desire to distance himself from the untimely demise of his predecessor or even to court favor with Chlothar. Domnolus may well have defended Rusticula to the king circa 613/14—there is no reason to doubt the veracity of Florentius's identification of the abbess's supporters—but more likely this defense took the form not of a prophetic threat but rather of a

---

69. Plausibly identified by Pietri and Heijmans, *Prosopographie de la Gaule chrétienne*, 1310, with Maximus of Die, who subscribed to the acts of the Council of Paris (614).
70. *Vita Rusticulae* chaps. 9–12.
71. Pietri and Heijmans, *Prosopographie de la Gaule chrétienne*, 590–91.
72. Sisebut, *Vita vel passio Sancti Desiderii*, chap. 4. On Chlothar's political motivations for patronizing the cult of Desiderius, see Ian Wood, "Forgery in Merovingian Hagiography," 374–75.
73. Fox, "Bishop and the Monk," 191.
74. *Passio Desiderii* chap. 16; *Vita Rusticulae* chap. 14. See also Pietri and Heijmans, *Prosopographie de la Gaule chrétienne*, 591.

supplication. If it did take place in the context of the Council of Paris, Domnolus may have hoped that the council's implicit endorsement of ecclesiastical unity under Neustrian leadership, as discussed in greater detail later, would encourage a conciliatory attitude on the king's part.

Chlothar seems to have been very conscious of the symbolic significance of the Council of Paris as a "universal" Gallic council. Seventy-nine bishops in all attended. By comparison, only fifty-four had attended the second-largest Frankish council, the Council of Mâcon (585), convoked by Guntram.[75] The attendees at Paris included a dozen metropolitan bishops, headed by a former loyalist of Brunhild and Theuderic, Aridius of Lyons.[76] In placing the presidency of the council in Aridius's hands—as opposed, for example, to those of the local metropolitan of Sens, Lupus, who actually was senior to Aridius—Chlothar signaled not only his ostensibly magnanimous embrace of the episcopal loyalists of his former political enemies but also, perhaps even more significantly, the implicit suggestion that, regardless of their former loyalties, all bishops in the *regnum Francorum* now served a common regime.[77]

The pairing of the council with a royal assembly, whose agenda would be partly informed by conciliar discussions, offered a similar reminder, as did the location of the council at the Basilica of Saint Peter in Paris. Paris, unlike Orléans, the location of the major interprovincial synods of the first half of the sixth century, had been a shared *civitas* during the second half of the century, although Chlothar's father, Chilperic, had attempted to dominate at the expense of his brothers. Now firmly under Neustrian control, its selection was a reminder that the center of political gravity had fundamentally shifted. The basilica itself—more specifically its *secretarium* (audience hall)—had been the site of at least two earlier synods, the Councils of Paris of 573 and 577; was dedicated to a saint of apostolic stature; and was not closely affiliated with a particular royal line but rather with Catholic orthodoxy and Roman imperialism.[78]

It would be hazardous to generalize about the reaction of the attending bishops to this calculated effort to redefine episcopal corporate unity within

---

75. The Council of Mâcon (585) also was attended by twelve clerical delegates.
76. Fox, "Bishop and the Monk," 189–93.
77. Lupus was in office no later than 592 (the death of Guntram of Burgundy), while Aridius did not assume his seat until 603. See Pietri and Heijmans, *Prosopographie de la Gaule chrétienne*, 196–98, 1212–15.
78. Council of Paris (573), Epistle to Egidius of Rheims; Gregory of Tours, *Decem libri historiarum* 5.18. On the political and religious associations of Saint Peter, see Bitel, *Landscape with Two Saints*, 86–87; and John Moorhead, "Some Principles of Church Dedication in the Early Medieval West," *Journal of the Australian Early Medieval Association* 5 (2009): 133–46, at 133–37.

the context of a Neustrian-dominated Gaul.[79] It seems reasonable to suppose that there was at least some variation in personal responses to this redefinition. Leaving aside the metropolitans, the suffragan bishops at Paris, by virtue of the scale of attendance, were predictably diverse in geographical origin and in seniority. Some had already spent years, even the entirety of their pontificates, as Neustrian subjects, and they already were accustomed to Chlothar's rule and even had occasion to collaborate with him. Berachundus of Amiens, for instance, roughly four years before the council gave his formal consent to Chlothar's grant of land for the founding of the monastery of Saint-Valéry-sur-Somme.[80] However, it is impossible to say how many of the more junior bishops were elected with Chlothar's own consent or nomination. We learn, for example, according to his eighth-century *vita*, that Austrigisilus of Bourges was ordained with the approval of the king circa 602.[81] But the challenge of even estimating ordination dates for the vast majority of conciliar attendees limits any efforts to identify additional beneficiaries of royal patronage. We might hypothesize that prelates ordained in Neustrian-controlled *civitates* during Chlothar's reign—for example, Magnobodus of Angers, ordained circa 609/10—received his explicit or implicit blessing, but this is as far as the evidence permits us to go.[82]

For those bishops less accustomed to Neustrian rule, the selection of Aridius as council president may have been an appreciated gesture. Additionally, it is perhaps telling that when the bishops at the council prefaced their acts with a standard statement of purpose, they borrowed their text from the *acta* of

---

79. It would be even more hazardous to hypothesize about the reasons for specific absences from the council. For example, Leudegasius of Mainz, a former admirer of Theuderic according to Fredegar, *Chronica* 4.38, likely was still in office in 614 but did not attend the council. While it is tempting to identify his former political loyalties as the reason for his absence, Chlothar encouraged, rather than discouraged, the attendance of bishops who earlier had served other regimes. On Leudegasius, see also Jonas of Bobbio, *Vitae Columbani* chap. 1.51. Similarly, Verus of Rodez, who collaborated with the *comes* Bulgar of Septimania ca. 610/12 to facilitate communications between Theudebert II and the Visigothic regnum, did not attend the council (although he did attend the later Council of Clichy), but there is no reason to suspect that he was uniquely fearful of the king's wrath: *Epistolae Wisigoticae*, ed. Wilhelm Gundlach, MGH Epistolae 3 (Berlin: Weidmann, 1892), nos. 11–12. On Verus, see also Frank Riess, *Narbonne and Its Territory in Late Antiquity: From the Visigoths to the Arabs* (Farnham, England: Ashgate, 2013), 171–72.

80. *Vita Walarici abbatis Leuconaensis*, ed. Bruno Krusch, MGH SM 4 (Hanover, Germany: Hahn, 1902), chap. 14. On Berachundus, see Pietri and Heijmans, *Prosopographie de la Gaule chrétienne*, 338–39. Chlothar also confirmed the testament of Bishop Sonnatius of Rheims, but this could have occurred any time after 613: Flodoard of Rheims, *Historiae Remensis Ecclesiae*, ed. Martina Stratmann, MGH SS 36 (Hanover, Germany: Hahn, 1998), chap. 2.5. On Sonnatius, see Pietri and Heijmans, *Prosopographie de la Gaule chrétienne*, 1826–27.

81. *Vita Austrigisili episcopi Biturigi*, ed. Bruno Krusch, MGH SRM 4 (Hanover, Germany: Hahn, 1902), chap. 1.8. On Austrigisilus, see Pietri and Heijmans, *Prosopographie de la Gaule chrétienne*, 303–5.

82. Pietri and Heijmans, *Prosopographie de la Gaule chrétienne*, 1225–26.

the Burgundian Council of Lyons (567/70), a text that may not have been known to the bulk of the assembled prelates before the council.[83] The subsequent *canones*, while written like all conciliar legislation for the present, were grounded in canonical precedents established by prior regional councils, as already has been observed in relation to the council's treatment of episcopal and comital jurisdiction. Chlothar, in his subsequent *edictum*, was comparatively less conservative in his respect for specific conciliar precedent, adjusting specific rules in order to forge "a compromise between the objectives of the bishops and a monarchy which was permanently dependent on local authorities, especially the Church," and to do so within a political-legal framework still heavily influenced by Roman traditions and models.[84]

The Paris acts themselves are conciliatory, rather than deferential, toward royal authority. Their authors neither explicitly criticized nor excessively challenged royal power, and found common ground in the conciliar rules of the past. This is not to suggest passivity, let alone obsequiousness, on the part of the episcopate, although the context of the council's assembly certainly was not conducive to any sort of coordinated effort to redefine royal authority vis-à-vis the church. Rather, Aridius and his colleagues strongly reaffirmed the continued relevance of their traditional prerogatives and jurisdictions within the context of Chlothar's expanded regnum. This was a legislative program to which all attending prelates could subscribe without guilt and that they had occasion to refer back to in subsequent decades as a touchstone for ecclesiastical norms and standards.[85]

---

83. Council of Lyons (567/70), *praefatio*: "Cum ... venissemus tam pro renovandis sanctorum patrum institutis, quae praesentis temporis necessario fecit opportunitas iterari, quam his, quae assurgentibus undecumque querelarum materiis recentis definitionis ordo poposcit institui, tracantes, quid saluti populi utilius competeret vel quid ecclesiasticus ordo salubriter observaret." Council of Paris (614), *praefatio*: "Cum in Dei nomine secundum priscorum sanctorum patrum constitutiones in orbem Parisius ex evocationem gloriosissimi principis domni Hlotharii regis in synodali concilio convenissimus tam pro renovandis antiquorum canonum statutis, quae praesentis temporis necessarum fecit oportunitas iterari, quam his, quae adsurgentibus undecumque querilarum materies recentes definitionis ordo poposcit insitui, tractantes, quid quomodo principis, quid salute populi utillius conpeterit vel quid ecclesiasticus ordo salubriter observaret." The council's full text was not included in the major chronological collections of the sixth century; see Friedrich Maassen, *Geschichte der Quellen und der Literatur des canonischen Rechts im Abendlande* (Graz, Austria: Akademische Druck-U. Verlagsanstalt, 1870), 211. Council of Paris (614), c. 12, also borrows language from Council of Lyons (567/70), c. 2. The council's acts were available to the bishop of Lyons, as four of its canons were included in the *Vetus Gallica* compilation, possibly during the pontificate of Aetherius (d. 602); see Hubert Mordek, *Kirchenrecht und Reform im Frankenreich: Die Collectio Vetus Gallica, die älteste systematische Kanonessammlung des fränkischen Gallien* (Berlin: Walter de Gruyter, 1975), 62–82.

84. Esders, *Römische Rechtstradition*, 340–57 (quote on 357). On Chlothar's willingness to offer "modest concession[s]" to these local authorities in his *Edictum*, see Murray, "Immunity, Nobility."

85. Most explicitly by Unknown (ca. 614), c. 1, and Council of Clichy (626/27), *praefatio*. Both councils, not coincidentally, also assembled in Chlothar's regnum.

Chlothar did not face any significant threats to his royal authority in the years following the Council of Paris (614). While his relationship with his son Dagobert, who was raised king in Austrasia, did suffer as the result of territorial and other disputes in the mid-620s, the latter (so far as we know) never directly threatened his father during his lifetime.[86] Instead, Chlothar had to deal with the less immediately dangerous but still insidious repercussions of aristocratic factionalism and regional disputes. Fredegar's *Chronica* includes two references to the involvement of bishops in political skirmishes during these years (614–29). The first is to the collaboration between Arnulf of Metz and Pippin I to undermine the credibility of the Agilolfing magnate Chrodoald in the eyes of Dagobert in 624.[87] Arnulf, the former *domesticus* of Theudebert II, only had been appointed to the episcopate—with Chlothar's approval—in 614.[88] His appointment may very well have been a reward for his devout partisanship during the first decade of the seventh century, when the episcopal see of Metz was occupied by loyalists of Brunhild.[89] If some of these prelates can be identified as Agilolfings on onomastic grounds, then it might be possible to see Arnulf's attacks on Chrodoald as an outcome of this earlier rivalry.[90]

---

86. Fredegar, *Chronica* 4.52–53. Fox, *Power and Religion*, 265–66, suggests that tensions lingered between father and son.

87. Fredegar, *Chronica* 4.52. Arnulf's own ancestry—about which little can be said for certain unless one gives credence to Carolingian-era genealogies—has been the subject of much speculation, as has been his alleged familial ties with the Pippinids. On the former question, the seventh-century *Vita Arnulfi*, ed. Bruno Krusch, MGH SRM 2 (Hanover, Germany: Hahn, 1888), chap. 1, merely notes his noble parentage. See also Eduard Hlawitschka, "Die Vorfahren Karls des Grossen," in *Karl der Grosse*, vol. 1, *Persönlichkeit und Geschichte*, ed. Helmut Beaumann (Düsseldorf, Germany: L. Schwann, 1965), 51–82, at 73. On the latter issue, see the helpful discussions of the evidence provided by Damien Kempf in his edition of Paul the Deacon, *Liber de episcopis Mettensibus* (Leuven, Belgium: Brepols, 2013), 10–21; and by Bouchard, *Rewriting Saints and Ancestors*, 113–16. Kempf notes that even if Arnulf was indeed an *avus* of later Pippinids—per *Die Urkunden der Arnulfinger*, ed. Ingrid Heidrich (Hanover, Germany: Hahn, 2011), nos. 2, 8 (6–8, 19–22)—subsequent generations of the family did not necessarily maintain a strong connection to Metz. On this same point, see also Fouracre, *Age of Charles Martel*, 44–45. The basic study of the early ninth-century *Commemoratio genealogiae*, which names Arnulf as a Carolingian ancestor, remains Otto Gerhard Oexle, "Die Karolinger und die Stadt des heiligen Arnulf," *Frühmittelalterliche Studien* 1 (1967): 250–364.

88. Lellia Cracco Ruggini, "The Crisis of the Noble Saint: The *Vita Arnulfi*," in *The Seventh Century: Change and Continuity*, ed. Jacques Fontaine and J. N. Hillgarth (London: Warburg Institute, 1992), 116–48, at 122–23.

89. I.e., Agiulfus and his nephew Arnoaldus, and possibly Pappolus, on whom see Halsall, *Settlement and Social Organization*, 15. Agiulfus and Arnoaldus's prior seizure of property granted by Bertram of Le Mans to Arnulf (Bertram of Le Mans, *Das Testament*, 36–37 [no. 50]) has been seen as an act with political overtones.

90. Jörg Jarnut, *Agilolfingerstudien: Untersuchungen zur Geschichte einer adligen Familie im 6. und 7. Jahrhundert* (Stuttgart, Germany: Anton Hiersemann, 1986), 12–35; Fox, *Power and Religion*, 63.

Caution here is necessary, however. Without denying a shared notion of family identity among the Agilolfings of Austrasia, Pippin and Arnulf's actions in 624 were directed first and foremost toward an individual rather than a family. The chronicle's account, brief though it is, in no way suggests that Chrodoald was targeted because of his Agilolfing birthright; it was rather because of his own actions and, presumably, his proximity to Dagobert.[91] It is unknown, of course, whether Chrodoald actually was guilty of the *cupiditas* and *superbia* of which he was accused. Additionally, the chronicler reports that it was not only Pippin and Arnulf but other Austrasian *proceres* as well who all resented the Agilolfing magnate. In short, there is no reason to imagine that a long-standing family feud was playing out in the court of Dagobert.

The aristocratic factionalism explicitly described as such in Fredegar's *Chronica* was the result of current conditions, with individual aristocrats—a number of whom, like Pippin and Arnulf, had abandoned Brunhild for Chlothar some years earlier—jockeying for the favor of a king only in his second year of rule, not ancient grievances.[92] So while it may be significant that in the past Arnulf had been a follower of Theudebert, and Chrodoald of Theuderic, it was Dagobert's arrival in Austrasia that precipitated current hostilities.[93] Allegedly, Dagobert was so swayed by the complaints of the Austrasian elites that he refused his own father's request that Chrodoald be spared.[94] This may suggest that Dagobert by this point had come to view the elimination of Chrodoald as a political necessity, and not simply as a sop to the two named political opponents of the Agilolfing magnate.

Dagobert's actions no doubt contributed to the tensions with Chlothar that rose to the surface the following year. That Arnulf himself was nominated in 625 as one of twelve mediators tasked with settling the territorial dispute between father and son speaks both to the latter's trust in Arnulf's counsel and perhaps to Chlothar's own gratitude for the bishop's prior support for his invasion of Austrasia.[95] It has been suggested that Arnulf's subsequent retirement into monastic life, perhaps circa 629/30, may have been the result of a

---

91. Jarnut, *Agilolfingerstudien*, 125, identifies him as a cousin to Agiulfus and Arnoaldus. On the question of Chrodoald's Agilolfing identity, cf. Carl I. Hammer, *From Ducatus to Regnum: Ruling Bavaria under the Merovingians and Early Carolingians* (Turnhout, Belgium: Brepols, 2007), 40–46.

92. Fox, *Power and Religion*, 95–97.

93. Jarnut, *Agilolfingerstudien*, 70.

94. Régine Le Jan, *Famille et pouvoir dans le monde franc (VIIe–Xe siècle): Essai d'anthropologie sociale* (Paris: Publications de la Sorbonne, 1995), 389, suggests that Chlothar's apparent sympathy for Chrodoald may reflect Faronid influence in his court.

95. Fredegar, *Chronica* 4.40, 4.53. The chronicler does not name the other bishops who served as mediators of the dispute but implies that they included both Austrasians and Neustrians.

144   CHAPTER 4

failure to arbitrate the dispute successfully.[96] A failure at reconciliation also might be suggested by the prolonged negotiations in 626 between Chlothar and Dagobert over the fate of Godinus, the son of the deceased Burgundian mayor Warnachar. While Chlothar initially agreed to spare Godinus, he later broke his promise.[97] Nevertheless, the chronicler is explicit that Arnulf and his colleagues had been entirely successful, so any speculation regarding the bishop of Metz's reasons for retirement must remain just that.

In the same chapter, the Fredegar chronicler also describes Chlothar's elimination of additional regional aristocratic threats in Étampes and southern Aquitaine. The latter case is particularly difficult to contextualize, not least of all because it supposedly involved not one but two bishops of Eauze: Palladius and his son Sidoc (Senotus). The entire episode is described in only a single, brief sentence, in which the chronicler records the exile in 626 of the two prelates, following an accusation by Duke Aighyna that they had helped foment a Basque revolt. The first problem with this brief notice is its identification of two prelates occupying the see of Eauze simultaneously, as indicated by the statement that they were exiled at the same time. Obviously, dual occupancy of an episcopal see was a serious canonical violation, so the means by which the *civitas* of Eauze became home to two bishops is a question that must be addressed.

Twelve years earlier, the city had been represented at the Council of Paris by a certain Leodomundus, about whom virtually nothing is known, so the appointment of Palladius and Sidoc must have occurred sometime in the intervening years. Perhaps significantly, one or possibly two other prelates from Novempopulana who subscribed to the council's acts, the bishops of Aire-sur-l'Adour and Latona (usually identified as either Losne or Lectoure), were named Palladius.[98] While Palladius by no means was an uncommon name in Merovingian Aquitaine, the coincidence of several Palladii holding episcopal office simultaneously in relatively close proximity to each other is somewhat surprising. We can do no more than speculate, however, as to the circumstances that led to this rather unusual situation. One possibility is that Palladius of Aire-sur-l'Adour—or possibly Lectoure—assumed some sort of authority over the metropolitan see of Eauze sometime between 614 and 626 and arranged for the formal appointment of his son as bishop so as to avoid

---

96. Fox, *Power and Religion*, 266. On the dating of Arnulf's retreat, see Ruggini, "Crisis of the Noble Saint," 125n19.

97. Fredegar, *Chronica* 4.54. For the familial context of the Godinus affair, see Fox, *Power and Religion*, 104–5.

98. Pietri and Heijmans, *Prosopographie de la Gaule chrétienne*, 1409, prefer Lectoure; Bouchard, *Rewriting Saints and Ancestors*, 42, prefers Losne.

the unseemliness of occupying multiple episcopal sees at once. This, again, is conjecture, but it is not unreasonable to assume that Palladius used his influence within Eauze to appoint his son prelate or co-prelate.

What also is not immediately clear from the Fredegar chronicler's account is what motivated the bishops to stir up the Basques, if indeed the charges against them were grounded in truth. The preceding decades had seen an increased interest on the part of the Franks in the lands of the Vascones. In 602, Theuderic II and Theudebert II had launched a successful campaign against the Basques, which may well have extended into the Iberian Peninsula proper, and subsequently appointed a *dux* over the Basques.[99] In the early decades of the seventh century the Visigoths also fought regularly with the Basques, often to discourage raiding.[100] Gundemar (r. 610–12), for instance, defeated the Basques in battle circa 611, while a decade later Suinthila (r. 621–23) fought another war against Basques who had invaded Tarraconensis. Supposedly, claimed Isidore of Seville, the Basques were utterly defeated and formally recognized Visigothic hegemony.[101] Roger Collins persuasively has argued that campaigns by both the Franks and the Visigoths against the Basques should be interpreted in the context of increased Frankish activity along the frontier zone between the two regna.[102] So, Sisebut's Cantabrian campaign circa 612, as reported by the Fredegar chronicler, apparently was aimed at recovering territory lost to Theuderic and Theudebert a decade earlier.[103]

Returning to the bishops of Eauze, whose city was located at some remove from the border with Iberia, they presumably had little to gain from extending independent Basque power into southern Francia. It is also not immediately clear how far into Novempopulana a Basque presence extended by 626. Collins suggests as far as Eauze proper, and while this certainly is feasible due to prior raiding this far north, it is not necessarily demonstrable from the text of the Fredegar chronicle alone.[104] But perhaps this detail matters less that the

---

99. I.e., the *dux* Genialis, whom Archibald R. Lewis, "The Dukes in the *Regnum Francorum*, A.D. 550–751," *Speculum* 51, no. 3 (1976): 381–410, at 396, hypothesizes to be a local tribal leader. Cf. Roger Collins, *The Basques*, 2nd ed. (Oxford: Blackwell, 1990), 91–93, who more persuasively identifies Genialis as a Frank and suggests that Frankish armies may have reached as far as Guipúzcoa and Vizcaya.

100. Collins, *Basques*, 82–98.

101. Isidore of Seville, *Las Historias de los godos, vándalos y suevos de Isidoro de Sevilla*, ed. and trans. Cristóbal Rodríguez Alonso (León, Spain: Centro de Estudios e Investigación San Isidoro, 1975), chap. 63.

102. Collins, *Basques*, 91. Cf. Edward James, *The Merovingian Archaeology of South-West Gaul* (Oxford: British Archaeological Reports, 1977), 12.

103. Fredegar, *Chronica* 4.33.

104. It would be ill advised to see in the decreased presence of bishops from Novempopulana at the Council of Clichy (626/67) compared to Paris (614) a reflection of regional destabilization, particularly as the latter council was nearly twice the size as the former.

likelihood that both the Franks and the Visigoths were finding it increasingly challenging to contain the Basques, a problem exacerbated by frequent conflict with each other.

If the bishops of Eauze were hoping to benefit personally from an increased Basque presence in Novempopulana, they might have had several possible motivations. One is that they hoped to increase their own regional power as a result of the further destabilization of Novempopulana. This, admittedly, would have been a risky, if not foolhardy, endeavor with very uncertain rewards. A second possibility is that Palladius and Sidoc were seeking to undermine the local authority of Chlothar's *dux* Aighyna, perhaps motivated by an unknown grudge or even some sense of loyalty to the previous regime. Once again, however, it is difficult to imagine that even committed political partisans would have preferred the disorder associated with increased Basque raiding to the order personified by the presence of a royal official. A third possibility is that the bishops were not seeking political destabilization in Novempopulana per se; rather, by encouraging a Basque revolt in the frontier zone between rival regna, they perhaps were serving the interests of the Visigothic kings, who may well have benefited from making the Basques a "Frankish" problem. With the Franks in recent decades venturing into Iberia, the Visigoths may have recognized the Basques as a possible device to force the Franks to refocus on stabilizing their own side of an increasingly porous border.[105] The bishops themselves thus would have anticipated a greater Frankish military presence in Novempopulana, not less. Aighyna's subsequent discovery of their guilt may be an indication of this increased royal interest in southern Aquitaine. Obviously, we never can know for certain what motivated the actions of Sidoc and Palladius, or even for that matter whether the duke's accusations were true. It certainly is conceivable that Aighyna perjured himself in order to undermine the authority of a powerful local family, native to a region in which he himself was a relative stranger.

Whatever the case may be, the Fredegar chronicler's pithy account of the circumstances surrounding their exile reflects the continuing threat posed by regional disputes to the stability of the regnum as a whole. The local and court maneuvering of Arnulf, Sidoc, and Palladius, in fact, transcended any theoretical divisions between the political periphery and center. And while all three prelates served a realm that was enjoying relative peace and stability, their own rivalries and personal loyalties had the effect of subtly undermining this

---

105. On Basque country as a "marcher territory," see Scott de Brestian, "Vascones and Visigoths: Creation and Transformation of Identity in Northern Spain in Late Antiquity," in *Romans, Barbarians, and the Transformation of the Roman World*, ed. Ralph Mathisen and Danuta Shanzer (Farnham, England: Ashgate, 2011), 283–97, at 297.

stability. Chlothar's victory over Brunhild, as total as it may have been on the level of the monarchy, did not eliminate the existence of factional politics. In this sense at least, Chlothar's experience was much the same as that of Clovis, whose triumph of political unity was not necessarily illusionary but never a completed process. This was especially true of the episcopate. The Council of Paris (614), like Orléans (511), suggested a corporate unity that continued to be tested even after Chlothar's victory and that almost certainly remained incomplete due to a combination of regional, interpersonal, and factional divisions.

These divisions are discernible in the actions of two subsequent ecclesiastical councils held in Chlothar's regnum, Mâcon (626/27) and Clichy (626/27), both of which assembled with royal permission near the end of the king's reign. A great deal has been written about the former synod, at which bishops and monks, under the presidency of Treticus of Lyons, debated the legacy of Columbanus.[106] While framed by Jonas of Bobbio as the result of a dispute between Abbot Eustasius of Luxeuil and the renegade monk Agrestius, a former *notarius* of Theuderic II, it was a quarrel complicated by the disputing parties' differing positions on the Aquileian schism, as well as their respective familial and political alliances. Prelates could be found on both sides of the dispute: Agrestius enjoyed the support of his relation Abelenus of Geneva, while Treticus himself and likely Donatus of Besançon backed Eustasius.[107]

Not surprisingly, some historians have preferred to view this initially intramonastic dispute alternatively as a thinly disguised excuse for regional factions to challenge each other's power, an opportunity for Burgundians hostile to the new royal regime to contest indirectly Chlothar's regional authority, or an effort by local prelates and nobles alike to undermine the influence of Luxeuil. Even Chlothar's precise role has been the subject of debate, since Jonas indicates that while he favored Eustasius, he nevertheless allowed Warnachar to exercise his influence over the council. Fortunately for Eustasius, Warnachar

---

106. Jonas of Bobbio, *Vitae Columbani* chap. 2.9. On this council and its context, see Pontal, *Histoire des conciles mérovingiens*, 225; Ian Wood, *Merovingian Kingdoms*, 196–97; Charles-Edwards, *Early Christian Ireland*, 364–69; Gauthier, *L'évangélisation*, 283–84; Felice Lifshitz, *The Name of the Saint: The Martyrology of Jerome and Access to the Sacred in Francia, 627–827* (Notre Dame, IN: University of Notre Dame Press, 2006), 16–19; Caitlin Corning, *The Celtic and Roman Traditions* (New York: Palgrave, 2006), 48–55; Bruno Dumézil, "L'affaire Agrestius de Luxeuil: Hérésie et régionalisme dans la Burgondie du VIIe siècle," *Médiévales* 52 (2007): 135–52; Fox, *Power and Religion*, 32–33, 92–97; Reimitz, *History, Frankish Identity*, 191–94; Andreas Fischer, "Orthodoxy and Authority: Jonas, Eustasius, and the Agrestius Affair," in *Columbanus and the Peoples of Post-Roman Europe*, ed. Alexander O'Hara (Oxford: Oxford University Press, 2018), 143–64; and Alexander O'Hara, *Jonas of Bobbio and the Legacy of Columbanus* (Oxford: Oxford University Press, 2018), 68–73.

107. Dumézil, "L'affaire Agrestius de Luxeuil," 145–49.

died before the synod could meet.[108] While Chlothar allowed the Burgundian mayor a great deal of autonomy in handling internal Burgundian affairs, it nevertheless seems likely that the king's sponsorship of the synod was intended to quell, rather than exacerbate, regional tensions. While the exact circumstances of the council will probably never be entirely understood, it is clear that royal involvement in Burgundy, both through the sponsorship of Columbanian monasticism and through the convocation of Mâcon (626/27), aggravated rather than quelled local factionalism, in which bishops were key players.

The surviving acts of the Council of Clichy, which met in close chronological proximity to Mâcon, less explicitly reflect the factionalism that persisted to the very end of Chlothar's regime.[109] Unsurprisingly, due to the long chronological gap between Paris (614) and Clichy, only nine bishops attended both councils.[110] With Aridius of Lyons by now deceased, the council's presidency fell to his successor, Treticus. Overall, the Council of Clichy was a far smaller meeting than Paris (614). While bishops from all of the Merovingian subregna attended Clichy, and nearly as many metropolitans, no bishops from Provence attended, and relatively few from the Burgundian heartland did, despite Treticus's presidency. This is rather surprising since the council singled out for condemnation the Bonosiacs, a heretical group attested in that region by several sixth- and seventh-century observers.[111]

The council's legislation was explicitly grounded in legal standards established at Paris over a decade earlier, and in the *praefatio* to their acts, the assembled bishops addressed Chlothar directly, requesting that the king continue to assist in the enforcement of the former council's *constitutiones*.[112] In a later canon, they went even further to threaten excommunication against *iudices* who scorned (*contemno*) the acts of both the Council of Paris and Chlothar's subsequent *edictum*, conveniently overlooking the discrepancies between the

---

108. Corning, *Celtic and Roman Traditions*, 52–53.
109. On the council's dating, attendance, and acts, see Pontal, *Histoire des conciles mérovingiens*, 212–16.
110. Sunnacius of Rheims, Magnobodus of Angers, Verus of Rodez, Agricola of Javols, Raurecus of Nevers, Hildoaldus of Avranches, Vuilligisilus of Toulouse, Gundoaldus of Meaux, and Ansericus of Soissons.
111. Council of Clichy (626/27), c. 5. For a review of the evidence on the Bonosiacs, see Shanzer and Wood, *Avitus of Vienne*, 165–66. Fischer, "Orthodoxy and Authority," 154–55, suggests that the council's reference to the Bonosiacs reflects ongoing Christological debates.
112. Council of Clichy (626/27), *praefatio*: "Ergo quando nobis vestrae bonitatis gratiam fiduciam contulit suggerendi, supplices speramus, ut eam constitutionis regulam nobis per omnia conservetis, quam Parisius actenus vobis presentibus in universali Gallearum et magna synodum iuxta prisca canonum institutionem constitui precepistis. Est nobis valde gratissimum, ut ea, quae vestro sunt imperio generaliter promulgata atque tantis sacerdotibus sunt edita vel digesta, in omnibus conserventur."

two publications.¹¹³ Such claims of legislative conservatism find some support in the bishops' stated reliance on canonical *libri* in crafting their own legislation, among them most likely the *Vetus Gallica*, as well as their relatively frequent quotation of earlier canons.¹¹⁴

So, while the Council of Clichy (626/27) was convoked, in part, to reaffirm the concordance between regnum and *ecclesia* enshrined in the ecclesiastical and secular legislation promulgated at Paris, it is worth considering the question of why Chlothar deemed such a reaffirmation desirable. The fact that it was largely a new generation of prelates who attended Clichy may very well have been one factor. Chlothar also may have thought it useful to reaffirm the *unitas* of the Gallo-Frankish church despite his recent decision (622) to place his son Dagobert on the Austrasian throne. Additionally, it is possible that among the council's goals was to affirm the unity of the episcopate amid the regionalism and factional politics that persisted post-614. Not only was Burgundy divided over the Agrestius affair at the time of the council, which may possibly help to explain its relative underrepresentation, recent years had also seen critical local disruptions erupt in Austrasia and Novempopulana in which prelates were involved. While the Council of Clichy by no means was unique in its professed legislative conservatism, its multiple references to the decisions enacted in 614 are suggestive of a conscious effort to recall a moment symbolizing the potential of a unified ecclesio-political regime under Chlothar's rule. So, while Clichy's convocation did not suggest that this moment was in any way illusionary, it was nevertheless an acknowledgment that Chlothar's decisive victory over Brunhild and her progeny prompted merely a realignment of local interests, and not their silencing. Perpetual vigilance and the continual *renovanda* of ecclesiastical norms remained necessary precautionary measures.

The Age of Pippin II

Of the three triumphant Frankish leaders examined in this chapter, it is Pippin II whose relationships with individual bishops have been most comprehensively surveyed by modern historians. In his seminal study of the *Liber historiae Francorum*, Richard Gerberding identifies over twenty certain or hypothetical episcopal allies of Pippin.¹¹⁵ Regarding the political loyalties of

---

113. Council of Clichy (626/27), c. 27.
114. Mordek, *Kirchenrecht*, 66–70; Pontal, *Histoire des conciles mérovingiens*, 214.
115. Gerberding, *Rise of the Carolingians*, 105–9.

the bishops of this period, Gerberding makes several important observations, not least of all the impossibility of identifying the allegiances of the majority of episcopal officeholders whose tenures coincided with Pippin's career. Additionally, Gerberding reaffirms Paul Fouracre's contention that Pippin's victory at Tertry (687) was more decisive militarily than politically, and that this inconclusive victory applied to the Neustrian church as well as to the court.[116]

While Pippin was able to instigate some personnel changes within the episcopal hierarchy—for example, his replacement of Bishop Ansbert of Rouen with his supporter (and possible kinsman) Gripho (ca. 689/91), as well as his appointment of Herlemund as bishop of Le Mans (ca. 698)—he was not immediately in a position to pack the Neustrian church with his own partisans.[117] This meant that some episcopal sees remained in the hands of bishops unlikely to have been Pippinid allies, such as Savaric of Auxerre, and also that Pippinid patronage did not extend equally to all major sees and institutions following Tertry.[118] As Ian Wood has observed on the latter point, the bulk of Pippin's ecclesiastical activity was "closer to the centres of his family's estates . . . [and his] ecclesiastical interventions were limited to those foundations to which circumstances and family connections gave him access."[119]

The sixth- and seventh-century Merovingians, of course, had been similarly selective in the allocation of their patronage. Additionally, despite his access to considerable personal and fiscal wealth, Pippin had to construct new patronage relationships in Neustria in particular, which necessitated a strategic approach.[120] If the Battle of Tertry's impact on Pippin's accumulation of episco-

---

116. Paul Fouracre, "Observations on the Outgrowth of Pippinid Influence in the 'Regnum Francorum' after the Battle of Tertry (687–715)," *Medieval Prosopography* 5 (1984): 1–31. On the battle's military decisiveness, cf. Bernard S. Bachrach, *Early Carolingian Warfare* (Philadelphia: University of Pennsylvania Press, 2001), 10–12.

117. On Gripho and his relationship with Pippin, see Gerberding, *Rise of the Carolingians*, 105; Fouracre, "Settlement of Disputes," 31–32; Eugen Ewig, "Die frankischen Teilreiche im 7. Jahrhundert (613–714)," in *Spätantikes und fränkisches Gallien*, 1:172–230, at 1:227; and Fouracre, "Observations on the Outgrowth," 15. On Herlemund, see Margarete Weidemann, "Bischofsherrschaft und Königtum in Neustrien vom 7. bis zum 9. Jahrhundert am Beispiel des Bistums Le Mans," in *La Neustrie: Les pays au nord de la Loire de 650 à 850*, ed. Hartmut Atsma (Sigmaringen, Germany: Jan Thorbecke, 1989), 1:161–93, at 172–73.

118. Gerberding, *Rise of the Carolingians*, 105, notes that this patronage did not extend to the houses of the upper Seine and Oise valleys or to Balthild's designated *seniores basilicae*. See also Fouracre, *Age of Charles Martel*, 49–50. On Savaric's hypothetical political loyalties, see Fouracre, "Observations on the Outgrowth," 8; see also 26n37.

119. Ian Wood, *Merovingian Kingdoms*, 265.

120. For useful summaries of the evidence for Pippinid family landholding, see Fouracre and Gerberding, *Late Merovingian France*, 311–12; and Fouracre, *Age of Charles Martel*, 47–48. See also Heinrich Bonnell, *Die anfänge des karolingischen hauses* (Berlin: Duncker und Humblot, 1866), 52–133; Eduard Hlawitschka, "Zur landschaftlichen Herkunft der Karolinger," *Rheinische Vierteljahrsblätter* 27 (1962): 1–17; Matthias Werner, *Der Lütticher Raum in frühkarolingischer Zeit: Untersuchungen zur Geschichte*

pal allies was indeed initially limited, it is important to determine why Pippin made overtures to specific prelates and why these individuals proved receptive. Most of the evidence for these relationships postdates the invasion of Neustria and is widely (if unevenly) distributed geographically. It is clear, however, that Pippin was interested not merely in establishing personal links with individual prelates (or placing his own loyalists in office) but also in forging potentially long-term relationships with specific sees and institutions of regional, or even transregional, significance.

In those regions east of the Seine, for instance, Pippin purposefully extended his influence over the major metropolitan sees of Rheims and Trier, and most likely Cologne as well. Sometimes the initiative, however, came from the bishops themselves. According to the eighth-century edition of Fredegar's *Chronica*, which Roger Collins has rebranded the *Historia vel Gesta Francorum*, Bishop Reolus of Rheims offered his support to Pippin shortly before the Battle of Tertry.[121] Reolus's support was both crucial and unexpected, as the bishop earlier had colluded in the assassination of Pippin's ally and probable kinsman the *dux* Martin following Ebroin's defeat of the Austrasians circa 676. Reolus's defection almost certainly was not the result of a change of heart about Pippin per se, let alone a desire to see his *civitas* dominated by an Austrasian magnate, but rather was a product of his personal opposition to the new Neustrian mayor Bercharius.[122]

Even after Reolus's death, Pippin maintained his influence in both Rheims and Belgica Secunda as a whole through his appointment of Bishop Rigobert as Reolus's successor.[123] It was at Pippin's request that Rigobert and several of his provincial suffragans assented in February 693 to a grant of privileges by Bishop Bertoendus of Châlons-sur-Marne to the monastery of Puteolus at Der (Montier-en-Der), as well as the latter's confirmation of the founding of the nearby convent of Puellemontier.[124] Several years earlier (686), Reolus too had offered his financial support to Montier-en-Der's founder, the abbot Bercharius, who had been attempting to establish a convent. Gerberding has plausibly

---

einer karolingischen Stammlandschaft (Göttingen, Germany: Vandenhoeck und Ruprecht, 1980), 341–475; and Frans Theuws, "Centre and Periphery in Northern Austrasia (6th–8th Centuries): An Archaeological Perspective," in *Medieval Archaeology in the Netherlands*, ed. J. C. Besteman, J. M. Bos, and H. A. Heidinga (Assen, Netherlands: Van Gorcum, 1990), 41–69.

121. Fredegar, *Chronica* Continuations chap. 5. See Gerberding, *Rise of the Carolingians*, 102–3; and Ian Wood, *Merovingian Kingdoms*, 265.

122. Gerberding, *Rise of the Carolingians*, 102–3; Bachrach, *Early Carolingian Warfare*, 10.

123. *Vita Rigoberti* chaps. 4–5.

124. *The Cartulary of Montier-en-Der, 666–1129*, ed. Constance Brittain Bouchard (Toronto: University of Toronto Press, 2004), no. 4 (52–58). I follow Bouchard in identifying the named episcopal addressees in the charter with Rigobert's suffragans.

suggested that Reolus's generosity was motivated by his expectation—and perhaps that of his new patron, Pippin—that Bercharius's other monastery of Hautvillers would fall under his protection upon its founder's death.[125] It is clear that Pippin's relationships with individual prelates in and around Rheims were closely linked to his *Klosterpolitik*: influence over Bercharius's foundations, for instance, would have strengthened Pippin's position in the strategically significant border region of Champagne, where his son Drogo had been appointed *dux* in 690.[126]

The aforementioned link is perceivable as well in Pippin's relationships with three other bishops from Belgica Secunda: Constantinus of Beauvais, Madalgar of Laon, and Bainus of Thérouanne. Constantinus of Beauvais, in the early eighth century, subscribed to two of Pippin's charters for the monastery of Echternach.[127] As for Madalgar, the *Vita Anstrudis* reports that he attempted to seize control of Anstrude's convent of Saint Jean-de-Laon. The abbess appealed to Pippin through her relation Wulfoald, and Pippin responded by sending his son Grimoald to appeal to the bishop of Laon. Madalgar relented, and Pippin's influence over the monastery was enhanced.[128] On a second occasion, Madalgar would accede again to the mayor's wishes, when Pippin requested in 711 that the bishop allow his subordinate Ermino to be appointed the new abbot of the monastery of Lobbes, located roughly halfway between Lille and Liège, and one of several monastic institutions in the Meuse region patronized by the Pippinids.[129] Bainus, with Pippin's backing, held several offices: bishop of Thérouanne until 701, then abbot of Fontenelle, and two years later rector of the daughter house of Fleury, the latter of which was a Pippinid foundation.[130] Bainus's abbatial appointment can be understood

---

125. *Cartulary of Montier-en-Der* no. 166 (337–40); Gerberding, *Rise of the Carolingians*, 102–3. Bouchard, however, is agnostic on the identification of Abbot Bercharius of Hautvillers with Abbot Bercharius of Montier-en-Der. Similarly, she notes the paucity of evidence for a relationship between the latter and the contemporary mayor (*Cartulary of Montier-en-Der*, p. 4).

126. *Liber historiae Francorum* chap. 48. On Champagne's strategic significance, see Fouracre, *Age of Charles Martel*, 49.

127. *Die Urkunden der Arnulfinger* nos. 4, 5 (11–15). On Echternach, see Friedrich Prinz, *Frühes Mönchtum im Frankenreich* (Munich: R. Oldenbourg, 1965), 200–202; and Gauthier, *L'évangélisation*, 316–28.

128. *Vita Anstrudis* chap. 16. A clear recounting of the complex family/factional dynamics at work in this brief episode can be found in Fox, *Power and Religion*, 155–59.

129. *Vita Erminonis abbatis Lobbiensis*, ed. Wilhelm Levison, MGH SRM 6 (Hanover, Germany: Hahn, 1913), chap. 3. The other institutions included Nivelles, Fosses, Maubeuge, Mons, and Andenne. See Fouracre, *Age of Charles Martel*, 49.

130. *Gesta abbatum Fontanellensium*, ed. and trans. Pascal Pradié (Paris: Les Belles Lettres, 1999), chap. 2.1. Charles Mériaux, "Thérouanne et son diocèse jusqu'à la fin de l'époque carolingienne: Les étapes de la christianisation d'après les sources écrites," *Bibliothèque de l'École des chartes* 158, no. 2

within the context of Pippin's ongoing efforts to consolidate his position in Rouen and the surrounding region after the Battle of Tertry, a process that had begun with the marriage of his son Drogo to Anstrude, the widow of the former Neustrian mayor Bercharius.[131]

Meanwhile, by the late seventh century, the metropolitan see of Trier had come to be dominated by the Widonids: first by Bishop Basinus, later with his nephew Liutwin (705–17/22), and most infamously by the latter's son Milo (717/22-761/2).[132] Basinus and Liutwin both participated in the founding and endowment of Echternach (ca. 697/98) by Pippin's mother-in-law Irmina, which became an explicitly avowed Pippinid house after 706.[133] While no biographical information is recoverable for the bishops of the metropolitan see of Cologne from the late seventh and early eighth centuries, Gerberding has argued for the probability of Pippinid influence over that episcopal office, citing Bede's reference to Pippin's order that martyred English missionaries be buried in Cologne.[134] There is no question that Cologne itself was situated well within the Pippinid geographic sphere of influence in Austrasia, so we might expect Pippin to have maintained an interest in the episcopal elections held in the metropolitan see.

Nevertheless, Rosamond McKitterick has suggested in regard to Pippin's patronage of the missionary and later bishop Willibrord that the mayor may have been motivated not only by a desire to extend Frankish political power over Frisia but also by a desire to establish an "independent church" in Utrecht, distant from the metropolitan see of Cologne. Pippin's intention, however, was not necessarily to undermine the authority of the bishops of Cologne so much as to ensure that he, and not the distant metropolitan, would act as the primary patron of Willibrord's enterprise.[135] The metropolitan bishop's other

---

(2000): 377–406, at 394, suggests that Bainus occupied his episcopal and monastic offices simultaneously.

131. Fouracre, *Age of Charles Martel*, 48.

132. For the dates, see Le Jan, *Famille et pouvoir*, 261n184. See also Ewig, *Trier im Merowingerreich*, 134; Ewig, "Milo et Eiusmodi Similes," 2:190–99; Gauthier, *L'évangélisation*, 357–68; and Hans Hubert Anton, "Die Trierer Kirche und das nördliche Gallien in spätrömischer und fränkischer Zeit," in Atsma, *La Neustrie*, 2:53–73, at 64.

133. Camille Wampach, ed., *Geschichte der Grundherrschaft Echternach in Frühmittelalter*, vol. 1.2, *Quellenband* (Luxembourg: Luxemburger Kunstdruckerei, 1930), no. 3 (17–20).

134. Gerberding, *Rise of the Carolingians*, 106, citing Bede, *Historia ecclesiastica gentis Anglorum*, ed. Bertram Colgrave and R. A. B. Mynors, rev. ed. (Oxford: Clarendon, 1992), 5.10. Although Gerberding does not cite it in this instance, elsewhere (88) he implies Pippin's control of Cologne in his reading of the *Vita Audoini episcopi Rotomagensis*, ed. Wilhelm Levison, MGH SRM 5 (Hanover, Germany: Hahn, 1910), chaps. 13–14, which describes the saint's embassy to Austrasia.

135. Rosamond McKitterick, "England and the Continent," in *The New Cambridge Medieval History*, vol. 2, *c. 700–c. 900*, ed. Rosamond McKitterick (Cambridge: Cambridge University Press, 1995),

suffragan see of Tongres/Maastricht also was of considerable interest, as well as concern, to the Pippinids. Bishop Lambert and Pippin had enjoyed at best a complicated relationship, with the prelate at times supporting the mayor but at other times opposing him.[136] Pippin's own *domesticus* was charged with the bishop's assassination circa 705. Pippin then arranged for Lambert to be succeeded by Hubert, a kinsman of his wife, Plectrude, whose loyalty was far more reliable.[137]

While not a metropolitan see like Rheims, Trier, and Cologne, Metz—located in Belgica Prima—long had enjoyed the status of a royal seat, and it retained its position as a major center of political power in the east into the late seventh century.[138] However, the Pippinids were not the only Austrasian noble family with links to Metz—the Wulfoald-Gundoinids in particular challenged their regional dominance—and until Charles Martel, their control over the *civitas* and its episcopate was not entirely secure.[139] Any assessment of their control of the episcopate depends to a considerable extent on how much weight one chooses to place on the reported familial link between Arnulf of Metz and the Pippinids. Arnulf had held the episcopal seat early in the century, and after a gap of several decades his son, Chlodulf, was able to secure election to the episcopacy in in the 650s.[140] By the late 660s Chlodulf had been succeeded by Abbo (II), likely the progeny of Arnulf's episcopal successor Goeric-Abbo and a probable ally of Pippin II.[141] The see of Metz, however, appears to have fallen outside the Pippinid orbit following Pippin's death with

---

64–83, at 66–70. But cf. James Palmer, *Anglo-Saxons in a Frankish World, 690–900* (Turnhout, Belgium: Brepols, 2009), 225–26, who stresses the uncertainties surrounding Willibrord's occupation of Utrecht as an episcopal (or archepiscopal) see. See also Eugène Honée, "St Willibrord in Recent Historiography," in *Missions and Missionaries*, ed. Pieter N. Holtrop and Hugh McLeod, Studies in Church History Subsidia 13 (Oxford: Boydell, 2000), 16–31, at 26–30.

136. On Lambert, see Gerberding, *Rise of the Carolingians*, 106; Matthias Werner, *Der Lütticher Raum in frühkarolingischer Zeit*, 241–74; J. L. Kupper, "Saint Lambert: De l'histoire à la légende," *Revue d'histoire ecclésiastique* 79 (1984): 5–49; Régis de La Haye, *De bisschoppen van Maastricht* (Maastricht, Netherlands: Stichting Historische Reeks Maastricht, 1985), 64–71; Ian Wood, *Merovingian Kingdoms*, 251–52; Theuws, "Maastricht as a Centre," 179–80, 183–85; and Kreiner, *Social Life of Hagiography*, 258.

137. On Hubert, see Gerberding, *Rise of the Carolingians*, 106, 129, 133–34; Theuws, "Maastricht as a Centre," 174–75, 181–82, 190–93; Fouracre, "Observations on the Outgrowth," 17.

138. On Metz's establishment as a royal seat, see Halsall, *Settlement and Social Organization*, 12. Cf. Bernard S. Bachrach, "Fifth-Century Metz: Late Roman Christian *Urbs* or Ghost Town?," *Antiquité Tardive* 10 (2002): 363–81, at 381n144. On the *sedes regiae* of Austrasia more generally, see Eugen Ewig, *Die Merowinger und das Frankenreich* (Stuttgart, Germany: W. Kohlhammer, 1988), 91–92; and Dierkens and Périn, "Les *sedes regiae* mérovingiennes," 289–92.

139. Halsall, *Settlement and Social Organization*, 14, 50–52; Fox, *Power and Religion*, 156–57, 267.

140. Halsall, *Settlement and Social Organization*, 16.

141. He is identified as such by Fouracre, "Observations on the Outgrowth," 15, and more tentatively by Gerberding, *Rise of the Carolingians*, 106.

the ordination of Sigibald in 715. Less than a decade earlier, Sigibald had provided Pippin's Austrasian nemesis Wulfoald with property in Verdun on which to construct a fort. M. A. Claussen has suggested plausibly that it was Sigibald's personal piety and local support that allowed him to remain in office while other episcopal nemeses of Charles Martel were less fortunate.[142] Pippin also seems to have been on friendly terms with Bishop Armoin of nearby Verdun, who participated in a land transaction with Pippin and Plectrude circa 701/2.[143] Another suffragan of the metropolitan of Trier, Garibald of Toul, subscribed to the aforementioned charters for Echternach.[144]

When we turn to the *civitates* of the west and south, evidence for possible Pippinid allies among the episcopate expectedly becomes scarcer. Gerberding, in his tally, identifies only four prelates, two of whom occupied the same episcopal seat: Clermont in Aquitanica Prima.[145] According to the *Vita Boniti*, the sainted bishop of Clermont was ordained thanks to Pippin, who urged Theuderic III to make the appointment circa 690 following the death of the previous occupant of the see, Bonitus's brother Avitus.[146] As Jamie Kreiner has observed regarding this episode, Bonitus's hagiographer stresses the legitimacy both of Pippin's petition to the king and Theuderic's own *auctoritas* to approve the ordination.[147] Bonitus's hagiographer similarly credits Pippin with the appointment of Bonitus's successor, Norbert, upon the former's resignation, circa 700.[148]

While Pippin may have exercised some influence in nearby Bourges as well, there is no further evidence of his involvement in the ecclesiastical affairs of either Aquitaine or Provence.[149] His lack of influence in the latter region is perhaps not all that surprising due to the political opposition that he faced there from the *patricius* Antenor, who resorted to open rebellion against Austrasian power circa 711, following the death of Childebert III.[150] It is more dangerous to generalize about Aquitaine. It has been suggested that Aquitaine progressively

---

142. M. A. Claussen, *The Reform of the Frankish Church: Chrodegang of Metz and the Regula Canonicorum in the Eighth Century* (Cambridge: Cambridge University Press, 2004), 44–45.
143. *Die Urkunden der Arnulfinger* no. 3, dep. 42 (8–11, 88).
144. *Die Urkunden der Arnulfinger* nos. 4, 5 (11–15). Other episcopal signatories of Pippin's charters for Echternach whose sees cannot be identified securely include Benarius, Witharius, and Josephus.
145. Gerberding, *Rise of the Carolingians*, 106–8.
146. *Vita Boniti* chap. 5.
147. Kreiner, *Social Life of Hagiography*, 76–77.
148. *Vita Boniti* chap. 15.
149. Ewig, "Die frankischen Teilreiche," 1:227.
150. Fouracre, "Observations on the Outgrowth," 8–9; Patrick Geary, *Aristocracy in Provence: The Rhône Basin at the Dawn of the Carolingian Age* (Philadelphia: University of Pennsylvania Press, 1985), 126–27; Patrick Geary, "Die Provence zur Zeit Karl Martells," in Jarnut, Nonn, and Richter, *Karl Martell in seiner Zeit*, 381–92. On Antenor, see also Horst Ebling, *Prosopographie der Amtsträger des Merowingerreiches von Chlothar II. (613) bis Karl Martell (741)* (Munich: Fink, 1974), 57–58.

had distanced itself from the rest of Francia during the later seventh century; however, this scenario has not convinced all scholars, not least of all because of the continued ownership of Aquitanian properties by northern religious institutions.[151] Any argument from the absence of evidence is, of course, dangerous, but there is no reason simply to assume a particularly pervasive Pippinid influence over Aquitanian episcopal sees and religious institutions during Pippin's lifetime.[152]

The evidence for Burgundy is nearly as sparse, and certainly as controversial due to the alleged presence of episcopal "republics" in several of the major sees of the region, as discussed earlier. According to the narrative originally proposed by Eugen Ewig and expounded by others, bishops in Orléans, Autun, Lyons, and elsewhere took advantage of an increasing gap between the political center (i.e., the Neustrian court) and periphery (Burgundy in particular) to take power into their own hands in the later seventh century.[153] This era of near-autonomous "republics" came to an end when Pippin II and Charles Martel set about to systemically dismantle them, recognizing them as threats to their own authority.[154]

This model has not gone uncriticized, with Paul Fouracre in particular questioning it in a series of publications.[155] Besides the issue of anachronistic nomenclature, Fouracre makes several objections to the model: (1) it takes on faith the criticism of the Merovingian episcopate and individual prelates in hagiographical and epistolary sources, especially the letters of Boniface; (2) there is inadequate documentary evidence for lay office holding in *civitates* supposedly dominated by bishops; (3) the model assumes that the episcopate had become more "secularized" by the late seventh century, a generalization that the evidence does not obviously support; and (4) the model theorizes a possibly exaggerated opposition between local power and the court. Regard-

---

151. Cf. Rouche, *L'Aquitaine*, 98–109, with Fouracre, *Age of Charles Martel*, 81–84.

152. Conversely, I am unconvinced by the suggestion by Rouche, *L'Aquitaine*, 105–7, that gaps in the relevant episcopal *fastes* are reflective of Aquitanian separatism in the later seventh and early eighth centuries.

153. Ewig, "Milo et Eiusmodi Similes," 2:207–19.

154. See, e.g., Josef Semmler, "*Episcopi potestas* und karolingische Klosterpolitik," in *Mönchtum, Episkopat und Adel zur Gründungszeit des Klosters Reichenau*, ed. Arno Borst, Vorträge und Forschungen 20 (Sigmaringen, Germany: Jan Thorbecke Verlag, 1974), 305–95, at 392–93; Reinhold Kaiser, *Bischofsherrschaft zwischen Königtum und Fürstenmacht* (Bonn, Germany: Ludwig Röhrscheid, 1981), 74–75; Reinhold Kaiser, "Royauté et pouvoir épiscopal au nord de la Gaule (VIIe–IXe siècles)," in Atsma, *La Neustrie*, 1:143–60, at 152–53 (German version: "Königtum und Bischofsherrschaft im frühmittelalterlichen Neustrien," in Prinz, *Herrschaft und Kirche*, 83–108, at 98–99); and Karl Ferdinand Werner, "La place du VIIe siècle dans l'évolution politique et institutionnelle de la Gaule franque," in Fontaine and Hillgarth, *Seventh Century*, 173–211, at 186–87.

155. E.g., Fouracre, *Age of Charles Martel*, 89–93; Fouracre, "Why Were So Many Bishops?," 18–20; and Fouracre and Gerberding, *Late Merovingian France*, 48–51.

ing Burgundy specifically, Fouracre has suggested in place of explanatory models that assume political separatism the alternative of political fragmentation. This latter model seems to fit the late seventh- and early eighth-century situation better than the alternative.

Certainly, the Burgundian episcopate was by no means united against Pippin. The metropolitan *civitas* of Lyons was home to one of Pippin's staunchest Burgundian supporters, Bishop Godinus. Like Bonitus and Norbert, Godinus had the Austrasian mayor to thank for his seat when he was elected circa 688. It also was almost certainly at Pippin's request that Godinus later assumed the abbacy of Jumièges circa 710.[156] Godinus's name also appears in several charters from the period, which reflect his consistent political allegiances. Barbara Rosenwein has identified, for instance, the significance of Godinus's appearance in Theuderic III's immunity charter of 688 as a "rapprochement" between two rival aristocratic factions.[157] In the charter, which grants the villa of Lagny-le-Sec to Abbot Chaino of Saint-Denis, a parcel of the property (Silly-le-Long) is retained and reassigned to Godinus himself. The (explicit) association of Chaino with Ebroin and (implicitly) Godinus with Pippin in a single legal transaction is thus an example of a peaceful effort to reward one of Pippin's Neustro-Burgundian supporters, but not at the expense of other aristocratic constituencies.

As for those episcopal republics that allegedly were coming to dominate local Burgundian politics, it is difficult to find much evidence for their dominance during Pippin's lifetime. The infamous conquests of Bishop Savaric of Auxerre of nearly half a dozen additional episcopal sees, including Orléans, for instance, only took place in the aftermath of Pippin's death.[158] Moreover, it is impossible to identify, let alone generalize about, either the regional authority or the political leanings of the majority of other Burgundian bishops who were contemporaries of Pippin.[159] What evidence we do possess is mostly circumstantial. For example, Ansbert of Autun participated—along with, among others, Godinus of Lyons—in a *placitum* of 692/93, convoked by Pippin's ally in the Neustrian court, the mayor Nordbert. This, however, is

---

156. Laporte, "Les listes abbatiales de Jumieges," 451; Gerberding, *Rise of the Carolingians*, 98.
157. *Chartae Latinae Antiquiores: Facsimile Edition of the Latin Charters prior to the Ninth Century* (hereafter *ChLA*), ed. Albert Bruckner et al. (Lausanne and Dietikon-Zürich, Switzerland: Urs Graf, 1954–2016), 13, no. 570, on which see Rosenwein, *Negotiating Space*, 84–89. Godinus's name also appears in *ChLA* 14, nos. 576, 577.
158. *Gesta episcoporum Autissiodorensium*, ed. and trans. Michel Sot, Guy Lobrichon, and Monique Goullet (Paris: Belles Lettres, 2002), chap. 26.
159. Gerberding, *Rise of the Carolingians*, 108, identifies Tetricus and Flocoald of Auxerre and Ansbert of Autun (among others) as prelates whose political allegiances are unknown.

not enough to prove Ansbert's own political loyalties.[160] The political loyalties of Wulfram of Sens are equally difficult to pin down. While Fouracre has noted the bishop's association with the Neustrian court, Gerberding sees evidence for possible Pippinid connections in his retirement to Fontenelle and in his missionary work among the Frisians.[161] If any generalizations are possible at all in regard to the Burgundian episcopate in the age of Pippin II, it is simply that some—but by no means all—prelates were involved in affairs of the court, and those who were involved were not unified in their political loyalties.

This conclusion holds for the Gallo-Frankish episcopate at large in this period. Without question, Pippin's activities before and especially after the Battle of Tertry encouraged a realignment of political alliances among elites, including bishops, in a manner similar to Clovis's victory over Alaric and Chlothar's over Brunhild. In all three cases, the victors followed up their military success with extensive efforts to win the loyalty of the leading figures of annexed territories through generous patronage. In Pippin's case, this most notably involved the benefaction of monastic institutions, but it also included the appointment of bishops and generous gifts to individual prelates. It even is possible that in modeling his efforts on well-established royal precedents, Pippin may have gone so far as to convoke an ecclesiastical council in 689 to address issues related to "the well-being of churches, orphans, and widows."[162] At no point, however, did Pippin enjoy the support of the entirety of the Gallo-Frankish episcopate, let alone dominate it. Moreover, the political uncertainty that resulted from his death effectively nullified many of those strategic relationships that he had worked so long to forge, in effect revealing their inherent fragility. It would fall to Pippin's son Charles Martel to fashion

---

160. *ChLa* 14, no. 576. On this case, see Fouracre, "'Placita,'" 28–29, 31–32. The editors of *Die Urkunden der Merowinger*, 355–57 (no. 141) prefer to the date the *placitum* to 694.

161. Fouracre, "Observations on the Outgrowth," 15; Gerberding, *Rise of the Carolingians*, 107–8. On the reliability of Wulfram's *vita*, see the discussions of Stéphane Lebecq, "Le baptême manqué du roi Radbod," in *Les assises du pouvoir: Temps médiévaux, territoires africains*, ed. Odile Redon and Bernard Rosenberger (Saint-Denis, France: Presses Universitaires de Vincennes, 1994), 141–50; and Ian Wood, *The Missionary Life: Saints and the Evangelization of Europe, 400–1050* (London: Longman, 2001), 92–94.

162. *Annales Mettenses Priores*, ed. Bernhard Simson, MGH SRG 10 (Hanover, Germany: Hahn, 1905), a. 692: "His itaque peractis sinodum adunare precepit, in quo de utilitatibus ecclesiarum, orphanorum ac viduarum consideratis, sese in opinatissimis regni sui sedibus cum suis fidelibus ad hibernandum locavit." This account is impossible to verify and may simply constitute an effort to exaggerate Pippin's near-monarchical status following Tertry; see Gregory Halfond, "Caring for Churches, Orphans, and Widows in Late Merovingian Francia: Contemporary and Carolingian Perspectives," *Revue d'histoire ecclésiastique* 113, nos. 3–4 (2018): 544–75. On the *annales*, see Yitzhak Hen, "The Annals of Metz and the Merovingian Past," in *The Uses of the Past in the Early Middle Ages*, ed. Yitzhak Hen and Matthew Innes (Cambridge: Cambridge University Press, 2000), 175–90.

new relationships with the Gallo-Frankish episcopal sees in a far more challenging political and military climate. And while his tactics were not inherently different from those of his father—or, indeed, earlier generations of Merovingians—it was Charles's reputation that would be irrevocably damaged by his efforts.[163]

---

163. For reassessments of Charles's ecclesiastical policies, see, e.g., Hans-Werner Goetz, "Karl Martel und die Heiligen: Kirchenpolitik und Maiordomat im Spiegel der spätmerowingischen Hagiographie," in Jarnut, Nonn, and Richter, *Karl Martell in seiner Zeit*, 101–18; and Fouracre, *Age of Charles Martel*, 122–45. On Charles's posthumous reputation, see Andreas Fischer, *Karl Martell: Der Beginn karolingischer Herrschaft* (Stuttgart, Germany: Kohlhammer, 2012), 188–97. See also Michel Rouche, "'Religio calcata et dissipata' ou Les premières sécularisations de terres d'Eglise par Dagobert," in Fontaine and Hillgarth, *Seventh Century*, 236–49, who argues for Dagobert I as "le premier qui ait vraiment sécularisé les biens d'Eglise, le premier qui ait, sans le savoir, fait apparaître les ambiguïtés de l'union de l'Etat et de l'Eglise" (246). Cf. Scholz, *Die Merowinger*, 207–8.

Conclusion

The Privilege of Saint-Pierre-le-Vif (660)

Around mid-November of the year 660, as many as twenty-six bishops assembled at the royal villa of Masolacus (Mâlay-le-Roi), where they approved Emmo of Sens's privilege for the monastery of Saint-Pierre-le-Vif in Sens.[1] Included among the subscribing prelates were four metropolitans: Emmo of Sens, Johannes of Arles, Choaldus of Vienne, and Aunemund of Lyons. Additionally, bishops from the provinces of Rouen, Rheims, Tours, Bourges, and

---

1. J. M. Pardessus, ed., *Diplomata, chartae, epistolae, leges aliaque instrumenta ad res Gallo-Francicas spectantia* (Aalen, Germany: Scientia Verlag, 1843–49), 2:112–14 (no. 335). On Saint-Pierre, see Brigitte Beaujard, "Sens," in *Province ecclésiastique de Sens*, ed. Jean-Charles Picard et al., Topographie chrétienne des cités de la Gaule 8 (Paris: Boccard, 1992), 19–32, at 28–29. For the dating of the meeting, see Ewig, "Das Privileg des Bischofs Berthefrid von Amiens," 2:575n82. Admittedly, it is not demonstrable that all of the subscribers attended; conceivably, some of their autographs could have been collected after the meeting dissolved, although to collect signatures from even half of the subscribers one by one would have required a significant effort on Emmo's part. The overlap between addressees and subscribers also may be significant in this regard. So, for example, as noted by Eugen Ewig, "Beobachtungen zu den Bischofsprivilegien für Saint-Maur-des-Fosses und Sainte-Colombe de Sens," *Spätantikes und fränkisches Gallien*, 2:485–506, at 2:503, the fact that the privilege is addressed to Eligius of Noyon (among others) but was subscribed to by Momolenus of Noyon may have been the result of its being posted before (or without knowledge of) Eligius's death. Odette Pontal, *Die Synoden im Merowingerreich* (Paderborn, Germany: Ferdinand Schöningh, 1986), 207, and Halfond, *Archaeology*, 253, both are neutral on whether this meeting should be considered an episcopal council proper. On the contents and form of the privilege, see also Eugen Ewig, "Markulfs Formular 'De privilegio' und die merowingischen Bischofsprivilegien," *Spätantikes und fränkisches Gallien*, 3:519–37.

Bordeaux subscribed.² Over 60 percent of the combined subscribers and addressees also had voted to approve Emmo of Sens's grant of privileges to the monastery of Saint Colombe a little over two months earlier.³ The subscriptions of some of these same prelates also appear on several other contemporary episcopal privileges, including those granted to Saint Denis (in 654), Sithiu (in 663), and Corbie (in 664). Eugen Ewig has identified the three aforementioned privileges, as well as that granted to Saint-Pierre-le-Vif, as products of the *Klosterpolitik* of Queen Balthild, the widow of Clovis II, whose regency lasted from 657 until 664.⁴ According to her *vita*, Balthild considered Saint-Pierre-le-Vif to be one of the six named *seniores basilicas sanctorum* of the Neustro-Burgundian kingdom, one of only two in Burgundy.⁵

The royal impetus behind the privilege is reflected in the decision to hold the meeting at Mâlay-le-Roi. This villa, which was located on the frontier between Neustria and Burgundy, was employed frequently as a seat of government by the seventh-century Merovingian rulers of the Neustro-Burgundian kingdom, who used it as a personal residence, an assembly place, and a hunting lodge.⁶ The villa was located only about six kilometers from the *civitas* of Sens, where two Roman highways intersected, connecting the metropolitan see directly to Paris, Troyes, Orléans, and Auxerre, thus offering travelers to the villa a relatively straightforward journey.⁷ It is unknown precisely when the villa was built. Archaeological and textual evidence alike suggests that before the Frankish arrival, the territory on which the villa eventually would be

---

2. The privilege is addressed by Emmo to his provincial suffragans Chrodobert of Paris, Faro of Meaux, Bertoaldus of Troyes, and Gauzbertus of Chartres, as well as to Audoin of Rouen and Eligius of Noyon. On the inclusion of Audoin and Eligius, see Ewig, "Bischofsprivilegien für Saint-Maur-des-Fosses," 2:503–4.

3. Pontal, *Die Synoden im Merowingerreich*, 206–7nn36, 39. For the Saint Colombe charter, see Paul Deschamps, "Critique du privilège épiscopal accordé par Emmon de Sens à l'Abbaye de Sainte-Colombe (660, 26 Août)," *Moyen Âge* 25 (1912): 144–65, at 160–64.

4. Ewig, "Das Privileg des Bischofs Berthefrid von Amiens," 2:576–83. Landeric's privilege for Saint Denis states that it was granted at the request of Clovis II without explicit mention of Balthild. Ewig argues that while the privilege for Saint-Pierre-le-Vif refers only to the *petitio* of the abbot and the *congregatio*, the document should still be considered the product of a royal initiative. On Balthild's *Klosterpolitik*, see also chapter 2.

5. *Vita Balthildis* chap. 9. The other named Burgundian monastery is Saint Aignan of Orléans.

6. Didier Perrugot, "Le palais merovingien de Malay (Yonne), histoire et archéologie," in *Palais royaux et princiers au Moyen Age*, ed. Annie Renoux (Le Mans, France: Centre d'édition et de publication de l'Université du Maine, 1996), 147–56, at 147. Malay was located near the forest of Othe. In general, royal residences were situated frequently near hunting grounds; see Carlrichard Brühl, "Remarques sur les notions de 'capitale' et de 'résidence' pendant le Haut Moyen Age," in *Aus Mittelalter und Diplomatik* (Hildesheim, Germany: Weidmann, 1989), 1:115–37, at 130; and Josiane Barbier, "Palais et terres du fisc en Neustrie," in Périn and Feffer, *La Neustrie*, 67–70, at 69.

7. Ernest Desjardins, *Géographie de la Gaule d'après la table de Peutinger* (Paris: Librairie de L. Hachette, 1869), 179. On the location of the villa, see Perrugot, "Le palais merovingien de Malay," 147.

constructed was Roman public land.[8] This land became part of the royal fisc with Clovis's conquest of the Kingdom of Soissons in the 480s, although Mâlay itself does not appear in the documentary record until the seventh century.[9] Nevertheless, the villa almost certainly existed before the Neustrian unification with Burgundy and was constructed as early as the late sixth century.[10] The estate was located on the right bank of the Vanne River to the east of what was once a Roman military camp.[11]

Similar in style to late imperial villas, the main building was a two-storied rectangular stone structure, comprising residential and public spaces. Mâlay remained in use throughout the seventh century but was abandoned as a royal residence probably in the eighth century and was finally destroyed in the tenth.[12] Contemporary sources refer to Mâlay as both a *villa* and a *palatium*.[13] The two terms are not mutually exclusive. In the context of royal landowning, the former term referred in this period simply to an individual unit of property or estate, although not necessarily to the residential building itself.[14] The latter term, with its suggestion of imperial *auctoritas*, indicated a nucleus of royal power that was not merely a residence but also an administrative center.[15] While villas such as Mâlay were modest residences by Roman imperial standards, they nevertheless were intended to impress visitors, as well as express the strength and status of the monarch himself.[16] They were centers, as well as embodiments, of political power.[17]

It was precisely at the moment that Mâlay appears in the historical record that strategically placed rural villas began to play a greater administrative role

---

8. Perrugot, "Le palais merovingien de Malay," 150–51.

9. Bachrach, *Merovingian Military Organization*, 4–5.

10. This dating is supported by ceramics found at the site: Perrugot, "Le palais merovingien de Malay," 153–54.

11. Perrugot, 151. Malay's location near a river was normal for Merovingian-era palaces: Ross Samson, "The Merovingian Nobleman's Home: Castle or Villa," *Journal of Medieval History* 13 (1987): 287–315, at 304.

12. Perrugot, "Le palais merovingien de Malay," 154.

13. Perrugot, 148.

14. Guy Halsall, "Villas, Territories and Communities in Merovingian Northern Gaul," in *People and Space in the Middle Ages, 300–1300*, ed. Wendy Davies, Guy Halsall, and Andrew Reynolds (Turnhout, Belgium: Brepols, 2007), 209–31, at 218–19; Samson, "Merovingian Nobleman's Home," 298–99.

15. Barbier, "Palais et terres du fisc en Neustrie," 69; Josiane Barbier, "Le système palatial franc: Genèse et fonctionnement dans le Nord-Ouest du regnum," *Bibliothèque de l'Ecole des Chartres* 148 (1990): 245–99, at 248–55.

16. Chris Wickham, *The Inheritance of Rome* (New York: Viking, 2009), 243–45.

17. Pierre Riché, "Les représentations du palais dans les textes littéraires du Haut Moyen Age," *Francia* 4 (1976): 161–71.

in the governance of the Merovingian kingdoms.[18] Just one royal residence among several, and by no means the favorite,[19] Mâlay, nevertheless, was an ideal location for assembling the gathered elites of the two subregna that made up the Neustro-Burgundian kingdom. In the bulk of the known occasions when assemblies of secular nobles and prelates gathered at the villa, their agendas dealt either implicitly or explicitly with the representation of the interests of the Burgundian ruling elite at the Neustrian court. In some cases, like the trial of Bishop Leudemund of Sion's coconspirator, the Burgundian *patricius* Aletheus, force was employed to remind these elites of their dependence on the court, while in others the message was expressed more collaboratively.[20] The message itself, however, remained very much the same.[21]

The attendance of the meeting of 660 likewise was reflective of its agenda. Although the privileges sponsored by Balthild explicitly weakened local episcopal control over the privileged establishments, as Barbara Rosenwein has suggested, we need not pity those bishops who subscribed to these documents as passive victims: their communal decision to bestow privileges strengthened their bonds with each other, with the honored institutions, and with the royal court.[22] Additionally, the substantial number of episcopal subscriptions attached

---

18. On the strategic placement of Attigny, Compiègne, and Ponthion, see Annie Renoux, ed., *Palais médiévaux (France-Belgique): 25 ans d'archéologie* (Le Mans, France: Université du Maine, 1994), 25, 37, 80.

19. The editors of *Die Urkunden der Merowinger*, xxv, observe that the geographic distribution of surviving Merovingian royal diplomas reveals a preference for the Frankish heartland between the Marne and Oise. The most frequently cited places of issue are Compiègne (seventeen); followed by Montmacq (seven); then Valenciennes, Quierzy, Nogent-sur-Marne, and Etrepagny (three each); and Clichy, Chatou, and Mâlay (two each).

20. Fredegar, *Chronica* 4.41–42. On Aletheus, see Ebling, *Prosopographie der Amtsträger des Merowingerreiches*, 45–46. Later, in 639, Neustrian and Burgundian nobles met at Mâlay, following the death of King Dagobert I, to raise Clovis II to the throne. Five years earlier, when Clovis II was born, Dagobert had announced his intentions of leaving Neustria and Burgundy intact as a single administrative unit under the rule of his newly born son when the latter came of age. On his deathbed, Dagobert left the matter of succession in the hands of his Neustrian adviser Aega and his widow, Nantechild, who called a kingdom-wide assembly to meet at Mâlay in order to confirm Dagobert's plan of succession (Fredegar, *Chronica* 4.76, 4.79–80). Similarly, on the trial of Bishop Chramlinus of Embrun at Mâlay (677/79), summoned by Ebroin, see *Die Urkunden der Merowinger* no. 122.

21. Karl Ferdinand Werner, "*Missus-marchio-comes*: Entre l'administration centrale et l'administration locale de l'empire carolingien," in *Histoire comparée de l'administration (IVe–XVIIIe siècle)*, ed. Walter Paravicini and Karl Ferdinand Werner (Munich: Artemis Verlag, 1980), 191–239, at 193–94, notes that in the Carolingian era, when kings met with the nobles of a peripheral region, they would often gather at a royal residence along the border of the residential zone and the route into that region.

22. Rosenwein, *Negotiating Space*, 80–81. Cf. Nelson, "Queens as Jezebels," 41. Albrecht Diem, "Who Is Allowed to Pray for the King? Saint-Maurice d'Agaune and the Creation of a Burgundian Identity," in *Post-Roman Transitions: Christian and Barbarian Identities in the Early Medieval West*, ed. Walter Pohl and Gerda Heydemann (Turnhout, Belgium: Brepols, 2013), 47–88, at 78, similarly recognizes the episcopal authors of seventh-century privileges as willing participants but suggests that as sponsors of Columbanian monasteries they "represented the interests of their own families rather

to this privilege charter is reflective of Balthild's efforts to work collaboratively with the episcopal elite of both Neustria and Burgundy. All but two ecclesiastical provinces in the Neustro-Burgundian regnum were represented at the meeting of 660.[23] Comparatively fewer subscribers, however, came from the Burgundian provinces of Lyons, Arles, and Vienne, which were represented by only seven bishops in all. Sens—the bulk of whose *civitates* traditionally had been oriented toward Burgundy, but which also included Paris—Rheims, Rouen, and Tours, in contrast, were represented by a significantly greater number of bishops (six, five, four, and two, respectively), which perhaps is not surprising considering the location of the privileged institution. Two prelates from the Aquitanian provinces of Bourges and Bordeaux were represented. It is significant that all four of the subscribing metropolitans had their sees in Burgundian territory. These were the senior prelates at the meeting, and the ones who presided over its agenda. It was their consensus above all that gave Emmo's privilege its legitimacy.

So, while the meeting's attendance tilted toward Neustria, including many bishops from dioceses in reasonably close proximity to the royal villa as well as the privileged institution, Balthild appears to have made a concerted effort to permit the few Burgundian bishops in attendance a leadership role, ensuring their support for her agenda by recognizing their prestige and their authority. Her efforts may have been in part influenced by her larger goal of ensuring internal political stability in Burgundy, which had been wracked by political factionalism since the 640s.[24] Bishops had been involved in these disputes, which were concerned, at least in part, with Neustrian influence in Burgundian affairs. Now that stability had been restored, Balthild had every reason to wish to strengthen relations between her court and the leading bishops of the region. So far as contemporary

---

than a structural episcopal interest or claim for control." More broadly, he argues in his study "Gregory's Chess Board: Monastic Conflict and Competition in Early Medieval Gaul," in *Compétition et sacré au Haut Moyen Âge: Entre médiation et exclusion*, ed. Philippe Depreux, François Bougard, and Régine Le Jan (Turnhout, Belgium: Brepols, 2015), 165–91, for increased "competition" between bishops and monks during the seventh century. I hope to address this issue myself in a future publication. On Columbanus's own relations with the Gallic episcopate, cf., e.g., Clare Stancliffe, "Columbanus and the Gallic Bishops," in *Auctoritas: Mélanges offerts à Olivier Guillot*, ed. Giles Constable and Michel Rouche (Paris: Presses de l'Université Paris Sorbonne, 2006), 205–15; Caitlin Corning, "Columbanus and the Easter Controversy: Theological, Social and Political Contexts," in *The Irish in Early Medieval Europe: Identity, Culture and Religion*, ed. Roy Flechner and Sven Meeder (New York: Palgrave Macmillan, 2016), 101–15; and O'Hara, *Jonas of Bobbio*, 51–55.

23. The exceptions were Eauze and Besançon.

24. *Vita Balthildis* chap. 5. On Burgundian factionalism, see Fredegar, *Chronica* chaps. 89–90. On Balthild's efforts to secure stability in Burgundy, see Fouracre and Gerberding, *Late Merovingian France*, 20, who identify Floachad's faction with the Neustrian court, and Willebad's with the "traditional Burgundian nobility."

sources reveal, her efforts were mostly successful, strengthened by the Burgundian aristocrats' recognition of the benefits of associating themselves with the Neustrian court.[25]

This study concludes with Emmo's privilege not because in itself it represents an ostensible "watershed" moment in episcopal-monarchical relations in the *regnum Francorum*. Without discounting the significance or innovative features of Balthild's *Klosterpolitik*, or its impact on targeted institutions and dioceses, the privilege issued at the royal villa of Mâlay in 660 exemplifies those long-standing features of the intersection between the ecclesiastical responsibilities of the Gallo-Frankish episcopate on the one hand and the expectations and demands of the court on the other. The bishops at Mâlay were not acting merely as royal agents in facilitating the queen's elaborate program of ecclesiastical patronage; they were collaborators, not servants, and it is clear that Balthild never lacked episcopal support for her agenda.[26] Similar to her royal predecessors, she assumed both her divinely mandated right and obligation to maintain the *pax et tranquilitas* of the Gallo-Frankish church and the necessity of working with the episcopal caretakers of the constituent administrative units that formed the federated church.[27]

Likewise, similar to her predecessors, Balthild recognized the special *auctoritas* of bishops as members of a unique *ordo*. And while her support for monasticism had the effect of limiting episcopal jurisdiction in specific circumstances, her goals never included undermining the order, its basic administrative structure, or its unique spiritual and institutional prerogatives. As her hagiographer later wrote, she esteemed bishops as *patres*.[28] And as Susan Wood has observed of Emmo's concession to Saint-Pierre-le-Vif specifically, this grant, as a "lesser" privilege, "promised barely more than was required already by the common canon law," and its episcopal subscribers, "for reasons of friendship, piety, or respect for monastic life," effectively agreed to abandon their own, more expansive, interpretation of

---

25. Nelson, "Queens as Jezebels," 21–22. On Balthild's possibly exaggerated involvement in the murder of the Mâlay attendee Aunemund of Lyons shortly after the meeting, see Nelson, 34–38. Nelson prefers to view the murder as the result of a regional factional conflict. See also Fox, *Power and Religion*, 41–42.
26. Ian Wood, *Merovingian Kingdoms*, 201.
27. Additionally, as noted by Yitzhak Hen, *Culture and Religion in Merovingian Gaul, AD 481–751* (Leiden: Brill, 1995), 55, there is no reason to doubt that personal piety was a significant factor influencing Balthild's *Klosterpolitik*.
28. *Vita Balthildis* chap. 4. Conversely, she loved monks as *fratres*.

episcopal jurisdictional power in the case of this particular institution.[29] Coercion, in other words, was unnecessary.

That said, in other instances Balthild certainly employed traditional methods of encouraging episcopal collaboration, including promoting her own candidates for ecclesiastical office.[30] And regardless of her culpability in the deaths of nine bishops, as infamously charged by Stephen of Ripon, she did share her royal predecessors' impatience for bishops resistant to her agenda.[31] While bishops like Nicetius of Trier and Germanus of Paris may have earned praise from Gregory of Tours for their bravery in refusing to yield in the face of royal power, such acts continued to be the exception, not the rule. The Gallo-Frankish bishops, as we have seen, generally were more strategic and cautious in their explicit challenges to royal power, in those instances both when they spoke as individual pastors and when they spoke in their corporate voice. When bishops more directly challenged monarchs, it typically was as members of broad political coalitions, as was the case, for instance, with one of Balthild's own episcopal appointees: Leudegar of Autun.

In Merovingian Gaul, bishops and kings did not "compete" for power or influence, nor did they seek to undermine each other as putative rivals. Nor did individual prelates represent "local" interests in perpetual opposition to the centralizing policies of the court. From Clovis onward, the Merovingians recognized the legitimacy and utility of episcopal authority, and they sought to align it with royal interests and initiatives. Threats and penalties aimed at individual bishops were justified on the grounds of the accused's own supposed crimes, and neither were intended to, or resulted in, the diminution of the order. While a king such as Chilperic I might generalize about the corporate episcopate in complaining about episcopal wealth and power, even he enthusiastically sought bishops' cooperation, loyalty, and service.

Abandoning an unnecessary and anachronistic opposition between a monolithic church and political state permits us to better appreciate the relationship between Gallo-Frankish bishops and the Merovingian monarchy on two levels: institutional and individual. The monarchy and the episcopate for the entirety of the Merovingian kingdom implicitly shared a mutual recognition of the benefits of collaboration. This collaboration not only had the acknowledged potential of encouraging peace and social order but also

---

29. Susan Wood, *Proprietary Church*, 193–94.
30. Fouracre and Gerberding, *Late Merovingian France*, 110.
31. Stephen of Ripon, *Vita Wilfridi episcopi Eboracensis*, ed. Wilhelm Levison, MGH SRM 6 (Hanover, Germany: Hahn, 1913), chap. 6.

ultimately helped to legitimize the acknowledged power of both institutions. Through their service to the court, bishops tacitly acknowledged the legitimacy of the royal regime and its institutions, while royal patronage provided the episcopate both with material support and with an acknowledgment of its spiritual and jurisdictional prerogatives. On the level of individuals, this ostensibly productive collaboration could, and sometimes did, break down due to an incompatibility of priorities, agendas, and personalities. In such cases, royal power usually prevailed, despite the ostensibly heroic counterexamples highlighted by hagiographers and episcopal chroniclers.

But even more significant than conflicts between individual prelates and monarchs were those instances in which the Merovingians succeeded in instigating collaboration through various inducements of patronage, not only because of the myriad benefits that such patronage offered but also because of the inequities and divisions that it created—or at the very least exacerbated—within the episcopal order. Bishops were drawn into partisan politics not simply as a consequence of aristocratic birth or the social status derived from their high office but also because the Merovingians recognized, and consistently attempted to take advantage of, the inherent quality of episcopal power to transcend the gap between the *civitas* and the court.

The consequence of this royal interference was not, as we have seen, the wholesale co-optation or disintegration of the episcopal order, either in terms of its moral authority or in terms of its institutional integrity and prerogatives. In the short term, royal patronage could, and on many occasions did, undermine consensus within the episcopal order, encouraging bishops to align themselves politically and sometimes causing them to lose their freedom or lives as a result. In the long term, however, its effects were far less dramatic, if no less significant. The Gallo-Frankish bishops remained a recognizably distinct *ordo* from secular officeholders, and this order did not undergo any sort of demonstrable secularization over the course of the Merovingian era. The seventh and early eighth centuries did witness new institutional manifestations of episcopal collaboration with the court, as well as new articulations of the venerable notion that such collaboration ultimately ensured the effective governance of the realm. However, the result was not a more politically engaged episcopate but only perhaps a more explicit acknowledgment by bishops, monarchs, and secular aristocrats alike of the obligation of ecclesiastical and secular elites to work collaboratively within the court to assist the monarchy in securing peace and stability. This acknowledgment did not necessitate a greater number of bishops engaging in court politics, let alone the secularization of those who did, neither of which is obviously demonstrable on the basis of prosopographical evidence.[32]

The endurance of the Gallo-Frankish corporate episcopate despite centuries of disagreements and divisions was a consequence, in part, of the exceptionality of the episcopal office, whose occupants assumed not only a unique spiritual authority but also a common fraternal identity that was expected to transcend existing familial, social, and political relationships. But this endurance also was a consequence of the nature of episcopal consensus itself. If consensus was a goal, and not a perpetual quality, of the order then it should not be surprising that bishops devoted so much necessary energy toward its continual maintenance and repair. To put it another way, the corporate integrity of the episcopate never was simply assumed; rather, it was akin to an eternal flame that each successive generation of bishops was expected to keep alight. And while political winds consistently—and sometimes violently—buffeted it, scattering numerous sparks in the process, the flame itself never went out.

---

32. More generally, any perceived decadence in the late seventh- and early eighth-century Gallo-Frankish church is complicated by the demonstrable widespread interest during this period in biblical, patristic, hagiographical, and canonical literature, although certainly not all relevant works and manuscripts can necessarily be associated with bishops or episcopal sees specifically. See in general Ian Wood, "The Problem of Late Merovingian Culture," in *Exzerpieren - Kompilieren - Tradieren: Transformationen des Wissens zwischen Spätantike und Frühmittelalter*, ed. Stephan Dusil, Gerald Schwedler, and Raphael Schwitter (Berlin: De Gruyter, 2017), 199–222. On canon law specifically, see Hubert Mordek, "Kanonistische Activität in Gallien in der ersten Hälfte des 8. Jahrunderts," *Francia* 2 (1974): 19–25.

Bibliography

Primary Sources

Acta Aunemundi alias Dalfini episcopi. AASS Sept. vol. 7, 744–46. Antwerp: Bernard Albert Van Der Plassche, 1760.
Ado of Vienne. *Chronicon.* Edited by J. P. Migne. PL 123. Paris: Garnier Brothers, 1879.
Annales Mettensis Priores. Edited by Bernhard Simson. MGH SRG 10. Hanover, Germany: Hahn, 1905.
Avitus of Vienne. *Opera.* Edited by Rudolf Peiper. MGH AA 6.2. Berlin: Weidmann, 1883. Translated by Shanzer and Wood as *Avitus of Vienne.*
Baudonivia. *Vita Radegundis Liber II.* Edited by Bruno Krusch. MGH SRM 2. Hanover, Germany: Hahn, 1888.
Bede. *Historia ecclesiastica gentis Anglorum.* Edited by Bertram Colgrave and R. A. B. Mynors. Rev. ed. Oxford: Clarendon, 1992.
Bertarius. *Gesta episcoporum Virdunensium.* Edited by D. G. Waitz. MGH SS 4. Hanover, Germany: Hahn, 1841.
Bertholdus. *Vita Maximini abbatis Miciacensis.* Edited by Luc d'Achéry and Jean Mabillon. AASS OSB 1. Paris: Louis Billaine, 1668.
Bertram of Le Mans. *Das Testament des Bischofs Berthramn von Le Mans.* Edited by Margarete Weidemann. Mainz, Germany: Verlag des Römisch-Germanischen Zentralmuseums, 1986.
The Bobbio Missal: A Gallican Mass Book. Edited by E. A. Lowe. Henry Bradshaw Society Publications 58. London: Harrison and Sons, 1920.
Boniface. *S. Bonifatii et Lulli epistolae.* Edited by Ernst Dümmler. MGH Epistolae 3. Berlin: Weidmann, 1892.
Caesarius of Arles. *Sancti Caesarii episcopi Arelatensis Opera omnia.* 2 vols. Edited by Germain Morin. Brugge, Belgium: Maretioli, 1937–42.
Capitularia regum Francorum. Edited by Alfred Boretius. MGH Legum Sectio 2: Capitularia regum Francorum. Hanover, Germany: Hahn, 1883.
The Cartulary of Montier-en-Der, 666–1129. Edited by Constance Brittain Bouchard. Toronto: University of Toronto Press, 2004.
Chartae Latinae Antiquiores: Facsimile Edition of the Latin Charters prior to the Ninth Century. 49 vols. Edited by Albert Bruckner, Robert Marichal, Olten Lausanne, and Dietikon-Zürich. Switzerland: Urs Graf, 1954–1998.
Concilia aevi Merovingici. Edited by Friedrich Maassen. MGH Legum Sectio 3: Concilia, Tomus 1. Hanover, Germany: Hahn, 1893.

BIBLIOGRAPHY

Concilia Galliae: A.314–A.506. Edited by Charles Munier. CCSL 148. Turnhout, Belgium: Brepols, 1963.

Concilia Galliae: A.511–A.695. Edited by Charles de Clercq. CCSL 148A. Turnhout, Belgium: Brepols, 1963. Translated by Gaudemet and Basdevant-Gaudemet as *Les canons des conciles mérovingiens*.

Cyprian of Carthage. *De catholicae ecclesiae unitate*. Edited by Maurice Bévenot. CCSL 3. Turnhout, Belgium: Brepols, 1972.

———. *Sancti Cypriani episcopi epistularium*. 3 vols. Edited by G. F. Diercks. CCSL 3B-D. Turnhout, Belgium: Brepols, 1994–99.

Decrees of the Ecumenical Councils. Edited by Norman P. Tanner. London: Sheed and Ward; Washington, DC: Georgetown University Press, 1990.

Desiderius of Cahors. *Epistulae S. Desiderii Cadurcensis*. Edited by Dag Norberg. Uppsala, Sweden: Almquist and Wiksell, 1961.

Epistolae aevi Merowingici collectae. Edited by Wilhelm Gundlach. MGH Epistolae 3. Berlin: Weidmann, 1892.

Epistolae Arelatenses genuinae. Edited by Wilhelm Gundlach. MGH Epistolae 3. Berlin: Weidmann, 1892.

Epistolae Austrasicae. Edited by Wilhelm Gundlach. MGH Epistolae 3. Berlin: Weidmann, 1892.

Epistolae Wisigoticae. Edited by Wilhelm Gundlach. MGH Epistolae 3. Berlin: Weidmann, 1892.

Flodoard of Rheims. *Historiae Remensis Ecclesiae*. Edited by Martina Stratmann. MGH SS 36. Hanover, Germany: Hahn, 1998.

Fortunatus, Venantius. *Carmina*. Edited by Friedrich Leo. MGH AA 4.1. Berlin: Weidmann, 1881.

———. *Vita Radegundis Liber I*. Edited by Bruno Krusch. MGH SRM 2. Hanover, Germany: Hahn, 1888.

Fouracre, Paul, and Richard Gerberding, eds. *Late Merovingian France*. Manchester: Manchester University Press, 1996.

Fredegar. *Chronica*. Edited by Bruno Krusch. MGH SRM 2. Hanover, Germany: Hahn, 1888.

Gaudemet, Jean, and Brigitte Basdevant-Gaudemet, trans. *Les canons des conciles mérovingiens (VIe–VIIe siècles)*. SC 354. Paris: Cerf, 1989.

Gesta abbatum Fontanellensium. Edited and translated by Pascal Pradié. Paris: Les Belles Lettres, 1999.

Gesta episcoporum Autissiodorensium. Edited and translated by Michel Sot, Guy Lobrichon, and Monique Goullet. Paris: Belles Lettres, 2002.

Gregory I. *Registrum epistularum*. Edited by Dag Norberg. CCSL 140. Turnhout, Belgium: Brepols, 1972.

Gregory of Tours. *Decem libri historiarum*. Edited by Bruno Krusch and Wilhelm Levison. MGH SRM 1.1. Hanover, Germany: Hahn, 1951.

———. *Liber in gloria confessorum*. Edited by Bruno Krusch. MGH SRM 1.2. Hanover, Germany: Hahn, 1885 [reprint 1969].

———. *Liber in gloria martyrum*. Edited by Bruno Krusch. MGH SRM 1.2. Hanover, Germany: Hahn, 1885 [reprint 1969].

———. *Liber vitae patrum*. Edited by Bruno Krusch. MGH SRM 1.2. Hanover, Germany: Hahn, 1885 [reprint 1969].

———. *Libri de virtutibus Sancti Martini episcopi*. Edited by Bruno Krusch. MGH SRM 1.2. Hanover, Germany: Hahn, 1885 [reprint 1969].

Hincmar of Rheims. *Vita Remigii episcopi Remensis*. Edited by Bruno Krusch. MGH SRM 3. Hanover, Germany: Hahn, 1896.

Isidore of Seville. *De ecclesiasticis officiis*. Edited by Christopher M. Lawson. CCSL 113. Turnhout, Belgium: Brepols, 1989.

———. *Las Historias de los godos, vándalos y suevos de Isidoro de Sevilla*. Edited and translated by Cristóbal Rodríguez Alonso. León, Spain: Centro de Estudios e Investigación San Isidoro, 1975.

Jonas of Bobbio. *Vitae Columbani abbatis discipulorumque eius libri duo auctore Iona*. Edited by Bruno Krusch. MGH SRM 4. Hanover, Germany: Hahn, 1902.

Le Blant, Edmond, ed. *Inscriptions chrétiennes de la Gaule antérieures au VIIIe siècle*. 2 vols. Paris: L'Imprimerie Impériale, 1856–65.

Leges Alamannorum. 2nd ed. Edited by Karl Lehmann and Karl August Eckhardt. MGH LL nat. Germ. 5.1. Hanover, Germany: Hahn, 1966.

Lex Baiwariorum. Edited by Ernst Maria Augustin Schwind. MGH LL nat. Germ. 5.2. Hanover, Germany: Hahn, 1926.

Lex Ribuaria. Edited by Franz Beyerle and Rudolf Buchner. MGH LL nat. Germ. 3.2. Hanover, Germany: Hahn, 1954.

Liber historiae Francorum. Edited by Bruno Krusch. MGH SRM 2. Hanover, Germany: Hahn, 1888.

Liber sacramentorum Romanae ecclesiae ordinis anni circuli (Sacramentarium Gelasianum). Edited by Leo C. Mohlberg, Leo Eizenhöfer, and Petrus Siffrin. Rome: Herder, 1960.

Marculfi formulae. Edited by Karl Zeumer. MGH Legum Sectio 5: Formulae. Hanover, Germany: Hahn, 1886. Translated by Rio as *Formularies of Angers and Marculf*.

Marius of Avenches. *Chronica*. Edited and translated by Justin Favrod. Lausanne: Université de Lausanne, 1993.

Mathisen, Ralph, trans. *Ruricius of Limoges and Friends: A Collection of Letters from Visigothic Gaul*. Liverpool: Liverpool University Press, 1999.

Missale Francorum. Edited by Leo C. Mohlberg. Rome: Herder, 1957.

Pactus legis Salicae. Edited by Karl Eckhardt. MGH LL nat. Germ. 4.1. Hanover, Germany: Hahn, 1962.

Pardessus, J. M., ed. *Diplomata, chartae, epistolae, leges aliaque instrumenta ad res Gallo-Francicas spectantia*. 2 vols. Aalen, Germany: Scientia Verlag, 1843–49.

Passio Desiderii episcopi Viennensis. Edited by Bruno Krusch. MGH SRM 3. Hanover, Germany: Hahn, 1896.

Passio Leudegarii episcopi et martyris Augustodunensis I. Edited by Bruno Krusch. MGH SRM 5. Hanover, Germany: Hahn, 1910.

Passio Praeiecti episcopi et martyris Arverneni. Edited by Bruno Krusch. MGH SRM 5. Hanover, Germany: Hahn, 1910.

Paul the Deacon. *Liber de episcopis Mettensibus*. Edited and translated by Damien Kempf. Leuven, Belgium: Brepols, 2013.

Pseudo-Jerome. *De septem ordinibus ecclesiae*. Edited by Athanasius Walter Kalff. PhD diss., University of Würzburg, 1935.

Remigius. *Testamentum*. Edited by Bruno Krusch. MGH SRM 3. Hanover, Germany: Hahn, 1896.
Rio, Alice, trans. *The Formularies of Angers and Marculf*. Liverpool: Liverpool University Press, 2008.
Ruricius of Limoges. *Fausti aliorumque epistulae ad Ruricium aliosque*. Edited by Bruno Krusch. MGH AA 8. Berlin: Weidmann, 1887. Translated by Mathisen as *Ruricius of Limoges and Friends*.
Shanzer, Danuta, and Ian Wood, trans. *Avitus of Vienne: Letters and Selected Prose*. Liverpool: Liverpool University Press, 2002.
Sisebut. *Vita vel passio Desiderii episcopi Viennensis*. Edited by Bruno Krusch. MGH SRM 3. Hanover, Germany: Hahn, 1896.
Les Statuta ecclesiae antiqua: Édition, études critiques. Edited by Charles Munier. Paris: Presses Universitaires de France, 1960.
Stephen of Ripon. *Vita Wilfridi episcopi Eboracensis*. Edited by Wilhelm Levison. MGH SRM 6. Hanover, Germany: Hahn, 1913.
Die Urkunden der Arnulfinger. Edited by Ingrid Heidrich. Hanover, Germany: Hahn, 2011.
Die Urkunden der Merowinger. Edited by Carlrichard Brühl, Theo Kölzer, Martina Hartmann, and Andrea Stieldorf. Hanover, Germany: Hahn, 2001.
Visio Baronti monachi Longoretensis. Edited by Wilhelm Levison. MGH SRM 5. Hanover, Germany: Hahn, 1910.
Vita Amandi prima. Edited by Bruno Krusch. MGH SRM 5. Hanover, Germany: Hahn, 1910.
Vita Anstrudis abbatissae Laudunensis. Edited by Wilhelm Levison. MGH SRM 6. Hanover, Germany: Hahn, 1913.
Vita Arnulfi. Edited Bruno Krusch. MGH SRM 2. Hanover, Germany: Hahn, 1888.
Vita Audoini episcopi Rotomagensis. Edited by Wilhelm Levison. MGH SRM 5. Hanover, Germany: Hahn, 1910.
Vita Austrigisili episcopi Biturigi. Edited by Bruno Krusch. MGH SRM 4. Hanover, Germany: Hahn, 1902.
Vita Baldomeri. AASS Feb. vol. 3, 683–84. Antwerp: J. Meursium, 1658.
Vita Balthildis. Edited by Bruno Krusch. MGH SRM 2. Hanover, Germany: Hahn, 1888.
Vita Bertilae abbatissae Calensis. Edited by Wilhelm Levison. MGH SRM 6. Hanover, Germany: Hahn, 1913.
Vita Boniti episcopi Arverni. Edited by Bruno Krusch. MGH SRM 6. Hanover, Germany: Hahn, 1913.
Vita Caesarii episcopi Arelatensis. Edited by Bruno Krusch. MGH SRM 3. Hanover, Germany: Hahn, 1896.
Vita Desiderii Cadurcae urbis episcopi. Edited by Bruno Krusch. MGH SRM 4. Hanover, Germany: Hahn, 1902.
Vita Eligii episcopi Noviomagensis. Edited by Bruno Krusch. MGH SRM 4. Hanover, Germany: Hahn, 1902.
Vita Erminonis abbatis Lobbiensis. Edited by Wilhelm Levison. MGH SRM 6. Hanover, Germany: Hahn, 1913.
Vita Filiberti abbatis Gemeticensis et Heriensis. Edited by Wilhelm Levison. MGH SRM 5. Hanover, Germany: Hahn, 1910.

Vita Gaugerici episcopi Camaracensis. Edited by Bruno Krusch. MGH SRM 3. Hanover, Germany: Hahn, 1896.
Vita Genovefae virginis Parisiensis. Edited by Bruno Krusch. MGH SRM 3. Hanover, Germany: Hahn, 1896.
Vita Goaris confessoris Rhenani. Edited by Bruno Krusch. MGH SRM 4. Hanover, Germany: Hahn, 1888.
Vita Landiberti episcopi Traeiectensis auctore Nicolao. Edited by Bruno Krusch. MGH SRM 6. Hanover, Germany: Hahn, 1913.
Vita Nicetii episcopi Lugdunensis. Edited by Bruno Krusch. MGH SRM 3. Hanover, Germany: Hahn, 1896.
Vita Rigoberti episcopi Remensis. Edited by Wilhelm Levison. MGH SRM 7. Hanover, Germany: Hahn, 1920.
Vita Rusticulae sive Marciae abbatissae Arelatensis. Edited by Bruno Krusch. MGH SRM 4. Hanover, Germany: Hahn, 1902.
Vita Vedastis episcopi Atrebatensis. Edited by Bruno Krusch. MGH SRM 3. Hanover, Germany: Hahn, 1896.
Vita Verani. AASS Oct. vol. 8, 467–70. Paris: Palmé, 1870.
Vita Walarici abbatis Leuconaensis. Edited by Bruno Krusch. MGH SRM 4. Hanover, Germany: Hahn, 1902.
Walstra, Gerard J. J., ed. *Les cinq épîtres rimées dans l'appendice des formules de Sens*. Leiden: Brill, 1962.
Wampach, Camille, ed. *Geschichte der Grundherrschaft Echternach in Frühmittelalter*, vol. 1.2, *Quellenband*. Luxembourg: Luxemburger Kunstdruckerei, 1930.
Weidemann, Margarete, ed. *Geschichte des Bistums Le Mans von der Spätantike bis zur Karolingerzeit*. 3 vols. Mainz, Germany: Verlag des Römisch-Germanischen Zentralmuseums in Kommission bei Habelt, 2002.

Secondary Sources

Althoff, Gerd. *Family, Friends, and Followers: Political and Social Bonds in Early Medieval Europe*. Translated by Christopher Carroll. Cambridge: Cambridge University Press, 2004.
——. "(Royal) Favor: A Central Concept in Early Medieval Hierarchical Relations." In Jussen, *Ordering Medieval Society*, 243–69.
Amidon, Philip R. "The Procedure of St. Cyprian's Synods." *Vigiliae Christianae* 37 (1983): 328–39.
Amiet, Robert. "Verano." In *Bibliotheca Sanctorum*, edited by Filippo Caraffa et al., 12:1017–21. Rome: Citta Nuova Editrice for Istituto Giovanni XXIII della Pontificia Universita Lateranense, 1969.
Anton, Hans Hubert. "'Bischofsherrschaften' und 'Bischofsstaaten' in Spätantike und Frühmittelalter: Reflexionen zu ihrer Genese, Struktur und Typologie." In *Liber amicorum necnon et amicarum für Alfred Heit*, edited by Friedhelm Burgard, 461–73. Trier, Germany: Verlag Trierer Historische Forschungen, 1996.
——. *Fürstenspiegel des frühen und hohen Mittelalters*. Darmstadt, Germany: Wissenschaftliche Buchgesellschaft, 2006.

———. "Königsvorstellungen bei Iren und Franken im Vergleich." In *Das frühmittelalterliche Königtum: Ideele und religiöse Grundlagen*, edited by Franz-Reiner Erkens (Berlin: De Gruyter, 2005), 270–330.

———. "Die Trierer Kirche und das nördliche Gallien in spätrömischer und fränkischer Zeit." In Atsma, *La Neustrie*, 2:53–73.

Atsma, Hartmut, ed. *La Neustrie: Les pays au nord de la Loire de 650 à 850*. 2 vols. Sigmaringen, Germany: Jan Thorbecke, 1989.

Bachrach, Bernard S. *Anatomy of a Little War: A Diplomatic and Military History of the Gundovald Affair (568–586)*. Boulder, CO: Westview, 1994.

———. *Early Carolingian Warfare*. Philadelphia: University of Pennsylvania Press, 2001.

———. "Fifth-Century Metz: Late Roman Christian *Urbs* or Ghost Town?" *Antiquité Tardive* 10 (2002): 363–81.

———. *Merovingian Military Organization, 481–751*. Minneapolis: University of Minnesota Press, 1972.

———. "Procopius and the Chronology of Clovis's Reign." *Viator* 1 (1970): 21–31.

Bailey, Lisa Kaaren. *Christianity's Quiet Success: The Eusebius Gallicanus Sermon Collection and the Power of the Church in Late Antique Gaul*. Notre Dame, IN: University of Notre Dame Press, 2010.

———. *The Religious Worlds of the Laity in Late Antique Gaul*. London: Bloomsbury, 2016.

Barbier, Josiane. "Palais et terres du fisc en Neustrie." In Périn and Feffer, *La Neustrie*, 67–70.

———. "Le système palatial franc: Genèse et fonctionnement dans le Nord-Ouest du regnum." *Bibliothèque de l'Ecole des Chartres* 148 (1990): 245–99.

Barrett, Graham, and George Woudhuysen. "Assembling the *Austrasian Letters* at Trier and Lorsch." *Early Medieval Europe* 24, no. 1 (2016): 3–57.

———. "Remigius and the 'Important News' of Clovis Rewritten." *Antiquité Tardive* 24 (2016): 471–500.

Barrow, Julia. "The Bishop in the Latin West 600–1100." In *Celibate and Childless Men in Power: Ruling Eunuchs and Bishops in the Pre-modern World*, edited by Almut Höfert, Matthew M. Mesley, and Serena Tolino, 43–64. London: Routledge, 2018.

Basdevant-Gaudemet, Brigitte. "Childebert et les évêques: Note sur une procédure de désignation épiscopale." *Revue historique de droit français et étranger* 74 (1996): 567–72.

Batiffol, Pierre. "Le règlement des premiers conciles africains et le règlement du sénat romain." *Bulletin d'ancienne littérature et d'archéologie chrétiennes* 3 (1913): 3–19.

Bayer, Clemons M. M. "Vita Eligii." In *Reallexikon der germanischen Altertumskunde*, 2nd ed., edited by Heinrich Beck, Dieter Geuenich, and Heiko Steuer, 35:461–524. Berlin: Walter de Gruyter, 2007.

Beaujard, Brigitte. "L'évêque dans la cité en Gaule aux Ve et VIe siècles." In Lepelley, *La fin de la cité antique*, 127–45.

———. "Sens." In *Province ecclésiastique de Sens*, edited by Jean-Charles Picard, Brigitte Beaujard, Elzbieta Dabrowska, Christine Laplace, Noël Duval, Patrick Périn, and Luce Piétri, 19–32. Topographie chrétienne des cités de la Gaule 8. Paris: Boccard, 1992.

Becher, Matthias. *Chlodwig I: Der Aufstieg der Merowinger und das Ende der antiken Welt*. Munich: C. H. Beck, 2011.

Beck, Henry G. J. *The Pastoral Care of Souls in South-East France during the Sixth Century*. Rome: Apud Aedes Universitatis Gregorianae, 1950.

Berger, Adolf. *The Encyclopedic Dictionary of Roman Law*. Philadelphia: American Philosophical Society, 1953.

Bergmann, Werner. "Untersuchungen zu den Gerichtsurkunden der Merowingerzeit." *Archiv für diplomatik* 22 (1976): 1–186.

Beyerle, Franz. "Das legislative Werk Chilperichs I." *Zeitschrift der Savigny-Stiftung für Rechtsgeschichte, Germanische Abteilung* 78 (1961): 1–38.

Bitel, Lisa. *Landscape with Two Saints*. Oxford: Oxford University Press, 2009.

Bloch, Marc. *Feudal Society*. Translated by L. A. Manyon. Chicago: University of Chicago Press, 1961.

Bonnell, Heinrich. *Die anfänge des karolingischen hauses*. Berlin: Duncker und Humblot, 1866.

Bouchard, Constance. *Rewriting Saints and Ancestors: Memory and Forgetting in France, 500–1200*. Philadelphia: University of Pennsylvania Press, 2015.

Brennan, Brian. "The Career of Venantius Fortunatus." *Traditio* 41 (1985): 49–78.

———. "The Conversion of the Jews of Clermont in AD 576." *Journal of Theological Studies* 36 (1985): 321–37.

———. "The Image of the Frankish Kings in the Poetry of Venantius Fortunatus." *Journal of Medieval History* 10, no. 1 (1984): 1–11.

———. "The Image of the Merovingian Bishop in the Poetry of Venantius Fortunatus." *Journal of Medieval History* 18, no. 2 (1992): 115–39.

Brent, Allen. *Cyprian and Roman Carthage*. Cambridge: Cambridge University Press, 2010.

Brestian, Scott de. "Vascones and Visigoths: Creation and Transformation of Identity in Northern Spain in Late Antiquity." In *Romans, Barbarians, and the Transformation of the Roman World*, edited by Ralph Mathisen and Danuta Shanzer, 283–97. Farnham, England: Ashgate, 2011.

Breukelaar, Adriaan. *Historiography and Episcopal Authority in Sixth-Century Gaul*. Göttingen, Germany: Vandenhoeck and Ruprecht, 1994.

Broome, Richard. "Approaches to the Frankish Community in the *Chronicle of Fredegar* and *Liber Historiae Francorum*." In *The Long Seventh Century: Continuity and Discontinuity in an Age of Transition*, edited by Alessandro Gnasso, Emanuele E. Intagliata, and Thomas J. MacMaster, 61–86. Oxford: Peter Lang, 2015.

Brown, Peter. *The Cult of the Saints*. Chicago: University of Chicago Press, 1981.

———. "From *Amator Patriae* to *Amator Pauperum* and Back Again: Social Imagination and Social Change in the West between Late Antiquity and the Early Middle Ages, ca. 300–600." In *Cultures in Motion*, edited by Daniel Rodgers, Bhavani Raman, and Helmut Reimitz, 87–106. Princeton, NJ: Princeton University Press, 2014.

———. *Poverty and Leadership in the Later Roman Empire*. Hanover, NH: University Press of New England, 2002.

———. *The Ransom of the Soul: Afterlife and Wealth in Early Western Christianity*. Cambridge, MA: Harvard University Press, 2015.

———. *The Rise of Western Christendom: Triumph and Diversity, A.D. 200–1000*. Rev. ed. Oxford: Wiley, 2013.

———. "The Study of Elites in Late Antiquity." *Arethusa* 33, no. 3 (2000): 321–46.

———. *Through the Eye of a Needle: Wealth, the Fall of Rome, and the Making of Christianity in the West, 350–550 A.D.* Princeton, NJ: Princeton University Press, 2012.

Brühl, Carlrichard. "Remarques sur les notions de 'capitale' et de 'résidence' pendant le Haut Moyen Age." In *Aus Mittelalter und Diplomatik*, 1:115–37. Hildesheim, Germany: Weidmann, 1989.

Buchner, Rudolf. *Die Provence in Merowingischer Zeit*. Stuttgart, Germany: W. Kohlhammer, 1933.

Cameron, Averil. "The Early Religious Policies of Justin II." In *The Orthodox Churches and the West*, edited by Derek Baker, 51–67. Studies in Church History 13. Oxford: Blackwell, 1976.

Candido da Silva, Marcelo. "Le prince, la *lex* et la *iustitia*: Le Bréviaire d'Alaric et l'Édit attribué à Clotaire II." In *Le Bréviaire d'Alaric aux origines du code civil*, edited by Michel Rouche and Bruno Dumézil, 199–212. Paris: Presses de l'Université de Sorbonne, 2008.

Casson, Lionel. *Travel in the Ancient World*. Baltimore: Johns Hopkins University Press, 1994.

Champagne, J., and R. Szramkiewicz. "Recherches sur les conciles des temps mérovingiens." *Revue historique de droit français et étranger* 49 (1971): 5–49.

Charles-Edwards, T. M. *Early Christian Ireland*. Cambridge: Cambridge University Press, 2000.

Claude, Dietrich. "Die Bestellung der Bischöfe im merowingischen Reich." *Zeitschrift der Savigny-Stiftung für Rechtsgeschichte Kanonistische Abteilung* 49 (1963): 1–75.

Claussen, M. A. *The Reform of the Frankish Church: Chrodegang of Metz and the Regula Canonicorum in the Eighth Century*. Cambridge: Cambridge University Press, 2004.

Coates, Simon. "Venantius Fortunatus and the Image of Episcopal Authority in Late Antique and Early Merovingian Gaul." *English Historical Review* 115, no. 464 (2000): 1109–37.

Collins, Roger. *The Basques*. 2nd ed. Oxford: Blackwell, 1990.

———. *Fredegar*. Authors of the Middle Ages 13. Aldershot: Ashgate, 1996.

———. *Die Fredegar-Chroniken*. Hanover, Germany: Hahn, 2007.

———. "Theodebert I, 'Rex Magnus Francorum.'" In Wormald, Bullough, and Collins, *Ideal and Reality*, 7–33.

Cooper, Kate, and Conrad Leyser, eds. *Making Early Medieval Societies: Conflict and Belonging in the Latin West, 300–1200*. Cambridge: Cambridge University Press, 2016.

Corbett, John H. "The Saint as Patron in the Work of Gregory of Tours." *Journal of Medieval History* 7 (1981): 1–13.

Corning, Caitlin. *The Celtic and Roman Traditions*. New York: Palgrave, 2006.

———. "Columbanus and the Easter Controversy: Theological, Social and Political Contexts." In *The Irish in Early Medieval Europe: Identity, Culture and Religion*, edited by Roy Flechner and Sven Meeder, 101–15. New York: Palgrave Macmillan, 2016.

Coville, Alfred. *Recherches sur l'histoire de Lyon*. Paris: Picard, 1928.
Curta, Florin. "Merovingian and Carolingian Gift Giving." *Speculum* 81, no. 3 (2006): 671–99.
Czock, Miriam. "*Wo gesündigt wird, kann der Sieg nicht gewonnen werden*: Plünderung von Kirchen im Krieg in den Werken Gregors von Tours (538–594)." In *Blick auf das Mittelalter: Aspekte von Lebenswelt, Herrschaft, Religion und Rezeption*, edited by Bodo Gundelach and Ralf Molkenthin, 13–23. Herne, Germany: Gabriele Schäfer Verlag, 2004.
Dailey, Erin T. *Queens, Consorts, Concubines: Gregory of Tours and the Women of the Merovingian Elite*. Leiden: Brill, 2015.
Daly, William M. "Clovis: How Barbarian, How Pagan?" *Speculum* 69, no. 3 (1994): 619–64.
De Clercq, Charles. *La législation religieuse franque de Clovis à Charlemagne (507–814)*. Leuven, Belgium: Bibliothèque de l'Université, 1936.
Decret, François. *Early Christianity in North Africa*. Translated by Edward L. Smither. Eugene, OR: Cascade Books, 2009.
De Jong, Mayke, Frans Theuws, and Carine Van Rhijn, eds. *Topographies of Power in the Early Middle Ages*. Leiden: Brill, 2001.
De La Haye, Régis. *De bisschoppen van Maastricht*. Maastricht, Netherlands: Stichting Historische Reeks Maastricht, 1985.
Delaplace, Christine, ed. *Aux origines de la paroisse rurale en Gaule méridionale, IVe–IXe siècles*. Paris: Editions Errance, 2005.
Delgado, Noel. "The *Grand Testamentum* of Remigius of Reims: Its Authenticity, Juridical *Acta* and Bequeathed Property." PhD diss., University of Minnesota, 2008.
Deliyannis, Deborah M. *Ravenna in Late Antiquity*. Cambridge: Cambridge University Press, 2010.
Deschamps, Paul. "Critique du privilège épiscopal accordé par Emmon de Sens à l'Abbaye de Sainte-Colombe (660, 26 Août)." *Moyen Âge* 25 (1912): 144–65.
De Nie, Giselle. *Views from a Many-Windowed Tower: Studies of Imagination in the Works of Gregory of Tours*. Amsterdam: Rodopi, 1987.
Desjardins, Ernest. *Géographie de la Gaule d'après la table de Peutinger*. Paris: Librairie de L. Hachette, 1869.
DeVries, Kirsten. "The Episcopate as *Ethnos*: Strategies of Distinction and Episcopal Identity in Merovingian Gaul." In *Emotions, Communities, and Difference in Medieval Europe: Essays in Honor of Barbara H. Rosenwein*, edited by Maureen C. Miller and Edward Wheatley, 143–59. Abingdon, England: Routledge, 2017.
Diefenbach, Steffen. "'Bischofsherrschaft': Zur Transformation der politischen Kultur im spätantiken und frühmittelalterlichen Gallien." In Diefenbach and Müller, *Gallien in Spätantike und Frühmittelalter*, 91–149.
Diefenbach, Steffen, and Gernot M. Müller, eds. *Gallien in Spätantike und Frühmittelalter: Kulturgeschichte einer Region*. Berlin: De Gruyter, 2013.
Diem, Albrecht. "Gregory's Chess Board: Monastic Conflict and Competition in Early Medieval Gaul." In *Compétition et sacré au Haut Moyen Âge: Entre médiation et exclusion*, edited by Philippe Depreux, François Bougard, and Régine Le Jan, 165–91. Turnhout, Belgium: Brepols, 2015.

———. "Monks, Kings, and the Transformation of Sanctity: Jonas of Bobbio and the End of the Holy Man." *Speculum* 82, no. 3 (2007): 521–59.

———. "Who Is Allowed to Pray for the King? Saint-Maurice d'Agaune and the Creation of a Burgundian Identity." In *Post-Roman Transitions: Christian and Barbarian Identities in the Early Medieval West*, edited by Walter Pohl and Gerda Heydemann, 47–88. Turnhout, Belgium: Brepols, 2013.

Dierkens, Alain, and Patrick Périn. "Les *sedes regiae* mérovingiennes entre Seine et Rhin." In *Sedes Regiae (ann. 400–800)*, edited by Gisela Ripoll and Josep M. Gurt, 267–304. Barcelona: Reial Academia de Bones Lletres, 2000.

Dill, Samuel. *Roman Society in Gaul in the Merovingian Age*. London: Macmillan, 1926.

Dörler, Philipp. "*The Liber Historiae Francorum*—a Model for a New Frankish Self-Confidence." *Network and Neighbours* 1 (2013): 23–43.

Drinkwater, John F. *The Alamanni and Rome, 313–496: Caracalla to Clovis*. Oxford: Oxford University Press, 2007.

———. "Patronage in Roman Gaul and the Problem of the Bagaudae." In Andrew Wallace-Hadrill, *Patronage in Ancient Society*, 189–203.

Duchesne, Louis. *L'eglise au VI siècle*. Paris: Fontemoing, E. de Boccard, Successeur, 1925.

———. *Fastes épiscopaux de l'ancienne Gaule*. 3 vols. Paris: Albert Fontemoing, 1907–15.

Dumézil, Bruno. "L'affaire Agrestius de Luxeuil: Hérésie et régionalisme dans la Burgondie du VIIe siècle." *Médiévales* 52 (2007): 135–52.

———. "La confiscation punitive en Gaule romano-barbare." In *Expropriations et confiscations dans les royaumes barbares: Une approche régionale*, edited by Pierfrancesco Porena and Yann Rivière, 51–68. Rome: École Française de Rome, 2012.

———. "Incarnating Authority, Exercising Authority: The Figure of the King in the Merovingian Era." In *Absentee Authority across Medieval Europe*, edited by Frédérique Lachaud and Michael Penman, 21–36. Woodbridge, England: Boydell, 2017.

———. "La royauté mérovingienne et les élections épiscopales au VIe siècle." In Leemans et al., *Episcopal Elections in Late Antiquity*, 127–43.

Duprat, E.-H. "Le couloir austrasien du VIe siècle." *Mémoires de l'Institut Historique de Provence* 20 (1943–44): 36–65.

Durliat, Jean. "Les attributions civiles des évêques mérovingiens: L'exemple de Didier, évêque de Cahors (630–655)." *Annales du Midi* 91 (1979): 237–54.

———. "*Episcopus, civis*, et *populus* dans les *Historiarum Libri* de Grégoire." In *Grégoire de Tours et l'espace gaulois*, edited by Nancy Gauthier and Henri Galinie, 185–93. Tours: Revue archéologique du Centre de la France, 1997.

———. "Evêque et administration municipale au VIIe siècle." In Lepelley, *La fin de la cité antique*, 273–86.

———. *Les finances publiques de Dioclétien aux Carolingiens (284–889)*. Sigmaringen, Germany: Jan Thorbecke Verlag, 1990.

Ebling, Horst. *Prosopographie der Amtsträger des Merowingerreiches von Chlothar II. (613) bis Karl Martell (741)*. Munich: Fink, 1974.

Effros, Bonnie. *Caring for Body and Soul: Burial and the Afterlife in the Merovingian World*. Philadelphia: University of Pennsylvania Press, 2002.

Engels, Donald. *Alexander the Great and the Logistics of the Macedonian Army*. Berkeley: University of California Press, 1978.
Epp, Verena, and Christoph H. F. Meyer, eds. *Recht und Konsens im frühen Mittelalter*. Ostfildern, Germany: Jan Thornbecke Verlag, 2017.
Erikson, Alvar. "The Problem of Authorship in the Chronicle of Fredegar." *Eranos* 63 (1965): 47–76.
Esders, Stefan. "Early Medieval Use of Late Antique Legal Texts: The Case of the *Manumissio in Ecclesia*." In *Configuration du texte en histoire*, proceedings of the Twelfth International Conference on Studies for the Integrated Text Science, edited by Osamu Kano, 55–66. Nagoya, Japan: Nagoya University, 2012.
———. *Die Formierung der Zensualität: Zur kirchlichen Transformation des spätrömischen Patronatswesens im früheren Mittelalter*. Ostfildern, Germany: Thorbecke, 2010.
———. "Rechtsdenken und Traditionsbewußtsein in der gallischen Kirche zwischen Spätantike und Frühmittelalter: Zur Anwendbarkeit soziologischer Rechtsbegriffe am Beispiel des kirchlichen Asylrechts im 6. Jahrhundert." *Francia* 20, no. 1 (1993): 97–125.
———. *Römische Rechtstradition und merowingisches Königtum*. Göttingen, Germany: Vandenhoeck and Ruprecht, 1997.
———. "Zwischen Historie und Rechtshistorie: Der *consensus iuris* im frühen Mittelalter." In Epp and Meyer, *Recht und Konsens im frühen Mittelalter*, 427–74.
Ewig, Eugen. "Beobachtungen zu den Bischofslisten der merowingischen Konzilien und Bischofsprivilegien." In Ewig, *Spätantikes und fränkisches Gallien*, 2:427–55.
———. "Beobachtungen zu den Bischofsprivilegien für Saint-Maur-des-Fosses und Sainte-Colombe de Sens." In Ewig, *Spätantikes und fränkisches Gallien*, 2:485–506.
———. "Beobachtungen zu den Klosterprivilegien des 7. und frühen 8. Jahrhunderts." In Ewig, *Spätantikes und fränkisches Gallien*, 2:411–26.
———. "Die frankischen Teilreiche im 7. Jahrhundert (613–714)." In Ewig, *Spätantikes und fränkisches Gallien*, 1:172–230.
———. "Die fränkischen Teilungen und Teilreiche (511–613)." In Ewig, *Spätantikes und fränkisches Gallien*, 1:114–71.
———. "Markulfs Formular 'De privilegio' und die merowingischen Bischofsprivilegien." In Ewig, *Spätantikes und fränkisches Gallien*, 3:519–37.
———. *Die Merowinger und das Frankenreich*. Stuttgart, Germany: W. Kohlhammer, 1988.
———. "Milo et Eiusmodi Similes." In Ewig, *Spätantikes und Fränkisches Gallien*, 2:189–219.
———. "Die Namengebung bei den ältesten Frankenkönigen und im merowingischen Königshaus." In Ewig, *Spätantikes und fränkisches Gallien*, 3:163–211.
———. "Das Privileg des Bischofs Berthefrid von Amiens für Corbie von 664 und die Klosterpolitik der Königin Balthild." In Ewig, *Spätantikes und fränkisches Gallien*, 2:538–83.
———. "Résidence et capitale pendant le Haut Moyen Age." *Revue historique* 230 (1963): 47–70.
———. *Spätantikes und fränkisches Gallien*. 3 vols. Edited by Hartmut Atsma, Matthias Becher, Theo Kölzer, and Ulrich Nonn. Munich: Artemis, 1976–2009.

———. *Trier im Merowingerreich: Civitas, Stadt, Bistum*. Trier, Germany: Paulinus Verlag, 1954.
———. "Zum christlichen Königsgedanken im Frühmittelalter." In Ewig, *Spätantikes und fränkisches Gallien*, 1:3–71.
Faivre, Alexandre. *Naissance d'une hiérarchie: Les premières étapes du cursus clérical*. Paris: Éditions Beauchesne, 1977.
Fischer, Andreas. *Karl Martell: Der Beginn karolingischer Herrschaft*. Stuttgart, Germany: Kohlhammer, 2012.
———. "Orthodoxy and Authority: Jonas, Eustasius, and the Agrestius Affair." In *Columbanus and the Peoples of Post-Roman Europe*, edited by Alexander O'Hara, 143–64. Oxford: Oxford University Press, 2018.
Fontaine, Jacques. "King Sisebut's *Vita Desiderii* and the Political Function of Visigothic Hagiography." In *Visigothic Spain: New Approaches*, edited by Edward James, 93–129. Oxford: Clarendon, 1980.
Fontaine, Jacques, and J. N. Hillgarth, eds. *The Seventh Century: Change and Continuity*. London: Warburg Institute, 1992.
Fouracre, Paul. *The Age of Charles Martel*. Harlow, England: Pearson Education, 2000.
———. "The Incidence of Rebellion in the Early Medieval West." In Cooper and Leyser, *Making Early Medieval Societies*, 104–24.
———. "Observations on the Outgrowth of Pippinid Influence in the 'Regnum Francorum' after the Battle of Tertry (687–715)." *Medieval Prosopography* 5 (1984): 1–31.
———. "'Placita' and the Settlement of Disputes in Later Merovingian Francia." In *The Settlement of Disputes in Early Medieval Europe*, edited by Wendy Davies and Paul Fouracre, 23–43. Cambridge: Cambridge University Press, 1986.
———. "The Use of the Term *Beneficium* in Frankish Sources: A Society Based on Favours?" In *The Language of Gift in the Early Middle Ages*, edited by Wendy Davies and Paul Fouracre, 62–88. Cambridge: Cambridge University Press, 2010.
———. "Why Were So Many Bishops Killed in Merovingian Francia?" In Fryde and Reitz, *Bischofsmord im Mittelalter*, 13–35.
Fox, Yaniv. "The Bishop and the Monk: Desiderius of Vienne and the Columbanian Movement." *Early Medieval Europe* 20, no. 2 (2012): 176–94.
———. "Image of Kings Past: The Gibichung Legacy in Post-conquest Burgundy." *Francia* 42 (2015): 1–25.
———. "New *Honores* for a Region Transformed: The Patriciate in Post-Roman Gaul." *Revue belge de Philologie et d'Histoire* 93 (2015): 249–86.
———. *Power and Religion in Merovingian Gaul*. Cambridge: Cambridge University Press, 2014.
Fryde, Natalie, and Dirk Reitz, eds. *Bischofsmord im Mittelalter*. Göttingen, Germany: Vandenhoeck and Ruprecht, 2003.
Garrison, Mary. "The *Missa pro principe* in the Bobbio Missal." In Hen and Meens, *Bobbio Missal*, 187–205.
Gaudemet, Jean. *Les sources du droit de l'Eglise en Occident*. Paris: Éditions du Cerf/Editions du CNRS, 1985.
Gauthier, Nancy. *L'évangélisation des pays de la Moselle: La province romaine de Première Belgique entre Antiquité et Moyen-Âge (IIIe–VIIIe siècles)*. Paris: E. de Boccard, 1980.

---. "Le réseau de pouvoirs de l'évêque dans la Gaule du Haut Moyen-Age." In *Towns and Their Territories between Late Antiquity and the Early Middle Ages*, edited by Gian Pietro Broglio, Nancy Gauthier, and Neil Christie, 173–207. Transformation of the Roman World 9. Leiden: Brill, 2000.

Geary, Patrick. *Aristocracy in Provence: The Rhône Basin at the Dawn of the Carolingian Age*. Philadelphia: University of Pennsylvania Press, 1985.

---. "Die Provence zur Zeit Karl Martells." In Jarnut, Nonn, and Richter, *Karl Martell in seiner Zeit*, 381–92.

George, Judith. "Poet as Politician: Venantius Fortunatus' Panegyric to King Chilperic." *Journal of Medieval History* 15, no. 1 (1989): 5–18.

---. *Venantius Fortunatus: A Latin Poet in Merovingian Gaul*. Oxford: Clarendon, 1992.

Gerberding, Richard. *The Rise of the Carolingians and the Liber Historiae Francorum*. Oxford: Oxford University Press, 1987.

Gillett, Andrew. *Envoys and Political Communication in the Late Antique West*. Cambridge: Cambridge University Press, 2003.

Glatthar, Michael. "Der Edictus Chilperichs I. und die Reichsversammlung von Paris (577)." *Deutsches Archiv für Erforschung des Mittelalters* 73 (2017): 1–74.

Godding, Robert. *Prêtres en Gaule mérovingienne*. Brussells: Société des Bollandistes, 2001.

Goetz, Hans-Werner. "Karl Martel und die Heiligen: Kirchenpolitik und Maiordomat im Spiegel der spätmerowingischen Hagiographie." In Jarnut, Nonn, and Richter, *Karl Martell in seiner Zeit*, 101–18.

Goffart, Walter. "The Frankish Pretender Gundovald, 582–585: A Crisis of Merovingian Blood." *Francia* 39 (2012): 1–27.

---. "The Fredegar Problem Reconsidered." *Speculum* 18 (1963): 206–41.

---. *The Narrators of Barbarian History*. Paperback ed. Notre Dame, IN: University of Notre Dame Press, 2005.

Goullet, Monique. "Les saints du diocèse de Toul." In Heinzelmann, *L'hagiographie*, 11–89.

Gradowicz-Pancer, Nira. "Femmes royales et violences anti-épiscopales l'époque a mérovingienne: Frédégonde et le meurtre de l'évêque Pretextat." In Fryde and Reitz, *Bischofsmord im Mittelalter*, 37–50.

Grahn-Hoek, Heike. "Quia Dei potentia cunctorum regnorum terminos singulari dominatione concludit: Kirchlicher Einheitsgedanke und weltliche Grenzen im Spiegel der reichsfränkischen Konzilien des 6. Jahrhunderts." In *Religiöse Bewegungen im Mittelalter: Festschrift für Matthias Werner zum 65. Geburtstag*, edited by Enno Bünz, Stefan Tebruck, and Helmut G. Walther, 3–54. Cologne, Germany: Böhlau, 2007.

Griffe, Elie. "Un évêque de Bordeaux au VIe siècle: Léonce le Jeune." *Bulletin de littérature ecclésiastique* 64 (1963): 63–71.

Guillot, Olivier. "'Assassins des pauvres': Une invective pour mieux culpabiliser les usurpateurs de biens d'église, aident à resituer l'activité conciliaire des Gaules entre 561 et 573." In *La culpabilité: Actes des XXèmes Journées d'histoire du droit*, edited by Jacqueline Hoareau-Dodinau and Pascal Texier, 329–66. Limoges, France: Presses Universitaires de Limoges, 2001.

---. "La justice dans le royaume Franc à l'époque merovingienne." In *La giustizia nell'alto medioevo, secoli V–VIII*, 653–731. Spoleto, Italy: Centro Italiano di Studi sull'Alto Medioevo, 1995.

Halfond, Gregory. "All the King's Men: Episcopal Political Loyalties in the Merovingian Kingdoms." *Medieval Prosopography* 27 (2012): 76–96.
———. *The Archaeology of Frankish Church Councils, AD 511–768*. Leiden: Brill, 2010.
———. "Caring for Churches, Orphans, and Widows in Late Merovingian Francia: Contemporary and Carolingian Perspectives." *Revue d'histoire ecclésiastique* 113, nos. 3–4 (2018): 544–75.
———. "Charibert I and the Episcopal Leadership of the Kingdom of Paris (561–567)." *Viator* 43, no. 2 (2012): 1–28.
———. "Contextualizing the Council of Tours (567)." In *Proceedings of the Fourteenth International Congress of Medieval Canon Law*, edited by Joseph Goering, Stephan Dusil, and Andreas Their, 289–301. Monumenta Iuris Canonici, Series C: Subsidia 15. Rome: Biblioteca Apostolica Vaticana, 2016.
———. "Corporate Solidarity and Its Limits within the Gallo-Frankish Episcopate." In *The Oxford Handbook of the Merovingian World*, edited by Bonnie Effros and Isabel Moreira. Oxford: Oxford University Press, forthcoming.
———. "Ecclesiastical Politics in the *Regnum Chramni*: Contextualizing Baudonivia's Vita Radegundis Ch. 15." *Journal of Ecclesiastical History* 68, no. 3 (2017): 474–92.
———. "The Endorsement of Royal-Episcopal Collaboration in the Fredegar *Chronica*." *Traditio* 70 (2015): 1–28.
———. "Negotiating Episcopal Support in the Merovingian Kingdom of Rheims." *Early Medieval Europe* 22, no. 1 (2014): 1–25.
———. "*Patrimoniolum Ecclesiae Nostrae*: The Papal Estates in Merovingian Provence." *Comitatus* 38 (2007): 1–18.
———. "Sis Quoque Catholicis Religionis Apex: The Ecclesiastical Patronage of Chilperic I and Fredegund." *Church History* 81 (2012): 48–76.
———. "Vouillé, Orléans (511), and the Origins of Frankish Conciliar Tradition." In Mathisen and Shanzer, *Battle of Vouillé*, 151–65.
———. "War and Peace in the *Acta* of the Merovingian Church Councils." In *The Medieval Way of War: Studies in Medieval Military History in Honor of Bernard S. Bachrach*, edited by Gregory Halfond, 29–46. Farnham, England: Ashgate, 2015.
Hall, Stuart George. "Institutions in the Pre-Constantinian *Ecclēsia*." In *The Cambridge History of Christianity*, vol. 1, *Origins to Constantine*, edited by Margaret M. Mitchell and Frances M. Young, 413–33. Cambridge: Cambridge University Press, 2006.
Halsall, Guy. "Childeric's Grave, Clovis' Succession, and the Origins of the Merovingian Kingdom." In *Cemeteries and Societies in Merovingian Gaul: Selected Studies in History and Archaeology, 1992–2009*, 169–87. Leiden: Brill, 2010.
———. *Settlement and Social Organization: The Merovingian Region of Metz*. Cambridge: Cambridge University Press, 1995.
———. "Villas, Territories and Communities in Merovingian Northern Gaul." In *People and Space in the Middle Ages, 300–1300*, edited by Wendy Davies, Guy Halsall, and Andrew Reynolds, 209–31. Turnhout, Belgium: Brepols, 2007.
———. *Warfare and Society in the Barbarian West, 450–900*. London: Routledge, 2003.
Hammer, Carl I. *From Ducatus to Regnum: Ruling Bavaria under the Merovingians and Early Carolingians*. Turnhout, Belgium: Brepols, 2007.
Handley, Mark A. *Death, Society and Culture: Inscriptions and Epitaphs in Gaul and Spain, AD 300–750*. Oxford: British Archaeological Reports, 2003.

Hannig, Jürgen. *Consensus Fidelium*. Stuttgart, Germany: Anton Hiersemann, 1982.
Harries, Jill. "Church and State in the *Notitia Galliarum*." *Journal of Roman Studies* 68 (1978): 26–43.
———. *Sidonius Apollinaris and the Fall of Rome*. Oxford: Clarendon, 1994.
Haubrichs, Wolfgang. "'Leudes, fara, faramanni und farones': Zur Semantik der Bezeichnungen für einige am Konsenshandeln beteiligte Gruppen." In Epp and Meyer, *Recht und Konsens im frühen Mittelalter*, 235–63.
Head, Thomas. *Hagiography and the Cult of Saints: The Diocese of Orléans, 800–1200*. Cambridge: Cambridge University Press, 1990.
Hefele, Karl Joseph von. *Histoire des conciles d'après les documents originaux*. Edited and translated by Henri Leclercq. 11 vols. Paris: Letouzey et Ané, 1907–52.
Heinzelmann, Martin. "L'aristocratie et les évêchés entre Loire et Rhin jusqu'à la fin du VII siècle." In *La christianisation des pays entre Loire et Rhin (IV–VII siècle)*, edited by Pierre Riché, 75–90. Paris: Éditions du Cerf, 1993.
———. *Bischofsherrschaft in Gallien*. Munich: Artemis Verlag, 1976.
———. "Bischof und Herrschaft vom spätantiken Gallien bis zu den karolingischen Hausmeiern: Die institutionellen Grundlagen." In Prinz, *Herrschaft und Kirche*, 23–82.
———. "Gallische Prosopographie (260–527)." *Francia* 10 (1982): 531–718.
———. "Gregor von Tours: Die ideologische Grundlegung fränkischer Königsherrschaft." In *Die Franken—Wegbereiter Europas*. 2 vols. Edited by Alfred Wieczorek, Patrick Périn, Karin von Welck, and Wilfried Menghin, 1:381–88. Mainz, Germany: Verlag Philipp von Zabern, 1996.
———. *Gregory of Tours: History and Society in the Sixth Century*. Translated by Christopher Carroll. Cambridge: Cambridge University Press, 2001.
———, ed. *L'hagiographie du haut moyen âge en Gaule du Nord*. Stuttgart, Germany: Jan Thorbecke, 2001.
———. "Prosopographie et recherche de continuité historique: L'exemple des V–VII siècles." *Mélanges de l'École française de Rome: Moyen Age, Temps Modernes* 100, no. 1 (1988): 227–39.
Hen, Yitzhak. "The Annals of Metz and the Merovingian Past." In *The Uses of the Past in the Early Middle Ages*, edited by Yitzhak Hen and Matthew Innes, 175–90. Cambridge: Cambridge University Press, 2000.
———. "Changing Places: Chrodobert, Boba, and the Wife of Grimoald." *Revue belge de philologie et d'histoire* 89, no. 2 (2012): 225–44.
———. "The Christianisation of Kingship." In *Der Dynastiewechsel von 751: Vorgeschichte, Legitimationsstrategien und Errinerung*, edited by Mathias Becher and Jörg Jarnut, 163–78. Münster, Germany: Scriptorium, 2004.
———. "The Church in Sixth Century Gaul." In Murray, *Companion to Gregory of Tours*, 232–55.
———. *Culture and Religion in Merovingian Gaul, AD 481–751*. Leiden: Brill, 1995.
———. *Roman Barbarians: The Royal Court and Culture in the Early Medieval West*. New York: Palgrave, 2007.
———. *The Royal Patronage of Liturgy in Frankish Gaul to the Death of Charles the Bald (877)*. Woodbridge, England: Boydell and Brewer, 2001.
———. "The Structure and Aims of the *Visio Baronti*." *Journal of Theological Studies* 47, no. 2 (1996): 477–97.

———. "The Uses of the Bible and the Perception of Kingship in Merovingian Gaul." *Early Medieval Europe* 7, no. 3 (1998): 277–89.
Hen, Yitzhak, and Rob Meens, eds. *The Bobbio Missal: Liturgy and Religious Culture in Merovingian Gaul*. Cambridge: Cambridge University Press, 2004.
Heuclin, Jean. "Le Concile d'Orléans de 511, un premier concordat." In *Clovis: Histoire et mémoire*, edited by Michel Rouche, 1:435–50. Paris: Presses de l'Université de Paris–Sorbonne, 1997.
Heyen, Franz Josef. "St. Goar im frühen und hohen Mittelalter." *Kurtrierisches Jahrbuch* 1 (1961): 87–106.
Hlawitschka, Eduard. "Die Vorfahren Karls des Grossen." In *Karl der Grosse*, vol. 1, *Persönlichkeit und Geschichte*, edited by Helmut Beaumann, 51–82. Düsseldorf, Germany: L. Schwann, 1965.
———. "Zur landschaftlichen Herkunft der Karolinger." *Rheinische Vierteljahrsblätter* 27 (1962): 1–17.
Holmberg, Erik. *Zur Geschichte des Cursus Publicus*. Uppsala, Sweden: A. B. Lundequistska Bokhandeln, 1933.
Honée, Eugène. "St Willibrord in Recent Historiography." In *Missions and Missionaries*, edited by Pieter N. Holtrop and Hugh McLeod, 16–31. Studies in Church History Subsidia 13. Oxford: Boydell, 2000.
Howe, John. "The Hagiography of Saint-Wandrille (Fontenelle) (Province of Haute-Normandie)." In Heinzelmann, *L'hagiographie*, 127–92.
Hummer, Hans. *Visions of Kinship in Medieval Europe*. Oxford: Oxford University Press, 2018.
Jäger, David. *Plündern in Gallien 451–592: Eine Studie zu der Relevanz einer Praktik für das Organisieren von Folgeleistungen*. Berlin: De Gruyter, 2017.
James, Edward. "*Beati Pacifici*: Bishops and the Law in Sixth-Century Gaul." In *Disputes and Settlements: Law and Human Relations in the West*, edited by John Bossy, 25–46. Cambridge: Cambridge University Press, 1983.
———. *The Franks*. Oxford: Blackwell, 1988.
———. *The Merovingian Archaeology of South-West Gaul*. Oxford: British Archaeological Reports, 1977.
———. *The Origins of France: From Clovis to the Capetians, 500–1000*. New York: St. Martin's, 1982.
Jarnut, Jörg. *Agilolfingerstudien: Untersuchungen zur Geschichte einer adligen Familie im 6. und 7. Jahrhundert*. Stuttgart, Germany: Anton Hiersemann, 1986.
Jarnut, Jörg, Ulrich Nonn, and Michael Richter, eds. *Karl Martell in seiner Zeit*. Sigmaringen, Germany: Jan Thorbecke Verlag, 1994.
Jones, A. H. M. "Church Finance in the Fifth and Sixth Centuries." *Journal of Theological Studies*, n.s., 11, no. 1 (1960): 84–94.
Jones, Allen E. *Social Mobility in Late Antique Gaul*. Cambridge: Cambridge University Press, 2009.
Jussen, Bernhard. "Liturgie und Legitimation: Wie die Gallo-Romanen das Römische Reich beendeten." In *Institutionen und Ereignis: Über historische Praktiken und Vorstellungen gesellschaftlichen Ordnens*, edited by Reinhard Blänkner and Bernhard Jussen, 75–136. Göttingen, Germany: Vandenhoeck and Ruprecht, 1998. Translated as "Liturgy and Legitimation, or How the Gallo-Romans Ended the Roman Empire," in Jussen, *Ordering Medieval Society*, 147–99.

———, ed. *Ordering Medieval Society: Perspectives on Intellectual and Practical Modes of Shaping Social Relations*. Translated by Pamela Selwyn. Philadelphia: University of Pennsylvania Press, 2001.

———. "Religious Discourses of the Gift in the Middle Ages, Semantic Evidences (Second to Twelfth Centuries)." In *Negotiating the Gift: Pre-modern Figurations of Exchange*, edited by Gadi Algazi, Valentin Groebner, and Bernhard Jussen, 173–92. Göttingen, Germany: Vandenhoeck and Ruprecht, 2003.

———. "Über 'Bischofsherrschaften' und die Prozeduren politisch-sozialer Umordnung in Gallien zwischen 'Antike' und 'Mittelalter.'" *Historische Zeitschrift* 260 (1994): 673–718.

———. "Zwischen Römischem Reich und Merowingern: Herrschaft legitimieren ohne Kaiser und König." In *Mittelalter und Moderne: Entdeckung und Rekonstruktion der mittelalterlichen Welt*, edited by Peter Segl, 15–29. Sigmaringen, Germany: Thorbecke, 1997.

Kaiser, Reinhold. *Bischofsherrschaft zwischen Königtum und Fürstenmacht*. Bonn, Germany: Ludwig Röhrscheid, 1981.

———. "Les évêques et leurs pouvoirs." In Périn and Feffer, *La Neustrie*, 99–101.

———. "Royauté et pouvoir épiscopal au nord de la Gaule (VIIe–IXe siècles)." In Atsma, *La Neustrie*, 1:143–60. Originally published as: "Königtum und Bischofsherrschaft im frühmittelalterlichen Neustrien," in Prinz, *Herrschaft und Kirche*, 83–108.

———. "Steuer und Zoll in der Merowingerzeit." *Francia* 7 (1979): 1–17.

Kaiser, Reinhold, and Sebastian Scholz. *Quellen zur Geschichte der Franken und der Merowinger: Vom 3. Jahrhundert bis 751*. Stuttgart, Germany: Kohlhammer, 2012.

Kershaw, Paul. *Peaceful Kings: Peace, Power and the Early Medieval Political Imagination*. Oxford: Oxford University Press, 2010.

Kéry, Lotte, ed. *Canonical Collections of the Early Middle Ages (ca. 400–1140)*. Washington, DC: Catholic University of America Press, 1999.

King, P. D. "The Barbarian Kingdoms." In *The Cambridge History of Medieval Political Thought, c. 350–c. 1450*, edited by J. H. Burns, 123–53. Cambridge: Cambridge University Press, 1988.

Kinney, Angela. "An Appeal against Editorial Condemnation: A Reevaluation of the *Vita Apollinaris Valentinensis*." In *Edition und Erforschung lateinischer patristischer Texte*, edited by Victoria Zimmerl-Panagl, Lukas J. Dorfbauer, and Clemens Weidmann, 157–77. Berlin: De Gruyter, 2014.

Klingshirn, William. *Caesarius of Arles: The Making of a Christian Community in Late Antique Gaul*. Cambridge: Cambridge University Press, 1994.

———. "Charity and Power: Caesarius of Arles and the Ransoming of Captives in Sub-Roman Gaul." *Journal of Roman Studies* 75 (1985): 183–203.

Krause, Jens-Uwe. *Spätantike Patronatsformen in Westen des Römischen Reiches*. Munich: C. H. Beck, 1987.

———. "Überlegungen zur Sozialgeschichte des Klerus im 5/6 Jh. n. Chr." In Krause and Witschel, *Die Stadt in der Spätantike*, 413–39.

Krause, Jens-Uwe, and Christian Witschel, eds. *Die Stadt in der Spätantike— Niedergang oder Wandel?* Stuttgart, Germany: Franz Steiner Verlag, 2006.

Kreiner, Jamie. "About the Bishop: The Episcopal Entourage and the Economy of Government in Post-Roman Gaul." *Speculum* 86, no. 2 (2011): 321–60.

———. *The Social Life of Hagiography in the Merovingian Kingdom.* Cambridge: Cambridge University Press, 2014.
Krusch, Bruno. "Das Leben des Bischofs Gaugerich von Cambrai." *Neues Archiv der Gesellschaft für ältere deutsche Geschichtskunde* 16 (1891): 227–34.
Kulikowski, Michael. "Ordo." In *Late Ancient Knowing: Explorations in Intellectual History*, edited by Catherine M. Chin and Moulie Vidas, 175–96. Oakland: University of California Press, 2015.
Kupper, J. L. "Saint Lambert: De l'histoire à la légende." *Revue d'histoire ecclésiastique* 79 (1984): 5–49.
Kurth, Godefroid. *Clovis.* 2 vols. Paris: Retaux, 1901.
Labande-Mailfert, Yvonne. "Les debuts de Sainte-Croix." In *Histoire de l'Abbaye Sainte-Croix de Poitiers*, edited by Yvonne Labande-Mailfert, Robert Favreau, Louise Coudanne, and Jacques Marcadé, 25–69. Poitiers, France: Société des antiquaires de l'Ouest, 1986.
Laporte, Jean. "Les listes abbatiales de Jumieges." In *Jumieges: Congres scientifique du XIII centenaire, Rouen, 10–12 June 1954*, 435–66. Rouen, France: Lecerf, 1955.
Lebecq, Stéphane. "Le baptême manqué du roi Radbod." In *Les assises du pouvoir: Temps médiévaux, territoires africains*, edited by Odile Redon and Bernard Rosenberger, 141–50. Saint-Denis, France: Presses Universitaires de Vincennes, 1994.
———. "Entre antique tardive et très Haut Moyen Age: Permanence et mutations des systèmes de communications dans la Gaule et ses marges." In *Morfologie sociali e culturali in Europa fra tarda Antichita e alto Medioevo*, 461–502. Spoleto, Italy: Centro Italiano di Studi sull'Alto Medioevo, 1998.
Leemans, Johan, Peter Van Nuffelen, Shawn W. J. Keough, and Carla Nicolaye, eds. *Episcopal Elections in Late Antiquity.* Berlin: De Gruyter, 2011.
Le Jan, Régine. *Famille et pouvoir dans le monde franc (VIIe–Xe siècle): Essai d'anthropologie sociale.* Paris: Publications de la Sorbonne, 1995.
Lepelley, Claude, ed. *La fin de la cité antique et le début de la cité médiévale.* Bari, Italy: Edipuglia, 1996.
Lesne, Emile. *La hiérarchie épiscopale: Provinces, métropolitains, primats en Gaule et Germanie.* Lille, France: Facultes Catholiques, 1905.
———. *Histoire de la propriété ecclésiastique en France.* 6 vols. Lille, France: Rene Giard, 1910–43.
Lewis, Archibald R. "The Dukes in the *Regnum Francorum*, A.D. 550–751." *Speculum* 51, no. 3 (1976): 381–410.
Lifshitz, Felice. *The Name of the Saint: The Martyrology of Jerome and Access to the Sacred in Francia, 627–827.* Notre Dame, IN: University of Notre Dame Press, 2006.
Loening, Edgar. *Geschichte des deutschen Kirchenrechts.* 2 vols. Strasbourg: Verlag Karl J. Trübner, 1878.
Loftus, Susan. "Episcopal Elections in Gaul." In Leemans et al., *Episcopal Elections in Late Antiquity*, 423–36.
———. "Suitable Men to Enter the Episcopate in Late Antique Gaul: Ideal and Reality." *Journal of the Australian Early Medieval Association* 10 (2014): 23–46.
Longnon, Auguste. *Géographie de la Gaule au VIe siècle.* Paris: E. Martinet, 1878.

Loseby, Simon T. "Arles in Late Antiquity: *Gallula Roma Arelas* and *Urbs Genesii*." In *Towns in Transition: Urban Evolution in Late Antiquity and the Early Middle Ages*, edited by Neil Christie and Simon T. Loseby, 45–70. Aldershot, England: Ashgate, 1996.

———. "Decline and Change in the Cities of Late Antique Gaul." In Krause and Witschel, *Die Stadt in der Spätantike*, 67–104.

———. "Discussion." In *Franks and Alamanni*, edited by Ian Wood, 270–84. Woodbridge, England: Boydell, 1998.

———. "Lost Cities: The End of the *Civitas*-System in Frankish Gaul." In Diefenbach and Müller, *Gallien in Spätantike und Frühmittelalter*, 223–52.

———. "Marseille: A Late Antique Success Story." *Journal of Roman Studies* 82 (1992): 165–85.

———. "Marseille and the Pirenne Thesis I." In *The Sixth Century: Production, Distribution, and Demand*, edited by Richard Hodges and William Bowden, 203–29. Leiden: Brill, 1998.

Lumpe, Adolf. "Zur Geschichte der Wörter *Concilium* und *Synodus* in der antiken christlichen Latinität." *Annuarium Historiae Conciliorum* 2, no. 1 (1970): 1–21.

Lupoi, Maurizio. *The Origins of the European Legal Order*. Translated by Adrian Belton. Cambridge: Cambridge University Press, 2000.

Maassen, Friedrich. *Geschichte der Quellen und der Literatur des canonischen Rechts im Abendlande*. Graz, Austria: Akademische Druck-U. Verlagsanstalt, 1870.

MacGeorge, Penny. *Late Roman Warlords*. Oxford: Oxford University Press, 2002.

Magnou-Nortier, Elisabeth. "À propos des rapports entre l'Eglise et l'Etat franc: La lettre synodale au roi Théodebert (535)." In *Societa, Istituzioni, Spiritualita: Studi in Onore di Cinzio Violante*, 519–34. Spoleto, Italy: Centro italiano di studi sull'alto Medioevo, 1994.

Mahl, Sibylle. *Quadriga virtutum, Die Kardinalugenden in der Geistegeschichte der Karolingerzeit*. Cologne, Germany: Böhlau, 1969.

Martindale, J. R., ed. *The Prosopography of the Later Roman Empire*. vol. 3. Cambridge: Cambridge University Press, 1992.

Mathisen, Ralph. *Ecclesiastical Factionalism and Religious Controversy in Fifth-Century Gaul*. Washington, DC: Catholic University of America Press, 1989.

———. "The First Franco-Visigothic War and the Prelude to the Battle of Vouillé." In Mathisen and Shanzer, *Battle of Vouillé*, 3–9.

———. *Roman Aristocrats in Barbarian Gaul*. Austin: University of Texas Press, 1993.

Mathisen, Ralph, and Danuta Shanzer, eds. *The Battle of Vouillé, 507 CE: Where France Began*. Berlin: Walter de Gruyter, 2012.

Mazel, Florian. *L'évêque et le territoire: L'invention médiévale de l'espace (Ve–XIIIe siècle)*. Paris: Éditions du Seuil, 2016.

McCormick, Michael. *Origins of the European Economy*. Cambridge: Cambridge University Press, 2001.

McDermott, William. "Felix of Nantes: A Merovingian Bishop." *Traditio* 31 (1975): 1–24.

McKitterick, Rosamond. *Charlemagne: The Formation of a European Identity*. Cambridge: Cambridge University Press, 2008.

———. "England and the Continent." In *The New Cambridge Medieval History*, vol. 2, c. 700–c. 900, edited by Rosamond McKitterick, 64–83. Cambridge: Cambridge University Press, 1995.

———. "Royal Patronage of Culture in the Frankish Kingdoms under the Carolingians: Motives and Consequences." In *Committenti e Produzione artistico-letteraria nell'alto medioevo occidentale*, 93–129. Spoleto, Italy: Centro Italiano di Studi sull'Alto Medioevo, 1992.

Meens, Rob. "The Sanctity of the Basilica of St Martin: Gregory of Tours and the Practice of Sanctuary in the Merovingian Period." In *Texts and Identities in the Early Middle Ages*, edited by Richard Corradini, Rob Meens, Christina Pössel, and Philip Shaw, 277–87. Vienna: Österreichischen Akademie der Wissenschaften, 2006.

———. "Violence at the Altar: The Sacred Space around the Grave of St. Martin of Tours and the Practice of Sanctuary in the Early Middle Ages." In *Ritual and Space in the Middle Ages*, edited by Frances Andrews, 71–89. Donington, England: Shaun Tyas, 2011.

Mériaux, Charles. "Du nouveau sur la *Vie de saint Éloi*." *Mélanges de science religieuse* 67, no. 3 (2010): 71–85.

———. "Thérouanne et son diocèse jusqu'à la fin de l'époque carolingienne: Les étapes de la christianisation d'après les sources écrites." *Bibliothèque de l'École des chartes* 158, no. 2 (2000): 377–406.

———. "Une Vita mérovingienne et ses lectures du IXe au XIe siècle: Le dossier de saint Géry de Cambrai." In *L'hagiographie mérovingienne à travers ses réécritures*, edited by Monique Goullet, Martin Heinzelmann, and Christiane Veyard-Cosme, 161–91. Ostfildern, Germany: Jan Thorbecke Verlag, 2010.

Mikat, Paul. *Die Inzestgesetzgebung der merowingisch-fränkischen Konzilien (511–626/27)*. Paderborn, Germany: Ferdinand Schöningh, 1994.

Mitchell, Kathleen. "Saints and Public Christianity in the *Historiae* of Gregory of Tours." In *Religion and Society in the Early Middle Ages: Studies in Honor of Richard E. Sullivan*, edited by T. F. X. Noble and John Contreni, 77–94. Kalamazoo, MI: Medieval Institute Publications, 1987.

Mitchell, Kathleen, and Ian Wood, eds. *The World of Gregory of Tours*. Leiden: Brill, 2002.

Moore, Michael E. *A Sacred Kingdom: Bishops and the Rise of Frankish Kingship, 300–850*. Washington, DC: Catholic University of America Press, 2011.

Moorhead, John. "Some Principles of Church Dedication in the Early Medieval West." *Journal of the Australian Early Medieval Association* 5 (2009): 133–46.

Mordek, Hubert. "Kanonistische Aktivität in Gallien in der ersten Hälfte des 8. Jahrhunderts." *Francia* 2 (1974): 19–25.

———. *Kirchenrecht und Reform im Frankenreich: Die Collectio Vetus Gallica, die älteste systematische Kanonessammlung des fränkischen Gallien*. Berlin: Walter de Gruyter, 1975.

Moreira, Isabel. "*Provisatrix Optima*: St. Radegund of Poitiers' Relic Petitions to the East." *Journal of Medieval History* 19 (1993): 285–305.

Müller, Christoph. "Kurialen und Bischof, Bürger und Gemeinde—Untersuchungen zur Kontinuität von Ämtern, Funktionen und Formen der 'Kommunikation' in der gallischen Stadt des 4.–6. Jahrhunderts." PhD diss., Albert-Ludwigs-Universität Freiburg, 2003.

Murray, Alexander C., ed. *A Companion to Gregory of Tours*. Leiden: Brill, 2015.

———. "The Composition of the *Histories* of Gregory of Tours and Its Bearing on the Political Narrative." In Murray, *Companion to Gregory of Tours*, 63–101.
———. *Germanic Kinship Structure*. Toronto: Pontifical Institute of Mediaeval Studies, 1983.
———. "Immunity, Nobility, and the Edict of Paris." *Speculum* 69, no. 1 (1994): 18–39.
———. "Merovingian Immunity Revisited." *History Compass* 8 (2010): 913–28.
———. "The Merovingian State and Administration in the Times of Gregory of Tours." In Murray, *Companion to Gregory of Tours*, 191–231.
———. "*Pax et Disciplina*: Roman Public Law and the Merovingian State." In *Proceedings of the Tenth International Congress of Medieval Canon Law*, edited by Kenneth Pennington, Stanley Chodorow, and Keith H. Kendall, 269–85. Vatican City: Biblioteca Apostolica Vaticana, 2001.
Nelson, Janet. "Gender and Genre in Women Historians of the Early Middle Ages." In *The Frankish World, 750–900*, 183–97. London: Hambledon, 1996.
———. "Queens as Jezebels: Brunhild and Balthild in Merovingian History." In *Politics and Ritual in Early Medieval Europe*, 1–48. London: Hambledon, 1986.
Nicholson, Oliver, ed. *The Oxford Dictionary of Late Antiquity*. Oxford: Oxford University Press, 2018.
Niermeyer, Jan Frederik. *Mediae Latinitatis Lexicon Minus*. Leiden: Brill, 2002.
Norton, Peter. *Episcopal Elections 250–600: Hierarchy and Popular Will in Late Antiquity*. Oxford: Oxford University Press, 2007.
Oexle, Otto Gerhard. "Die Karolinger und die Stadt des heiligen Arnulf." *Frühmittelalterliche Studien* 1 (1967): 250–364.
O'Hara, Alexander. *Jonas of Bobbio and the Legacy of Columbanus*. Oxford: Oxford University Press, 2018.
Palmer, James. *Anglo-Saxons in a Frankish World, 690–900*. Turnhout, Belgium: Brepols, 2009.
Patzold, Steffen. "Die Bischöfe im Gallien der Transformationszeit: Eine sozial homogene Gruppe von Amtsträgern?" In *Antike im Mittelalter: Fortleben, Nachwirken, Wahrnehmung*, edited by Sebastian Brather, Hans Ulrich Nuber, Heiko Steuer, and Thomas Zotz, 179–93. Ostfildern, Germany: Thorbecke, 2014.
———. "Bischöfe, soziale Herkunft und die Organisation lokaler Herrschaft um 500." In *Chlodwigs Welt: Organisation von Herrschaft um 500*, edited by Mischa Meier and Steffen Patzold, 523–43. Stuttgart, Germany: Steiner, 2014.
———. "L'épiscopat du haut Moyen Âge du point de vue de la médiévistique allemande." *Cahiers de Civilisation Médiévale* 48 (2005): 341–58.
———. "'Konsens' und 'consensus' im Merowingerreich." In Epp and Meyer, *Recht und Konsens im frühen Mittelalter*, 265–97.
———. "Zur Sozialstruktur des Episkopats und zur Ausbildung bischöflicher Herrschaft in Gallien zwischen Spätantike und Frühmittelalter." In *Völker, Reiche und Namen im frühen Mittelalter*, edited by Mathias Becher and Stefanie Dick, 121–40. Munich: Wilhelm Fink, 2010.
Patzold, Steffen, and Conrad Walter. "Der Episkopat im Frankenreich der Merowingerzeit: Eine sich durch Verwandtschaft reproduzierende Elite?" In

Verwandtschaft, Name und soziale Ordnung (300–1000), edited by Steffen Patzold and Karl Ubl, 109–39. Berlin: De Gruyter, 2014.

Pauly, Ferdinand. *Die Stifte St. Severus in Boppard, St. Goar in St. Goar, Liebfrauen in Oberwesel, St. Martin in Oberwesel*. Erzbistum Trier 2. Berlin: De Gruyter, 1980.

Périn, Patrick, and Laure-Charlotte Feffer, eds. *La Neustrie: Les pays au nord de la Loire de Dagobert à Charles le Chauve (VIIe–IXe siècles)*. Rouen, France: Musées et monuments départementaux de Seine-Maritime, 1985.

Perrugot, Didier. "Le palais merovingien de Malay (Yonne), histoire et archéologie." In *Palais royaux et princiers au Moyen Age*, edited by Annie Renoux, 147–56. Le Mans, France: Centre d'édition et de publication de l'Université du Maine, 1996.

Peterson, Leif Inge Ree. *Siege Warfare and Military Organization in the Successor States (400–800 A.D.)*. Leiden: Brill, 2013.

Petre, Hélène. *Caritas: Etude sur le vocabulaire latin de la charité chrétienne*. Leuven, Belgium: Spicilegium Sacrum Lovaniense, 1948.

Picard, Jean-Charles, Brigitte Beaujard, Elzbieta Dabrowska, Christine Laplace, Noël Duval, Patrick Périn, and Luce Piétri, eds. *Province ecclésiastique de Sens (Lugdunensis Senonia)*. Topographie chrétienne des cités de la Gaule 8. Paris: De Boccard, 1992.

Pietri, Luce. *La ville de Tours du IVe au VIe siècle: Naissance d'une cité chrétienne*. Rome: Ecole française de Rome, 1983.

Pietri, Luce, and Marc Heijmans, eds. *Prosopographie de la Gaule chrétienne (314–614)*. Prosopographie chrétienne du Bas-Empire 4. Paris: Association des amis du Centre d'histoire et civilisation de Byzance, 2013.

Pontal, Odette. *Histoire des conciles mérovingiens*. Paris: Éditions du Cerf, 1989. Originally published as *Die Synoden im Merowingerreich* (Paderborn, Germany: Ferdinand Schöningh, 1986).

Poveda Arias, Pablo. "Clovis and Remigius of Reims in the Making of the Merovingian Kingdoms." *Europan Review of History / Revue européenne d'histoire*, published online, November 23, 2017, 1–22.

Prinz, Friedrich. "Die bischöfliche Stadtherrschaft im Frankenreich vom 5. bis zum 7. Jahrhundert." *Historische Zeitschrift* 217 (1974): 1–35. Revised version published in *Bischofs- und Kathedralstädte des Mittelalters und der frühen Neuzeit*, edited by Franz Petri, 1–26 (Cologne, Germany: Böhlau, 1976).

——. "Der fränkische Episkopat zwischen Merowinger- und Karolingerzeit." In *Nascita dell'Europa ed Europa carolingia*, 101–33. Spoleto, Italy: Centro Italiano di Studi sull'Alto Medioevo, 1981.

——. *Frühes Mönchtum im Frankenreich*. Munich: R. Oldenbourg, 1965.

——. "Herrschaftsformen der Kirche vom Ausgang der Spätantike bis zum Ende der Karolingerzeit: zur Einführung ins Thema." In Prinz, *Herrschaft und Kirche*, 1–21.

——, ed. *Herrschaft und Kirche*. Stuttgart, Germany: Hiersemann, 1988.

——. *Klerus und Krieg im früheren Mittelalter: Untersuchungen zur Rolle der Kirche beim Aufbau der Königsherrschaft*. Stuttgart, Germany: Hiersemann, 1971.

Rapp, Claudia. *Holy Bishops in Late Antiquity: The Nature of Christian Leadership in an Age of Transition*. Berkeley: University of California Press, 2005.

Reimitz, Helmut. "After Rome, before Francia: Religion, Ethnicity, and Identity Politics in Gregory of Tours' *Ten Books of Histories.*" In Cooper and Leyser, *Making Early Medieval Societies,* 58–79.
———. *History, Frankish Identity and the Framing of Western Ethnicity, 550–850.* Cambridge: Cambridge University Press, 2015.
Renard, Étienne. "Le *Pactus legis Salicae,* règlement militaire romain ou code de lois compilé sous Clovis?" *Bibliothèque de l'École des chartes* 167 (2009): 321–52.
Renna, Thomas. "The Idea of Peace in the West." *Journal of Medieval History* 6 (1980): 143–67.
Renoux, Annie, ed. *Palais médiévaux (France-Belgique): 25 ans d'archéologie.* Le Mans, France: Université du Maine, 1994.
Reuter, Timothy. "Kirchenreform und Kirchenpolitik im Zeitalter Karl Martells: Begriffe und Wirklichkeit." In Jarnut, Nonn, and Richter, *Karl Martell in seiner Zeit,* 35–59.
Reydellet, Marc. *La royauté dans la littérature latine de Sidoine Apollinaire à Isidore de Séville.* Rome: École Française de Rome, 1981.
Reynolds, Roger E. *The Ordinals of Christ from Their Origins to the Twelfth Century.* Berlin: Walter de Gruyter, 1978.
Riché, Pierre. "Note d'hagiographie mérovingienne: La *vita Rusticulae.*" *Analecta Bollandiana* 72 (1954): 369–77.
———. "Les représentations du palais dans les textes littéraires du Haut Moyen Age." *Francia* 4 (1976): 161–71.
Riess, Frank. *Narbonne and Its Territory in Late Antiquity: From the Visigoths to the Arabs.* Farnham, England: Ashgate, 2013.
Rio, Alice. *Legal Practice and the Written Word in the Early Middle Ages.* Cambridge: Cambridge University Press, 2009.
———. *Slavery after Rome, 500–1100.* Oxford: Oxford University Press, 2017.
Ristuccia, Nathan J. *Christianization and Commonwealth in Early Medieval Europe.* Oxford: Oxford University Press, 2018.
Roberts, Michael. *The Humblest Sparrow: The Poetry of Venantius Fortunatus.* Ann Arbor: University of Michigan Press, 2009.
Rosenwein, Barbara. *Emotional Communities in the Early Middle Ages.* Ithaca, NY: Cornell University Press, 2006.
———. *Negotiating Space: Power, Restraint, and Privileges of Immunity in Early Medieval Europe.* Ithaca, NY: Cornell University Press, 1999.
———. "One Site, Many Meanings: Saint-Maurice d'Agaune as a Place of Power in the Early Middle Ages." In de Jong, Theuws, and Van Rhijn, *Topographies of Power,* 271–90.
Rosser, Gervase. *The Art of Solidarity in the Middle Ages: Guilds in England, 1250–1555.* Oxford: Oxford University Press, 2015.
Rouche, Michel. *L'Aquitaine, des Wisigoths aux Arabes, 418–781: Naissance d'une region.* Paris: Éditions Touzot, 1979.
———. *Clovis.* Paris: Fayard, 1996.
———. "'Religio calcata et dissipata' ou Les premières sécularisations de terres d'Eglise par Dagobert." In Fontaine and Hillgarth, *Seventh Century,* 236–49.

Ruggini, Lellia Cracco. "The Crisis of the Noble Saint: The *Vita Arnulfi*." In Fontaine and Hillgarth, *Seventh Century*, 116–48.

———. "Guilds." In *Late Antiquity: A Guide to the Postclassical World*, edited by Glen Warren Bowersock, Peter Brown, and Oleg Grabar, 479–81. Cambridge, MA: Belknap Press of Harvard University Press, 1999.

Saller, Richard P. *Personal Patronage under the Early Empire*. Cambridge: Cambridge University Press, 1982.

Samson, Ross. "The Merovingian Nobleman's Home: Castle or Villa." *Journal of Medieval History* 13 (1987): 287–315.

Sarti, Laury. "The Military, the Clergy, and Christian Faith in Sixth-Century Gaul." *Early Medieval Europe* 25, no. 2 (2017): 162–85.

———. *Perceiving War and the Military in Early Christian Gaul*. Leiden: Brill, 2013.

Scheibelreiter, Georg. *Der Bischof in merowingischer Zeit*. Vienna: Bohlau, 1983.

———. "Church Structure and Organisation." In *The New Cambridge Medieval History*, vol. 1, *c. 500–c. 700*, edited by Paul Fouracre, 675–709. Cambridge: Cambridge University Press, 2005.

———. "The Death of the Bishop in the Early Middle Ages." In *The End of Strife*, edited by David Loades, 32–43. Edinburgh: T. and T. Clark, 1984.

Scholz, Sebastian. *Die Merowinger*. Stuttgart, Germany: Kholhammer Verlag, 2015.

Schwedler, Gerald. "Lethe and 'Delete'—Discarding the Past in the Early Middle Ages: The Case of Fredegar." In *Collector's Knowledge: What Is Kept, What Is Discarded*, edited by Ania-Silvia Goeing, Anthony T. Grafton, and Paul Michel, 71–96. Leiden: Brill, 2013.

Semmler, Josef. "*Episcopi potestas* und karolingische Klosterpolitik." In *Mönchtum, Episkopat und Adel zur Gründungszeit des Klosters Reichenau*, edited by Arno Borst, 305–95. Vorträge und Forschungen 20. Sigmaringen, Germany: Jan Thorbecke Verlag, 1974.

———. "Zum Testament des gallofränkischen Bischofs." In *Herrscher- und Fürstentestamente im westeuropäischen Mittelalter*, edited by Brigitte Kasten, 573–97. Cologne, Germany: Böhlau Verlag, 2008.

Servatius, Carlo. "'*Per ordinationem principis ordinetur*': Zum Modus der Bischofsernennung im Edikt Chlothars II vom Jahre 614." *Zeitschrift fur Kirchengeschichte* 84 (1973): 1–29.

Settipani, Christian. "Ruricius Ier évêque de Limoges et ses relations familiales." *Francia* 18, no. 1 (1991): 195–222.

Shanzer, Danuta R. "Dating the Baptism of Clovis: The Bishop of Vienne vs. the Bishop of Tours." *Early Medieval Europe* 7, no. 1 (1998): 29–57.

———. "The Tale of Frodebert's Tail." In *Colloquial and Literary Latin*, edited by Eleanor Dickey and Anna Chahoud, 376–405. Cambridge: Cambridge University Press, 2010.

Shoemaker, Karl. *Sanctuary and Crime in the Middle Ages, 400–1500*. New York: Fordham University Press, 2011.

Sieben, Hermann Josef. *Die Konzilsidee in der Alten Kirche*. Paderborn, Germany: Ferdinand Schöningh, 1979.

Sogno, Christiana, Bradley K. Storin, and Edward J. Watts. "Introduction: Greek and Latin Epistolography and Epistolary Collections in Late Antiquity." In *Late*

Antique Letter Collections: A Critical Introduction and Reference Guide, edited by Christiana Sogno, Bradley K. Storin, and Edward J. Watts, 1–10. Oakland: University of California Press, 2017.

Spencer, Mark. "Dating the Baptism of Clovis, 1886–1993." *Early Medieval Europe* 3, no. 2 (1994): 97–116.

Stancliffe, Clare. "Columbanus and the Gallic Bishops." In *Auctoritas: Mélanges offerts à Olivier Guillot*, edited by Giles Constable and Michel Rouche, 205–15. Paris: Presses de l'Université Paris Sorbonne, 2006.

Sternberg, Thomas. *Orientalium more secutus: Räume und Institutionen der Caritas des 5. bis 7. Jahrhunderts in Gallien*. Münster, Germany: Aschendorff, 1991.

Stocking, Rachel L. *Bishops, Councils, and Consensus in the Visigothic Kingdom, 589–633*. Ann Arbor: University of Michigan Press, 2000.

Stroheker, Karl Friedrich. *Der senatorische Adel im spatantiken Gallien*. Tübingen, Germany: Alma Mater Verlag, 1948.

Theuws, Frans. "Centre and Periphery in Northern Austrasia (6th–8th Centuries): An Archaeological Perspective." In *Medieval Archaeology in the Netherlands*, edited by J. C. Besteman, J. M. Bos, and H. A. Heidinga, 41–69. Assen, Netherlands: Van Gorcum, 1990.

———. "Maastricht as a Centre of Power in the Early Middle Ages." In de Jong, Theuws, and Van Rhijn, *Topographies of Power*, 155–216.

Thier, Andreas. *Hierarchie und Autonomie: Regelungstraditionen der Bischofsbestellung in der Geschichte des kirchlichen Wahlrechts bis 1140*. Frankfurt am Main: V. Klostermann, 2011.

Tyrrell, Vida Alice. "Merovingian Letters and Letters Writers." PhD diss., University of Toronto, 2012.

Ubl, Karl. *Inzestverbot und Gesetzgebung: Die Konstruktion eines Verbrechens (300–1100)*. Berlin: Walter de Gruyter, 2008.

———. "L'origine contestée de la loi salique: Une mise au point." *Revue de l'Institut français d'histoire en Allemagne* 1 (2009): 208–34.

———. *Sinnstiftungen eines Rechtsbuchs: Die* Lex Salica *im Frankenreich*. Ostfildern, Germany: Thornbecke, 2017.

Uhalde, Kevin. *Expectations of Justice in the Age of Augustine*. Philadelphia: University of Pennsylvania Press, 2007.

Valliere, Paul. *Conciliarism: A History of Decision-Making in the Church*. Cambridge: Cambridge University Press, 2012.

Van Dam, Raymond. *Leadership and Community in Late Antique Gaul*. Berkeley: University of California Press, 1985.

———. *Saints and Their Miracles in Late Antique Gaul*. Princeton, NJ: Princeton University Press, 1993.

Wallace-Hadrill, Andrew, ed. *Patronage in Ancient Society*. London: Routledge, 1989.

Wallace-Hadrill, J. M. *Early Germanic Kingship in England and on the Continent*. Oxford: Clarendon, 1971.

———. *The Frankish Church*. Oxford: Clarendon, 1983.

———. "Gregory of Tours and Bede: Their Views on the Personal Qualities of Kings." In *Early Medieval History*, 96–114. New York: Harper and Row, 1976.

———. *The Long-Haired Kings*. London: Methuen, 1962.

Weidemann, Margarete. "Bischofsherrschaft und Königtum in Neustrien vom 7. bis zum 9. Jahrhundert am Beispiel des Bistums Le Mans." In Atsma, *La Neustrie*, 1:161–93.

——. "Die kirchliche Organisation der Provinzen Belgica und Germania vom 4. bis zum 7. Jahrhundert." In *Willibrord, zijn wereld en zijn werk*, edited by Petronella Bange and Anton Gerard Weiler, 285–316. Nijmegen, Netherlands: Centrum voor Middeleeuwse Studies, 1990.

——. *Kulturgeschichte der Merowingerzeit nach den Werken Gregors von Tours*. 2 vols. Mainz, Germany: Verlag des Römisch-Germanischen Zentralmuseums, 1982.

Werner, Karl Ferdinand. "*Missus-marchio-comes*: Entre l'administration centrale et l'administration locale de l'empire carolingien." In *Histoire comparée de l'administration (IVe–XVIIIe siècle)*, edited by Walter Paravicini and Karl Ferdinand Werner, 191–239. Munich: Artemis Verlag, 1980.

——. "La place du VIIe siècle dans l'évolution politique et institutionnelle de la Gaule franque." In Fontaine and Hillgarth, *Seventh Century*, 173–211. London: Warburg Institute, 1992.

Werner, Matthias. *Der Lütticher Raum in frühkarolingischer Zeit: Untersuchungen zur Geschichte einer karolingischen Stammlandschaft*. Göttingen, Germany: Vandenhoeck und Ruprecht, 1980.

Wickham, Chris. *Framing the Early Middle Ages*. Oxford: Oxford University Press, 2005.

——. *The Inheritance of Rome*. New York: Viking, 2009.

Widdowson, Marc. "Merovingian Partitions: A Genealogical Charter." *Early Medieval Europe* 17, no. 1 (2009): 1–22.

Woll, Ingrid. *Untersuchungen zu Überlieferung und Eigenart der merowingischen Kapitularien*. Frankfurt: Peter Lang, 1995.

Wood, Ian. "Administration, Law, and Culture in Merovingian Gaul." In *The Uses of Literacy in Early Medieval Europe*, edited by Rosamond McKitterick, 63–81. Cambridge: Cambridge University Press, 1990.

——. "The Ecclesiastical Politics of Merovingian Clermont." In Wormald, Bullough, and Collins, *Ideal and Reality*, 34–57.

——. "Entrusting Western Europe to the Church, 400–750." *Transactions of the Royal Historical Society* 23 (2013): 37–73.

——. "Forgery in Merovingian Hagiography." In *Fälschungen im Mittelalter*, 5:369–84. Monumenta Germaniae Historica: Schriften 33. Hanover, Germany: Hahn, 1988.

——. "The Franks and Papal Theology, 550–660." In *The Crisis of the Oikoumene*, edited by Celia Martin Chazelle and Catherine Cubitt, 233–41. Turnhout, Belgium: Brepols, 2006.

——. "Gregory of Tours and Clovis." *Revue belge de philologie et d'histoire* 63 (1985): 249–72.

——. "Incest, Law and the Bible in Sixth-Century Gaul." *Early Medieval Europe* 7, no. 3 (1998): 291–303.

——. "Jural Relations among the Franks and Alamanni." In *Franks and Alamanni in the Merovingian Period*, edited by Ian Wood, 213–26. Rochester, NY: Boydell, 1998.

——. "Liturgy in the Rhone Valley and the Bobbio Missal." In Hen and Meens, *Bobbio Missal*, 206–18.

———. *The Merovingian Kingdoms: 450–751*. London: Longman, 1994.

———. *The Missionary Life: Saints and the Evangelization of Europe, 400–1050*. London: Longman, 2001.

———. "The Problem of Late Merovingian Culture." In *Exzerpieren - Kompilieren - Tradieren: Transformationen des Wissens zwischen Spätantike und Frühmittelalter*, edited by Stephan Dusil, Gerald Schwedler, and Raphael Schwitter, 199–222. Berlin: De Gruyter, 2017.

———. "Saint-Wandrille and Its Hagiography." In *Church and Chronicle in the Middle Ages: Essays Presented to John Taylor*, edited by Ian Wood and G. A. Loud, 1–14. London: Hambledon, 1991.

———. "The Secret Histories of Gregory of Tours." *Revue belge de philologie et d'histoire* 71 (1993): 253–70.

———. *The Transformation of the Roman West*. Leeds: Arc Humanities Press, 2018.

———. "The *Vita Columbani* and Merovingian Hagiography." *Peritia* 1 (1982): 63–80.

Wood, Susan. *The Proprietary Church in the Medieval West*. Oxford: Oxford University Press, 2006.

Woodruff, Jane. "The *Historia Epitomata* (Third Book) of the Chronicle of Fredegar: An Annotated Translation and Historical Analysis of Interpolated Material." PhD diss., University of Nebraska, 1987.

Wormald, Patrick, Donald Bullough, and Roger Collins, eds. *Ideal and Reality in Frankish and Anglo-Saxon Society: Studies Presented to J. M. Wallace-Hadrill*. Oxford: Blackwell, 1983.

Index

abducted nuns, 92
Abelenus of Geneva, 147
Ado of Vienne, 80
Aetherius of Lyons, 79
Aetius (Parisian archdeacon), 30
Agde, Council of (506), 103, 126, 127n30, 129, 130
Agen, episcopal see of, 126
Agilolfings, 117, 142–43
Agrestius (monk), 106, 147, 149
Agricola of Javols, 148n110
Aighyna (*dux*), 144, 146
Aix, episcopal see of, 102
Alais, episcopal see of, 60, 106
Alamanni, 124, 128
Alaric II (Visigothic king), 42, 152
Albinus of Uzès, 73n41
Albofledis (sister of Clovis I), 35
Aletheus (*patricius*), 137, 163
Alodius of Toul, 128
Amandus of Tongeren-Maastricht, 12n43, 100
Amelius of Bigorra-Tarbes, 134n51
Ansbert of Autun, 157–58
Ansbert of Rouen, 74n44, 150
Ansericus of Soissons, 148n110
Anstrude of Laon (abbess), 85, 152
Antenor (*patricius*), 155
Antidius of Agen, 61n137
Aper (Epvre) of Toul, 128
Aquileian schism, 147
Aquitaine: aristocratic threats to Chlothar II from, 144; Clovis I and, 125, 126, 129; Gundovald in, 111; Pippin II and, 155–56; Sigibert I's stake in, 57n121, 77
Arians and Arianism, 105, 124
Aridius of Lyons, 33, 45, 79, 138, 139, 140, 148
Arles, *civitas* and episcopal see of, 55, 57–58, 60, 101
Arles, Second Council of: 50, 66n11

Armoin of Verdun, 155
Arnulf of Metz, 32, 43n56, 74n44, 117, 142–44, 146, 154
asylum/sanctuary, right of, 48–49, 84n97
auctoritas of bishops independent of royal delegation, 4, 17, 29, 32, 40–42, 165, 166
Audoin of Rouen, 24, 61, 66, 74n44, 84–85, 86, 118, 161n2
Aunacharius of Auxerre, 28, 50
Aunemund of Lyons, 80, 84, 160
Aurelianus (Provençal bishop), 37
Aurelianus of Arles, 37n30, 78n61
Austrapius of Champtoceaux, 74n42
Austrasia: Agilolfings of, 117, 142–43; Burgundy, broken treaty with, 43; Chlothar's invasion of, 143; Dagobert as king of, 142, 143, 149; Ebroin's defeat of, 151; Pippinid influence in, 153; regional disruptions in, 149
Austrenus of Orléans, 28–29, 117, 136
Austrigisilus of Bourges, 140
Auxerre, Synod of (561/605), 50, 51–52
Avitus of Clermont, 76–77, 155
Avitus of Vienne, 1–2, 3, 8n24, 16, 36–37, 103n35, 105–6, 125, 132

Baddo (*legatus*), 135
Bainus of Thérouanne, 152–53
Balthild (queen of Clovis II), 80, 85, 87n114, 161, 163–66
Basinus of Trier, 153
Basques, 144–46
Bede, 153
Belgica Prima, 124, 128, 154
Belgica Secunda, 34–35, 122–24, 125, 127, 129, 131, 151, 152
Benarius (bishop), 155n144
Beracharius of Le Mans, 83
Berachundus of Amiens, 140
Bercharius (abbot of Hautvillers), 152n125

197

Bercharius (abbot of Montier-en-Der), 151–52
Bercharius (Neustrian mayor), 151, 152n125, 153
Berny, council of (580), 45, 89, 90n130
Bertarius, *Gesta episcoporum Virdunensium*, 128
Bertilla of Chelles, 85
Bertoald (Burgundian mayor), 28–29, 117, 136
Bertoaldus of Troyes, 161n2
Bertoendus of Châlons-sur-Marne, 151
Bertram of Bordeaux, 30, 45, 61n137, 109n62, 111–14
Bertram of Le Mans, 88n119, 89, 134, 142n89
Bertrude (queen of Chlothar II), 137
Bigorre, episcopal see of, 132
Bischofsherrschaft, 17, 20, 41, 64, 93, 115
bishops in Merovingian Gaul, 1–27, 160–68; administrative structure of, 12–14; anonymity of majority of, 6; *auctoritas* of bishops independent of royal delegation, 4, 17, 29, 32, 40–42, 165, 166; burdens and benefits of office, 1–2, 14–16; Burgundy, Frankish assimilation of, 1–4; as corporate body, 5–6, 8–16, 17, 19, 42, 168 (*See also* corporate episcopate; limits of corporate episcopal solidarity); map of ecclesiastical provinces and *civitates*, x–xi; number of episcopal sees and dioceses, 12; political engagement of, 109–19, 120, 167–68 (*See also specific rulers*); promotion of episcopal unity, 4; relationship between monarchy and, 2–3, 4–5, 29, 165–68; socioeconomic and familial backgrounds, 6–8, 41, 118; sources for, 19–27. *See also* patronage relationships; services of episcopal *ordo* to court
Bobbio Missal, 29n2, 65
Bobo of Valence, 109n62, 114
Boniface, 12n43, 100n24, 115, 156
Bonitus of Clermont, 74n44, 106, 155, 157
Bonnelles, villa of, Étampes, 89, 134
Bonosiacs, 148
Bourges, episcopal see of, 155
Brown, Peter, 8, 63
Brunhild of Austrasia, 19, 38, 45, 61, 133, 134, 136–39, 142, 143, 147, 149, 158
building projects, 15, 89
Bulgar, *comes* of Septimania, 140n79
Burgundaefarones, 61, 136–37
Burgundofaro of Meaux, 74n44, 86, 87

Burgundy: Austrasia, broken treaty with, 43; Austrenus of Orléans and Bertoald, 28–29; Epaone, bishops asked to attend council of, 1–2; Frankish annexation of, 1–4, 28–29, 98; Neustria and, 28–29, 117, 137, 162–65; Pippin II and, 156–58; regional sentiment in, 4

Caesarius of Arles, 55, 64n6, 98, 102, 103–4, 132
Cain (biblical figure), 38
Camillianus of Troyes, 127n30
Candericus of Lyons, 80n76
canones et leges, 32, 46
capitularies, royal, 54, 92–93
Cariatto of Geneva, 74n43
Cato, priest of Claremont, 14n51
Cautinus of Clermont, 99, 100
Chaino, abbot of Saint Denis, 157
Chalcedon, Council of (451), 14
Chalon-sur-Saône, Councils of: 579, 44n57; 647/53, 10n32, 53, 66n11, 72, 79–80, 103n35, 107
Champagne, 152
Charibert I: administrative and legislative episcopal support of, 40n42, 46n65; conflicts between bishops and, 104–5; patronage of, 69, 83, 86, 88; territorial partitions and, 55–57, 58
Charles Martel, 61, 80, 108–9, 154, 155, 156, 158–59
Charterius of Périgueux, 45
Chartres, *civitas* of, 34, 59–60
Châteaudun, episcopal see of, 34, 39, 59–60, 106
Chelidonius affair, 106n49
Childebert I, 4, 37n30, 39–40, 68–69, 78, 102
Childebert II, 43, 49nn77–78, 51, 73n41, 81, 86, 89, 133, 134
Childebert III, 155
Childeric I, 121n3
Childeric II, 61, 100, 114, 118
Chilperic I: administrative and legislative support from bishops, 44–46; assassination of, 133, 135; *civitas* of Paris and, 139; on corporate episcopate, 92–93, 166; counsel, advice, and criticism from bishops, 29–31, 33–34, 38; Gregory of Tours and, 18n61, 89, 111; patronage relationships and, 65, 82, 89; territorial partitions and, 55, 57
Chlodoswintha (Lombard queen), 124
Chlodulf of Metz, 154

Chlothar I, 31, 44, 48–49, 55, 57, 60, 70, 88, 133
Chlothar II, 19, 120, 133–49; aristocratic factionalism and regional disputes under, 142–48; Austrenus of Orléans and Bertoald, 28–29; Brunhild of Austrasia, downfall of, 61, 147; Clovis I compared, 147; on corporate episcopate, 90, 92, 116; Council of Clichy (626/27) and, 140n79, 141n85, 145n104, 147, 148–49; Council of Mâcon (626/627) and, 147–48; Council of Paris (614) and, 135, 138–42, 147; Desiderius of Vienne, cult of, 138; elections of bishops, involvement in, 70–73, 75; episcopal canons and royal legislation of, 47, 51–53; episcopal counsel and, 32–33; Fredegar chronicler and, 28n1, 117–18, 136–37, 140n79, 142–45; patronage employed by, 89, 133, 140; petitioned by bishops, 85; Pippin II compared, 158; reunification efforts and episcopal allies, 133–39
Chlothar III, 83, 84
Choaldus of Vienne, 160
Chramlius of Embrun, 45, 72, 163n20
Chrodebert of Paris, 161n2
Chrodoald (Agilolfing magnate), 117, 142–43
Chrodobert of Tours, 109n62
civitates: administrative significance of, 108; new bishops required to be natives of *civitas* they represent, 71; petitions by bishops on behalf of, 85–86. *See also specific civitates*
Claudius (ordained by Remigius of Rheims), 96, 127, 130–31
Claussen, M. A., 155
clerics and their dependents, jurisdiction over, 48, 49–53
Clermont, *civitas* and episcopal see of, 76–77, 155
Clermont, Council of (535), 34n19, 50n87, 56n115, 66n11, 68
Clichy, Council of (626/27), 43n52, 49n80, 51, 52, 54n107, 71, 72, 140n79, 141n85, 145n104, 147, 148–49
clientage. *See* patronage relationships
Clovis (son of Chilperic I), 58, 59
Clovis I, 19, 120–33; Chlothar II compared, 147; conversion and baptism, 91, 122, 124–25; corporate episcopate under, 121, 129–33; Council of Orléans (511) and, 42–43, 66, 121, 123, 125–30; counsel, advice, and criticism of bishops, 34–37, 38; election of bishops, involvement in, 68, 96, 127; epistle to bishops of Aquitaine (ca. 507/8), 84; epistolary evidence from reign of, 121–22, 125; grants of patronage offered by, 88; military campaigns and cultivation of episcopal allies, 121–25, 162; petitioned by bishops, 85; Pippin II compared, 158; *urceus* carried off by, 85–86, 122–23.
Clovis II, 37–38, 72, 80, 85, 107, 161, 163n20
Clovis III, 87–88
collegiality. *See* councils and conciliarism
Collins, Roger, 145, 151
Cologne, metropolitan see of, 102, 151, 153, 154
Columbanus and Columbanian monasticism, 8, 87, 106, 147–48, 163–64n22
Commemoratio genealogiae, 142n87
conflict between bishops. *See* limits of corporate episcopal solidarity
consensus, as episcopal priority, 9n28, 11, 27, 90, 91, 97–98, 168
consensus populi/consensus civium (for election of bishop), 68, 72, 74–76
Constantinus of Beauvais, 152
Contumeliosus of Riez, 104
Corbie, monastery of, 161
corporate episcopate: under Clovis I, 121, 129–33; collaborative projects, 106; functioning of bishops as corporate body, 5–6, 8–16, 17, 18, 19, 27, 32, 42, 168; royal patronage of, 90–94; structural integrity of provincial governance and, 106–9. *See also* limits of corporate episcopal solidarity
councils and conciliarism: administrative and legislative services of, 42–54; definition of conciliarism, 18n60; episcopal conflict over, 103–5; hardships of attending councils, 1; judicial tribunals, councils as, 29–31, 43–46, 103–4; local concerns primarily addressed by councils, 11–12; mixed (secular/episcopal) councils, 116–17; order of bishops in subscription to conciliar acts, 127n30; origins and development of concept of conciliar governance, 9; patronization of corporate episcopate and, 90–91; provincial identities and, 107; royal embrace of, 18; royal legislation and conciliar canons, 32. *See also specific councils*

counts, episcopal role in selection of, 71–72
courtiers, bishops as, 91
Cronopius of Périgueux, 99, 127n30
Cunibert of Cologne, 32, 117
Cyprian of Bordeaux, 129
Cyprian of Carthage, 9
Cyprian of Toulon, 98–99, 105

Dagobert I, 7n23, 32, 38–39, 43n56, 66, 80, 84, 117n93, 118, 136, 142–44, 149, 159n163, 163n20
Dagobert II, 24
Daly, William, 121
David (biblical king), 37
De septem ordinibus ecclesiae (attrib. Jerome), 10n32
Desideratus (Diddo) of Chalon-sur-Saône, 109n62, 114
Desiderius of Cahors, 34n19, 38n33, 39, 74n44, 82n88, 96n5
Desiderius of Eauze, 74n42
Desiderius of Vienne, 33, 45, 79, 138
Diddo (Desideratus) of Chalon-sur-Saône, 109n62, 114
Dido of Poitiers, 24–25
Diefenbach, Steffen, 11
doctrinal/theological controversies, 98–99, 105–6
Domitianus of Angers, 105n46
Domnolus of Le Mans, 105n46
Domnolus of Vienne, 85, 109n62, 138–39
Donatus of Besançon, 147
Drogo (*dux*; son of Pippin II), 152, 153
Dumézil, Bruno, 73
Dynamius (*patricius*), 73n41

Eauze, Council of (551), 50, 51n89, 66n11, 103n35
Eauze, dual bishoprics of, 144–45
Ebrachar, Duke of Brittany, 55
Ebroin (mayor), 45, 61, 114, 118, 151, 157, 163n20
Echternach, monastery of, 152, 153, 155
Egidius of Rheims, 33n13, 59, 82n90, 139n78
elections of bishops, royal involvement in, 67–81; Clermont, elections in, 76–77; Clovis I and, 68, 96, 127; conciliar legislation on, 68–73; *consensus populi/consensus civium*, 68, 72, 74–76; former courtiers, appointment of, 73–74; Marculf's formulary and, 74–76; *pontifices et proceres*, consultation with, 75–76

Eligius of Noyon, 74n44, 84, 160n1, 161n2
Emerius of Saintes, 70, 104
Emmo of Sens, 160–65
Epaone, Council of (517), 1, 2, 3–4, 48n76, 49, 50, 103n35, 132
"episcopal republics," 115–16, 156–58
episcopate, Merovingian. *See* bishops in Merovingian Gaul
epistolary communications: between bishops, 95–97, 102; Clovis I and, 121–22, 125; episcopal counsel offered in, 34–40; as sources, 26
epitaphs, episcopal, 6, 25, 78
Epvre (Aper) of Toul, 128
Erchinoald (mayor), 72
Ermelenus of Saint Denis, 83
Ermenulfus of Evreux, 134
Ermino, abbot of Lobbes, 152
Erpo (*dux*), 137
Esther (biblical queen), 38
Étampes: aristocratic threats to Chlothar II from, 144; villa of Bonnelles in, 89, 134
Eucherius of Lyons, 78
Eufrasius of Clermont, 76, 77, 127n30
Eufronius of Tours, 15, 22, 58, 59, 88, 104–5
Euspicius (presbyter of Verdun), 128
Eustasius of Luxeuil, 137, 147–48
Ewig, Eugen, 109, 115, 156, 161

Falco of Maastricht, 102, 131
Faro of Meaux, 161n2
Faustianus of Dax, 44, 61n137, 111–13
Felix of Nantes, 15, 100, 101, 105n46
Ferreolus of Limoges, 61n137
Filibert, abbot of Jumièges, 85
Firminus, *comes* of Clermont, 76–77
Firminus of Verdun, 128
Flavius of Chalon, 23, 73n41, 74n43
Flocoald of Auxerre, 157n159
Florentius, *Vita Rusticulae*, 85, 137–38
Foaldus of Lyons, 80n82
formulae and law, 47n70
Fortunatus (Venantius Fortunatus), 9n32, 15, 22, 25, 65, 105n45
Fouracre, Paul, 84, 150, 156–57, 158
Fox, Yaniv, 8, 79
Fredegar chronicler: Aletheus, on trial of, 163n20; on Austrenus of Orléans and Bertoald, 28–29; on Basques, 145; on Brunhild of Austrasia, 61; on Burgundian factionalism, 164n24; on capture/retaking of Le Mans (596), 89n129; on Chlothar II, 117n93, 118, 136–37, 140n79,

142–46; on Clovis I, 122n9; on elections of bishops, 74n43, 79; on episcopal envoys, 55n111; Gregory of Tours' *Historiae* used by, 117n91; on petitions by bishops, 85; on Pippin II, 151; on political engagement of episcopate, 117–18; on services of bishops to monarchy, 32–33, 43n56, 45; as source, 22–23
Fredegund (queen of Chilperic I), 89, 133–36
Frodebert of Tours, 95–96, 97, 109–10

Gaiso, *comes* of Tours, 88
Gallus (uncle of Gregory of Tours), 75
Garibald of Toul, 155
Gaugericus of Cambrai, 137
Gauzbertus of Chartres, 161n2
Gemiliacum (Jumilhac-le-Grand), episcopal claims to, 99
Genesius of Lyons, 74n44, 80, 85
Genialis (*dux*), 145n99
Gennadius of Marseilles, 10n32
Genovefa of Paris, 121, 125n24
Gerberding, Richard, 84, 118, 149–50, 151–52, 153, 155, 158
Germania, Council of (742), 103n35
Germanus of Paris, 34, 38–39, 57, 85, 105n46, 166
Goar (hermit), 33, 128
Godinus, son of Warnarchar (Burgundian mayor), 144
Godinus of Lyons, 80, 106, 157
Gregory I the Great (pope), 101
Gregory of Langres, 74n42
Gregory of Tours: Berny, on council of (580), 45, 89, 90n130; on Chilperic I and Fredegund, 18n61, 89, 111, 135; on Chlothar II, 134, 139n78; on Clovis I, 122, 124n16; on conciliar tribunals, 44, 45–46; on conflicts between bishops, 99, 100, 101, 103, 104, 105n47, 111–14; on discontented clerics, 14; election as bishop of Tours, 80; on elections of bishops, 70n27, 73n41, 74n45, 76, 77–79; on episcopal counsel, 30–31, 33, 34, 43; on episcopal envoys, 55nn110–11; family of, 8n24; Fredegar chronicler and, 23, 117n91; Gallus (uncle), on ordination of, 75; on Gundovald affair, 44, 60–61; *Historiae*, 20–22, 23, 117; *Liber vitae patrum*, 31n8, 58n125, 75n49; *Libri de virtutibus Sancti Martini episcopi*, 86; *Miracula*, 21; on Nantes cathedral, 15; *ordo* as used by, 9n32; on patronage relationships, 64–65, 66; on petitions by bishops, 81–83, 85n105, 86, 88n121; on political engagement of episcopate, 111–14, 117, 119; praise for bishops defying royal power, 166; on Radegund's Convent of the Holy Cross, 59n129; on royal grants of patronage, 89; as source, 19–22; territorial partitions and, 57, 58n123, 58nn125–28, 59n131
Grimoald (mayor), 24–25, 82n88, 109–10
Grimoald (son of Pippin II), 152
Gripho of Rouen, 150
Gundemar (Visigothic king), 145
Gundoaldus of Meaux, 148n110
Gundovald (royal pretender), 23, 44, 60–61, 111–13, 133, 135
Guntram of Burgundy: administrative and legislative episcopal support for, 43, 44–45, 46, 47; Chlothar II and, 133, 134, 135; conflicts between bishops and, 111–13; on corporate episcopate, 93; Council of Mâcon (585) and, 139; counsel, advice, and criticism from bishops, 39; elections of bishops and, 70, 73n41, 74, 77, 78, 79, 89; petitioned by bishops, 82–83, 85; Saint-Jean-de-Maurienne, creation of new episcopal see of, 101; territorial partitions, episcopal support for, 55, 57–61

hagiography, 25–26, 118–19
Haimoaldus of Rennes, 134
Handley, Mark, 25
Hautvillers, monastery of, 152
Hector (*patricius*), 83–84, 100
Heinzelmann, Martin, 20, 93
Heraclius of Paris, 130
Heraclius of Saintes, 70, 83, 104
Herlemund of Le Mans, 150
Herpin (*comes*), 137
Hilary of Poitiers, 98
Hildoaldus of Avranches, 148n110
Hincmar of Rheims, *Vita Remigii*, 123
Hubert of Maastricht-Tongres, 154
Hugo of Rouen, 116n87

immunities, royal, 86–88
Importunus of Paris, 95–96, 97, 99, 109–10, 109n62
Innocentius of Rodez, 100, 105
Irmina (mother-in-law of Pippin II), 153
Isidore of Seville, 10n32, 145
Iulianus of Vienne, 3n8, 132

James, Edward, 84
Jews, episcopal canons on, 47, 50n87
Johannes of Arles, 160
John II (pope), 104
John III (pope), 82
Jonas of Bobbio, 136, 147
Josephus (bishop), 155n144
jurisdiction: conflicts between bishops over, 98, 99–101; of corporate episcopate in law codes and capitularies, 91–93; divide between ecclesiastical and royal law, 48–54

Klingshirn, William, 104, 132
Klosterpolitik, 87, 152, 161, 165
Königsnähe, 5, 84
Kreiner, Jamie, 15, 25, 26, 118, 155

Laban of Eauze, 111–12
Lagny-le-Sec, villa of, 157
Lambert of Maastricht-Tongres, 88, 154
Landeric (Neustrian mayor), 136, 137n68
Landeric of Paris, 86–87, 161n4
Lantbert of Lyons, 74n44, 80
Latinus of Tours, 107
law codes, Frankish, on corporate episcopate, 91–92
Le Mans, *civitas* and episcopal see of, 89, 134
Leges Alamannorum, 52–53, 92
Leo of Sens, 39–40, 130
Leontius of Bordeaux, 22, 69–70, 83, 104–5
Leontius or Licontius of Lyons, 77, 78n61
Leporius, *Libellus emendationis*, 98
letters. *See* epistolary communications
Leudast, *comes* of Tours, 58
Leudegar of Autun, 24, 45, 74n44, 100, 109n62, 114, 118, 166
Leudegasius of Mainz, 140n79
Leudemund of Sion, 117, 137, 163
Leudesius (mayor), 118
Leudovald of Bayeux, 135
Leuvigild of Spain, 134n51
Lex Baiwariorum, 52n97, 91, 92
Lex Ribuaria, 53, 91
Liber historiae Francorum, 22, 23–25, 33n13, 118, 149, 152n126
Licerius of Arles, 74n43
Liliola of Arles, 85
limits of corporate episcopal solidarity, 18–19, 95–119; councils, conflict over, 103–5; epistolary communications evidencing, 95–97, 102; interpersonal conflicts between bishops, 97–106;

mediators and arbiters of conflict, 97–98, 105; metropolitan prerogatives, conflict over, 101–3; political engagement and, 109–19, 120, 167–68; property-based and jurisdictional disputes, 98, 99–101; structural integrity of provincial governance and, 106–9; theological/doctrinal controversies, 98–99, 105–6
Limoges, episcopal see of, 126
Liutwin of Trier, 153
Loening, Edgar, 121
Loseby, Simon T., 108
Lupicinus of Angoulême, 127n30
Lupus of Lyons, 4, 77
Lupus of Sens, 139
Lupus of Soissons, 126
Lyons, *civitas* and episcopal see of, 77–81, 108, 157
Lyons, councils of: 518/23, 2–3; 567/70, 44n57, 97–98, 105, 141; 572/73, 116n89; 581, 43, 44n57, 116n89

Maastricht, Church of Saint Mary, 87–88
Mâcon, Councils of: 581/83, 47–48, 50, 66n11; 585, 42n48, 44, 45n60, 46, 50–51, 93, 103n35, 113–14, 116, 139; 626/627, 147–48
Madalbertus of Lyons, 80n82
Madalgar of Laon, 152
Magnericus of Trier, 55
Magnobodus of Angers, 140, 148n110
Magnus Maximus (Roman emperor), 12
Mâlay-le-Roi, Council of (677/79), 72
Mâlay-le-Roi, royal villa of, 160, 161–63
Malluf of Sens, 82
Mappinus of Rheims, 103
Maracharius of Angoulême, 74n42
Marculf's formulary, 29n2, 52, 57n121, 64n3, 74–76, 87n114, 88
Marius of Avenches, *Chronica*, 24
Maroveus of Poitiers, 59, 86
Marseilles, Council of (533), 103–4
Martin (*dux*), 151
Martin of Tours, 21, 81, 89, 124
Masolacus. *See specific entries at* Mâlay-le-Roi
Maximus (bishop; see unknown), 109n62, 137–38
Maximus of Aix, 102n31
Maximus of Die, 138n69
Maximus of Geneva, 98–99, 105
McKitterick, Rosamond, 153
Medard of Noyon, 85
Melun, *castrum* of, 39

Merovech (son of Chlothar II), 136
Merovingian episcopate. *See* bishops in Merovingian Gaul
Merovingian rulers: *auctoritas* of bishops independent of, 4, 17, 29, 32, 40–42, 165, 166; conciliar canons and royal legislation, 32; corporate episcopal order recognized by, 16; councils and conciliarism, royal embrace of, 18; political engagement of episcopate and, 109–19, 120; relationship between episcopacy and, 2–3, 4–5, 29, 165–68. *See also* elections of bishops, royal involvement in; patronage relationships; services of episcopal *ordo* to court; *specific rulers*
metropolitan prerogatives, conflicts over, 101–3
Metz, *civitas* and episcopal see of, 154–55
"micro-Christendoms," 2, 11, 17
Milo of Trier, 116n87, 153
mirrors for princes, 37, 38
Missa pro principe, Bobbio Missal, 65
Mitchell, Kathleen, 21
Momolenus of Noyon, 160n1
monarchy. *See* Merovingian rulers
monasteries and monasticism: Columbanus and Columbanian monasticism, 8, 87, 106, 147–48, 163–64n22; exemptions, privileges, and benefactions, 86–87, 151–52, 158, 160–65; Pippinids, monastic and episcopal influence of, 152, 153. *See also specific monasteries*
Montier-en-Der, monastery of, 151–52
Mouzon, church of, 102
Mummolus of Uzès, 100
Mundericus (archpriest of Tonnerre and bishop-elect of Langres), 60
Murray, Alexander C., 21, 71, 88

Nantes, cathedral of, 15
Nazelles, villa of, 86
Neustria: Burgundy and, 28–29, 117, 137, 162–65; Charles Martel and, 61; under Chlothar II, 133–35, 137, 139, 140; factionalism in, 114; Le Mans retaken by, 134; loss of territory after death of Chilperic, 133; Pippin II and bishops of, 150–51
Nicasius of Angoulême, 61n137
Nicetius of Auch, 127n30
Nicetius of Dax, 74n42, 111
Nicetius of Lyons (great-uncle of Gregory of Tours), 78, 79

Nicetius of Trier, 31, 32, 33, 36n25, 45, 55, 101, 103, 124, 166
Nivardus of Rheims, 74n44
Norbert (Neustrian mayor), 157
Norbert of Clermont, 106, 155, 157
Notitia Galliarum, 12, 130
Novempopulana, 126, 130, 144–46, 149

Orange, Council of (441), 50, 103n35
Orestes of Bazas, 61n137, 112n74
Orléans, *civitas* of, 28–29
Orléans, Councils of: 511, 12n40, 34n19, 36, 42, 48, 49, 66, 68, 121, 123, 125–30, 132, 147; 533, 103n35, 127n30, 132; 538, 3–4, 48, 50, 51n89, 66n11, 68, 103n35; 541, 48, 49, 50, 51, 66n11, 69n24, 97, 98, 103n35, 132; 549, 48, 49, 68–69, 86n110, 103n35, 128
Ostrogoths, 126, 131

Pactus legis Salicae, 91, 93, 121n2.
Palladius of Aire-sur-l'Adour, 144
Palladius of Eauze, 117, 144–46
Palladius of Latona (Losne or Lectoure), 144
Palladius of Saintes, 61n137, 109n62, 111–14, 134n51
Pantagatus of Vienne, 4
Pappolus of Chartres, 83
Paris, *civitas* of: Saint Peter, Basilica of, 29–30, 46, 139; as shared *civitas*, 139; territorial partitions and, 57
Paris, councils of: 556/73 (561/64), 34, 39, 40, 42n48, 44n57, 56–57, 60, 69, 70, 139; 577, 29–30, 45–46, 139; 614, 42n48, 47, 52, 53, 66n11, 70, 71, 90–91, 98, 135, 138–42, 144, 145n104, 147, 148
Paris, Edict of (614), 47, 51, 52, 53, 66n11, 70–72, 75, 92, 141, 148
Passio Leudegarii, 118
Paternus of Avranches, 56n114
patronage relationships, 17–18, 63–94; *civitas* or diocesan church, episcopal petitions on behalf of, 85–87; concept of, 64; corporate episcopate, patronizing, 90–94; courtiers, bishops as, 91; dual episcopal roles of client and patron, 64; episcopal acceptance of, 63–67; immunities, royal, 87–88; intercessions of bishops on behalf of others, 84–85; lower clerics and, 65–66; monastic exemptions, privileges, and benefactions, 86–87, 151–52, 158, 160–65; petitions by bishops, 81–88; royal extensions of, 88–89, 167. *See also* elections of bishops, royal involvement in

INDEX

Patzold, Steffen, 7
Pelagius I (pope), 82n89
petitions by bishops, 81–89
Pientius of Poitiers, 85
Pippin I, 117, 142–43
Pippin II, 19, 149–59
Pippinids: Arnulf of Metz and, 142n87; Fredegar chronicler and, 118, 136; *Liber historia Francorum* on, 24; monastic and episcopal influence of, 152, 153; patronage of, 80, 88; politico-military agenda, episcopal support for, 61, 117
Plectrude (queen of Pippin II), 154, 155
Poitiers, *civitas* of, 58–59
political engagement of episcopate, 109–19, 120, 167–68. *See also specific rulers*
Praejectus of Clermont, 83–84, 100
Praetextus of Rouen, 30, 32, 43, 45, 61, 82, 103, 105n46, 135
Principius of Soissons, 123
Priscus of Lyons, 74nn42–43, 78–79
Priscus Valerianus (*praefectus praetorio*), 78
Promotus of Châteaudun, 34, 39, 59, 82–83
Protadius (*patricius*), 19
Provence: Council of Lyons (518/23) and, 3–4n9; Frankish annexation of, 98; papal estates in, 58n123; Pippin II and, 155; territorial partitions and, 57n121, 60

Quintianus of Clermont, 132n44

Radegund (saint and queen of Chlothar I), 59, 85
Ragnachar of Cambrai, 122
Ragnemodus of Paris, 30, 45, 57, 134
Rapp, Claudia, 11
Rebais, exemption for, 86
Regalis of Vannes, 55
Remigius of Rheims: advice, criticism, and counsel provided by, 34–35, 36, 37; Clovis I and, 122, 123, 125, 127, 129–31; conflict between bishops and, 96–97, 102, 103, 130–32; patronage relationships and, 85, 88n120, 131
Reolus of Rheims, 74n44, 151–52
Rheims, episcopal see of, 108
Ricomer *(patricius)*, 137
Riculf, priest of Tours, 14n51
Riez, Council of (439), 103n35
Rigobert of Rheims, 61, 151
Rio, Alice, 74–75
Rodez, *civitas* of, 60
Rosenwein, Barbara, 86–87, 157, 163

Ruarecus of Nevers, 148n110
Rufinus of Comminges, 61n137
Ruricius of Limoges, 8n24, 96n5, 99, 103, 126
Rusticius of Cahors, 74n44
Rusticula of Arles, 95, 137–38
Rusticus of Lyons, 78n61
Rusticus of Trier, 33n14

Sacerdos of Lyons, 77–78
Sadalberga of Laon, 85
Sagittarius of Gap, 82
Saint Columbe, monastery of, 161
Saint Denis, 83, 87, 89, 157, 161
Saint Marcel, Basilica of, 86
Saint Peter, Basilica of, Paris, 29–30, 46, 139
Saint Symphorian, Basilica of, 86
Saintes, Council of (561/67), 70, 83, 104–5
Saint-Jean-de-Losne, Council of (673/75), 51–52, 72, 103n35
Saint-Jean-de-Maurienne, episcopal see of, 101, 106
Saint-Pierre-le-Vif, Sens, monastery of, 160–66
Salonius of Embrun, 82
Salustius of Clermont, 77
sanctuary/asylum, right of, 48–49, 84n97
Sapaudus of Arles, 58, 82n89, 102
Savaric of Auxerre, 116n87, 150, 157
Secundinus of Lyons, 79
services of episcopal *ordo* to court, 17, 28–62; administrative and legislative support, 40–54; counsel, advice, and criticism, 29–40; judicial tribunals, councils as, 30–31, 43–46; peace and order, promotion of, 43, 62; prayers, royal solicitation of, 29; in territorial partitions and military conflicts, 28–29, 54–61
Sidoc (Senotus) of Eauze, 117, 144–46
Sidonius Apollinaris, 8n24, 64n6
Sigibald of Metz, 155
Sigibert I: administrative and legislative support of bishops, 43; counsel, advice, and criticism of bishops, 33–34, 38–39; elections of bishops and, 76–77, 81; petitioned by bishops, 86; territorial partitions and, 55, 57–60
Sigibert III, 38n33
Sigismund (Burgundian ruler), 2–3
simony, 70
Sisebut (Visigothic king), 145; *Vita Desiderii*, 10n32, 136, 138
Sithiu, monastery of, 161

Soissons, conquest of kingdom of, 111, 122–23, 124, 125, 162
Soissons, Council of (744), 103n35
Solomon (biblical king), 37
Sonnatius of Rheims, 140n80
Stephanus (royal treasurer), 2
Stephen of Ripon, 166
Suinthila (Visigothic king), 145
Sunnacius of Rheims, 148n110
Syagrius, *rex* of Soissons, and Syagrian War, 122–23, 124, 125
Syagrius of Autun, 23, 85, 101
Symmachus (pope), 102

territorial partitions, episcopal support in, 54–60
Tertry, Battle of (687), 19, 150, 151, 153, 158
testaments, episcopal, 26–27n85
Tetricus of Auxerre, 79, 157n159
Tetricus of Langres (great-uncle of Gregory of Tours), 79
Theodorius of Arles, 107
Theodosius of Auxerre, 130
theological/doctrinal controversies, 98–99, 105–6
Theudebert I, 31, 37, 39, 56n115, 66, 68, 86
Theudebert II, 101, 140n79, 142, 143, 145
Theuderic I, 31, 75, 129n39
Theuderic II, 19, 28, 29, 45, 101, 136, 138, 139, 140n79, 143, 145, 147
Theuderic III, 72, 80, 155, 157
Toul, Council of (550), 103
Toul, episcopal see of, 128
Tours, *civitas* of: national following of cult of Saint Martin of, 108; Saint Martin, Church of, 66, 86, 88; territorial partitions and, 58
Tours, Council of (567), 10n32, 42n48, 43n52, 51, 56n114, 97–98, 103n35, 104–5
travel in Merovingian Gaul, 1, 81–82, 126
Treticus of Lyons, 79, 147–48
Trier, episcopal see of, 128, 153, 155
Troyes, Council of (585), 44n57
True Cross relic installed in Radegund's convent, Poitiers, 59

Turin, episcopal see of, parishes seized from, 101

Unknown, Councils of: 588, 44n57; ca. 614, 141n85
Ursicinus of Cahors, 44, 61n137, 73n41, 100, 105
Ursicinus of Turin, 101
Ursus of Toul, 128

Valence, Council of (583/85), 86
Van Dam, Raymond, 64, 78
Venantius Fortunatus, 9n32, 15, 22, 25, 65, 105n45
Ver, Council of (755), 103n35
Veranus of Cavaillon, 60
Verdun, episcopal see of, 128
Verus of Rodez, 140n79, 148n110
Vetus Gallica, 141n83, 149
Victorius of Rennes, 105n46
Vienne, episcopal see of, 101, 108
Visigoths, 12n42, 35, 42, 124, 125, 126, 131, 140n79, 145, 146
vitae and hagiographies of individual bishops, 25–26, 118–19
Vito of Verdun, 128
Viventiolus of Lyons, 2–3, 2n4, 78n61, 80n76
Viventius of Lyons, 79–80
vocati episcopi, 109, 116
Vouillé, Battle of (507), 42–43, 124, 125, 126, 130
Vuilligisilus of Toulouse, 148n110

Warnarchar (Burgundian mayor), 137, 144, 147–48
wergild, 91–92
Widonids, 153
Willibrord of Utrecht, 153, 154n135
Witharius (bishop), 155n144
women: abducted nuns, episcopal responsibility for, 92; petitioning bishops, 85
Wood, Ian, 76–77, 150
Wood, Susan, 165
Wulfoald (Austrasian mayor), 152, 154
Wulfoald-Gundoinids, 154
Wulfram of Sens, 158

CPSIA information can be obtained
at www.ICGtesting.com
Printed in the USA
BVHW032339080819
555467BV00005B/32/P